The Legal Foundations of Inequality

The long revolutionary movements that gave birth to constitutional democracies in the Americas were founded on egalitarian constitutional ideals. They claimed that all men were created equal and with similar capacities and that the community should become self-governing. Following the first constitutional debates that took place in the region, these promising egalitarian claims, which gave legitimacy to the revolutions, soon fell out of favor. Advocates of a conservative order challenged both ideals and wrote constitutions that established a national religion and created an exclusionary political structure. Liberals proposed constitutions that protected individual autonomy and rights but established severe restrictions on the principle of majority rule. Radicals favored an openly majoritarian constitutional organization that, according to many, directly threatened the protection of individual rights. This book examines the influence of these opposing views during the founding period of constitutionalism in countries including the United States, Argentina, Bolivia, Colombia, Chile, Ecuador, Mexico, Peru, Uruguay, and Venezuela and explores their legacy to our time.

Roberto Gargarella is Professor of Constitutional Theory and Political Philosophy at the Law School of the Universidad de Buenos Aires and the Universidad Torcuato Di Tella and a researcher for CONICET in Buenos Aires and the Christian Michelsen Institute in Norway. He has been a Visiting Fellow at Columbia, New York University, and Harvard and a Visiting Professor at universities in Europe, Latin America, and the United States. He received a John Simon Guggenheim grant in 2000 and a Harry Frank Guggenheim grant in 2002–2003 and has published on issues of legal and political philosophy, as well as on U.S. and Latin American constitutionalism.

Cambridge Studies in the Theory of Democracy

General Editor
ADAM PRZEWORSKI *New York University*

OTHER BOOKS IN THE SERIES

Robert Barros, *Constitutionalism and Dictatorship: Pinochet, the Junta, and the 1980 Constitution*

Jon Elster, ed., *Deliberative Democracy*

José María Maravall and Adam Przeworski, eds., *Democracy and the Rule of Law*

José María Maravall and Ignacio Sánchez-Cuenca, *Controlling Governments: Voters, Institutions, and Accountability*

Adam Przeworski, Susan Stokes, and Bernard Manin, eds., *Democracy, Accountability, and Representation*

Adam Przeworski et al., *Democracy and Development: Political Institutions and Well-Being in the World, 1950–1990*

Melissa Schwartzberg, *Democracy and Legal Change*

The Legal Foundations of Inequality
Constitutionalism in the Americas, 1776–1860

Roberto Gargarella

CAMBRIDGE UNIVERSITY PRESS
Cambridge, New York, Melbourne, Madrid, Cape Town,
Singapore, São Paulo, Delhi, Mexico City

Cambridge University Press
32 Avenue of the Americas, New York NY 10013-2473, USA

Published in the United States of America by Cambridge University Press, New York

www.cambridge.org
Information on this title: www.cambridge.org/9781107617810

© Roberto Gargarella 2010

This publication is in copyright. Subject to statutory exception
and to the provisions of relevant collective licensing agreements,
no reproduction of any part may take place without the written
permission of Cambridge University Press.

First published 2010
First paperback edition 2013

A catalogue record for this publication is available from the British Library

ISBN 978-0-521-19502-7 Hardback
ISBN 978-1-107-61781-0 Paperback

Cambridge University Press has no responsibility for the persistence or
accuracy of URLs for external or third-party internet websites referred to in
this publication, and does not guarantee that any content on such websites is,
or will remain, accurate or appropriate.

Contents

Acknowledgments		*page* ix
Introduction		1
1	Radicalism: Honoring the General Will	9
	THE ENGINE OF AMERICAN HISTORY	9
	THE HISTORY OF RADICAL CONSTITUTIONALISM IN AMERICA	12
	"A GOVERNMENT BY ITS CITIZENS IN MASS"	19
	THE PEOPLE AGAINST "THE FEW AND THE GREAT"	23
	MORAL POPULISM: ON THE TENSIONS BETWEEN RADICALISM AND INDIVIDUAL RIGHTS	30
	THE ECONOMY: THE AGRARIAN REPUBLIC	38
	THE NEED FOR NEW POLITICAL INSTITUTIONS	45
	CONSTITUTIONALISM	49
	THE ORGANIZATION OF POWER: A STRICT SEPARATION OF POWERS	54
	RIGHTS AND THE CULTIVATION OF VIRTUE	74
	FROM POLITICAL RIGHTS TO THE RIGHT TO THE LAND: THE CONSTITUTION AS *LA LEY DE LA TIERRA*	78
	RADICALISM AND CONSTITUTIONALISM IN THE AMERICAS: A BALANCE	82
2	Conservatism: The Moral Cement of Society	90
	THE ENDLESS INFLUENCE OF CONSERVATISM	90
	MORAL PERFECTIONISM: PREVENTING THE LOOSENING OF MORAL BONDS	92
	POLITICAL ELITISM: THE IMPOSSIBILITY OF DEMOCRACY IN A SOCIETY "FULL OF VICES"	103
	THE CONSTITUTION	111

vii

	CONSERVATIVE CONSTITUTIONS AND THE STRUCTURE OF POWER: "A SINGLE WELL-DIRECTED MAN"	117
	RIGHTS: "TO FORM CUSTOMS AND NATIONAL CHARACTER"	130
	THE REGENERATION OF AMERICAN CITIZENS	136
	PRIVATE PROPERTY AND POLITICAL RIGHTS: THE REALM OF THE WEALTHY	141
	CONSERVATISM AND CONSTITUTIONALISM IN THE AMERICAS: A BALANCE	146
	THE CONSERVATIVE LEGACY	150
3	Liberalism: Between Tyranny and Anarchy	153
	THE SOVEREIGNTY OF THE INDIVIDUAL	153
	MORAL NEUTRALITY: A WALL OF SEPARATION	157
	POLITICAL NEUTRALITY: THE PROCEDURAL VIEW	163
	FROM THE SOVEREIGNTY OF THE PEOPLE TO THE SOVEREIGNTY OF REASON	167
	THE ECONOMY: THE POLITICS OF LAISSEZ FAIRE	172
	CONSTITUTIONALISM	178
	RIGHTS: THE FIGHT AGAINST ALL PRIVILEGES	180
	THE ORGANIZATION OF POWER: A SYSTEM OF CHECKS AND BALANCES	194
	LIBERALISM AND CONSTITUTIONALISM IN THE AMERICAS: A BALANCE	208
4	The Quest for Equality	215
	ULYSSES' DISLOYALTY	215
	THE UNFULFILLED PROMISE OF RADICALISM	217
	LIBERALISM: STABILIZING ITS OWN PROGRAM	220
	LIBERALS, CONSERVATIVES, AND POLITICAL INEQUALITY	223
	POLITICAL INEQUALITIES: WERE THEY UNAVOIDABLE?	227
	EGALITARIANISM AND POLITICS: RECOGNIZING THE VALUE OF PUBLIC DISCUSSION	230
	EGALITARIANISM AND RIGHTS: THE EQUAL VALUE OF EACH PERSON'S OPINIONS	235
	THE EGALITARIAN CONSTITUTION	241
Bibliography		249
Index		267

Acknowledgments

I want to give special thanks to Adam Przeworski, who read the first version of this book, made useful and stimulating comments, and encouraged me to publish my manuscript in English. My project benefited greatly from many discussions with friends, colleagues, and students that took place at the Universidad de Buenos Aires and the Universidad Torcuato Di Tella in Buenos Aires; the Universidad de los Andes and the Universidad Nacional in Colombia; the Universidad Católica in Uruguay; the ITAM in Mexico; the Universidad de Chile; the Universitat Pompeu Fabra in Spain; Columbia, Cornell, and Yale universities in the United States; and the Club de Cultura Socialista in Buenos Aires. I thank all those who participated in these debates, particularly Juan Carlos Torre, who helped me with the publication of parts of this manuscript in Spanish. I am thankful to Julia Maskivker and Marisol Yakimiuk, who collaborated with me as research assistants at an early stage of my research. I also took advantage of numerous dialogues at the annual Seminario Latinoamericano (SELA), coordinated by my friend Owen Fiss. My research was made possible, in part, by the financial help I received from the Simon Guggenheim Foundation and the Christian Michelsen Institute in Norway. During these years, I had the enormous privilege of having access to the wonderful library of the Universidad Di Torcuato Tella, the New York Public Library, and the libraries of Columbia, Cornell, New York, and Yale universities.

The Legal Foundations of Inequality

Introduction

Most constitutional democracies are in trouble: significant numbers of people do not trust their representatives and do not participate in party politics. Surveys reveal alarming figures on how citizens evaluate the worth and functioning of different public institutions and suggest a disconnection between what the citizenry wants and what the political decision-making process produces. Among the many factors that might explain this situation, one is undoubtedly the structure of the institutional system itself, as organized by its constitution. Many of the problems that we presently attribute to modern constitutional democracies are not unfortunate distortions of a properly organized institutional design but are the foreseeable effects of that framework. My aim in this book is not to overemphasize the role of our constitutional history in explaining future political events but rather to pay due regard to an important and often neglected topic.

Constitutional democracies, as we presently know them, were born after long revolutionary movements in defense of the community's independence or against aristocracy. These movements were profoundly egalitarian and expressed this egalitarianism in two basic dimensions. At the personal level, the revolutions claimed, and this was actually their main claim, that all men are created equal and that all have similar basic capacities.[1] At the collective level, they claimed that the community should become self-governing; in other words, they maintained that neither a foreign country nor a particular family or group should rule the country in the name of the people at large.

In practice, though, these promising egalitarian claims, which gave legitimacy to the revolutions, soon fell out of favor. The main

---

[1] A similar distinction is made between "private" and "public" autonomy in Habermas (1996).

constitutional projects that grew after the revolutions severely distorted the original egalitarian goals. Clearly hostile to the ideal of personal autonomy, some of these constitutions commanded the use of the coercive powers of the state in favor of a particular religion. Moreover, the majority of the constitutions actually obstructed the idea of having a self-governing community. In this sense, for example, they discouraged civic participation, reduced popular controls to a minimum expression, reserved the "last institutional word" to the least democratic branch of government, and organized a countermajoritarian political system to replace rather than to "discover" or "refine" the will of the people. In the following chapters, I examine the decreasing influence of egalitarian ideals in American constitutional life and begin to defend a philosophical argument about the importance of these complex ideals. In sum, I explore how our constitutional order came to dishonor the valuable egalitarian promises that gave foundation to our communities.

In analyzing the origins of American constitutionalism, I concentrate primarily on the ideological debates that took place during the founding period of constitutionalism in the region. I examine not only the basic content and impact of the main constitutional ideas that were present then but also their strengths and weaknesses.

When I refer to American constitutionalism, I mean mostly, though not exclusively, the constitutional developments that took place in the United States and in nine Latin American countries, namely, Argentina, Bolivia, Colombia, Chile, Ecuador, Mexico, Peru, Uruguay, and Venezuela. These countries deserve particular attention, among other reasons, because of the richness and variety of their constitutional discussions, especially those concerning the organization of their main public institutions. My focus is mainly on the period when the basic features of their constitutions were shaped – from 1776 to 1801 in the United States and from 1810 to 1860 in the Latin American countries.

Neverthless, by "constitutional organization" I mean more than just the constitutional debates and the constitutional text. Constitutional documents represent a fundamental but not exclusive part of the enterprise of organizing the "basic structure" of society. This structure includes the most important institutions of society – those in charge of distributing the fundamental rights and duties and dividing the advantages that derive from social cooperation.[2] The constitution

---

[2] Rawls (1971), chap. 1. For Rawls, the main institutions of society include the political constitution of the country and also its main social and economic dispositions.

plays a particularly important role in the organization of this basic structure: it expresses the philosophical assumptions and the political aspirations of this enterprise. It also tells us about the costs that society is prepared to pay in order to ensure these goals.

In the study of constitutional documents, I make an important distinction between what are normally considered their two main parts: the bill of rights, which establishes the rights and obligations of the people; and the organization of power, which refers to the distribution of functions and capacities between different branches of government. This distinction helps me to compare the different constitutional models that appeared during the period, each of which organized these two parts of the text in different ways. I describe these three models as radical, conservative, and liberal:

- Radical or majoritarian or populist constitutions may be characterized by their political majoritarianism and their normally implicit defense of moral populism. They try to strengthen the authority of the people, in constrast to conservative constitutions.[3] Radical constitutions also tend to include a list of rights in their texts but, as in conservative constitutions, these rights also seem conditional: they are defended as long as they do not contradict – or as long as they foster – the fundamental interests of the majority.
- Conservative models are characterized by their defense of political elitism and moral perfectionism. They tend to concentrate power and strengthen the authority of the executive while making individual rights dependent on "external" values, such as the values of the Catholic religion. For instance, a conservative constitution may include in its text the right to publish ideas freely in the press but make this right conditional on not attacking the church. My definition of conservatism is very close to a standard definition of political conservatism.[4]
- Liberal constitutions emphasize political moderation and moral neutrality and are fundamentally aimed at solving the main

---

[3] My definition of majoritarianism overlaps with the concept of "strict majoritarianism" used in Macmillan's *International Encylcopedia*, which asserts that "not only may a minority never override a majority but also it can never check a majority: a majority vote is conclusive for the whole group." Ibid., vol. 9, p. 536.

[4] For example, Macmillan's *International Encyclopedia of the Social Sciences* defines political conservatism as the ideology that "celebrate[s] inherited patterns of morality and tested institutions, that are skeptical about the efficacy of popular government, that can be counted upon to oppose both the reforming plans of the moderate Left and the deranging schemes of the extreme Left, and that draw their heaviest support from men who have a substantial material and psychological stake in the established order." Sills (1968), vol. 3, p. 291.

problems that they attribute to the former models. They try to limit and control the exercise of power, ensuring equilibrium between the different branches of government. Liberals want to avoid the risk of both "tyranny" and "anarchy," which, they assume, derives from the absence of adequate institutional controls. In addition, they try to ensure a very particular protection of individual rights, which they reasonably assume to be unprotected under the previous formulations. Liberals present these rights as unconditional: in their opinion, they should depend neither on the will of one person in particular nor on any person's conception of the good. My definition of liberalism is also close to the standard international definition of political liberalism.[5]

These different constitutional models refer, in the end, to ideal types or ideal models, which means that in reality we should not expect to find exact or pure expressions of them.[6] These ideal models help us to classify and finally understand the basic organization of the enacted constitutions.[7] Of course, constitutions in most American countries represented strange mixtures of the models just described. This fact does not deny that these constitutions emphasized certain perfectionist features or that other documents tried to foster the state's moral and political "abstinence." Some constitutions were more conservative, or liberal, or radical than others. Moreover, in early American history we find paradigmatic constitutions that resembled very closely the pure or ideal models just described. For example, the U.S. Constitution

---

[5] According to Macmillan's *International Encyclopedia* "[Liberal] thought and practice have stressed two primary themes. One is the dislike for arbitrary authority, complemented by the aim of replacing that authority by other forms of social practice. A second theme is the free expression of individual personality." Ibid., vol. 9, p. 276.

[6] I focus on these three basic models because, in my opinion, they represent the main constitutional models that were established in the Americas during the founding period. However, I do not assume this classification to be exhaustive. There are other possible theoretical combinations that I do not explore in this work.

[7] The differences that separate these projects from each other stem from multiple sources. Undoubtedly, one of them has to do with their assumptions about the intellectual and political capacities of the people. Conservatives are normally very skeptical about people's abilities to take control over their own lives. They assume that there are certain valuable plans of life that need to be followed by each, independent of what each particular person thinks about that option. In their opinion, the state has to use its coercive powers in order to enforce these good ways of life. Liberals, by contrast, assume that each person has to be the only sovereign regarding his or her own life. Paradoxically, perhaps, this confidence in the judgments of each individual is normally translated into a strict distrust of collective opinions. Radicals assume, as do liberals, that people are fundamentally equal with regard to their intellectual capacities. However – and in contrast with liberals – they give priority to the collective decisions of the majority, which many times imply the removal of particular individual choices.

of 1787 represents a very good illustration of a liberal model. The Chilean Constitution of 1823 and 1833, the one sanctioned in Ecuador in 1869, the one defended by Bartolomé Herrera in Peru in 1860, or the constitutional proposals suggested by Lucas Alamán in Mexico represent excellent examples of conservative constitutions. Finally, the 1776 constitution of Pennsylvania (and many other states after that), the short-lived Mexican Constitution of 1814 (the Apatzingán Constitution), and some of the constitutional initiatives proposed by José Gervasio Artigas in Uruguay or by the Chilean Francisco Bilbao seem close to the radical model. These paradigmatic constitutions help us to understand the nature and ideological affiliation of other documents sanctioned or proposed during the same period.

A question underlying the entire project is whether it makes sense to take constitutions, and particularly Latin American constitutions, so seriously, especially when we recognize how much the political leaders of the time tended to ignore the commands and limits established by these early texts. An extreme example of this attitude was Bolivian president Mariano Melgarejo's assertion that the 1886 constitution, whose enactment he was then celebrating, was very nice, but, that fact notwithstanding, he would rule as he wanted. Granted, if we had to write a definitive history of the political life of these countries, we would probably not dedicate more than a chapter to the development of their constitutions. Yet this would be a very important chapter: constitutions do not represent a mere footnote in the history of the American nations. In the way they designed new constitutions, some politicians and their legal advisers decisively contributed to shaping a new political and legal practice. Undoubtedly, the numerous constitutions sanctioned in Latin America during the nineteenth century provide evidence not only of the fragility of these documents but also of the importance acquired by these constitutions. Even cases like Melgarejo's do not refute the fact that most politicians, including the most authoritarian ones, conceived of the constitution as important, at least in symbolic terms, to the institutional revival of their countries. These documents, despite their mistakes and defects, actually defined the main features of the institutional structure of the countries in question. Also, the old constitutional discussions and documents represent a valuable antecedent, which is indispensable if we want to understand contemporary constitutional discussions. They played a significant role in shaping American "public philosophy."[8]

[8] I take the idea of a "public philosophy" from Sandel (1996), p. 4.

Of equal importance is the need to define the limits of this enterprise. My analysis of constitutionalism should not be read as a way of minimizing the weight of other causes in determining the success or failure of different political experiences in America. Undoubtedly, the religious fanaticism of certain sectors, the economic voracity of other groups, and the political ambition of certain leaders may be more important than any legal change in explaining the political evolution of the examined countries. However, we should not neglect the impact of constitutionalism. The evidence suggests that certain institutional arrangements favored political stability whereas others did not and that some constitutions contributed to the cause of liberty or equality whereas others cleared the path to authoritarianism. In sum, I assume that constitutions matter when we want to understand and explain the political life of the communities in which we live, even though other factors may be more influential than these pieces of paper.

There is the risk of placing too much emphasis on certain speeches or written documents, or on certain intellectual figures, and thereby neglecting the importance of social processes. After all, does it make sense to dedicate so much attention to written materials that nobody read or to oratorical pieces that only a small and very exclusive elite listened to? Although in most cases the majority of the population was indifferent to all those abstract and seemingly unimportant discussions, even this fact does not deny the value of my research, which, in the end, depends partly, on the scope and ambition of my purposes. For example, I believe that the information that we analyze may be relevant to studying the evolution of certain political ideas in America. The fact that, when formulated, these ideas circulated mainly within a closed elite says nothing against the project. These ideas had and continue to have an impact on the way we organize our daily lives. Many of the political debates that we witness today transmit the echoes of those older discussions.

Another point worth noting is that, although a particular person, say, James Madison, wrote many pieces clearly associated with a certain constitutional conception, such as liberalism, that person is not necessarily a liberal. In fact, many of the political figures I discuss changed their basic ideas dramatically during their lives. The Argentinean Juan Bautista Alberdi, for example, can serve as a good representative of liberal or conservative thinking, depending on what period of his life we consider. For this reason, my references to certain works or a certain author should be taken only as examples of the constitutional conception under examination. This explains why,

Introduction

in certain exceptional cases, a name that I associate with a specific concept may later appear associated with another one.

Given the large-scale dimension of this project, the very idea of studying "American constitutionalism" may seem too vast. Because there are too many important differences to take into account when dealing with so many different countries,[9] there is always the risk of making incorrect generalizations about all cases when comparing them with the peculiarities of the countries one knows best. In defense of the scope of the project one could say, first, that this is not a historical project: I am interested mostly in highlighting the influence of certain constitutional ideas in America and examining their weaknesses and strengths. I am not interested in giving an exhaustive account of early constitutional ideas and their influence across different countries. Second, in spite of the significant differences between the countries under scrutiny, many similarities join them together. For example, many of these countries were influenced by similar texts. In Latin America, the Constitution of Cadiz was enormously influential at one time, whereas the U.S. Constitution prevailed at other periods. The same holds true about the influence of Catholicism or the radicalism of the French Revolution in Latin America, or of republicanism in the United States. Throughout the hemisphere, at different periods, different movements and organizations contributed to strengthening certain ideas and disregarding others. Not surprisingly, then, liberals, conservatives, and radicals tended to advance similar constitutional projects even when they lived in different countries and at different times.

My work is to a great extent descriptive. However, the more egalitarian view that I try to reconstruct always accounts for my normative view. I describe this egalitarian conception as one that defends both the individual's right to self-government and society's right to self-determination. In this sense, the egalitarian view radically differs from the conservative view, which actually denies both claims. In contrast with the liberal-individualist position, egalitarians say that the constitution has to leave more room for the will of the people, which is in some ways diluted in liberal constitutions because of the specific system of checks and balances that they adopt. In addition, egalitarians say that the defense of rights should include the defense of certain fundamental interests (e.g., the right to shelter) normally

---

[9] For a similarly ample comparative project, Frank Safford properly describes the limits and possibilities of the task ahead. See Safford (1985). I clearly subscribe to his view.

neglected in liberal models, interests that should be deemed of fundamental importance if one were committed to defending the value of individual autonomy. Finally, and in contrast with radicals, egalitarians assume that rights have to be defended unconditionally and that the will of the people needs always to be refined. In this sense, they disagree with the radicals' assumption that "the voice of the people is the voice of God."

Comparing these different constitutional proposals should allow us to evaluate the achievements, merits, and defects of each of these projects. In my final assessment, I claim that, after the founding period examined here, the structure of most American constitutions reflected the liberal ideals or, as occurred in many Latin American countries, a combination of liberal and conservative ideals. I also claim that, in the end, these constitutions undermined, at least in part, the egalitarian commitments that were present at the time of the various revolutions seeking independence: a commitment to the idea that all men are created equal as much as a commitment to the idea of collective self-government. Through these constitutional documents, the new political leaders dishonored the egalitarian faith that distinguished their societies' main social commitment: an egalitarian faith that they themselves displayed in the declarations of independence of their countries and in the first articles of the constitutions that they proposed.

Chapter One
Radicalism: Honoring the General Will

The Engine of American History

The existence or the possibility, real or imagined, of a government "by its citizens in mass" has been one of the most important causes of the development of American constitutionalism. Legal reforms were often adopted to prevent the radicalization of politics, that is, a situation where the rules simply enforced the norms preferred by the majority.

An illustration of this situation is the development of so-called radical constitutionalism in the United States soon after independence was declared. Following the revolutionary spirit of the time, many states enacted constitutions – the first "radical" constitutions – that came to empower a very active citizenry. These constitutions had a remarkable impact on the minds of the main political leaders of the country, who realized that such institutional systems adopted at the national level would subvert the already fragile order.[1] Many of the fundamental features of the federal constitution may be explained by this historical fact: the early local constitutions taught the leaders what *not* to do at a national level. For example, the system of checks and balances, probably the main creation of the American Federalists, was a direct reaction to the system of "strict separation

---

[1] According to Gordon Wood, "By the mid-1780s many American leaders had come to believe that *the state legislatures, not the governors, were the political authority to be most feared*. Not only were some of the legislatures violating the individual rights of property-owners through their excessive printing of paper money and their various acts on behalf of debtors, but in all the states the assemblies also pushed beyond the generous grants of legislative authority of the 1776 Revolutionary constitutions and were absorbing numerous executive and judicial duties – directing military operations, for example, and setting aside court judgements." Wood (2002), pp. 142–143, emphasis added.

9

of powers" organized by the radical state constitutions.[2] Thus, we may understand many of the defensive tools reserved to the different branches – the executive's powers of veto, the newly developed practice of judicial review, the ample legislative functions of the senate – as means that came to weaken the powerful legislatures created by those radical constitutions. Similarly, we may read the strong protections created in favor of property rights and, particularly, against the issuing of "paper money" as a reaction to the policies promoted by the strong state legislatures at the time.

The situation was not substantially different in Latin America. Typically, the Rousseauean ingredients of the constitutions enacted in countries such as Venezuela and Peru after declarations of independence help us to understand many of the exceptional political decisions that followed their approval, including the sudden desire to concentrate the political powers in the hands of a dictator. Although those early and quite radical constitutions were condemned to failure, it is surprising to see how much they were blamed for the political difficulties that ensued. Simon Bolívar's "Memorial to the Citizens of New Granada by a Citizen of Caracas," written in 1813, represents an exceptional example of this attitude. In the "Memorial," Bolívar specified that "among the causes that brought about Venezuela's downfall the nature of its constitution ranks first, which, I repeat, was as contrary to Venezuela's interests as it was favorable to those of her adversaries."[3] Notably, Bolívar faulted the seemingly radical constitution of 1811, which survived only a few days, for making the consolidation of independence impossible. Bolívar, as we know, would soon become one of the most influential (and conservative) constitutional thinkers in Latin America.

---

[2] I define the "Federalists" as the group responsible for drafting and defending the U.S. federal constitution. Those who rejected the constitution are defined as the "Anti-Federalists."

[3] See Bolívar (1951), vol. 1, p. 22. He also stated, "The most grievous error committed by Venezuela in making her start on the political stage was, as none can deny, her fatal adoption of the system of tolerance, a system long condemned as weak and inadequate by every man of common sense, yet tenaciously maintained with an unparalleled blindness to the very end." Ibid., p. 18. A few years later, in the speech he delivered at the inauguration of the second national Congress of Venezuela in Angostura, he went back to his criticisms of the original Venezuelan Constitution, now in order to object to its federalist character. He stated that "no matter how tempting this magnificent federative system might have appeared, and regardless of its possible effect, the Venezuelans were not prepared to enjoy it immediately upon casting off their chains. We were not prepared for such good, for good, like evil, results in death when it is sudden and excessive. Our moral fiber did not then possess the stability necessary to derive benefits from a wholly representative power; a power so sublime, in fact, that it might more nearly befit a republic of saints." Ibid., p. 181.

Similarly, in Peru the authoritarian general Agustin Gamarra faulted the first national constitutions and especially the progressive document of 1828 for the country's subsequent crisis. Gamarra interpreted those documents as implementing a feeble institutional system, unable to reestablish political order, while promoting a deep hostility toward the executive power. "The [1828] constitution," declared Gamarra, "is what is dissolving the country: there is no obedience, no authorities; in this situation of immorality nobody seems ready to work. The prisons are full of assassins: this is the fruit of impunity and license.... I find no other remedy but to promote the reform of our Fundamental Code, because with two more years like these, Peru will be lost forever."[4] Gamarra fulfilled his promise immediately, enacting the authoritarian Constitution of Huancayo.

In Mexico, too, the early radical actions developed by political activists against rich property owners had a tremendous impact on the evolution of the political life of the country. One important example involves the case of Lucas Alamán, the main right-wing ideologist during the nineteenth century. Lucas Alamán's family was directly affected by the radical measures adopted by the revolutionaries regarding the distribution of property. Lucas Alamán never forgot this attack and consequently aimed all his constitutional proposals at weakening majority rule and protecting property. His defense of a "conservative senate," composed of representatives of the upper classes, and his proposals for restricting the political rights of the majority are only two among the multiple initiatives he promoted in defense of those who had been threatened in the early revolutionary years. "The proprietors generate envy and rapacious feelings, that is why they need protection...we need to ensure the proprietors...a direct influence over the creation of law...in many states a war has been declared against them...that is why so many nations limited the right to suffrage only to the proprietors, and in accordance with their contributions."[5]

Such tendencies were common in all the American countries and show how the more radical experiences of the region shaped constitutional practice.[6] That radicalism was one of the fundamental "engines"

---

[4] Quoted in Planas (1998), p. 145.
[5] Alamán (1997), pp. 187–192.
[6] In various passages of his excellent work, Frank Safford also describes the impact of the populists' mobilizations upon the most conservative minds. For example, in one of these passages he tells us, "In New Granada conservatives feared not the possibility of peasant rebellion but rather the mobilization of artisans in Bogotá and, after a time, of popular elements in Cali. In Peru and Chile also urban insurrection was more of a threat than the peasantry." Safford (1985), p. 398.

of the constitutional process is emphasized by the antiradical testimonies that were advanced by some of the region's most important political figures. The influence of radicalism and the fears that it generated are not difficult to explain. In a period marked by the revolutions of independence in America, no other discourse turned out to be more attractive than the one based on the idea of self-government. This fact explains not only the failure of the radical theorists in England and their extraordinary success in America a few years later but also the spectacular diffusion of French revolutionary literature in America. The Americans were anxiously waiting for these ideas: they wanted to provide their claims with solid theoretical foundations. All of them, even the more conservative ones, acclaimed and propagated the ideology of selfgovernment during the fight for independence.

The immediate hostility generated by these radical ideas, once the independence process was finished, is also not surprising. At that moment, different groups were fighting to define who would be in charge of restructuring the new societies institutionally, socially, and economically. For that reason, none of these groups were comfortable with attempts to consolidate of the radical project; this alternative, they assumed, would come to subvert the entire organization of society. Paradoxically, then, they made enormous efforts to prevent the triumph of the same ideology that they themselves had been promoting a short while ago. They had awakened the "sleeping giant" and now did not know how to send him back to his cave. The people, as Federalist Fisher Ames put it, were now turning "against their teachers the doctrines which were inculcated in order to effect the late revolution."[7]

The History of Radical Constitutionalism in America

Before exploring in detail the content, scope, and limits of the radicals' approach to constitutionalism, we should consider the context in which their views emerged. Social and political circumstances contributed to the appearance of radical ideas about the organization of society, both in the United States and in Latin America.

In the United States, radical ideas grew rapidly after independence. The reasons for this growth seem apparent: the North Americans had already developed a practice of self-government; their fight against England was made in the name of self-government; and their

[7] Wood (1969), p. 397.

revolutionary leaders demanded their political mobilization invoking self-governing ideals. The practice of the "town meetings," which was common before and after the revolution, allowed the people to intervene directly in the political affairs of the community: these meetings enabled them to have a clear say in public matters and taught them about the importance of their participation.[8] These people, in fact, assumed that their political will should prevail and, for that reason, demanded new institutions that facilitated this result.

Probably the first and most important document that reflected this view was the 1776 Pennsylvania Constitution, which was the product of the British radical Thomas Paine. The text had a decisive influence over other states, being followed by a wave of new constitutions that reproduced its fundamental structure. It launched what was called a period of "radical constitutionalism."[9]

---

[8] According to Wood, "During the 1780s the people had organized various committees, conventions, and other extralegal bodies in order to voice grievances or to achieve political goals. By doing so, they had continued common practices that had been used during the Revolution itself. Vigilante and mob actions of various kinds had done quickly and efficiently what the new state governments were often unable to do, control prices, prevent profiteering, and punish Tories. Everywhere people had extended the logic of 'actual' representation and had sought to instruct and control the institutions of government. Unlike the British in relation to their House of Commons, the American people never surrendered to any political institutions or even to all political institutions together their full and final sovereign power." Wood (2002), p. 160.

[9] Paine had traveled to the United States after an opaque public life in England. His ideas, however, became enormously popular in America. His *Common Sense*, for instance, went through twenty-five editions in the year 1776 alone. Paine was touching very sensitive cords: he criticized the British political system, wrote about the decadence of the hereditary British government, and praised the ideal of self-government. The constitution that he proposed reflected some of these concerns. It reserved a central role to the legislature and created a weak executive; it suppressed the institution of senate; and it attempted to ensure a more transparent decision-making process, opening it up to the public. It provided for the annual election of representatives (art. 9), declared that "the doors of the house [of representatives] shall be and remain open for the admission of all persons who behave decently" (art. 13), proclaimed the obligation of publishing the votes and proceedings of the assembly (art. 14), and declared that all the elections would be "free and voluntary" (art. 32). In addition, and in order that "laws before they are enacted may be more maturely considered, and the inconvenience of hasty determinations as much as possible prevented, all bills of a public nature shall be printed for the consideration of the people, before they are read in general assembly the last time for debate and amendment; and, except on occasions of sudden necessity, shall not be passed into law until the next session of assembly; and for the more perfect satisfaction of the public, the reasons and motives for making such laws shall be fully and clearly expressed in the preambles" (art. 15). Its bill of rights, in addition, asserted that all power "derived from the people"; that all officers of government were "their trustees

13

Following the example of Pennsylvania, many other states implemented radical reforms to their constitutions after independence. We find unicameral legislatures in Georgia and Vermont; executives that were elected by the legislature (in nine of the eighteen constitutions enacted at that time); an executive deprived of its powers of veto; a popularly elected council aimed at preserving the constitution (Vermont); popular elections for most of the political officers; a senate directly elected by the citizenry in all the new state constitutions, with the exception of Maryland; rotation for most public positions (in Delaware, Georgia, Maryland, North Carolina, and Virginia); and a declaration of rights in almost all cases.[10] Clearly, many of these new constitutions greatly differed from what would come to be the federal constitution. They tended to create weak executives, reserved a larger role to the citizenry, provided for a "strict separation of powers," and ensured a closer relationship between the people and their representatives.

Undoubtedly, the intense political activism that distinguished the postrevolutionary years was at least in part due to the nature of the state constitutions. This intensity, as a final consequence, led many state legislatures to adopt decisions that were very favorable to the people's claims. At that time, the most important demand was the issuance of paper money. Most people were highly indebted after the war, and the printing of paper money appeared to offer the only escape from this situation; the alternatives seemed to be the loss of their few properties or prison. Under strong popular pressure, many legislatures decided to accept the popular demands. A first wave of money creation concluded in 1777, and then a second one extended that until 1781. However, for Allan Nevins, if at that time "the paper money doctrine was endemic, [it became] epidemic and virulent" in 1785.[11] This

and servants, and at all time accountable to them" (art. 4); and that the people had the right to "assemble together, and to apply to the legislature for redress of grievances, by address, petition, or remonstrance" (art. 16). Profoundly republican, it declared "a firm adherence to justice, moderation, temperance, industry, and frugality," virtues that, assumedly, were necessary to "preserve the blessings of liberty, and keep a government free" (art. 14).

[10] See Lutz (1988), pp. 104–105.

[11] What happened in Rhode Island during those years is particularly telling. In 1786 the leader of the debtors' group, Jonathan Hazard, was directly elected as the governor of the state. Controlling both the executive and the legislative branches of the state, the debtors' group advanced diverse laws favorable to its interests. The laws provoked serious concern among the creditors and also among the national political elite. In a letter to his brother Ambrose expressing his concern about the events that were taking place in Rhode Island, James Madison wrote: "In Rhode Island a large sum has been struck and made a tender, and coin. The consequence is that

situation, without doubt, created an intense social climate that would have a serious impact on the forthcoming constitutional debate.[12]

Radicals had achieved a strong influence at the state level: they participated in the writing of some of their constitutions and took an active role in the political debates of the time, through articles they wrote in the newspapers and the political activities that they organized. In spite of this, radicals did not play a significant role during the debates of the federal convention: those debates were mainly reserved to a more exclusive elite.

Even though radicals were not present during the constitutional debates, their viewpoints were sometimes represented by the so-called Anti-Federalists, that is, the delegates who did not sign the final version of the document. The Anti-Federalists were in the main well-established and powerful representatives of their states and not radical ideologists: they denounced democracy as the source of "all political evils" and attacked, rather than promoted, popular participation. However, it is also true that, by defending the decentralization of politics and attacking all those proposals that favored the concentration of public authority, they contributed toward advancing at least some of the populists' demands.

From those who were "outside" the federal convention, probably the clearest radical voice was Thomas Jefferson's. As happens with most active people, Jefferson is not easy to classify. This notwithstanding, it is clear that he made a very significant contribution to the radical cause. His profuse and articulate writing may represent for the radicals what the *Federalist Papers* represent for the ardent defenders of the North American constitution. As we know, Jefferson played a fundamental role in the draft of the Declaration of Independence; was politically very active in his state of Virginia; collaborated with the U.S. government as an ambassador in France, where he became well acquainted with the new revolutionary ideologies; and became the third president of the United States.[13]

---

provisions are withheld from the Market, the Shops shut up – a general distress and tumultuous meetings." Nevins (1927), p. 518.

[12] "Madison to Ambrose Madison," Aug. 7, 1786, Madison (1979), vol. 9, p. 89.

[13] In contrast with what many of his contemporaries maintained, Jefferson always defended an active role for popular majorities. Because of his confidence in the majority will, he objected to the decision to write the federal constitution behind the closed doors of the convention, as well as many of the proposals advanced by the delegates. He assumed, as many radicals assumed, that the constitution relied too heavily on internal types of control, neglecting the importance of external, popular ones.

Radicalism

In early Latin American history we find two significant waves of radicalism, although radicals had little direct influence in the regional constitutional conventions. Unsurprisingly, the history of Latin American radicalism also begins with the independence revolutions and the increasing importance of the ideas of collective self-government and the sovereign people. Latin Americans, as did their U.S. counterparts, confronted a powerful and monarchical authority and asserted the rights of the locals to rule by themselves. The early revolutionary years (1810–1812) are characterized by the growing influence of U.S. and, particularly, French revolutionary ideas. Most of the early Latin American constitutions – the 1811 Constitution of Venezuela being the best example of them – were inundated with Rousseauean phraseology: the social contract, the general will, the sovereignty of the people. The early revolutionary leaders appeared to be radical, bellicose, and extremist in their defense of independence. The Argentines Mariano Moreno (one of the main translator of Rousseau's works in the region) and Bernardo Monteagudo are two good representatives of this early and violent version of radicalism.[14] The Uruguayan José Gervasio Artigas appears as one of the more consistent and influential radicals in this early period, with his claims for a more egalitarian distribution of land and a more decentralized political authority.[15] The early revolutionary movement against landowners in Mexico is also a good illustration of the force and influence of this early radicalism: this was a movement accompanied with constant appeals to the lower classes and extremist plans for the redistribution of lands.[16]

This first wave of radicalism was promptly defeated, however, as a consequence of the serious crisis of independence that followed the declarations of independence in most of the new nations. In effect, after 1810 Spain made significant military efforts for reestablishing its authority upon the old colonies, and local military leaders, unfairly, began to fault those early radical constitutionalists for the crisis. Thus, shortly after the declaration of independence and the earliest wave of radicalism, conservatism reemerged in most countries of the region: in Chile, General Diego Portales led this military reaction (which would install the most stable conservative regime

---

[14] Showing the extremism of his views, Moreno claimed that "the foundations of a new republic have never been laid except by rigor and punishment mixed with the spilt blood of those members who might oppose its progress." I take this translation from Shunway (1993), p. 35. See also Moreno (1937).
[15] Halperín Donghi (1973; 1985).
[16] Bazant (1977); Churruca Peláez (1983).

in the region); in Argentina, some of the early revolutionary leaders promoted monarchical solutions; Mexicans directly established a monarchical government; and Bolívar and his allies led the conservative response in Colombia, Peru, and Venezuela.

The second wave of Latin American radicalism emerged after the 1848 revolutions in Europe. Shortly afterward, many Latin Americans who took part or became somehow involved in those events returned to their countries, bringing with them some of the aspirations of the revolutionary movement. In many cases, the revolutionary demands seemed to have a clear correspondence in the Latin American world. In America, as in Europe, the demands for the democratization of society sound relevant, given the concentration of power that characterized the new independent nations. In America, as in Europe, the complaints of the lower classes also seem to be reasonable, given the level of exploitation that they suffered. In America, as in Europe, artisans were beginning to organize themselves in associations in order to protect their interests.

The Chileans Francisco Bilbao and Santiago Arcos represent good illustrations of these phenomena: they were Latin American intellectuals who participated in the 1848 European revolution and then returned to their country to reproce and continue that battle for democracy. Both of them had been directly involved in the belligerent actions of the artisans in France and were in close contact with progressive intellectual elites of the time. Back in Chile, they launched the Sociedad de la Igualdad in order to help organize the lower classes and fight against the "conservative order" in place since the end of the 1820s.[17] This democratizing wave, promoted by artisans' organizations, also became important in other Latin American countries, such as Peru[18] and Colombia (New Granada). The Colombian artisans' associations became the most relevant social actor of the country during the mid-1850s.[19] Also in Ecuador, intellectuals such as Juan

---

[17] Collier (1967); L.A. Romero (1978), pp. 180–181. The Sociedad de la Igualdad was created in Chile, at the middle of the century, by two young activists, Santiago Arcos and Francisco Bilbao, who were disappointed with the political situation in their country and particularly with the lack of social roots among the existing political forces. One of the first decisions of the Sociedad was to foster a popular upheaval in San Felipe, where the Sociedad supported an artisan insurrection that ended with the imprisonment of San Felipe's mayor. Soon afterward, the group supported another popular rebellion in Santiago. In both cases, the national government reacted strongly: it declared a state of siege, arrested many of the members of the Sociedad, and even demanded the group's dissolution. By that time, Bilbao and Arcos had both left the country and continued their militant activities abroad.
[18] Gootenberg (1993).
[19] Jaramillo Uribe (1964); Molina (1973).

Montalvo led an incipient movement in defense of democratization, associationism, and land reform.

At the same time, in Mexico the Revolución de Ayutla took place, led by radical liberals who, in this way, put an end to decades of authoritarianism (the revolution marked the overthrow of General Antonio de López de Santa Anna's autocratic regime). Following this revolutionary movement, the new authorities called a constitutional convention that produced the constitution of 1857. Its debates were characterized by many well-articulated presentations of radical constitutional projects and proposals, including the ones presented by Melchor Ocampo, Ponciano Arriaga, Ignacio Ramírez, and Castillo Velasco.

It seems undeniable that radical political discourse gained popular adherence over time and finally contributed to the gradual democratization of the new societies.[20] However, what I would describe as a "partial success" of radicalism was achieved in spite of the desires of the dominant political coalitions. In fact, radical groups and the associative movement that was linked to radicalism suffered from heavy political repression. Many of these groups were fiercely opposed (e.g., in Peru) or simply declared illegal (e.g., the Sociedad de la Igualdad, after one year in existence), and many of their members were sent into exile.[21] In Colombia, the associations played a crucial role in the election of José Hilario López as the country's president. Despite their extraordinary contribution, however, the new administration did not pay much attention to the artisans' claims: López's government, although radically liberal, promoted economic liberalism instead of protectionism, something that seriously hurt the interests of the artisans.[22] Meanwhile, in countries such as Argentina, the dominant elite developed a strong sense of distrust to the new democratic ideals because (rightly or wrongly, in good or bad faith) they associated

---

[20] In spite of its ephemeral character, it seems clear that the Sociedad de la Igualdad and its sequels (e.g., the Partido Radical) played a fundamental role in the gradual moderation of Chile's conservative regime and that the artisans' movement in Colombia, which had ramifications throughout the country, decisively contributed to popularizing the democratic ideal in New Granada.

[21] Gootenberg (1993); Collier (1967).

[22] After these events, some of the artisans' leaders, in association with members of the armed forces, tried to impose their authority through coercive means. Under General José María Melo's command, they then promoted a disgraceful military coup that ended very badly – for them and for the country. Other political figures such as Murillo Toro, at one point closely associated with the artisans' group, followed a different and more interesting path. In particular, Murillo Toro became a serious advocate of social and political reforms. He was one of the strongest defenders of universal suffrage and one of the most radical supporters of land reform.

these new claims with the despotic government of General Juan Manuel de Rosas, who had ruled in a completely discretionary way but employed a democratic phraseology and eventually resorted to populist means (i.e., plebiscites held under conditions of repression for political dissidents).

In the end, the fears generated by the increasing importance of radicalism helped local elites – mainly composed of conservatives and liberals – to merge, in a surprising move. After all, these two forces had spent decades fighting against each other. Because both conservatives and liberals viewed radicalism as an unacceptable threat to their desire for stability and order, they decided to take advantage of their many points of agreement and began to cosign constitutional documents that they had each refused to sign before. The result was a rejection of the radicals' approach to constitutionalism. What were, then, the radicals' main theoretical contributions?

"A Government by Its Citizens in Mass"

Above all, the radicals made a significant contribution to the cause of political equality. They believed in the moral principle that *all people were born equal*. Radicals recognized the tremendous potential of this principle and translated it into a political one: the principle of *self-government*. The connection between the notion of basic human equality and the principle of self-government was quite obvious: if we are all equal, why should we accept the discretionary rule of a few? If we want to count each person as equal, why should we not accept majority rule?[23]

In England, the notion of self-government had appeared under the banners of radical groups ever since the famous "Putney debates" in the late 1640s. At that time, the "levellers" began to manifest a profound social discontent with the British monarchy.[24] More significantly, during the following century different radical groups directly challenged the authority of the crown after the so-called Wilkes affair. These different radical associations – the "Radical Dissenters," the "Constitutional Society," the "Society of the Supporters of the Bill of Rights" – proposed strict reforms of the existing political system in the name of the people's right to self-government. Richard Price, a member of the Radical Dissenters, defended these reforms as a way of ensuring that each person would become "his own legislator."

---

[23] See, for example, Waldron (1999), p. 111.
[24] See, for example, Aylmer (1975).

Joseph Priestley, famous for his sermon in defense of the French revolutionary movements, which was ferociously attacked by Edmund Burke in his *Reflections on the French Revolution*, defended the "frequent interchange" between the people and their representatives as a way of honoring that principle of self-government.[25] Because of similar commitments, James Burgh wrote his well-known book *Political Disquisitions*, in which he proposed a radical reform of the political system that would ensure a more intense popular participation in politics.[26] John Cartwright, a leading political figure of British radicalism during the eighteenth century, developed Burgh's ideas in his work *Take Your Choice*. This book represented one of the most advanced political programs of the period.[27] The Briton Thomas Paine clarified, simplified, and organized many of these radical views, making them accessible for Americans. In his main books, and particularly in *The Rights of Man*, Paine defended the people's right to selfgovernment against those who, like Edmund Burke, denied it in the name of existing political tradition.

In both the United States and Latin America, political leaders had access to these ideas, which were enormously important during the revolutionary years. Thomas Jefferson made a clear connection between the principle of self-government and the principle of basic human equality in the U.S. Declaration of Independence. The idea that "all men are created equal" appeared at the very beginning of it, as the first "self-evident" "truth" of politics. In his opinion, that principle was simply "the common sense" of the age.[28] Jefferson shared a profound commitment to the idea of self-government with Paine, which they reproduced in their famous defense of the independence of generations. In Paine's view, "the earth belongs to the living."

A few years later, many Latin Americans became acquainted with Paine's works as well as with many of the early radical constitutions adopted in the United States. The Latin Americans read versions

---

[25] Priestley (1791), p. 257.
[26] Hay (1979), especially chap. 6.
[27] Cone (1957), pp. 56, 76.
[28] Wood (2002), p. 102. In Wood's opinion, by the end of the eighteenth century to be enlightened was to believe in the natural equality of all men. Even those as aristocratic as William Byrd and Governor Francis Fauquier of Virginia conceded that all men, even men of different nations and races, were born equal and that "the principal difference between one people and another proceeds only from the differing opportunities of improvement.... Thus despite the patrician sense of gentlemanly distinctiveness expressed by the Revolutionary leaders – a frank and unabashed commitment to elitism that profoundly separates them from us today – what in the end remains remarkable is the degree to which they accepted the equality of all people." Ibid.

of these works translated by the Venezuelan Manuel García de la Sena in his book *La independencia de la Costa Firme justificada por Thomas Paine treinta años ha*.[29] Through his translation, Sena, who was intensely involved in the development of the constitutional life of his country, managed to influence many important political leaders of his time. Most notably, José Artigas, the radical revolutionary leader of the Banda Oriental, read Sena's work, which would have an important impact on the first radical constitutions of his country.[30] Acknowledging this influence, Artigas wrote a letter to the Cabildo of Montevideo in which he said: "I would celebrate if each of the *orientales* had a copy of [this book edited by Sena]. Fortunately, I have an exemplar myself, but this is not enough to illustrate how much [I value this work]."[31] Following these egalitarian influences, the Banda Oriental's constitution of 1813 began with a clear reference to the idea that "all men are born free and equal" and a strong affirmation of the right to self-government. The noted Chilean radical Francisco Bilbao translated this idea of self-government into a particular understanding of freedom, which we could name *freedom as nondependency*: "Every man is free. No man can depend on another man. The freedom that makes a person sovereign prevents him from violating or establishing the dependency of another man."

The radicals' commitment to the idea of self-government revealed something still more fundamental, which was their *confidence* in the intellectual capacities of the people. Clearly, during the revolutions of independence in America, most political leaders appealed to the people, praised their abilities, and attacked the political domination exercised by foreign governments over their countries. However, not many of them maintained those claims when the revolutions of independence were over. The same leaders who had fostered the political participation of the people during the war and

---

[29] Among other works, the book included "The Articles of Confederation"; the early constitutions of Pennsylvania, Connecticut, New Jersey, Massachusetts, and Virginia; and different commentaries written by Paine on American independence, finance, governmental authority, and the British monarchy.

[30] A hero of the revolution of independence in the River Plate area, Artigas showed himself to have an egalitarian spirit unmatched by most of his contemporaries. Two constitutional projects created during his government reaffirmed his federalist and egalitarian commitments. One, written by Felipe Cardozo in 1813, created a confederation of states in which the president was elected by lottery through the senate. The second, presented by the first autonomous government in 1813, created a federal structure; divided the power among three branches after the 1780 Constitution of Massachusetts, on which it was based; reorganized the working of the *cabildos*; and provided for a weak executive with mandate lasting only one year.

[31] Grases (1961), p. xviii.

had encouraged the people to sacrifice even their lives in favor of the revolution were then the main advocates of their passivity and subordination. Surprisingly, they assumed that the people had to offer their bodies to the new nations but that the new nations could do without their will.

Radicals instead upheld their commitments untouched, in spite of the sharp condemnations that they received for doing so. In a letter to William Jarvis, Thomas Jefferson discussed this point and concluded by saying: "I know no safe depository of the ultimate powers of society but the people themselves; and if we think them not enlightened enough to exercise their control with a wholesome discretion, the remedy is not to take it from them, but to inform their discretion by education."[32] This was the best answer that a radical could provide in the face of attack. In Latin America, a Colombian politician, Manuel Murillo Toro, gave a similar response to his critics. In Colombia, in fact, radicals and radical liberals had fostered the adoption of universal suffrage but became very disillusioned after they saw the results of the first free and open elections. What happened was that the large majority of the people, following the counsel of the conservative leaders of the church, favored the Conservative Party at the polls: the people voted for the same politicians who, radicals argued, had been oppressing them for years. Murillo Toro, then one of the few radical political leaders who kept his confidence in the people's capacities, replied: "We need to start our work in order to serve the political education of the people. The people cannot be educated in abstract. It is only by acting that the people can learn. The very practice of voting educates the people."[33]

This view implied a new and very significant epistemic position that said that "fundamental truths could be arrived at by anyone with the perseverance to examine the world carefully and to cogitate on his experience."[34] From this starting point, according to which all were endowed with reason, many radicals jumped to a different and more polemical idea – that the greater the number of people participating in politics, the greater the chances of obtaining a "just" or impartial political decision. "The more numerous state assemblies and conventions have universally discovered more wisdom, and as much order, as the less numerous ones," stated the "Federal Farmer."[35] "Great social ideas require the sanction of a numerous and

[32] Jefferson (1999), p. 382.
[33] Murillo Toro (1979), p. 95.
[34] See, for example, Kuklick's introduction, in Paine (1989), p. x.
[35] Quoted in Storing (1981a), vol. 2, p. 284.

august body," said the Ecuadorian Juan Montalvo.[36] The assumption that helped radicals go from their confidence in the people's capacity to their preference for "large numbers" was probably something like the "Millean" premise that said that each person is the "best judge" of his or her own interests, a premise that was not at all foreign to the American constitutional writers.[37] If one takes into account all these ideas, one can reasonably conclude, with many radicals, that the decisions tend to become more impartial after a *process of collective reflection*.[38] In fact, radicals may say, if the decision makers do not consult *all those potentially affected*,[39] they probably lose fundamental information regarding the decision they want to make. Without that information, it is more difficult for them to adequately recognize and balance all the different viewpoints existing in society: their choice, therefore, runs the risk of being less impartial than it should be. In line with these arguments, Jefferson defined the ideal of a "republican government" – *his* ideal of government – as "a government by its citizens in mass, acting directly and personally, according to rules established by the majority." "[E]very other government is more or less republican," he added, "in proportion as it has in its composition more or less of this ingredient of the direct action of the citizens."[40]

The People against "the Few and the Great"

American radicals distrusted, above all, not the will of the majority but, by contrast, systems of political representation that left the people with very little authority in the decision-making process. Power, they believed, "often convert[ed] a good man in private life to a tyrant in

---

[36] He defended this view in the discourse that he pronounced upon the installation of the "Republican Society." MacDonald Spindler and Cook Brooks (1984), p. 27.
[37] For example, the Colombian Murillo Toro explicitly defended the idea that "the best judge of his own interests is the same individual." See Murillo Toro (1979), p. 90. Also, during the Mexican constitutional convention of 1857, the radical Ignacio Ramírez proclaimed that the legislative task required no more wisdom than that of the people. The laws had to take into consideration the needs of the people and for that reason the people, needed to be trusted and consulted. See, for example, Zevada (1972), p. 182. His colleague Melchor Ocampo reaffirmed this view, contrasting the principle of the "despot" with the principle of "democracy."
[38] See, for example, Nino (1991).
[39] See, for example, Habermas (1996).
[40] Jefferson (1999), p. 207. "In general," he added, "I believe that the decisions of the people, in a body, will be more honest and disinterested than those of the wealthy men." He presented this view in a letter to John Taylor, from May 28, 1816. See Jefferson (1984), p. 1392.

office."[41] That was why, for example, many of them suggested not delegating the "power for making laws...to any man for a longer time than one year."[42]

This antirepresentative trend was quite important during the early years of the revolution, particularly in the United States. Using a rhetoric that resembled the French revolutionaries, they said, for example: "You fought, conquered and gained your liberty, then keep it....Trust it not out of your own hands; be assured, if you do, you will never more regain it."[43] Similarly, others assumed that, "as soon as the delegate power gets too far out of the hands of the constituent power, a tyranny is in some degree established."[44] The populists feared the creation of a new national government and considered it the source of future oppression. They predicted that "all the power [would] fall in the hands of the few and the great."[45] This was, in fact, what Jefferson stated in his famous dictum – that "173 despots would surely be as oppressive as one....As little ill it avail us that they are chosen by ourselves. An *elective despotism* was not the government we fought for."[46]

For similar reasons, they also criticized the way in which the first local governments were organized. In many cases, the new institutions were integrated by a small number of representatives (which hindered the expression of all the different viewpoints existing in society), who shared their social origins (transforming the representative system into a government by a homogeneous and economically powerful social group). Even worse, these new institutions favored the separation of the representatives from their constituency. Not surprisingly, then, the critics of the new governments began to refer to the "aristocratic" composition of the new political class. "Centinel," a noted Anti-Federalist, foresaw, for example, "a government that w[ould] give full scope to the magnificent designs of the well-born." In an article in the *Boston Gazette*, over the signature of "A Federalist," an anonymous Anti-Federalist expressed his belief that the constitution was written by a group of self-serving aristocrats.[47] A pamphlet written by "A Farmer and a Planter" stated that "aristocracy, or

---

[41] Demophilus (1776), p. 5.
[42] *Pennsylvania Packet* (Philadelphia), Sept. 20, 1778.
[43] "A Farmer and a Planter," in Borden (1965), p. 72.
[44] Thomas Young, from Vermont. Included in Sherman (1991), p. 190.
[45] Melancton Smith, "Speech at the Constitutional Convention," June 21, 1788, quoted in Storing (1981), vol. 6.
[46] Jefferson, "Notes on the StateVirginia," reprinted in Ford (1968), pp. 223–224.
[47] See Borden (1965), pp. 1–2.

government in the hands of a very few nobles, or RICH MEN, is therein concealed in the most artful wrote plan that ever was formed to entrap a free people."[48] Similar concerns about the "low-born" were expressed by "Montezuma"[49] and John Humble.[50] "Aristocratis" wrote a satirical antiaristocratic pamphlet objecting to the national constitution, where "a few [were designed] to rule, and many to obey."[51] For John Mercer, an Anti-Federalist from Maryland, the Anti-Federalist creed was based on a distrust of representative government in general and aristocratic government (like the one just created) in particular.[52] "Philadelphiensis" objected that the federal constitution would create a "despotic monarchy," given that the "president general will be a king to all intents and purposes, and one of the most dangerous kind too – a king elected to command a standing army... [a] tyrant."[53] Likewise Cato: "The mode in which [the representatives] are appointed and their duration, will lead to the establishment of an aristocracy."[54]

In Latin America, the same Rousseauean trend nourished the populists' critique of the old authoritarian regimes and was directly incorporated into the texts of the new constitutions. The early Constitution of Venezuela, written in 1811, represented one of the first significant documents inspired by French ideology.[55] In this constitutional text, the Venezuelan patriots made reference to the new social pact that would allow the people to leave the "savage" state of nature that distinguished the former period of Spanish domination. The authors of the constitution justified their work by making reference to the "unlimited and licentious freedom" and the unconstrained "passions" that existed before the adoption of this new document.

[48] Ibid., p. 70, emphasis in the original.
[49] Ibid., pp. 20–23.
[50] Ibid., p. 73.
[51] Ibid., p. 144.
[52] Ibid., p. 175.
[53] Ibid., p. 212.
[54] Cato, in the *New York Journal*, 1787, included in Allen and Gordon (1985). Other examples of the same ideas appear in George Mason, "Objections to the Constitution of Power Formed by the Convention, 1787"; Richard Lee, Oct. 10, 1787; "Letters of Centinel," Oct. 5, 1787; "John De Witt," Nov. 5, 1787; "The Address and Reasons of Dissent of the Minority of the Convention of the State of Pennsylvania," Dec. 18, 1787, all in Allen and Gordon (1985).
[55] Written by a commission composed of Juan Germán Roscio, Francisco Javier Ustáriz, and Francisco Isnardi, among others, the constitution was arduously debated. Among other things, the constitution purported to establish a federal political regime and it radically diluted the power of the president, dividing that function among three different persons, which sounded amazing at that time. One of the main people to take issue with the text, Francisco Miranda, refused to sign it, asserting that it did not fit in with local needs and habits. A few weeks later, the constitution was suppressed and Miranda appointed as the country's dictator.

The constitution was described as the "free expression of the general will," and the "sovereignty" of the country as resident in the "general mass of its inhabitants."

In Artigas's famous *Oración de Abril*, we find a very similar approach to the constitution, also inspired by the French revolutionary style. In that case, Artigas defended the urgent need for adopting a new constitution as a way of protecting the rights of the people. "We are still ruled by the faith of men," he said, "and we still lack the safeguards of the contract." Similarly, the Apatzingán Constitution of 1814 settled that national sovereignty resided in the people, that the law was the "expression of the general will," that it was aimed at securing "common happiness," and that the government's only purpose was to protect the citizens "assembled by their own will." By the middle of the century, the Chilean Francisco Bilbao would still radicalize these claims and directly demand the "abolition of delegation."

In fact, after independence, this anti-authoritarian trend constituted one of the most salient notes of the populists' discourse and practice. Radicals fought not only against any return to Spanish authoritarianism but, more important, against the concentration of political power in the hands of a few. They attacked Bolívar's exceptional powers in Venezuela, proposed the curtailment of the powers of the executive in Peru, fought against the establishment of a theocratic regime in Ecuador and in favor of a radically decentralized regime in Colombia, and battled against the perpetuation of an authoritarian government in Chile. A proclamation by the Chilean Sociedad de la Igualdad summarized some of these goals: the people are fighting against the future government of Manuel Montt because it represents "the state of siege, the deportations, the expatriations, the military tribunals, the corruption of the Judiciary, the massive killing of the people, torture in the criminal procedures, censorship, usury, repression, and especially the impairment of the national interests and the right of association."[56]

Of course, the radicals' hostility toward authoritarian regimes did not cure them of the evils of authoritarianism. In fact, the blind confidence that they often showed in the people's collective capacities moved them to defend very despotic regimes. Asserting the strongest version of this view, some radicals maintained that collective reflection constituted not only a necessary but also a *sufficient* condition for the adoption of correct political decisions. From this point of view, the majority was infallible, and for that very reason it was necessary

---

[56] Barros Arana (1913), vol. 2, p. 520.

to adhere closely to its opinions. A thing was just or correct, therefore, simply *because* it was the product of majority rule. Following these assumptions, many radical politicians defended the existence of some sort of predefined "general will" that had to be in some way discovered and implemented by the people. This idea was summarized in the exaggerated claim that equated the "voice of the people" with "the voice of God," a claim promptly adopted and ridiculed by the Federalists.[57]

In Latin America, we also find these attitudes among the most populist of leaders. For example, the Argentinean Bernardo de Monteagudo, an extreme radical at the beginning of the revolutionary process and an extreme conservative by the end of it, argued in 1812 that "any constitution that lacked the seal of the general will is arbitrary; there is no reason, no pretext, no circumstance that could authorize it. The people are free and they will never err if they are not corrupted or forced by violence."[58] We find similar ideas, for example, in the demands of the first Mexican revolutionaries. In the well-known pamphlet *Elementos circulados por el señor [Ignacio] Rayón,* which constitutes one of the most important antecedents of the radical Mexican Constitution of 1814, the author made clear references to the "infallible" (*inerrante*) character of the will of the legislature. Similar considerations appear in the writings of Mariano Moreno in Argentina; in the proclamations of the radical Chilean priest Camilo Enríquez; in the papers of José-Fernández de Lizardi, "the Mexican thinker"; in the writings of the patriots Manuel Vidaurre and Benito Laso in Peru; and in the work of the Venezuelan Juan Germán Roscío.[59]

The reasonable assertion that a collective process of reflection favored the adoption of impartial decisions was transformed into an

---

[57] In this sense, for example, Hamilton stated that "the voice of the people has been said to be the voice of God; and however generally this maxim has been quoted and believed, it is not true in fact." See Farrand (1937), vol. 1, p. 299. Similarly, the Federalist Fisher Ames objected to the "democrats" who thought "nothing so sacred than their voice, which is the voice of God." In the influential and well-known paper "The Essex Result," Theophilus Parsons directly objected to the ambitions and strong optimism of those whom he also described as the "democrats." He argued, in this sense, that "all democrats maintain that the people have an inherent, unalienable right to power; there is nothing so fixed that they may not change it; nothing [as sacred as] their voice." See H. Storing (1981a), vol. 2, p. 369. While the Federalists attributed a tendency to irrationality to the common people, many Anti-Federalists responded that the "disordered passions" criticized by the Federalists actually belonged to the will of "wicked and ambitious men." They argued that "tyrants have always made use of this plea [about a chaotic situation]; but nothing in our circumstances can justify it." See an essay by "Brutus Junior," in Borden (1965), p. 102.
[58] Quoted in J. L. Romero (1969), p. 78.
[59] See, for example, Lewin (1980).

unreasonable claim stating that whatever the majority decided was correct, simply because it was a majority decision. Probably, those who favored this view assumed that majority will was identical to universal will. Clearly, if the will of the many summarized the will of all, then there were good reasons for respecting it: by doing so, each individual would become his or her "own legislator." The assumedly universal character of the decision made it completely legitimate. However, the truth is that, in most cases, what appeared to be the will of the majority did not represent more than the will of a very few. Even worse, in many cases the decisions of a group that included, among its members, some representatives of the lower class, the most numerous of all, were assumed to be the expression of the majority will, and therefore of the universal will. The acts of a small minority were described, then, as the acts of "the people."

Clearly, these linguistic abuses did not simply come from the ambitious dreams of genuine radicals. Many authoritarian demagogues and many caudillos also tried to legitimize their arbitrary actions through the invocation of the popular will. More important, the critics of radicalism were eager to associate every episode of violence against their interests with the notion of "democracy." The term came to represent all that the elite feared. Similarly, these critics described any attempt to "open" the existent elitists' political systems as an attempt to establish an uncontrolled "direct democracy." They appealed to such a robust and expansive concept of "individual rights" that almost any move aimed at modifying the "status quo" appeared immediately to be classified as a violation of rights. Moreover, they identified the interests of the "rich and well born," the interests of a particular "minority," with the interests of *the* minorities. Then, they transformed the reasonable demand to protect minority rights into an unreasonable demand for the protection of the rights of the rich.

In *Federalist* 10, Madison dedicated a long part of the document to criticizing the example of the ancient "popular models" of government. But he did not proceed in this way merely as a result of his passion for history. Madison wanted to show the unacceptable character of the more democratic models of government that appeared during those years in the United States at a local level. Without making direct references to that period, he asserted that "pure democracy" could "admit of no cure for the mischiefs of faction," that these systems "ha[d] ever been the spectacles of turbulence and contention," and that they were always "incompatible with personal security or the rights of property." Madison's attempt to identify the timid democratic experiments of the postrevolutionary period with "pure democracy," and "pure democracy" with "turbulence and contention," was surely excessive. The same can be said of his attempts, clearly shared by most of the Federalists, to describe as strict violations of the right of property what were, in the end, the polemical but still reasonable efforts of local legislatures to prevent the worse effects of a dramatic social crisis.[60] What the state legislatures were doing, under the pressure of a desperate majority, was to try to limit a crisis that for many people implied losing the little property they had or being put in jail.

Similarly, in Latin America, many important political thinkers had harsh words against democracy when fighting against dire authoritarian and "vertical" regimes. Typically, Argentina's "founding fathers" described the despotic government of General Rosas as the local expression of the new democratic movements that grew in both Europe and America during the 1850s. For Frank Safford, intellectuals such as Juan Bautista Alberdi or Domingo Faustino Sarmiento in Argentina adopted a very "negative view" of all these new democratic movements because of the widespread support that Rosas received from the popular sectors.[61] It is true, of course, that Rosas organized and won different plebiscites in order to legitimize his authority. However, it is also true that he organized these plebiscites in a context of terror, censorship, and violence against his opponents. Therefore, the association of Rosas's government with a democratic experience appears to be a clear attempt to bastardize the idea of popular government. It is not by chance that three of the greatest Argentinean political thinkers of the century, Alberdi, Sarmiento, and Estaban Echeverría, grounded their theory of government on a sharp distinction between the "sovereignty of the majorities," which they all repudiated, and the "sovereignty of reason," which they unanimously defended.

We can say similar things about what happened in other Latin American countries. Only an abusive use of the term democracy allows us to understand why sanguinary caudillos, such as Juan Boves or Francisco José Rangel in Venezuela, were presented as democratic

[60] Here I am basically referring to the issuing of "paper money" decided by most state legislatures during the "most critical period of American history." See Fiske (1916).
[61] Safford (1985), p. 394. For Safford, in effect, "In the Río de la Plata...the dictatorship of Juan Manuel Rosas in Buenos Aires, like the regimes of lesser caudillos in the provinces, had enjoyed widespread support from the popular classes. In the Plata, therefore, younger intellectual politicians tended to take a more negative view of democratic revolution. In exile in Chile in the 1840s, Domingo Faustino Sarmiento and Juan Bautista Alberdi, even before the European revolutions, expressed the belief that popular sovereignty, in the hands of the ignorant mass, would inevitably lead to dictatorship."

caudillos.[62] In Mexico, too, the conservative ideologist Lucas Alamán, among many others, identified the violent sackings that took place in El Parián, after the radical leader Vicente Guerrero came to power, with the usual expressions of democratic regimes.[63]

Moral Populism: On the Tensions between Radicalism and Individual Rights

The populists' assertion of the radical principle comes together with many other important consequences. The one we examine here is the idea that majority will must prevail in *all* cases. Clearly, this view conflicts with other intuitions that we also have, which say that there are certain values and certain areas of our personal lives that should be absolutely free from the interference of others. Many affirm, in effect, that the community should always protect predetermined moral values, for example, those associated with a particular religion; goods, such as private property in land; or acts, such as those that belong to what many call "private morality."[64] Particularly, they continue, the community should prevent the majorities from interfering with these actions and values.

The populists, however, did not find good reasons for accepting that claim. Why should the majorities be prevented from acting in areas where they want to act? What reasons could justify the dismissal of the "general will"? The populists' attitude brought alarm and distress among their opponents. They were not only asking their opponents to accept their favored decisions but also assuming that these decisions were "right" and "just." The political extremism of the revolutionaries was usually supported by the conviction that what was being done was right and unquestionable. The most dramatic measures were justified by the idea that what was being done was the result of radical preferences and, for that reason, right; or just and, for that reason, beneficial to the majorities.

In Mexico, the first radical rebels demonstrated the tragic scope of these convictions, asserting that all individual interests had to be subordinated to the greater good of the nation.[65] In his *Plan de*

---

[62] Recalling these violent experiences, Juan Vicente González, one of the intellectual leaders of the conservative group, asserted that rejecting the conservative's power was a way of restoring anarchy.

[63] The fact that Lorenzo Zavala, at that time Guerrero's main ally, did not condemn the sackings but, to the contrary, tried to justify them undoubtedly favored the conservatives' strategy. See, for example, Bazant (1977), pp. 41–42.

[64] That is, by now, those acts that do not seriously harm other people.

[65] See Churruca Peláez (1983), p. 89.

Operaciones, the Argentinean revolutionary leader Mariano Moreno gave a clear idea of the extremism and dogmatism of his commitments: Moreno, like many other revolutionaries of his time, was totally sure that he was fighting for a just cause. For this reason, he believed that all the measures he favored, even the most extreme ones, were fully justified. In a well-known paragraph of his *Plan*, Moreno, the so-called Argentinean Robespierre, wrote:

> [T]he foundations of a new republic have never been laid except by rigor and punishment mixed with the spilt blood of those members who might oppose its progress.... No one should be scandalized by the intention of my words, to cut off heads, spill blood, and sacrifice at all costs, even when they [my words] resemble the customs of cannibals and savages.... No decrepit state or province can regenerate itself nor cut out its corruption without spilling rivers of blood.[66]

These are just a few examples of the tensions that existed between radicalism and certain basic individual interests. Under this approach, individual rights were seriously threatened: they seemed unable to do what they were supposed to, namely, to successfully resist the majoritarians' attacks. From this radical point of view, rights were subordinated to the majority will and needed to be at its service. In addition, for many radicals, rights were merely the product of the majority will. They could not be seen, as many (still) see them, as external constraints, as barriers that the majority cannot trespass.

In the opinion of the legal philosopher Herbert Hart, we need to distinguish "the acceptable principle that political power is best entrusted to the majority from the unacceptable claim that what the majority do with that power is beyond criticism and must never be resisted," an attitude that he names populism.[67] This tension between the radical – populist – position and individual rights was additionally fostered, as we already explored, by the peculiar conception of rights prevalent at the time of independence. In fact, when the wealthy minorities fenced their privileges by appealing to the idea of "rights," the very concept of rights was devalued. Everything that the rich had come to possess, by whatever means, was now protected by seemingly unquestionable natural rights. Lucidly, Jefferson recognized the dimensions of this maneuver and refused to include the right to property among the sacred rights incorporated into the U.S. Declaration of Independence. Other revolutionary leaders did

---

[66] I take this translation from Shunway (1993), p. 35. See also Moreno (1937).
[67] See Hart (1988), p. 79.

not have, like Jefferson, the opportunity to defy this elitist view of rights from the "inside." In many cases, they did not occupy positions of power in their societies, or even expect to, and, as a consequence, they felt freer to directly attack the entire legal and philosophical apparatus defended by their opponents. The dire extremism of the latter, who tried to shape the legal structure of the country for their own exclusive needs, undoubtedly favored the radicalization of the populists.

The tension between this radical position and the idea of rights has, at least, one additional foundation that comes from the writings of thinkers like Rousseau. Intelligently, Rousseau recognized that self-government was not possible in every type of society. More particularly, he recognized the importance of ensuring certain economic and social preconditions in order to make the formation and expression of the "general will" possible. First of all, he said, the formation of the "general will" required the existence of a homogeneous community, that is, one in which each person identified with and was committed to the interests of the others. All the people should be able to recognize and pursue certain shared and preexisting values. The absence of these social ties as well as the proliferation of multiple and diverse interests threatened the formation of the "general will." The more the people felt identified with certain specific interests, the more difficult it would be for them to recognize what they had in common. In other words, in heterogeneous and divided societies, each person tends to primarily defend the interest of his or her own group. In these cases, it becomes impossible to constitute the "general will": what we find is social conflict and not a common good.

Because of these types of belief, many thinkers assumed that in order to make self-government possible it was necessary to foster a homogeneous society first. For example, many Anti-Federalists believed that in a proper society the "manners, feelings and interests of the people should be similar." If this did not occur, the outcome was a "permanent clash of opinions." The representatives of one part of the community would be in continuous conflict with representatives of the other part. Obviously, these conflicts prevented "the operation of government" and hindered the promotion of the "common good."[68]

Of course, the goal of having a homogeneous society composed of socially committed individuals is not easily obtainable. Many radicals, however, recognizing the importance and urgency of this

[68] See Storing (1981b), pp. 19–20.

objective, decided to resort to the coercive powers of the state as a way of "cultivating" new and better citizens. For Rousseau, for example, the task of the legislator is "to change human nature, to transform each individual...into a part of a larger whole from which this individual receives, in a sense, his life and his being."[69] His defense of a "civil religion" goes in the same direction. In his opinion, this civil religion was important in order to inculcate "social sentiments without which a man cannot be a good citizen or a faithful subject."[70] The idea of "cultivating" new citizens was an old republican idea that became very popular in America,[71] too, after the revolutions of independence. In fact, many Americans considered that in order to build the new societies it was necessary to first reconstruct their social basis. Benjamin Rush adopted an extreme version of this view, asserting that it was necessary "to convert men into republican machines," to teach each person "that he does not belong to himself, but that he is public property."[72] Also, while some believed that for that objective it was necessary to "import" the best European citizens,[73] they defended the need for "recreating" the American people by "inculcating" certain civic virtues and "eradicating" certain social vices.[74]

This discourse of vices and virtues was very common in America, particularly during the years that followed the revolutions of independence. The prestigious Chilean priest Camilo Henríquez, for example, wrote in the newspaper *La Aurora*: "Industrious communities have habits that...[make liberty possible]. Work makes the people stronger and accustoms them to frugality, it fosters the simplicity of manners, which is necessary for the conservation of the republican systems....When the simplicity of manners disappeared, when luxury was introduced...the republic found its death, liberty was buried with the glory and vigor of Rome."[75] In a similar line, Bernardo Monteagudo complained about the way in which the Spanish educated Americans in the habits of "obedience." For him, the Spanish made American citizens "unable to be governed by democratic principles."[76]

[69] Quoted in Sandel (1996), p. 319.
[70] Rousseau (1984), book IV, chap. 8.
[71] See, among others, Wood (1969; 1992); Sandel (1996).
[72] Quoted in Sandel (1996), p. 319.
[73] See, typically, Alberdi (1920).
[74] Among the virtues, we would find, for example, those of patriotism, austerity, courage, frugality, solidarity, simplicity, and industry. Among the vices, instead, we would find those of cowardice, selfishness, or vagrancy. The former seemed indispensable for enriching communal life, whereas the latter represented a fundamental obstacle to its constitution.
[75] See Henríquez (1970), pp. 132–135.
[76] See Safford (1992), p. 87.

The inculcation of certain habits, or the absence of certain virtues, appeared again as key elements for explaining the consolidation of, or the impossibility of consolidating, the new republics.

When we assume a position like this, it becomes impossible not to combine the state with the moral formation of its members. The question is, What is the state supposed to do in order to inculcate those virtues and eradicate those vices? To many radicals, the best way to achieve these objectives was through the promotion of religion. In this way, they assumed, it would be possible to improve the people's character, while society would remain united by certain common beliefs. This assumption was common, among many Anti-Federalists in the United States, who campaigned for the protection of the dominant religion in order to avoid the evils that were becoming more and more common in Europe. "Religion," wrote Richard Henry Lee in a letter to Madison, had to be "the guardian of morals." The people's opinions should be reoriented "in favor of virtue and religion."[77] He, like many other Anti-Federalists, believed that the opinions of men needed to be formed "in favour of virtue and religion." He stated that "it is not more difficult to build an elegant house without tools to work with, than it is to establish a durable government without the public protection of religion."[78] They wanted to revitalize religion because, as Charles Turner asserted, "without the prevalence of Christian piety and morals, the best republican constitution can never save us from slavery and ruin." Turner, particularly, stressed the importance of fostering religion for those who cared about self-government. The diffusion of religion, he believed, would make government less necessary by rendering "the people more capable of being a Law to themselves."[79]

In Latin America, radicals also formulated these types of judgments. We find a crucial and crude example of this attitude in the orders advanced by the revolutionary priests Miguel Hidalgo and José María Morelos in Mexico.[80] For both of them, and for Morelos in particular, it was perfectly coherent to combine an egalitarian distribution of wealth with the violent appropriation of their enemies' properties and the forceful imposition of the Catholic creed "without toleration of any other religion." Also, they assumed it was justified to destroy or "set fire to" their enemies' most appreciated goods. In their opinion,

---

[77] Storing (1981b), p. 22.
[78] Ibid.
[79] Ibid., p. 23.
[80] The two notable priests, Hidalgo and Morelos, were very successful in mobilizing the Indians and the poor in favor of the revolution of independence. Hidalgo, a pioneer

in order to "rebuild [the New Society,] it [was] necessary to destroy the ancient."[81] In addition, the revolutionary priests also found it reasonable to strictly punish all "vicious" acts and behaviors, such as gambling. They prohibited the consumption of tobacco – in order to avoid this "detestable vice, so harmful to the people's health"[82] – and forced their followers to work hard for the common good, in accordance with the teachings of the Bible. In the "Bando" that he publicized from Oaxaca, for example, Morelos explained these views, asserting that in the new nation there would be no place for "unearned leisure or for indolent attitudes." Making reference to the "incurable evils" that laziness brought to society, he asserted that under his government "no vice would be countenanced" and that all dissolute behaviors would be eradicated.[83]

The moral regeneration of society also ranked high among the priorities that the Chilean radicals from the Sociedad de la Igualdad defended. Not surprisingly, given that the principal members of the Sociedad had studied with "Catholic Socialists," such as Henri Lacordaire or Hugues Lammenais,[84] in France, the association proposed as one of its main objectives to achieve "unity and to fight against poverty and the vicious behaviors."[85] Francisco Bilbao, in the newspaper that he published with his brother Manuel, Santiago Arcos, and Victorino Lastarria, defended the need for "scaring away vices and indolence from the working class."[86] In his opinion, the moral education of the new workers would help them improve their character. This reeducation would take place in "associations with few members, family meetings, small circles, where the oral and spoken words will recreate the holy doctrines of the republican system."

---

of these radical demands, called not only for political change but also for drastic economic change. His famous *Bando sobre tierras y esclavos*, written in December 1810, demanded both the immediate abolition of slavery and the redistribution of the national lands: each community, he believed, had to decide the use of its own lands. Morelos, a former student of the Colegio de San Nicolás while Hidalgo was the head there, followed the teachings of his predecessor and was as successful as him in recruiting the lower classes for the revolution. Like Hidalgo, he also organized a redistribution of land and promoted a profound change in the political system. In order to advance the latter goal, he proposed a new national constitution, the 1814 Apatzingán Constitution, which showed a clear "Rousseauean" inspiration.

[81] Quoted in J. L. Romero and Romero (1977), p. 57.
[82] Ibid.
[83] See Churruca Peláez (1983), pp. 205–208.
[84] Lammenais, particularly, attracted the attention of the new generations with his defense of religion outside the control of the church: the church was, in his opinion, an oppressive institution distinguished only by its money and privileges.
[85] Gazmuri (1992), p. 60.
[86] Ibid., pp. 77–79.

These practices, he believed, "would have a marvelous effect, habituating the people to the [goods that belong to] these pacific, noble and moral meetings."[87] "Liberty, democracy, and solidarity," he assumed, would finally be achieved.[88]

Similarly, the Uruguayan caudillo José Artigas defended the importance of cultivating virtue in the Rio de la Plata.[89] The main measures of his government provide us with many examples of this attitude. Artigas commanded, in effect, the diffusion of reading materials among the population; used the press as an educational tool; asked the help of "progressive" priests in order to promote the dissemination of new revolutionary ideas; and was obsessively concerned with the way in which the Uruguayans were living.[90] These increasing controls also became apparent in the way he distributed punishments and rewards. Artigas, in effect, was determined to strictly penalize even those who committed insignificant crimes and to reward those who behaved in accordance with his project.[91] After the Portuguese invasions, from 1816 onward, these controls over people's private behavior became still greater: at that time, Artigas asked his collaborators to produce periodic and detailed reports regarding the people's behavior.[92] He knew that it was difficult to develop this moral reformism successfully – to "remove the people's passions with only one stroke" when "they had never been virtuous."[93] However, he still reaffirmed that "the perverse should never be confused with the good ones." In his opinion, the best representatives of the people, those who deserved the people's confidence, should become the "exemplar." "All the other citizens," he added, "should learn the virtues" from those representatives. For that reason, he believed that each flaw in one of the representatives deserved the highest condemnation.[94]

Clearly, many radicals recognized that, in order to attain the desired moralization of society, the use of the coercive powers of the

---

[87] Ibid., p. 78.
[88] Ibid. Bilbao wanted to use the Sociedad in order to produce the "emancipation of citizens and workers, the political revolution of reason, and the destruction of property; to ensure each person's right to think and be as he wanted, the right of the power in each person...the independence of reason; [and] the sovereignty of the people." Ibid.
[89] See particularly Frega (1998).
[90] Ibid. See also Fernández Cabrelli (1968); Street (1959), pp. 260–261.
[91] Street (1959), chap. 6. Many among Artigas's critics, for example, point to the military establishment of Purificación as the main example of his rather arbitrary political style. In Purificación, in fact, Artigas imprisoned and mistreated his enemies.
[92] Frega (1998), p. 111.
[93] Sala Touron et al. (1978), p. 201.
[94] Frega (1998), p. 109.

state and the educational system were only two of the tools at their disposal. Notably, many of them realized the profound connections that linked society's economic organization with particular models of conduct.

As Morelos acknowledged, a more egalitarian economy could "improve the habits of the people, distancing them from ignorance, rapine, and theft."[95] In line with this assumption, many believed that an adequate form of economic organization could favor the promotion of certain fundamental moral and personal values, such as solidarity, simplicity, frugality, and austerity.

The discussion on the impact of different economic models on people's personal morality was particularly important in the United States, even before the revolution seeking independence. At that time, for example, nonimportation and nonconsumption movements rejected the importation of British goods because, they believed, these imports would bring with them luxury and vices. In this way, "the colonists hoped not only to retaliate against Britain but also to affirm republican virtue, to assert economic independence, and to save themselves from the corruption of imported luxuries."[96]

During the 1780s, once again, the North Americans conducted a substantial debate about ways in which to think about the economy. For most of them, it seemed obvious that society was faced with a crucial choice between opposing "commercial" and "agrarian" models of economic organization. The populists were certain of the benefits of the agrarian model with regard to matters of personal morality. In their opinion, this way of structuring the economy promoted the types of moral values that they favored. Also, they assumed that the alternative economic model fostered selfish and competitive conduct. José Artigas in the Banda Oriental, Juan Montalvo in Ecuador, and Manuel Madiedo in Colombia were also certain about the importance of redistributing the land and the impact of these measures on the people's character. Only through the reorganization of the land into small and collective shares, asserted Madiedo, "the selfishness of the single proprietor may come to an end."[97]

Radicals could have been right or wrong about the causal connections that they established. Perhaps it was not so obvious that an agrarian life fostered cooperation and a commercial life selfishness. However, their point was important because they perceived something

[95] Churruca Peláez (1983), p. 206.
[96] Sandel (1996), p. 142.
[97] Abramson (1999), p. 87.

that most others did not and still do not: that our choice of a certain form of economic organization has a significant impact on other areas of our social life. In other words, they recognized that our economic choices were not neutral with regard to questions of morality. For example, they assumed that the preference for an agrarian model implied a preference for more cooperative or less competitive beings. Moreover, given the strength of these connections and the importance they attributed to the moral character of the citizenry, they decided to subordinate their economic choices to their moral ideal. Then, they chose to develop an agrarian society *because* they wanted to have less selfish citizens, just as they chose to reject alternative forms of organization because they rejected the impact these models had on the character of the people.

Their reasoning seems more complete now. Above all, radicals wanted to achieve a self-governing society; they assumed that the attainment of self-government required the presence of active citizens; and they recognized that, in order to have active citizens, the basic institutions of society had to be arranged in very particular ways. Regarding the economic organization of society, they typically assumed that a commercial, capitalist organization would undermine rather than favor the moral qualities that an active citizenry required. As George Mason put it, "If virtue is the vital principle of a republic, and it cannot long exist, without frugality, probity and strictness of morals, will the manners of populous commercial cities be favorable to the principles of our free venality, and corruption, which invariably prevail in great commercial cities, be utterly subversive of them?"[98]

The Economy: The Agrarian Republic

At the beginning of this chapter, we examined one of the populists' most important ideas, that of *popular self-government*. The populists wanted a popular government, which ruled "for the people" and "by the people" – a government that "embodi[ed] the will of the people and execute[d] it."[99] In the previous section, we began to explore the importance that radicals attributed to certain economic arrangements for the cultivation of virtue. In this section, we focus more directly on the *material preconditions* – more specifically, on the type of economic equality – that they found indispensable for making that

---
[98] Quoted in Sandel (1996), p. 126.
[99] Jefferson, in letter to Samuel Kercheval. See Jefferson (1999), p. 210.

self-government possible.[100] By defending this position, radicals contradicted other alternative and very common views, which said that it was possible to design new political institutions completely independently from the way in which the economy and social life were organized.

Their defense of a certain economic equality was, at least in part, instrumental. In their opinion, if the nation's wealth were distributed very unequally, society would become divided into many different factions, with different and contradictory interests. Such a society would be heterogeneous and would have difficulty in forming a common will. Ultimately, such a society would have problems in ensuring its self-government.

On the one hand, they believed that economic institutions, like political institutions, had to be the product of the majority will. On the other hand, however, economic institutions had to facilitate the formation and expression of the majority will. The question is whether these two objectives were coherent. In other words, radicals believed that certain forms of economic organization impaired self-government or made it almost impossible. Clearly, if only a small part of the population had a proper job and somewhere decent to live, then the promise of self-government would become frustrated. In a context like this, the majority would be subordinated to the will of the few and most individuals would depend on the arbitrary will of others. Many radicals believed, however, that in America the promise of self-government had good chances of becoming true: there was a lot of "free" land, open to all. In the new continent, each could have what he or she needed for becoming a free person. Within these conditions, the poorest could also have their share: the dream of a "republic of small proprietors" was at least conceivable.

Jefferson's works provide us with a good example of the radicals' approach to the economic organization of society. He, like many others, conceived of the concentration of land as one of the most important problems in society and the redistribution of land as a feasible cure for that evil. "The property of this country," he wrote in a 1785 letter to James Madison, "is absolutely concentrated in a very few hands.... I asked myself what could be the reason so many should be permitted to beg who are willing to work, in a country where there

---

[100] Characterizing the republican theory, Mark Philp argued that this conception "offers a persuasive account of the interconnection between social, material, and normative conditions in the polity, and that it recognizes the importance of a high degree of civic virtue in the state." See Philp (1996), p. 386.

is a very considerable proportion of uncultivated lands?"[101] Jefferson suggested different ways for repairing this situation[102] and concluded by stating: "Whenever there are in any country uncultivated lands and unemployed poor, it is clear that the laws of property have been so far extended as to violate natural right. The earth is given as a common stock for man to labor and live on. If for the encouragement of industry we allow it to be appropriated, we must take care that other employment be provided to those excluded from the appropriation. If we do not, the fundamental right to labor the earth returns to the unemployed.... The small landholders are the most precious part of a state."[103] Jefferson's defense of an "agrarian republic" was inscribed within his more general criticisms of the "commercial republic," an alternative model that would become dominant a few years after independence.

The Jeffersonians defended the agrarian model as a way of allowing the people to become more independent, more committed, and more attached to the interests of their country. As Michael Sandel notes, many Americans, with Jefferson, feared that "manufactures on a scale beyond that of the household or small workshop would create a propertyless class of impoverished workers, crowded into cities, incapable of exercising the independent judgement citizenship require[d]."[104] An agrarian society, instead, appeared to favor a fuller development of the civic and personal qualifications of each person. "[W]hen people live principally by agriculture, as in America," they believed, "every man is in some measure an artist, he makes a variety of utensils, rough indeed, but such as will answer his purpose, he is a husbandman in summer and a mechanic in winter, he travels about the country, he converses with a variety of professions, he reads public papers, he has access to a library and thus becomes acquainted

---

[101] Jefferson (1984), p. 841.
[102] And he added: "These lands are undisturbed only for the sake of game. It should seem then that it must be because of the enormous wealth of the proprietors which places them above attention to the increase of their revenues by permitting these lands to be labored. I am conscious that an equal division of property is impracticable, but the consequences of this enormous inequality producing so much misery to the bulk of mankind, legislators cannot invent too many devices for subdividing property, only taking care to let their subdivisions go hand in hand with the natural affections of the human mind. The descent of property of every kind therefore to all the children, or to all the brothers and sisters, or other relations in equal degree, is a politic measure and a practicable one. Another means of silently lessening the inequality of property is to exempt all from taxation below a certain point, and to tax the higher portions or property in geometrical progression as they rise." Ibid.
[103] Ibid., pp. 841–842.
[104] Sandel (1996), p. 143.

with history and politics.... Knowledge is diffused and genius roused by the very situation of America."[105]

In Latin America, some political leaders advocated a better distribution of the land, appealing to certain basic egalitarian claims. Using the same types of argument as Jefferson, the Mexican leader Ezequiel Zamora asserted: "God made all humans equal in their bodies and souls. Why, then, should a few thieves and factious people live from the work of the poor, especially those who have a dark skin?" And again: "When God created the world he gave the water, the sun, the land, as a common stock. Why, then, have the [few] appropriated the best land, the forest and the water, that belong to the entire people?"[106]

Much earlier than Zamora, the revolutionary priests Hidalgo and Morelos had recognized the importance of the problem of land for explaining and resolving the most important difficulties confronted by the Mexican people. As early as 1810, Hidalgo promulgated his famous *Bando sobre tierras y esclavos*, where he commanded that, in each community, the land should be cultivated by the "naturals" of the place. In addition, Hidalgo prohibited renting this land, assuming that, in this way, the land could again fall in the hands of a few.[107] Following Hidalgo's policies, Morelos also defended the redistribution of lands to the people who worked them and called for the confiscation of all property belonging to the enemies of the revolution. Morelos's *Plan político* proposed that "the rich, the nobles, and their employees" should lose all their properties, which should go to the poor and increase military revenues too. Francisco Severo Maldonado was another early Mexican reformist who recognized that the uneven distribution of land was the country's main problem. Until recently, he said, social reformers believed that "it was possible to destroy the tree of evil by attacking its fruits but leaving its roots untouched." In contrast with this position, he believed that the only possible way "for restoring the lost social equilibrium and securing the triumph of democracy" was that of redistributing all the national goods.[108] Following similar lines, Fernández de Lizardi proposed

---

[105] Noah Webster, quoted in Sandel (1996), pp. 144–145.
[106] Quoted in Brito Figueroa (1975), p. 56.
[107] See Bazant (1977), pp. 17–19.
[108] Noriega (1980), p. 196. In his opinion, in Mexico there was "more land to be distributed than people to whom to distribute it." For that reason, he proposed to divide the national territory in a multiplicity of shares that would allow the subsistence of each family. The state, which had to buy most of the land, financed by a national bank (also to be created), would have the mission of distributing and renting out the land.

the redistribution of all the lands of the country and the formation of a community of small proprietors. The government, he believed, should refuse to satisfy the greed of the richest and promote, instead, "justice and the general good of the nation." In accordance with his plan there would be no more "uncultivated lands."[109] Later on, during the 1850s, Francisco García also campaigned for the redistribution of lands and, acting as a governor in the state of Mexico, Lorenzo de Zavala, "the father of the agrarian movement in Mexico,"[110] advanced a public plan aimed at redistributing the state's land. Zavala's plan included, in addition, taxing property owners who lived outside the country and the imposition of limitations on the amount of property that each person could possess. With the "Ayutla Revolution," led by Juan Álvarez against Santa Anna's authoritarian regime, Mexico inaugurated a new period of debate on the distribution of land.[111]

Although in Mexico many important political leaders took the problem of redistribution of land seriously, this debate was not so common in most other Latin American countries. In the Banda Oriental, José Artigas was one of the few leaders who promoted a radical reorganization of the economy. Through his Reglamento provisorio de la Provincia Oriental para el fomento de la campaña, Artigas set into motion an important plan for the redistribution of lands. Notably, the plan, launched on September 10, 1815, established that the most disadvantaged groups of society – "free blacks," *zambos*, Native Americans, insolvent widows with children, and *criollos* among them – would be those most favored by the new plan. The idea was to provide each of them with the bare necessities for their subsistence.[112] The Reglamento, in addition, created the obligation to work the assigned land as well as the maximum amount of land that each person could accumulate in his own hands. Under Artigas's plan, within two months of having received his property, each person had to have built his own cattle ranch. Those who failed to fulfill this

---

[109] Chávez Orozco (1985), p. 195.
[110] Thus, for Ramond Estep. See Estep (1949), p. 140.
[111] It was the group of "pure liberals" that advanced these discussions on most occasions. However, the same Juan Álvarez, a famous caudillo from the South, argued for these reforms in the property of land. Particularly, he defended the Native Americans' right to acquire and possess property. Álvarez wrote, in addition, a famous pamphlet, the *Manifiesto a los pueblos cultos de Europa y América*, in which he denounced the ignominy and oppression of the poor in the hands of the landowners. See Díaz Díaz (1972b), pp. 144–145.
[112] See Street (1959). Before the adoption of this Reglamento, Artigas had already commanded the distribution of lands to the "laborious people who wanted to cultivate them." See Reyes Abodie et al. (1968), p. 15.

commitment had to return their assigned land, which would go to a new candidate.

In Ecuador, too, Juan Montalvo famously campaigned for a redistribution of land, a claim that he rooted in the writings of the classical republicans.[113] In Chile, the two most important leaders of the Sociedad de la Igualdad, Santiago Arcos and Francisco Bilbao, were severe critics of the inequalities that distinguished Chilean society during the 1850s. "Everywhere there are poor and rich people," argued Arcos, "but not everywhere do we find poor people as in Chile." Arcos proposed an agrarian reform, aimed at creating a class of small proprietors. "We need to take the land from the hands of the rich," he asserted, "in order to distribute it to the poor. We need to take the cattle from the rich in order to distribute it to the poor... it is necessary to distribute the entire country, without attention to its former divisions."[114] "Bread and freedom" was, for Arcos, the banner of the disadvantaged in Europe, which had also to become the banner of poor Americans.[115] The experiment of the Sociedad de la Igualdad, however, was fundamentally marginal and ephemeral.

In Colombia, we find at least one instance of a political leader who articulated an appealing conception about how to organize society, both politically and economically. This was Manuel Murillo Toro, who would become the president of Colombia on two occasions. Murillo knew how to articulate a strong case for universal suffrage with the defense of a different distribution of property. As the minister of finance for Hilario López's government during the 1850s, he promoted a system of progressive taxation together with a redistribution of nonoccupied land. "Economic reforms," argued Murillo, "are an integral part of democratic reform."[116] Murillo was a significant protagonist of the intellectual debates held in Colombia during the nineteenth century. In a bitter polemic with Miguel Samper, one of the most important defenders of laisssez faire, Murillo wrote a pamphlet,

---

[113] Inspired by Rousseau's writings and the examples of republican Rome, Montalvo defended, for example, the division of the land into small portions. He believed that through this division it would be possible to obtain enormous social benefits that were impossible to obtain by leaving land in the hands of a few. "In a democracy, it is not enough to divide the land equally. These portions, in addition, should be small, as the Romans did." Each share should be sufficient, he added, to allow the subsistence of a man. See Roig (1984), p. 111.

[114] See Arcos (1977), p. 162. Arcos wrote that it was necessary to simply take these goods from the rich, and not to buy them, because even in that case "they will say that these measures constitute a robbery, and they will call us thieves and communists." Ibid.

[115] Ibid.

[116] Molina (1973), p. 75.

Dejad hacer, in which he attacked the "selfish and fatal doctrines defended by John Baptist Say and his school, summarized in the simple maxim laissez faire or, what is the same: let them rob, let them oppress, let the wolves eat the lambs."[117] "The only remedy we have, in order to cure the evils you have exposed," he concluded, "is to forbid the accumulation of land: that is the only remedy, and we should not be afraid of it."[118]

To a greater or lesser extent, all these debates contained another discussion regarding the proper role of the state in divided and unequal societies: should they adopt a passive role and leave individuals free to shape the economy as they wanted? Should the state, by contrast, intervene and try to shape it in accordance with certain predefined goals? As we have seen, particularly through Murillo's example, the arguments in favor of an active state were not easy to make at a moment when most intellectuals were fascinated by the British liberal economic school. The latter alternative found its place in Latin America: it not only favored the economic interests of the

---

[117] Murillo recognized that, at a certain point, Miguel Samper had acknowledged the dramatic social evils that predominated in the country. However, he continued, Samper had finally closed his eyes again and claimed: "We must shut up, we must let them do what they want, let them oppress, let the lion eat the lamb; let them put at risk the most important industry of the country, let it grow into the worst of all tyrannies." Morales Benítez (1997), p. 208. In his opinion, "the only fruit of the economic school that you Samper] defend...has been an enormous increase in the richness of those who were already rich, and the impoverishment of all those who were already poor. This extreme inequality of wealth or, to put it better, the lack of adequate rules securing the fair distribution of wealth...that make impossible for most people to participate in the progress of civilization, that allow the increase of inequality, and that create the misery of those who are at the bottom and the unrest of those who are at the top, is a fundamental fact that we must study and remedy. We cannot continue saying 'go on.'" Ibid. Manuel María Madiedo was another distinguished member of the so-called Republican school. Radical, Catholic, and a strong defender of artisans' rights, Madiedo, like Murillo, confronted those who defended laissez faire in his country. In this sense, he also entered into bitter polemics with his ideological enemies. "Poor people," he argued, "cannot keep their needs in a closet, waiting for their salary to grow" (González González, 1997, p. 264). He attacked the inegalitarian distribution of wealth that was prevalent in Colombia and the upper classes, which were favored by that system. He repudiated the rich "not for being rich...but for being rich as they are and for becoming rich as they become" (Abramson, 1999, p. 266). Like Murillo, he also proposed a reorganization of the economic structure of society and, particularly, a redistribution of land. See ibid., p. 87.

[118] Morales Benítez (1997), p. 210. He added, "I do not attack the appropriation of land. By contrast, I believe it can be useful and necessary, if we put limits to this appropriation that the whole society will be in charge of controlling...men can appropriate without limits the fruits of their work; but they cannot appropriate what nature gave to all us gratuitously, for our sustenance and conservation." Ibid., p. 212. See also Torres Almeida (1984).

dominant elite but also looked very attractive for a majority that had suffered the consequences of Spain's monopoly. The alternative interventionist view, however, would also get some attention later, when many began to recognize the dark side of the liberal policies.

The Need for New Political Institutions

For radicals, the basic institutions of society had to be shaped in specific ways in order to foster certain moral qualities in the citizenry and thus make self-government possible. Clearly, the civic commitments that radicals favor cannot be possible and cannot flourish in just any type of institutional setting. If, for example, the political institutions prevent participation or make it very difficult, then the ideal of self-government is seriously affected. Within a hostile political system, even virtuous and politically committed individuals tend to lose their civic energies. Political apathy may indeed be the *outcome* of a certain institutional organization rather than an innate human quality that we have to condemn.

In addition, because of their confidence in the people's capacities and their general distrust of representatives, radicals defended an institutional system that not only allowed but also encouraged the people's active participation in politics. It is important to emphasize this point because most alternative institutional proposals were designed to block this possibility. In the proposal that most radicals favored, the institutions did not appear as a mere "procedural" structure, aimed at allowing free agreements among free people, or consist of a general framework, open to any kind of "substantive" content. Instead, it required an institutional system that advanced the majority interests. This system was linked to certain basic substantive values, shaped in their light, and aimed at honoring them.

What was required to favor the political commitments of the citizenry? First, the institutions should be open to the people, an ideal that was not at all obvious in America at the time of the revolutions of independence. Both in the United States and in Latin America, there were elitist and restrictive political regimes that concentrated political rights on only a very small group, the "select few." Second, the new political regimes had to open their institutions to the people's claims and actions. Finally, they had to provide incentives for the political participation of the community.

In their opinion, the existing political institutions were not only unjust but also incompatible with the production of adequate, impartial decisions. Even an altruistic leader aiming to promote the interests of the community, they assumed, would be unable to properly defend the common good. In their opinion, as we explored earlier, impartiality required a process of collective reflection and not simply the goodwill of the enlightened few.

Not surprisingly, many radicals defended the adoption of systems of direct democracy. They knew about this possibility through the literature, particularly through references from the classical period but also through their own political practices. In effect, the practice of "town meetings," which was very important in the United States but not in Latin America during the postrevolutionary period, confirmed to them that it was possible to organize the political life of the community through radically democratic means.[119] These local popular conventions allowed and encouraged the political participation of most of the members of the community. The restrictions normally imposed on voting in both local and national matters were usually ignored at town meetings. The idea is that "in the actual meetings participated many people who did not meet the proper requirements, but who were known and established inhabitants of the town";[120] and that "when concerned with local matters," the community "seldom counted the contents of a man's pocket before it counted his vote."[121] Normally, in the town meetings the community had the opportunity to openly discuss the evolution of local affairs and decide about its own future. After the approval of the federal constitution, however, this way of organizing the political life of the community was generally abandoned. The growth of the population, the conflicts sometimes generated by the meetings, and the extreme hostility of some powerful groups toward popular participation affected this practice and reduced its initial importance.[122] Jensen has argued that

---

[119] See, for example, Jensen (1967), pp. 118–121; Patterson (1981), pp. 50–52.
[120] See Brown (1970), p. 5.
[121] See Starkey (1955), p. 10. This is according to studies made by C. Grant, who said that "[during the 1720s] towns tended to ignore the complex legal distinctions" that differentiated between classes of inhabitants and established restrictions in the suffrage. Also, "in nearly all Connecticut towns after 1740, all adult males were allowed to vote" at the local level. See Grant (1961), pp. 128–130. For Pole, through the town meetings "even the humblest members of the town felt that their interests, involved with those of their town, were included in its representation." See Pole (1966), p. 54.
[122] James Madison, for example, believed that the town meetings tended to end with "tumult" and caused "distress." Letter from James Madison to Ambrose Madison, Aug. 7, 1786, in Rutland and Rachal (1975), vol. 9, p. 89. In their private complaints, many of these critics asserted that the practice of communal assemblies had only pandered to the "creatures of the populace" and "the lowest sort of people." However, in their public arguments they defended their initiatives by saying that

"conservative-minded men sought to avoid further unpleasantness by doing away with town government, substituting for it a corporation by which the towns could be governed by mayors and councils."[123]

Many representatives of the radical view came to defend representative systems of democracy only as "necessary evils," as "second best" options, whereas most of the defenders of the representative system at the time considered this to be the preferred alternative, the best of all possible choices. Many of those who viewed the representative system as the "first choice" considered that this system served to expropriate the last institutional say from the people. Representation, they believed, favored the concentration of political decisions in the hands of the "educated few," who were better able than the people themselves to "discover" and serve the general interests of the country. In accordance with this view, the adoption of a representative system implied the complete displacement of the people from politics.

Radicals did not share that view. They believed that "political sovereignty" resided in the people and that the people could recover that sovereignty, if they had delegated it, whenever they wanted. The Banda Oriental Constitution of 1813 was so emphatic on the people's ultimate right to their self-government that it even included an explicit reference to the right to abolish the government, if the people found it unable to ensure the general welfare. "Because all men are born free and equal," it proclaimed, "and have certain natural, essential, and inalienable rights, among them, the right to enjoy and defend their life and liberty, the right to acquire, possess and protect their property and, finally, the right to demand and obtain security and happiness, it is the duty [of the Government] to ensure these rights...and if it cannot achieve these great objectives, the people have the right to alter the Government, and to adopt all the measures required to

---

they were based "on the need for better municipal administration." See Brunhouse (1942), p. 153. More significantly, after their appointment to the high court in New York, the influential Federalists John Jay and Robert Livingston launched an explicit campaign against all those bills that recognized "the existence and the power of the committee system." See Countryman (1981), p. 184. See also Rakove (1979), chap. 22. Also, following similar lines, the chief justice of the supreme court in Worcester concluded that the conventions were totally repugnant to the constitution. By that time, most conservatives agreed on the idea that "[having a state constitution], Committees and Conventions of the people were [no more] lawful." See Brooke (1989), pp. 119–120. It is worth comparing these views with the idea that town meetings always promoted "the peaceful and legal settlement of disputes." In fact, most scholars agree that local meetings tended to lessen the proportion and intensity of social conflicts. See, for example, Douglas (1971), pp. 141–143; or Richard Brown (1970), p. 214.

[123] Jensen (1967), pp. 118–121.

ensure its safety, prosperity and happiness." Artigas had ratified this view in his famous speech Oración de Abril, when he "restored" to the people the authority that they had delegated to him. "My authority," he claimed, "emanates only from you and it ceases before your sovereign presence." Also, as in the Banda Oriental Constitution of 1813, the Apatzingán Constitution of 1814 made reference to the people's "undeniable right" to "establish...alter, modify, or totally abolish the government, whenever this is required for their happiness" (art. 4). Once again, the idea was that the final political authority was in the people, who could recover it whenever they deemed it necessary.

The same principles that induced radicals to distrust the representative system moved them to urge a much closer relationship between the representatives and the people. This strong relationship between the two groups would ensure that the representatives not only would have an adequate knowledge of the will of the people but also would be unable to act simply as they wished – that is, it would avoid the "alienation" of power. This second goal ranked very high among the populists' political interests: they always feared the existence of "autonomous" representatives acting for their own selfish interests. For this reason, too, they usually claimed that an adequate government was the one that had the same feelings, opinions, and viewpoints as the people.[124] Of course, in order to achieve these goals, they needed something more than campaigning for the election of the best representatives or relying on the civic virtues of the citizenry. Radicals required, in addition, institutional tools that allowed them to punish the representatives every time they ignored or betrayed the interests of the people. They became experts in the design of these tools, even though most of their proposals were not in the end incorporated into national constitutions.[125]

Finally, their distrust of representation contributed to strengthening their defense of decentralized political systems. In fact, the defense of federalism became one of the most distinctive banners of radicalism. Through federalism, radicals believed, the representatives would have less power and the citizenry would have greater chances of imposing and implementing its own will: the majority interests, in sum, would end up being better protected. The enemies of radicalism, however, found this demand for a decentralized government unacceptable. In fact, the fight for and against federalism

---

[124] See, for example, "The Federal Farmer," in Storing (1981a), vol. 2, p. 230.
[125] Typically, this is what happened with most of the Anti-Federalist proposals, which were ultimately not incorporated into the U.S. Bill of Rights.

constituted one of the main causes of political violence all across the American continent. In the United States, its critics argued that a radically decentralized political system represented a fundamental threat to the protection of individual rights. In Latin America, for its critics the federal system was also seen as a threat to the same consolidation of independence.

Politicians of radical inspiration such as Ezequiel Zamora in Venezuela, Lorenzo de Zavala in Mexico, and the same Artigas in the Banda Oriental were exemplary defenders of the federalist cause, which they perceived as the almost magical solution to most of the national problems they confronted. "Federation," said Zamora, "embodies the cure for all the evils of the nation." Zamora's faith in federalism was unlimited: federalism not only cured those evils but "ma[de] them impossible."[126]

Constitutionalism

The history of radical constitutionalism in America is the history of failure. In most cases, radicals did not manage to put their constitutional ideas into practice – sometimes because they were defeated in the constitutional debates, at other times because they disrespected these discussions. Obviously, this failure does not necessarily mean that their ideas were in some way wrong or unacceptable. On some occasions, in fact, they could not participate in these debates because they were arbitrarily excluded from them, and on others they chose not to participate because they realized that those who engaged in them were simply attempting to advance their own interests.

The fact that radicals did not manage to enforce a radical constitution does not mean that they did not play a significant role in the discussions about how to design the new constitutions. On the contrary, their participation was, in many cases, extremely relevant to an explanation of the finally adopted legal documents. In the United States, for example, it is difficult to explain the content of the federal constitution without making reference to the populists' ideas. The early state constitutions that they had written and the objections they advanced against the proposed national constitution both had a profound impact on the document's final draft. In Latin America, the

---

[126] "With a federal system," argued Zamora, "each state will be in charge of its own necessities, using its own resources. Meanwhile, through their union in a general power, the different states will contribute to the great good, the glorious good of the national unity. Public order will be no longer a pretext for tyranny but, instead, it will be the first characteristic of each particular power." Gabaldón (1987), p. 319.

initial revolutionary movements brought with them impetuous initiatives aimed at securing a complete reorganization of the institutional system. Typically, many of these new ideas reflected the influence of French revolutionary thought. The independence leaders made, at that time, the usual references to the idea of "general will" and to the need for recreating a "social pact." In addition, many of them drafted new constitutions that reflected some of those ideas. In most cases, however, these early drafts did not go very far in their radicalism: they reproduced the revolutionary phraseology but without establishing radical institutions. What they did, however, was establish the basis of an alternative constitutional tradition that was hostile to the very common idea of having a strong executive, a kind of monarch, and which favored the incorporation of a bill of rights into the constitution.

The Venezuelan Constitution of 1811 was an early and important constitutional document of Rousseauean inspiration. Although it cannot properly be deemed a radical constitution, the 1811 text was clearly written in radical language and included some initiatives that were at least compatible with some of the populists' more fundamental demands. The Venezuelan Constitution was soon followed by similar documents in other Latin American countries, including Peru and New Granada. Radical ideas spread all over the continent. From Argentina, people like Mariano Moreno and Bernardo de Monteagudo wrote significant populist pieces that were also read beyond the Argentinean borders. In Mexico, there was a very important and extremist revolutionary movement, led by the priests Hidalgo and Morelos. The latter, among other things, promoted the adoption of a curiously radical constitution, which was drafted in Apatzingán in 1814 (later on, in the same country, we find some other interesting radical proposals like the ones made by Severo Maldonado and Fernández de Lizardi). In the Banda Oriental, José Gervasio Artigas was also concerned with constitutional questions from a radical viewpoint but even more with advancing an entire set of social and political reforms that could radically transform the structure of his country.

Shortly after this interesting beginning, radicalism began to lose force, partly because of the difficulties that radicals faced in carrying out their project. Undoubtedly, many of them attributed magical effects to the revolutions of independence and the new ideas that lay behind these movements. In Latin America, the populists assumed that the new societies would become more egalitarian once they were relieved of the heavy burdens of Spanish dominance. This was obviously not true. In part, the effects of four hundred years of Spanish colonization had gone too deep: the new Latin American societies had no experience of self-government. Most of the people had been directly and brutally excluded from the organization of the basic structure of society. Profound social, political, and economic inequalities existed that proved impossible to cure in just a few years. Even worse, very active forces began to work against these initial egalitarian tendencies. On the one hand, the Spanish tried to reconquer their lost territories, a decision that moved the Americans to reorganize their recently drafted institutions. To many revolutionary leaders, this initial military challenge required the locals to concentrate political authority and strengthen their military organization, two objectives that worked against the egalitarian ambitions of radicals. On the other hand, many of the local political leaders also played an active role, trying to prevent possible radical changes: they rightly assumed that in the new societies they would benefit the most, politically and economically speaking, and did not want to lose this chance. Because of these external and internal pressures, radicals were removed from the political scene when they were just beginning to have some influence. What came after this breeze of timid radicalism was a strong conservative wind. The military officers reaffirmed their influence, and the legal authorities began to think about monarchist alternatives.

During the second half of the nineteenth century, Latin American radicalism recovered part of the energy it had enjoyed during the 1810s. Undoubtedly, the artisans' revolutions that took place in Europe during the late 1840s help to explain this rebirth. In America at that time, there were also significant groups of artisans claiming their rights: they were both politically excluded from the decision-making process and economically affected by the prevalent laissez faire economic programs. In addition, many Latin Americans who were working or studying in Europe at the time returned to their countries and attempted to re-create there what they came to know abroad. One fantastic example in this respect is that of the Chilean Francisco Bilbao, who studied in France with Quinet and Michelet, two of the most important critics of the role of the church, particularly of the Jesuits, in educational matters. Bilbao went back to Chile and, as we know, organized the short-lived but still quite influential Sociedad de la Igualdad. Forced to leave his country because of his political activity and his anticlerical writings, he developed a radical life as an agitator. Among other things, he became a key figure in the rebirth of egalitarian thinking in Peru and an active intellectual in Argentina, where one of his many activities was to lead a support campaign in favor of Benito Juárez, the famous liberal leader in Mexico. Santiago Arcos, who also studied in France during the revolutionary period and who accompanied Bilbao in the creation of the Sociedad de la Igualdad, followed a similar path, both in Chile and abroad, advocating the egalitarian cause.[127]

In no other country did the artisans become as strong as in Colombia. Here, too, we find an active intellectual elite, which was also very well acquainted with the new radical and socialist ideas. In a very short period more than one hundred artisans' associations appeared throughout the country.[128] Important political leaders developed extremist rhetoric, trying to mobilize the artisans in favor of radical political reform. Something similar happened in Peru, which was, with Chile, the third important country that registered a rapid growth in its associational movement. After a short time of social unrest, however, none of these countries achieved a socialist revolution or a radical change in its political organization. The more radical leaders were exiled, imprisoned, or simply ignored. The more radical associations, such as the famous Sociedad Democrática in New Granada, lost their decisive battle to establish economic protectionism. However, this wave of radicalism had an interesting, though very gradual impact on the entire Latin American continent, making a fundamental contribution to the diffusion of new democratic demands.

After this wave of radicalism, the politically egalitarian way of thinking needed many years to recover its strength. With the new century, Latin America came to know some new thinkers and

---

[127] Arcos moved first to Argentina, then to Paris, and later to Spain, where he took part in the elections, accompanied by a group of federalists and leftist republicans, then to Italy, and finally back to France, where he committed suicide. Gazmuri (1992).

[128] In New Granada, the artisans' associations were numerous, and the influence of the French Revolution was heavier than in most other countries (see Jaramillo Uribe, 1997, 239–260). The first association of this type, the Sociedad Democrática, was created in 1847 at the initiative of an artisan, Artemio López. In a very short time, the Sociedad Democrática managed to gather numerous members and, as a result, much attention. Its example was followed all throughout the country, and the artisans' group suddenly evolved into a principal interest group. The artisans developed a radical discourse that included demands for a more active state, economic protectionism, and social reform (see, e.g., Camacho Roldán, 1946, vol. 2, chap. 21). Politically speaking, they sided with the liberal candidate, José Hilario López, and played a fundamental role in his victory. Despite their extraordinary contribution, though, the new administration did not attend to their claims: López's government, although radically liberal, promoted economic liberalism instead of protectionism, something that seriously hurt the interests of the artisans. After that, some of the artisans' leaders, in association with members of the armed forces, tried to impose their authority through coercive means.

social activists who favored this recovery. The Chilean typographer Luis Recabarren, the more moderate Argentineans Juan B. Justo and Alfredo Palacios, the Mexican anarchist Ricardo Flores Magón (founder of the Partido Liberal Mexicano), the Peruvian Marxists José Carlos Mariátegui and Víctor Raúl Haya de la Torre, and the remarkable radical González Prada would participate in this late recovery of radicalism.[129]

In the United States, the situation had always been substantially different. In contrast with what happened in Latin America, the British colonists in North America were forced to organize by themselves. In most cases, they had to design their own institutions and decide how to solve their own affairs. Briefly stated, they developed a practice of self-government, whereas their Latin American peers were subjected to an extremely hierarchical political organization. The revolution of independence brought into existence and helped to promote a very active citizenry, ready to petition for its rights before local authorities. Here, the ground seemed well prepared for the advancement of radicalism: the North Americans were accustomed not only to a radical political rhetoric but also to a radical political practice. They knew how to take advantage of an institutional system more open to the people's demands and wanted to reproduce this system at the national level. In the end, however, their efforts also proved futile. The years that preceded the federal convention were extremely problematic, both politically and socially . On the one hand, the prevalent Articles of Confederation could not ensure a good political coordination among the states. On the other hand, many different states experienced both popular rebellions and strong pressures against their legislatures, which resulted in certain laws that favored the popular majorities.

All these events worked, in the end, against the more radical initiatives. Many people, and most within the dominant political elite, viewed this picture as too chaotic and attributed its cause to the populists' pressures. Once again, disorder seemed to prevail at both the national and local levels, and the elites began to press not only for a more centralized political government but also for national and local institutions less sensitive to the people. An active citizenry simply seemed to promise more violence and social unrest. A decentralized country, meanwhile, promised more years of internal disorder and international isolation. Here, too, the radical project began to lose part of its initial influence.

[129] For an excellent summary of the evolution of these ideas, see Hale (1986).

The Organization of Power: A Strict Separation of Powers

In general terms, radicals had a difficult relationship with constitutional matters. The enactment of a constitution represented an interesting promise, a way of giving legal support to the self-governing ideal, but also a threatening risk, that of preventing the future generations' self-government. This was what Thomas Paine denounced when he claimed that the "right of the living" was much more important that "the authority of the dead" and maintained that "every generation is equal in rights to the generations which preceded it, by the same rule that every individual is born equal in rights with its contemporary."[130] In conclusion, he argued that "every age and generation must be as free to act for itself, in all cases, as the ages and generations that preceded it."[131] Thomas Jefferson, as we know, followed these ideas and, because of them, suggested in his "Notes on the State of Virginia" the adoption of a more "flexible" constitution, which would be changed every nineteen years, for example. This would imply, in his opinion, that every new generation would have its own constitution. In this manner, and only in this way, he believed, would the adoption of a constitution be a development in the self-governing enterprise and not an obstacle to it.

With regard to the constitutional particulars, in most cases the populists favored the establishment of republican and federal governments, organized through a "strict" separation of powers. Within this general structure, the populists promoted a strong congress and subordinated the other two branches to its will. Also, they favored the political participation of the people. In this sense, for example, they proposed substantial changes in the distribution of political rights: they knew that most people were legally excluded from politics and fought to reverse this situation. Their approach to rights was, once again, very different from the one that was prevalent at the time. They conceived of constitutional rights as a tool for expanding the political participation of the community and facilitating the self-governing ideal. In sum, they subordinated the structure of rights to a collective goal that was totally unacceptable to other, alternative views.

Their constitutions – or, more frequently, their constitutional proposals – were also unusual because of their "Rousseauean" vocabulary and their strong declarations of republican faith. During the revolutionary period, radicals seemed particularly enthusiastic

---

[130] Paine (1989), p. 56.
[131] Ibid., p. 76. See also Holmes (1988).

for the idea of writing or rewriting their constitutions. This decision, they believed, symbolized the radical reorganization of society. The new constitution would come to say that the old regime of domination and oppression was over. The new constitution represented, for them, the promise of a *new social pact*, the transition from the state of nature to civilization. This assumption explains, for example, Artigas's disquiet at the absence of a new constitution for the Banda Oriental: "Citizens," he proclaimed, "people must be free. This has to be the only goal and reason for its concern. However, after three years of our revolution, we still lack a general protection for the popular right. We are still [governed] by the people's faith and we do not see the securities of the contract... only a Constitution [can check the ambitions of men]."[132]

One of the most extreme expressions of the influence of Rousseau in Latin American constitutionalism appears in the work of Francisco Bilbao, particularly in his quite spectacular project *El gobierno de la libertad*.[133] In that document, Bilbao claimed that the "government of liberty" he proposed implied "the abolition of delegation, the abolition of the presidency, the abolition of the Army, the suppression of the *fueros*."[134] Also, in the opening paragraphs of his work, he stated: "All Constitutions recognize the sovereignty of the people, but they immediately add that, given the practical impossibility of exercising it [through direct democracy], or the people's incapacity to exercise it, the people were obliged to delegate it."[135] Confronting this view, he wondered: "Do we need to delegate sovereignty? Do we need to delegate our liberty? If this were true, I would prefer abandoning the idea of sovereignty and affirm the legitimacy of despotism, rather than deceive the true sovereign, transforming it into a slave." And he concluded: "To delegate means to transmit, to renounce, to abdicate sovereignty.... He who delegates... becomes a machine or a slave.... We do not have the right to delegate our sovereignty. We have the duty to be immediately, permanently and directly sovereign." "Delegation," he proclaimed, "is slavery disguised as sovereignty."[136]

---

[132] See his "Oración," for example, in Petit Muñoz (1956).
[133] This document, in which he presented his view on the constitution, is one of the most complete, well-argued, and coherent documents written by a Latin American radical. In addition, the document is remarkable as a consequence of its radicalism, which is illustrated, for example, in Bilbao's description of the French 1793 Jacobin constitution as the only constitution in history that "deserved to be remembered" – a claim that none of the most revolutionary of the time would have been ready to subscribe. See Bilbao (1886), vol. 1, 278 (see also Bravo 2007).
[134] Bilbao (1886), vol. 1, p. 279.
[135] Ibid., p. 246.
[136] Ibid., p. 247.

In accordance with these principles, Bilbao's proposed constitution instituted a peculiar form of political representation. Bilbao wanted to challenge a political system where representatives "do what they want: legislate, adjudicate, execute, becoming the true sovereigns."[137] For him, if the people were not given a chance "to discuss, deliberate, and vote what the law should be," then the whole idea of citizens as legislators became false. Trying to give sense to the idea of the "sovereignty of the people," he suggested a representative system where representatives received mandatory instructions from the people and acted as mere "agents" or "commissioners" of the latter.[138]

Most American constitutions did not reach so far as Bilbao's project, but they did show a clear commitment to majority rule.[139] Within the threefold organization of power generally approved at the time, radicals placed congress as the most important branch, the "fixed point" of the constitution, and the "most popular" branch of government. This choice seems easy to justify given that no institution other than the legislature can represent and express the majority interests. Congress is composed of numerous members who come from different parts of society and, ideally, represents all or at least many of the different viewpoints existing in the community. In addition, its members are, at least in part, chosen by popular election and can be removed by the people when their interests and demands are not taken seriously. The short-term mandates of its members contributed to these goals: most members of the legislature are subject to a close scrutiny by the people.

Clearly, radicals knew, as we know, that in its daily working many problems threatened and, to some extent, undermined the representative character of congress. Because all representative institutions suffer from similar or worse problems, however, the representative assembly remains the most representative institution, at least in relative terms.

While they tried to preserve the authority of congress, radicals tended to reject institutional arrangements that allowed other

---

[137] Ibid.
[138] Ibid.
[139] At the beginning of the revolutionary process, this commitment found expression in very basic things such as "an expanded suffrage, the use of the ballot rather than the customary oral voting, the opening of legislative meetings to the public, the printing of legislative minutes, and the recording of votes taken in the legislatures. All these proposals enlarged the political arena and limited the power of those who clung to the traditional ways of private arrangements and personal influence." Wood (2002), p. 51.

branches of power to interfere with the decisions of the legislature. More specifically, they rejected all those proposals that allowed the executive or the judiciary to obstruct the decisions of the majority. Radicals favored a system of "strict separation of powers" in which no power had the right to interfere with the actions of the others. As Maurice Vile explained, in his study on the first constitutional discussions in the United States, the radicals "all adhered to the doctrine of the separation of powers, and they all rejected, to a greater or a lesser degree, the concept of checks and balances."[140]

Seemingly, the system of "strict separation" had many virtues when compared to other alternatives. First, it was based on a mechanism that was clear, simple, and easy to understand. Through its implementation, everyone would know what branch of power was doing what. There would be no confusions. Second, the system of "strict separation" helped to prevent an undesirable scenario: through its functioning, none of the different branches of power would feel the temptation to subtly begin to replace the others. In other words, when the institutional system allowed one of the branches to interfere with the actions of the others, then it suddenly "opened the door" to unacceptable encroachments. Each power would use each possible situation for taking the place of the others. Clearly, for people who assumed, as did radicals, that most public officers tended to behave selfishly, this possibility was obviously threatening. Third, the system made clear that, in order to check the government, what was necessary was to ensure "exogenous" or "popular" controls. Fourth, and most important, the system of "strict separation" fenced the congress against the intrusive actions of the countermajoritarian branches of power.[141] Particularly, it helped to strengthen the powers of the congress vis-á-vis a tradition of strong executives, namely, of strong royal governors.[142] In the end, the populists' defense of the system of "strict" separation was, above all, a way of preserving the radical character of the republican government.

Most of the first radical constitutions in the United States, the state constitutions approved before the adoption of the federal constitution of 1787, created these systems of "strict separation." In Latin America, too, this idea acquired a certain importance among the advocates

---

[140] Vile (1967), p. 133.
[141] I take the term "countermajoritarian" from Alexander Bickel's work. See Bickel (1962). By now, we can define an institution as countermajoritarian when it does not embody and represent the preferences of the majority.
[142] In Pennsylvania, for example, the institution of the governor was directly eliminated from the constitutional text.

of populism. The Mexican Constitution of 1814, the Constitution of Apatzingán, seemed committed to that principle. More polemically, some scholars describe the Mexican Constitution of 1857, at least in its first version, as an example of this conception.[143] More clearly, the first constitution proposed for the Banda Oriental, in 1813, explicitly excluded "mutual interference" between different branches. In article 21 it proclaimed that "the Government of this province will never exercise legislative and judicial functions, or the functions of one of them; the legislative branch will never exercise executive and judicial functions, or the functions of one them. The Judiciary will never exercise legislative or executive functions, or the functions of one of them." In this way, they assumed, they would guarantee "the government of the laws, and not a tyranny."

The populists' preference for a "popular" government did not necessarily imply a preference for an unchecked government, although most of their enemies raised this point against them. Actually, radicals were also concerned with the establishment of checks and controls, although they wanted controls of a different type. They did not think that the only possible way for preventing the abuse of power was through the adoption of "internal" or "endogenous" controls, that is, controls exercised by one branch of power upon the others. Rather, radicals preferred the adoption of "external," "exogenous," or "popular" controls, that is, controls exercised directly by the people and not mediated by public officers. These controls gave the citizenry, as "the only legitimate source of power," the "last say" in cases of institutional crisis.

In this sense, for example, and showing his fears about the conduct fostered by the system of "endogenous" controls, Samuel Williams stated that "the security of the people is derived not from the nice ideal application of checks and balances, and mechanical powers, among the different parts of the government, but from the responsibility, and dependence of each part of the government, over the people."[144] For those who shared this view, the basic idea was that "the branches of power should be separate from each other, and each answerable directly to the people, not to the other branches."[145]

One of the most interesting debates on the subject was the one held between Thomas Jefferson and James Madison. In his "Notes on the State of Virginia," Jefferson defended "exogenous" controls, suggesting, among other things, that every time it was necessary to "correct

[143] See, for example, Aguilar Rivera (2000).
[144] Quoted in Vile (1991), p. 678.
[145] Ibid.

[breaches]" of the constitution, "a convention [should be called]" for that purpose. Concerned about the possible implications of Jefferson's view, Madison promptly reacted to this suggestion, clarifying, at the same time, the profound theoretical disagreements that separated their respective views.

Madison dedicated the whole of *Federalist* 49 to replying to the author of the "Notes." For him, the appeal to the people was inconvenient because of the "danger of disturbing the public tranquility by interesting too strongly the public passions." Also, he thought, the "appeal to the people would carry an implication of some defect in the government," depriving it of its necessary "veneration." Finally, he suggested that this way of solving the interbranch difficulties would be too favorable to and, as a result, improperly biased in favor of the legislative branch. The legislators had "connections of blood, of friendship and of acquaintance" with the people at large.

The Madisonian reply did not fully convince the critics of the federal constitution. In fact, these critics had some other reasons for arguing against the framers' proposal of a balanced government. For example, they believed that the strategy of giving "defensive tools" to each department would promote a situation of political stalemate or, in the worst case, a state of "war" between different branches of power. Nathaniel Chipman, for example, foresaw a state of permanent tension between the different interests at stake, because of the proposed system. Chipman depicted this situation as one of "perpetual war of each [interest] against the other, or at best, an armed truce, attended with constant negotiations, and shifting combinations, as if to prevent mutual destruction; each party in its turn uniting with its enemy against a more powerful enemy."[146]

Radicals aimed to preserve the authority and popular character of congress: no other institution represented the popular will like the legislature, and for that reason, they assumed, it was commonly under the attack of the other branches. As an additional safeguard to the popular character of the institution, as a way of preserving its representative character, radicals defended the creation of ample legislatures, composed of numerous people. This was a common claim among some American Anti-Federalists, who wanted congress to become a "mirror of society." An adequate government, they assumed, should possess the same interests, feelings, opinions, and views as the people themselves.[147]

---

[146] See Chipman (1833), p. 171.
[147] See "The Federal Farmer," in Storing (1981a), vol. 2, p. 230.

In fact, many of the critics of the U.S. federal constitution defended similar ideas, associating the more numerous assemblies with greater wisdom. They said, for example, that "the most respectable assemblies we have any knowledge of and the wisest, have been those, each of which consisted of several hundred members."[148] Actually, the "Federal Farmer" seemed to defend a general principle about the virtues of large collective bodies, to which "[the] more numerous state assemblies and conventions have universally discovered more wisdom, and as much order, as the less numerous ones."[149] Others defended the creation of large assemblies for instrumental reasons, arguing that "the variety prevents combination, and the number excludes corruption."[150] Similarly, in Latin America, the radical liberal Ponciano Arriaga argued that "legislation becomes wiser when the legislative assembly is more numerous." "It is not true," he asserted, contradicting the judgments of his opponents, "that when we have more deputies we find less conscience and less patriotism among the elected. These difficulties we will have even if we restrict the numbers. However, experience teaches that the more dispersed and fragmented is the authority, the more public spirit and respect for the democratic institutions we find." "What happens," he concluded, "is that many are still horrified with the people.... If we increase the number [of deputies] Congress will be filled by new and humbler men, who won't believe they are wise. Perhaps, then, everything will be better, because we will find more faith and stronger commitments [among the representatives]." Following the same line of thought, Ignacio Ramirez criticized the creation of small legislative bodies, arguing that they would be more easily corrupted.[151]

Because of these beliefs, radicals commonly rejected the indirect election of representatives, as they opposed bicameral legislatures. On the one hand, radicals rejected indirect elections because, to their mind, they favored corruption[152] and the distortion of the people's will. Above all, however, the radicals disliked indirect elections because of their elitist foundations. As the Mexican deputy José Gamboa asserted, indirect elections were based only on "fear of the people."[153] On the other hand, and more importantly, radicals rejected bicameralism

---

[148] Ibid., p. 369.
[149] Letter from the "Federal Farmer" in Storing (1981a), vol. 2, p. 284.
[150] Paine, in *Pennsylvania Packet* (Philadelphia), Dec. 5, 1778.
[151] See Zarco (1957).
[152] See, in this respect, the opinion of the radical Ignacio Ramírez in the Mexican constitutional convention. Zevada (1972), p. 182.
[153] Ibid.

because they rejected the particular type of bicameral legislature that their opponents proposed. The critics of populism wanted to build a "conservative" senate, which would not only restrain the decision-making powers of the majority but also, and more importantly, guarantee a "fixed" legislative place for the powerful "few." In addition, the populists' Rousseauean ideology provided them with additional good reasons for combating the institution of a senate. In their opinion, to accept a bicameral legislature meant to accept the "division" of the popular will: the popular will, however, was one and indivisible. Any attempt to fragment it had to be resisted and rejected.

In France, the revolutionary agents did not want to annex another chamber to the most popular branch. The first two constitutions that they approved, those of 1791 and 1793, created a *unicameral* legislature. Only after intense debates and the spectacular failure of the revolutionary constitutions did they decide to accept the institution of a bicameral congress in the constitution of 1795. However, we must acknowledge, this constitution did not incorporate a conservative type of senate, one that represented the landed and clerical interests, but only a second chamber composed of older representatives of the people.

In America, the most interesting antecedent of unicameralism was the one adopted in Pennsylvania in its 1776 constitution. For Thomas Paine, bicameral systems "always admit[ed] of the possibility...that the minority govern[ed] the majority."[154] The influential Benjamin Franklin recognized that "it had always been his opinion that the legislative body should consist of one house only."[155]

Paine's proposal, however, was severely criticized by those who saw it as too complacent and too sensitive to the interests of the majority. At that time, many depicted the initial policies of the new congress – the abolition of slavery, the confiscation of William Penn's properties, the issuing of paper money, the regulation of prices, and the proposal for closing down the Bank of North America – as expressions of the furious and unchecked will of the populace. For its enemies, the

---

[154] See in Forner (1945), p. 389. Paine, like many Pennsylvanian radicals, associated the introduction of a senate with the creation of a new aristocracy, and the senators with people who "having once obtained [the power], used it as their own property." The senate, they assumed, was designed to ensure the presence of "the minority of the rich" within the structure of power. For "Eudoxus," the defenders of a bicameral system proposed the senate as a mere means for "setting up distinctions...and jarring interests." In his opinion, those who opposed unicameralism were those who feared "agrarian law[s from a] democratic power." See "Eudoxus," *Pennsylvania Packet* (Philadelphia), Apr. 22, 1776.
[155] See Rollins (1989), p. 148.

constitution was unable to produce "sedate," moderate decisions: any popular initiative, they believed, was immediately transformed into a new law. With the unicameral system, they argued, the "common farmers, unread in history, law, and politics," were governing the country, while "educated and well-read men" were prevented from correcting "the errors [of the people]."[156] John Adams considered the project to be "too democratic," a way of establishing "simple democracy."[157] In their objections to the constitution, the critics put into question even the basic egalitarian principle on which the constitution was built, rendering their elitist assumptions evident. The following statement is a clear example of this: "Mr. Thomas Paine's writings abound with this sort of specious falsehoods and perverted truths. Of all his doctrines, none perhaps has created more agitation and alarm than that which proclaims to all men that they are created free and equal." The people "believed that by making their own and other men's passions sovereign, they should invest man with immediate perfectibility; and breath into their regenerated liberty an ethereal spirit that would never die.... With opinions so wild, and passions so fierce, the spirit of democracy has been sublimated to extravagance."[158]

Paine recognized the force and intensity of these attacks and proposed different amendments to his favored constitutional project. In *The Rights of Man*, for example, he suggested the following: "[I]n order to remove the objection against a single house (that of acting with too quick an impulse) and at the same time to avoid the inconsistencies, in some cases absurdities, arising from the two houses, the following method has been proposed as an improvement on both. First, to have but one representation. Second, to divide that representation, by lot, into two or three parts. Third, that every proposed bill shall first be debated in those parts, by succession, that they may become hearers

---

[156] Quoted in Shaeffer (1974). Similarly, Rufus King made reference to "the great Body of the people" that he described as a body "without Virtue, and not governed by any internal constraints of Conscience." It was necessary, in his opinion, to put immediate checks upon "the madness of Democracy."

[157] See Baylin (1992), pp. 290–293; and Walsh (1969), chap. 5. Also, Koch and Peden (1946), pp. 77–114; and Knight (1989). In a letter to Charles Lee, Benjamin Rush wrote about "poor Pennsylvania.... They call this a democracy, a mobocracy in my opinion would be more proper. All our laws breathe the spirit of town meetings and porter shops" (Butterfield, 1951, p. 244). Similarly, Fisher Ames reasoned that "democracy is the volcano which conceals the fiery materials of its own destruction. These would produce an eruption, and carry desolation in their way" (Bernhard, 1965, p. 59; Butterfield, 1951). The conservative Noah Webster also criticized the Pennsylvania Constitution, pointing out the demands of "publicity" that were included in the text.

[158] F. Ames, in Ames (1983), vol. 2, pp. 208–209.

of each other, but without taking any vote. After which the entire representation to assemble for a general debate and determination by vote."[159] In this way, Paine managed to consistently keep the radical character of his proposed constitution while dismissing the most common objections to it.

The proposal for a unicameral congress was quite successful in the United States during the years that followed the revolution of independence. Some constitutions, in Vermont and Georgia, for example, copied the Pennsylvanian model, and many politicians and journalists adopted its principles and also criticized the idea of including a conservative senate in the federal constitution. They objected to this proposal, emphasizing that it would favor only the "select few," the aristocracy, the minority of "rich and well-born."[160]

In Latin America, too, many political leaders suggested adopting a unicameral congress and considered the senate to be an aristocratic institution. The Uruguayan liberal José Ellauri, who led the constitutional debates in his country, argued against including provisions for a senate in the constitution.[161] However, confronting the intense attacks of his critics, he suggested, like Thomas Paine, an alternative solution that still resisted the incorporation of a senate: the idea was to replace the senate with a new body composed of nine members selected from the same lower house.[162]

In Peru, the idea of a unicameral legislature was popular from the start of the country's constitutional history. The first constitutional delegates, for example, defended unicameralism as a way of preserving the unity of the popular "voice." This idea was repeatedly defended during the constitutional debates that produced the constitution of 1823. The Peruvians' distrust of bicameral legislatures was also evident in the liberal constitutions of 1856 and 1867. The 1856 constitution created a "heterodox" legislative model, where congress had only one chamber but functioned with two: each year, the legislature was divided into two parts, through a lottery. Then, in its actual functioning, congress appeared as a bicameral body, a solution that, once again, seemed to follow Paine's teachings. The 1867 constitution, however, returned to the model of a "pure" unicameral system. In

---

[159] Paine (1944), p. 214.
[160] A long list of examples, from the Anti-Federalist files, can be found in Borden (1965) and Allen and Gordon (1985).
[161] It is true that Ellauri and many other Uruguayans, resisted the idea of creating a senate as a result of the aristocratic character that they attributed to it. However, it is also true that Ellauri, like many of his colleagues, was equally afraid of the power of the "unchecked masses." See Pivel Devoto (1955), p. 24.
[162] See Bauzá (1887), p. 288. See also Pivel Devoto (1956), chap. 2.

Ecuador, early constitutions such as those of 1830 and 1850 adopted the unicameral proposal. However, none of these experiments had other significant populist overtones.

Another early, and more genuine, defense of a unicameral legislative body appeared in Mexico in 1814. In effect, the Apatzingán Constitution, following the French revolutionary constitutional model, incorporated a unicameral congress into its text, inaugurating a significant tradition of unicameralism.[163] In nineteenth-century Mexico, in effect, the unicameral proposal would always be a controversial issue but one that was taken seriously by all constitutional theorists. The creation of ultraconservative senates, as in the constitution of 1843, may be seen at least in part as a reaction to the unicameral model. Subsequently, these very conservative bodies reinforced the existing prejudices against the senate. Not surprisingly, one of the most important discussions within the constitutional convention of 1857 was the one aimed at suppressing the second legislative chamber. At that time, and for a few years, the *liberales puros* were successful with their proposals: most of the delegates recognized the need for avoiding the aristocratic features of the senate.[164]

The populists' fundamental aim of strengthening the powers of congress had, as an obvious counterpart, the aim of limiting the powers of the executive. We should not forget that, in both the United States and Latin America, the populists identified a strong executive with monarchy. For most of them, then, the creation of a powerful executive implied the return to an ancient model of domination. Typically, the Venezuelan Constitution of 1811, a constitution that Bolívar described as the source of all the institutional problems suffered by the country after its enactment, "dissolved" the executive power, creating a plural executive. Undoubtedly, the decision to have three different executive heads responded to the delegates' fear of a new tyranny and their absolute confidence in the regenerative force of the new laws.

---

[163] This constitution represents an interesting example of the use of lottery mechanisms for the selection of representatives. See articles 49, 75, 88, 98, 132, 133, 182, 218, 212, 222, among others.

[164] The delegate Ramiro Gamboa asserted that the senate was an antidemocratic institution. The essence of representative democracy, he claimed, resided in the radical vote. Through the senate, however, the minority imposed its own view upon the majority. The delegate Espiridion Moreno declared that in a democratic system it should not be surprising that the most populated areas imposed their views upon the less populated ones. More directly, Ignacio Ramírez claimed that the institution of a senate constituted an abuse of the representative system that simply made the creation of new laws more difficult.

In 1823 the Peruvian constitutional delegates decided to follow the example of Venezuela and created a plural executive, composed of three persons. We should remember that Peru, like Mexico, gained its independence from Spain rather late, so these were its first constitutional creations. On that opportunity, the influential deputy José Faustino Sánchez Carrión, who shortly afterward would dramatically change his ideological position, stringently condemned the alternative of a strong executive.[165] In his opinion, "three people will not get together to oppress the rest of us." He declared that "a government by one is efficient if what we want is to treat human beings as beasts...but what I want to defend is freedom, this is also what the people want. Without freedom I do not want anything: the idea of having only one person in charge of the government brings me back the image of the king...of the tyranny."[166] "If we want to ensure political freedom," he concluded, "we cannot give more powers to the Executive." This alternative was, in his opinion, the worst and most threatening of all possibilities, given that the executive controlled the military and the purse.[167] Because of these assumptions, the 1823 constitution not only divided the executive in three but also reduced its military and legislative capacities and suppressed its powers of veto.

In Chile, too, the fight against the "excessive" powers of the executive constituted one of the main political goals of the populist groups throughout the century. This fight became particularly intense after 1848, when groups such as the Sociedad de la Igualdad and the Asamblea Constituyente[168] began to press for the adoption of immediate political reforms and obtained its initial fruits by the end of the century, through the work of Manuel Antonio Matta and his Radical Party.[169]

---

[165] In the letters he signed as the Solitario de Sayán, Sanchéz Carrión ferociously attacked the monarchist alternative, defended by important military leaders such as the Argentinean general San Martín. Given the character of Peruvian people, he stated, "[if we accepted a constitutional monarchy,] we would become excellent vassals and never again citizens: we would have servile attitudes, we would find pleasure in kissing the hand of the Majesty." González Portacarrero (1987), p. 92.
[166] See Basadre (1949), vol. 1, p. 12.
[167] See ibid., vol. 2, p. 267.
[168] The Asamblea, which was closely connected to the Sociedad de la Igualdad was composed of Benjamín Vicuña Mackenna, Guillermo and Antonio Matta, and Angel Gallo, among others, and advocated the adoption of radical political reform through newspapers and demonstrations.
[169] As the president of the Radical Party, Matta defined the main political goals of his organization. These goals included promoting a constitutional reform that reduced the atrocious powers of the executive, an electoral reform that put an end to the privileges of the rich, the decentralization of political authority, and the restriction of the powers of the church.

65

Another common strategy for reducing the powers of the executive was to limit the term of its mandate. During the famous Río Negro Convention in Colombia, the representatives of the so-called Radical Olimpo proposed, among other things, restricting each presidential mandate to only two years. The radicals justified this remarkable decision by making reference to their fears of tyrannical governments. They had come to power with the help of the authoritarian general Tomás Mosquera, but they seriously distrusted his intentions and ambitions. The exceptional adoption of a two-year term of mandate represented the actions that most radicals were ready to take in order to reduce the powers of the executive. Similarly, the early constitutional proposal in the Banda Oriental in 1813 not only restricted the military and legislative powers of the executive but also reduced its mandate to a one-year term.

In other cases aimed at achieving similar goals, the populists put the election of the executive in the hands of congress, an initiative that was very common among the new independent states in the United States. In fact, this system was adopted in nine of the eighteen state constitutions after independence. Similarly, many of these constitutions (e.g., in the cases of Pennsylvania, Delaware, Maryland, Virginia, North Carolina, and Georgia) provided for a system of mandatory rotation for the main public positions. By the same token, the Apatzingán Constitution of 1814 adopted a system of mandatory rotation, divided executive authority in three, and deposited the election of the latter in the hands of congress. Through these initiatives, radicals tried to restrict the powers of representatives and also to foster the political participation of the citizenry.

In Latin America, the limitation of executive powers came together with other initiatives aimed at reducing the power of the military and the clergy. For those who defended a radical government, the persistent influence of these two groups was as threatening as the concentration of powers in the hands of the executive. The direct and indirect influence of the church and the military in politics was enormous: they both concentrated political and economic power and had numerous allies within the dominant groups. The church's extensive landed possessions were the source of social unrest throughout the century. In countries such as Mexico, these conflicts generated constant and very violent disputes among different political groups: many of them suffered from extreme poverty, while the church kept most of its properties uncultivated. In Chile, the struggles against the privileges of the church resulted in the creation of the Radical Party, whose members belonged to the Liberal Party and decided not to accept the alliance that the latter had established with the conservative groups.

During those years, many radicals had suffered persecution because of their ideas. Bilbao, for example, was expelled from his work because of his anticlerical writings and his radical proposals, after being denounced by Mariano Egaña, taken to the tribunals, and finally forced into exile. In Peru, distinguished political figures such as Mariano Amézaga, Manuel González Prada (one of the first significant Peruvian anarchists), and even the influential priest Francisco de Paula González Vigil also tried to reduce the political influence of the church. At the same time, Ignacio Escudero led an important legislative battle to reduce the powers of the military. In the constitutional convention of 1856, for example, Escudero proposed the direct suppression of the standing army. On that occasion, he said that during the war a standing army was useless, whereas in periods of peace it was too dangerous.[170] In Mexico, the *liberales puros* played an extraordinary role in the fight against the abusive powers of the church and the military. Melchor Ocampo led a personal battle against the church's economic impositions that affected the poorest sectors of society. The Mexican constitutional convention of 1857 (like the Argentinean convention of 1853) illustrates the scope and intensity of these confrontations regarding the privileges of the church. In Colombia, a relatively minor decision, the suppression of small monasteries in the locality of Pasto, triggered the extremely violent "War of the Supremes" during the 1830s. At the beginning of the 1850s, the political debates were once again concentrated on the privileges of the church and the military. In particular, the group of so-called *gólgotas* campaigned for radically liberal reforms that reduced the power and influence of both groups. This battle surfaced once again during the time of the Radical Olimpo, as well as in the subsequent Río Negro Convention of 1863.[171]

Another significant part of the populists' political program related to the idea of strengthening relations between the representatives and the people. These initiatives turned out to be particularly important, especially when we consider how much alternative political views pressed in the opposite direction, namely, in favor of separating the people from their delegates. Three reasons seemed to justify the populists' initiatives: radicals aimed at empowering the citizenry, which

---

[170] Paz Soldán (1943), p. 99.
[171] See, for example, the famous vote by Salvador Camacho Roldán, B. Herrera, and Justo Arosamena, against the collaboration between the state and the church.

required greater popular access to the political arena; they wanted to improve the representative character of congress; and they distrusted representatives and wanted to reduce the risk of having self-serving politicians, whom they did not want acting independently without paying attention to the people's claims.

Radicals had been applying systematic pressure in favor of this objective since the eighteenth century. In England, because of the political scandals that surrounded the famous Middlesex affairs during the 1760s, radicals placed the issue of political reform at the top of their agenda. James Burgh advanced many reform proposals in his 1774 book *Political Disquisitions*. There, he defended the need to "restore the spirit of the constitution" by securing three important political changes: annual parliaments, the exclusion of placemen and pensioners from the Commons, and adequate parliamentary representation.[172] Also, as additional measures oriented toward improving the representative character of the system, he proposed mandatory rotation for most representative positions and defended the people's right to write instructions to their delegates. The claim for this right was normally based on the assumption that the representatives were, essentially, the people's attorneys, advocates, or servants. Joseph Priestley and Richard Price shared Burgh's enthusiasm for these reforms. In his *General Introduction and Supplement to the Two Tracts on Civil Liberty, the War in America, and the Finances of the Kingdom*, Price wrote that "civil governments are only public servants and their power, by being delegated, is by its nature limited." Shortly after, in his *Additional Observations in the Nature of Civil Liberty, the Principles of Government, and the Justice and Policy of the War with America*, he reaffirmed the idea that the representatives should be "accountable to their constituents" in "all their acts."[173]

Not surprisingly, radicals in the United States adopted some of the proposals advanced by their British counterparts shortly before. Favored by a long-standing practice of self-government, the Americans soon became concerned with these issues. During the period of "radical constitutionalism," we find numerous initiatives aimed at improving the representative character of the political system. For example, many of the first state constitutions provided for mandatory rotation and very short mandates also for the legislators. A traditional principle had taught them to associate the elimination

---

[172] See Hay (1979), chap. 6.
[173] Cone (1968), chap. 3.

of "annual elections" with the "beginning of slavery." The right to give written instructions to the representatives, accompanied by a threatened right of recall, was also popular among the radical activists. Once again, Pennsylvania's Constitution of 1776 represented a good example of the way in which radicals pursued these innovations. The constitution, in effect, granted the people's right to instruct their representatives and to "apply to the legislature for redress of grievances" (art. 16 of its Bill of Rights). It also instituted the principle of annual elections (sec. 9) under the widespread belief that long mandates would imply something like a renunciation to the ideal of popular sovereignty. In addition, in section 14 the constitution provided for the principle of mandatory rotation. For many Pennsylvanian intellectuals of the period, like "Demophilus," the ideal was that of promoting radical democracy in small communities. The introduction of representatives highly dependent upon their constituents appeared to be the best means for obtaining the desired objective.[174] All of the previously mentioned constitutional clauses were aimed at ensuring the goal of a strong popular government.

In Latin America, these radical reforms were much less successful, either in theory or in practice. However, they still had advocates who defended them. The Bolivian Lucas Mendoza de Tapia, for example, proposed adopting the right to make written instructions to the representatives, appealing to North American antecedents and affirming the importance of making the representatives dependent on popular will. "If the deputy wants to represent the people, then I cannot understand why he should become independent of the people's opinion."[175] In Argentina, too, the debate on the right to make written instructions was quite popular during the first half of the century.

Another significant area of reform was the judicial system. This area was always problematic because of its implications for the democratic organization of the country: it should be clear that, at least in principle, an increase in the powers of the judiciary seems to imply a decrease in the democratic powers of the citizenry. The dispute over the functions of the judicial branch was commonly translated into a dispute over the question of who, or which institution, should have the "last say" within the political system. For radicals, obviously, the "last say" had to be in the hands of the citizenry or, within a representative system, in the hands of their delegates in congress: the political

---

[174] See "Demophilus" (1976). "Demophilus" defended the idea of a radical democracy as presumably practiced in early England by the "Saxons."

[175] Mendoza de Tapia recalled that "Edmund Burke, who received from his constituency a strict parliamentary program, refused to follow it, asserting that the people

branches should prevail over the nonpolitical ones. The critics of radicalism favored instead the opposite solution, which implied the adoption of countermajoritarian institutions, such as the judiciary, empowered to prevail over the radical ones.

In France, the first revolutionary delegates had immediately showed their hostility toward judicial bodies. Of course, this hostility was grounded on diverse reasons, not all of them theoretically interesting. However, it was also true that the radical doctrine gave them many good arguments against the role of judges. Montesquieu's principle that "the judges are the mouth through which the law speaks" was then clearly popular. It symbolized a strong commitment to majority rule and the superiority they attributed to congress. In line with this principle, during the constitutional convention of 1791, the deputy Nicolas Bergasse defended the idea that the judges should be subordinated to the law. More specifically, he argued that the magistrates should not distort the meaning of the law by way of interpreting it: if they did not understand the actual meaning of the law, they had to go back to its creators in search of clarification.

Thomas Jefferson's opinions on the issue were certainly influenced by the hostility of the French toward the judiciary. In a letter to William Jarvis, he criticized his colleague for assuming the judges to be "the ultimate arbiters of all constitutional question." In his opinion, this was "a very dangerous doctrine...and one which would place us under the despotism of an oligarchy. Our judges are as honest as other men, and not more so. They have, with others, the same passions for party, for power, and the privilege of their corps...their power [is] the more dangerous as they are in office for life, and not responsible, as the other functionaries are, to the elective control."[176] In the same letter, Jefferson clarified who should, in his opinion, have the "last institutional say" in cases of political crisis. "When the legislature or executive functionaries act unconstitutionally," he argued, "they are responsible to the people in their elective capacity. The exemption of the judges from that is quite dangerous enough. I know

---

should not impose their views upon the representative. However, this Burkean claim has its limits. When the people become more enlightened, the horizons of public reason become broader, and the independence of the deputy from his electors diminishes. In the United States it is very common that the electors write specific programs that their representatives are obliged to follow." See Jordán de Albarracín (1978), p. 125.

[176] He continued: "The constitution has erected no such single tribunal, knowing that to whatever hands confined, with the corruptions of time and party, its members would become despots. It has more wisely made all the departments co-equal and co-sovereign within themselves." Jefferson (1999), p. 381.

no safe depositary of the ultimate powers of the society but the people themselves."[177]

The Jeffersonian John Taylor shared the opinion of his friend, stating that "a judicial sovereignty over constitution and law, without responsibility to the national sovereignty [was] an unprincipled and novel anomaly, unknown to any political theory, and fitted to become an instrument of usurpation."[178] Similar complaints also came from "Brutus," who argued that "the supreme court under this constitution would be exalted above all other power in the government, and subject to no control."[179] Against him, Hamilton dedicated his thoughtful and now famous *Federalist* 78.

Other radicals had defended jury nullification, that is, the doctrine that jurors have the right not to enforce a law they consider unjust. This doctrine reflected the radicals' "view of the jury as a democratic institution in which citizens deliberate, not only about the facts of the case but also about the justice of the law as applied to the case."[180]

Also, because of their distrust of countermajoritarian institutions, the populists of Pennsylvania decided to create a novel body of popular origin aimed at ensuring respect for the constitution.[181] The new organization, the "council of censors," was severely criticized, among other things, because of its composition. Madison, for example, in *Federalist* 50, objected to it because its current members had previously taken part in the political life of the state, which, for him, affected the impartiality of their decisions and prevented them from carrying out adequate deliberations. The main objections to the council, however, made reference to its supposed inefficiency. Madison asserted, in this respect, that "the decisions of the council on constitutional questions, whether rightly or erroneously formed, have [not] had any effect in varying the practice" of the political branches. Curiously, the council was also heavily criticized in postrevolutionary France, where the revolutionaries presented it as an example of what should not be done in order to protect the constitution. Above all, however, they used this example in order to reject the system of judicial review as an appropriate alternative and therefore to reaffirm the predominance of the national assembly.

---

[177] Ibid., p. 382.
[178] See J. Taylor (1814), p. 217.
[179] See Kenyon (1966), p. 350. "Brutus" published his view as newspaper letters. Apparently it was his view that triggered Hamilton's famous defense of the role of the judiciary in *Federalist* 78.
[180] Sandel in Allen and Regan (1998), p. 331. See also Abramson (1994).
[181] See the text of the constitution in Blaustein and Singler (1988), pp. 29–30.

The initial hostility of U.S. radicals toward the judiciary was fueled, in addition, by circumstantial reasons, which were, in the end, not totally independent from their theoretical reasons. During the post-revolutionary period, judges were in charge of prosecuting the majority group, mostly composed of the debtors who were unable to repay their debts in hard currency. Literally thousands of people were judicially prosecuted, and, as a result, properties were sold, and debtors were imprisoned. Between 1784 and 1786, there was a more than 200 percent increase in trials over a similar period between 1770 and 1772. At that moment, the majority, following the practices that it had learned during the revolution, tried to force judges to suspend or adjourn the processes until the following term. Mobilizations to prevent the sitting of the courts multiplied everywhere. Samuel Ely led a massive mobilization in Northampton. Luke Day followed his example, leading fifteen hundred men. Other comparable attempts were made in Taunton, Concord, and Great Barrington. Undoubtedly, however, the most significant of all these popular insurrections was the one promoted by Daniel Shays with a thousand men. Shays's Rebellion was the object of serious concern and discussion among the members of the federal convention: they acknowledged that the new national institutions should be able to prevent these types of counter-institutional reaction. As Gordon Wood argued, these rebellions had an extraordinary impact on their deliberations.[182]

In Latin America, the judicial institutions were born weak. Their members were normally too close to the political authorities in charge of appointing them. Perhaps, given its lack of "independent life," radicals were not particularly concerned with the judicial branch. However, we still find some interesting initiatives aimed at reducing the scope of its powers and enhancing legislative authority. In the very peculiar Colombian Constitution of 1863, for example, the delegates positioned the senate as the supreme national institution: in this case, it was not the supreme court but the senate that was in charge of pronouncing the "last institutional word." In fact, the senate took the place of the judiciary in the task of reviewing the constitutionality of the laws. Inspired by similar principles, a group of federalist Venezuelan rebels drafted a radical program, the "Saint Thomas program," in 1858, aimed at challenging the authority of the conservative groups that had ruled the country during most of the century.[183] The program included, among other proposals, the

---
[182] Wood (1966).
[183] See Picón Salas (1962); Díaz Sánchez (1950).

popular election of judges.[184] In Mexico, also inspired by federalist beliefs, the brilliant theorist Mariano Otero presented a significant constitutional project that also reduced the powers of the judiciary in order to preserve certain federalist principles. Therefore, in Otero's project the state legislatures received the power to declare a national law unconstitutional.

During the constitutional convention, many of the Mexican *liberales puros* went even further in their reflections, recognizing the deep theoretical problems involved in the design of countermajoritarian institutions. Because of this, they denounced the way in which their opponents were trying to organize the senate and the judiciary. By this means, they condemned the senate as an antidemocratic institution and objected to the requisite of being "instructed in the science of law" in order to become a supreme court member. For Melchor Ocampo, for example, a knowledge of the contents of the "official science" did not guarantee the adoption of impartial and just decisions. Ponciano Arriaga shared Ocampo's judgment and asserted that lay judges tended to adopt better decisions than professional ones.

The radicals' hostility toward the judiciary would become even more intense in the following years. The brilliant Chilean radical Luis Recabarren summarized this view by stating that "the judicial organization is the safest bridge" created by the rich against those "who want to transform the present social order."[185]

Finally, radicalism tried to strengthen popular control over public affairs by decentralizing the decision-making process – that is, by defending federalism. Federalism became, in fact, one of the most significant and problematic issues during the postrevolutionary period. In the United States, the issue of federalism was, arguably, the topic that organized most of the constitutional debates during the federal convention. In addition, many of the critics of the constitution, those who worked "outside" the closed doors of the convention, objected to the document for organizing a centralized regime that undermined the democratic and autonomous life of the states.

In Latin America, federalism also constituted a significant political issue. In this case, however, most of the disputes were not solved through discussion in the press and in democratic forums but in battle camps. In Venezuela, the wars over federalism divided the country

---

[184] The program also included, for example, the absolute freedom of the press; the administrative independence of the provinces; direct, secret, and universal suffrage; the congressional right to remove executive ministers; and strict limits on the use of the armed forces. See Gil Fortoul (1954), vol. 3, pp. 135–136.
[185] Recabarren (1972), p. 249.

for most of the century. The early constitution of 1811 was aimed at establishing a certain form of federalism. However, the constitution was immediately suspended and the original federalist formula replaced with "center-federalist" alternatives during the long regime commanded by General José Antonio Páez. From the 1840s, the tensions originated by this scheme began to explode and finally produced the so-called Federal War, beginning in 1859. This bloody war began shortly after the approval of the 1858 constitution, which appeared to be a desperate attempt to reinstall federalism to its original dominant position. In Colombia, the dispute between federalist and antifederalist groups also defined the history of the century. The constitutions of 1821, 1832, 1853, and 1863 reflected in their contents the triumph of the federalist band. However, the new century would begin with a reversal of the situation, which included the approval of the conservative constitution of 1886 and the victory of the centralist forces.

In Mexico, many of the most distinguished political leaders of the century – Vicente Guerrero, Lorenzo de Zavala, Juan Alvarez, and Benito Juárez, among many others – defended the federalist cause. Constitutions such as those of 1824 and 1857 partially incorporated the demands of federalist groups, although none of them, and particularly the first one, fully satisfied their claims. In Ecuador, the polemical leader Vicente Rocafuerte, a devoted admirer of U.S. federalism, greatly contributed to the dissemination of federalist ideology, although he actually repudiated many of its principles during his presidential mandate. In Chile, the most important and stable constitution of the century, the one approved in 1833, represented a direct reaction to the exceptional federalist constitution of 1828. In Argentina, the pressure of federalist groups was decisive in the defeat and final abrogation of the 1819 and 1826 constitutions and was also important during the debates that ended in the constitution of 1853. It is worth noting, though, that in this case, beside certain extraordinary exceptions, such as the one represented by General Manuel Dorrego, the federalist banner was not in the hands of the more progressive and democratic forces.

Rights and the Cultivation of Virtue

With regard to rights, radicalism had always had a problematic relationship. Undoubtedly, the harsh experience of the initial years of the revolution, when radicals played a significant role, combined with the ill-intentioned propaganda advanced by their enemies, contributed toward shaping the poor image of radicals in this respect. For their enemies, an eventual political victory of the populists would necessarily imply the destruction of all liberties, the triumph of chaos and anarchy. Obviously, the memory of the barbarous Haitian Revolution of 1791, made in the name of the egalitarian ideals of the French Revolution, did not favor the populists' cause. Since then, many associated radicalism with bloody revolution, the violent mobilization of the people and the destruction of private property. Many other examples contributed toward reinforcing these ideas. The Mexican popular leader Vicente Guerrero came into power while his adherents sacked El Parián; the federalist leaders in Venezuela fought for their cause by the most brutal means; the Argentinean caudillos mobilized their people under the banner "Religion or Death." All these cases may, or may not, represent good examples of the way in which the populists tended to act. They all served to strengthen the ideas that the conservatives wanted to promote, namely, that any appeal to the people was fated to provoke the most atrocious social conflict. In fact, situations such as those quoted here always favored the conservatives' elitist proposals. Against those who proposed the social integration of the most disadvantaged groups, the conservatives argued that the time had not yet come: any new attempt to integrate these groups would necessarily trigger a further period of unruly violence.

In spite of these apocalyptic images, promoted by the enemies of radicalism, it is also true that radical doctrine was not very well prepared for counteracting those attacks. There are obvious tensions between the defense of majority claims and the defense of individual rights, and radical theory was not well equipped to confront them. Most of all, radicals wanted to defend the "will of the majority," and this attitude forced them to subordinate the promotion of rights. For many, the triumph of the radicals simply implied the triumph of populism: the end of all rights. In addition to this, their concern with the "cultivation" of a virtuous citizenship reinforced the idea that their project was incompatible with making autonomous choices about plans of life.[186]

The Apatzingán Constitution of 1814 provides us with an example of the risks associated with the radical proposals. After declaring that law was "the expression of the general will" aimed at obtaining the "common happiness" (art. 18) and affirming legal equality (art. 19),[187] the constitution evinced its populist features. In article 20

---

[186] See Sandel (1996).
[187] The conservative forces would later reject even this modest adherence to egalitarianism. Thus, the constitution of 1824 did not even mention equality before the law.

it stipulated that all citizens should obey the laws, even if they personally disapproved of them. For the constitution, this statement did not imply an offense against their freedom or their reason: it merely represented "the sacrifice of the particular intelligence to the general will." Meanwhile, article 41 defined the heavy duties of revolutionary citizens. It stated that "the citizens' duties to their country include: a complete submission to the laws, the absolute respect for its authorities, their immediate disposition to contribute to the public expenses and the voluntary sacrifice of their goods and their life when it became necessary to do so." "The exercise of these virtues," it asserted, "represents the real form of patriotism." Finally, reinforcing the idea that the populists did not leave room for each person to pursue an autonomous life, the constitution declared the Catholic religion to be the only religion in the country, proclaimed its "intolerance" toward all other sects, and mandated the loss of citizenship in case of crimes such as treachery or heresy (art. 15).[188]

The revolutionaries' blind defense of the general will was the product of their belief in the infallibility of the radical decision. As Ignacio Rayón argued, the majority will was *inerrante,* infallible. Article 6 of his *Elementos,* one of the most important intellectual pieces written in order to shape and justify the constitution, clarified the scope of the revolutionaries' populist thought. The *Elementos* said, for example, that "no other right can be attended, no matter how unquestionable it appears to be, when it is prejudicial to the independence and felicity of the nation."[189] Similarly, in his influential paper *Sentimientos de la Nación,* José María Morelos also made reference to these perfectionist ideas and ratified the absolute supremacy of the will of congress. Article 12 of his document, for example, stated that, "given that good law is superior to every person, the ones approved by our Congress must enforce patriotism and constancy among our people, moderate opulence and indigence, increase the earnings of the poor, improve their habits, and distance them from ignorance, robbery, and theft."

In line with this view, Artigas's main constitutional project also included clear references to the moral prerequisites of the good republic. For instance, in article 3 it proclaimed that the "country's felicity and prosperity, as well as the good order and the preservation of the civil government are essentially dependent on its piety, religion, and morality of its inhabitants." In spite of his general defense of these

---

[188] In addition, the constitution established that, in order to become a Mexican citizen, the foreigners had to declare their respect for the country's independence and demonstrate their adherence to the Catholic religion (art. 14).
[189] See Churruca Peláez (1983), p. 89.

moral habits, however, Artigas refused to establish any particular faith through the constitution.

Similarly, Bilbao's 1855 constitutional project left an ample place to associations and moral education. Thus, for example, he reserved the distribution of credits to people organized in associations that occupied themselves in solidarity missions, and he also organized a system of gratuitous and mandatory "moral education."

In the United States, all the new revolutionary constitutions in some way affirmed religious freedom. As Gordon Wood claims, however, these declarations "did not necessarily mean that the government would abandon its traditional role in religious matters."[190] Through such constitutions, Maryland, South Carolina, and Georgia "authorized their state legislatures to create in place of the Anglican Church a kind of multiple establishment of a variety of religious groups, using tax money to support 'the Christian religion,' [while] both Connecticut and Massachusetts continued to recognize the modified but still official status of the established Congregational church."[191] During the time of the national constitutional debates, many Anti-Federalists refused to include in the constitution a principle of state neutrality regarding religion. In this sense, for example, Charles Turner asserted that, "without the prevalence of Christian piety and morals, the best republican constitution can never save us from slavery and ruin." Turner, like many Anti-Federalists, expected the new constitution to include all educational means "as shall be adequate to the divine, patriotic purpose of training up the children and youth at large, in that solid learning, and in those pious and moral principles, which are the support, the life and soul of a republican government and liberty, of which a free Constitution is a body." The promotion of religion, he assumed, would favor a decrease in the importance of government. In this way, "the people [would be] more capable of being a Law to themselves."[192]

The fact that the Anti-Federalists were so prone to restrict individual rights may sound strange, given that the same Anti-Federalists, and not the Federalists, were the ones who wanted to annex a bill of rights to the constitution. However, this seemingly paradoxical situation seems easy to explain. The Anti-Federalists wanted mainly to defend the autonomy of the states and demanded the bill of rights as a way of defending the states from the intrusive intervention of the national government. Their hearty defense of the bill of rights was

[190] Wood (2002), p. 130.
[191] Ibid., pp. 130–131.
[192] Storing (1981b), p. 23.

compatible with the limitation of individual rights at the state level. As Michael Sandel explains,

> Even Virginia's famous Declaration of Rights, drafted by Anti-Federalist George Mason, contained no rights to freedom of speech, assembly, or petition, to habeas corpus, grand jury proceedings, counsel, or separation of church and state, or any protection against double jeopardy or bills of attainder or ex post facto laws. The only right ensured by all these twelve states that had constitutions was trial by jury in criminal cases. Only two guaranteed freedom of speech, and five permitted establishments of religion. A national bill of rights was not simply a way of assuring continued protection for rights the states already protected, but primarily a way of restraining the power of a national government that threatened the independence of the states.[193]

From Political Rights to the Right to the Land: The Constitution as *La Ley de la Tierra*

Even though in both the United States and in Latin America populists proposed or accepted the limitation of individual rights, it is also true that they sometimes pressed for the expansion of certain specific rights. In the end, the common assumption that the triumph of radical governments would imply the end of rights was false: populists defended only *some* rights: *the rights that appeared as a precondition to the government of the majorities*. For example, not surprisingly, populists were frequently behind the demands for more political rights: they wanted the entire community to be in charge of its own life. The fight for expanding the list of "citizens," in fact, defined the life of radicalism since its origins.

In England, radical groups always had this demand at the top of their political agenda. This commitment, which often took the form of a claim for universal suffrage, promised to bring a revolutionary change to the organization of society. For that reason, too, conservatives and radicals always saw each other as enemies: the former wanted to preserve exactly what the latter wanted to change.

In America, the demand for the expansion of political rights was a natural consequence of the revolutionary battles; these revolutions of independence had grown out of a situation of political exclusion. The Chilean radicals, for example, continually demanded the political integration of the most disadvantaged groups in a society traditionally governed by just a few families. To Santiago Arcos, the very

[193] Sandel (1996), p. 35.

existence of the Sociedad de la Igualdad demonstrated the intelligence and capacity of the working class; he argued that "they showed us that they can take part in the public life of the community, even when they cannot read."[194] In the end, the Sociedad did not succeed in its fight to create a more egalitarian society, although its influence proved crucial in the gradual democratization of the country. In Venezuela and Peru, the populists' crusade for the expansion of political rights had its initial victories during the 1850s. The noted Peruvian politician Pedro Gálvez led a significant campaign to ensure the political rights of the *indígenas* and the *mestizos*."[195] Appealing to the "principle of human dignity," he advocated expanding the right to vote, which, he proposed, should be conferred regardless of the voters' ability to read and write.[196] The Venezuelan federalist general Juan Falcón questioned the conservatives' defense of restrictive political rights, noting that "it does matter if you enact good or bad laws. What also matters is that you do not have the exclusive right to create them: that right resides in the majority…this is the real cause of the present revolution."[197] At the same period, the Mexican radicals began to assert their authority and to press for a broader distribution of political rights. In fact, the delegates to the constitutional convention of 1857 were elected by universal suffrage for the first time.

In Colombia, radicals were also behind the fight to adopt universal suffrage. This right became prevalent during the 1850s and was immediately incorporated into the constitution. However, despite the exceptional force of the Colombian radicals, its defenders had to confront a very early challenge given that the most conservative groups won New Granada's first free election. This circumstance forced many of them to reevaluate the worth of having free elections in a country where the priests and the landowners exercised such influence over the people. Notably, Manuel Murillo Toro was once again one of the few politicians who, in spite of that early defeat, kept his populist commitments and continued campaigning for universal suffrage. Murillo challenged those who wanted to reestablish limits on the political rights of the population. Contrary to them, he suggested instead to accompany universal suffrage with the redistribution of land.

---

[194] Arcos (1977), p. 146.
[195] In association with other men of egalitarian inclination, such as Francisco Quirós and José Sevilla, Pedro Gálvez created the Club Progresista in order to discuss and propagandize their ideas. They published a well-known newspaper, *El Progreso*, which also contributed to those goals.
[196] See Basadre (1949), vol. 3, p. 228.
[197] Quoted in Gil Fortoul (1949), vol. 3, p. 136.

In the end, we should acknowledge that, within their conception of rights as preconditions to democracy, radicals included not only the right to vote. Their program also included other fundamental rights, such as those that guaranteed the people's subsistence and independence. Some radicals argued against large-scale manufactures and wage labor, assuming that it would foster the dependency of workers. They believed that "the dependency of workers under industrial capitalism" would "deprive workers of the independence of mind and judgment necessary to meaningful participation in self-government."[198] Similarly, many of them defended a radical revision of the status quo, proposing, for example, a far-reaching redistribution of land. We have already explored some of these initiatives and made reference, for example, to Paine's and Jefferson's defense of "agrarian republicanism." In the Latin American context, we also examined the very progressive Reglamento Provisorio advanced by José Artigas.

The Mexican constitutional debates of 1857 represented a singular event in nineteenth-century Latin American history: for the first time, a constitutional convention was filled with proposals regarding the redistribution of land. The issue was so central to the debates that the president of the convention, the *liberal puro* Ponciano Arriaga, summarized his reformist view in claiming that the entire constitution should be seen as the legal expression of land reform: the constitution, he said, is *la ley de la tierra*.[199] The proposals for agrarian reform appeared particularly in the debate over article 17 of the constitution, related to the right to property. At that time, deputies Ponciano Arriaga and Castillo Velasco presented two separate and individual votes, while delegate Isidro Olvera presented an "Organic Law" dedicated to the same issue.

In his vote, Castillo Velasco asserted that political institutions should be basically aimed at securing social welfare. He admitted, though, that the people were already frustrated with these institutions because they were being used for other, private purposes. Particularly concerned with the destiny of the Native Americans, he proposed to distribute land for "common use" by the members of the community (art. 2). Article 3 of his proposal was also dedicated to the disadvantaged groups, establishing that each person without a job should receive a plot of land that allowed him to ensure his

---

[198] Sandel, in Allen and Regan (1998), p. 326.
[199] Zarco (1957), pp. 388–389.

subsistence.[200] Meanwhile, Olvera justified his project by making reference to the aggressions suffered by the Mexican people during the country's history and the fact that most of the land was kept uncultivated in the hands of a few. Olvera recommended the adoption of numerous measures aimed at alleviating the suffering of the poor and limiting the property rights of the landowners.[201] Finally, Ponciano Arriaga maintained that the whole enterprise of writing a new constitution was senseless without a due consideration of the agrarian problem. "This country," he argued, "cannot be free or republican or even less successful – no matter how many constitutions and laws we approve asserting abstract rights and beautiful but impossible theories – as a consequence of the absurd economic system that we have." A land reform was necessary, he continued, for securing "democratic equality" and "popular sovereignty."[202]

Ignacio Ramírez was perhaps the most salient member of the convention regarding issues of social reform, consistently defending the rights of disadvantaged groups. He did so at the convention, as he had done during the previous years.[203] During the constitutional debates, the present focus of our attention, Ramírez proposed to write a document simply aimed at favoring the disadvantaged. He complained about the official project, asserting that it said "nothing about children's rights, the orphans, the abandoned child.... Some codes lasted centuries, because they protected women, children, the elderly, those who were weak and hungry. Today we have to do the same through our constitution."[204] His progressive proposals included, for example, workers' sharing in the profits of the firms where they worked and a basic salary that guaranteed the subsistence of all. "The real, the greatest of all social problems has to do with the workers' emancipation from the capitalists; the solution is easy: we have to transform work into capital...this will ensure

---

[200] Ibid., pp. 362–365.
[201] Ibid., pp. 694–697.
[202] Ibid., pp. 388–389.
[203] Signing his articles with the nickname of "El Nigromante," Ramírez engaged in numerous polemics with the writers of the newspaper *El Tiempo*, edited by Lucas Alamán. Defending the rights of the working class, Ignacio Ramírez wrote, "We the workers ask you, the landowners, why you eat our bread and enjoy it with your prostitutes and servants, without doing any effort?...We cultivate [your lands] so we may ask you: what do you do with the money we give you. [Why can't we ask you for] part of your lands that you keep uncultivated." Reyes Heroles (1957), vol. 3, p. 657.
[204] Sayeg Helú (1972), p. 92.

the subsistence of the worker and give him the right to share the earnings with the capitalists."[205]

Radicalism and Constitutionalism in the Americas: A Balance

The contribution of radicalism to the history of American constitutionalism was significant at different levels, all of them important. First of all, radicals forced the dominant elites to confront and discuss social issues that they had wanted to avoid. In contexts where political life was in the hands of a few, a rich and cultivated minority united by commercial and family bonds, the presence of radicals was fundamental. Radicalism became the voice of the disadvantaged and the marginalized, and the claims for social integration were very important. Radicalism organized, publicized, and gave theoretical support to the pressing demands for the redistribution of land. Because they were among the first critics of the pervasive social inequalities, they deserve part of the credit for the slow social improvements that ensued.

In addition, their role in the adoption of political reforms was also fundamental. Once again, they were among the first critics of a political system that strictly limited the participatory rights of the population. Of course, radicals' defense of broader political rights was only a part of their reformist agenda. Political institutions, they claimed, should evolve into institutions that worked for the interests of the common people. The idea of a "mixed constitution," implicitly or explicitly defended by many of their opponents, was, in their opinion, totally unacceptable: there were no social orders to preserve, as the "mixed constitution" purported to do, beyond what the majorities decided to preserve.

Moreover, they objected to all proposals that suggested a mere "virtual" representation of the people – a government by the people without the people. In their opinion, nobody knew the interests of the people better than the people themselves. Their view was totally revolutionary: it implied a complete reconsideration of the political system, its purposes, and its representative character.

In most cases, however, the populists' pressures were incapable of forcing substantial changes in the elite's preferred choices. Manuel María Madiedo wrote his most important work about the life of Colombian political parties after 1810 in order to explain just these

[205] Ibid., p. 93.

problems. Madiedo wanted to show how much the political parties favored the interests of the oligarchy and how much they ignored the demands of the needy. A defender of egalitarian policies himself, the social-Christian Madiedo attacked the economic choices of the dominant elite, asserting that they had been aimed simply at transforming "the rich into the master, a semigod; and the poor into a beast."[206] In Chile, Bilbao and Arcos tried to provoke a revolutionary change in their country's political life, organizing and educating the working class and trying to foster the interests of the poor. They both ended their political careers, however, recognizing the tremendous difficulties they found in advancing these ideas. In Argentina, Manuel Dorrego led a solitary fight to combine federalist ideals with more egalitarian policies. His political career, though, was violently interrupted, and his labor promptly forgotten. In Peru, González Vigil was for years the lucid voice of the disadvantaged.

Activists such as the Chilean Bilbao and the Gálvez brothers, who also proposed the use the state's resources in order to eliminate existing inequalities, accompanied González Vigil in his campaign. However, their battle was to be fundamentally unsuccessful: General Castillo, who came to power backed by most progressive liberals and radicals, would soon frustrate their desire for creating a new and more egalitarian society. In Bolivia, General Manuel Belzu also gained the attention of some radical groups through his progressive speeches, which were sometimes based on Pierre-Joseph Proudhon's ideas. Nonetheless, his government did not produce any relevant advance for the populists' cause. In Mexico, the populists controlled some of the most important positions within the constitutional convention. However, in spite of the importance of the positions they occupied and the value of the proposals they advanced, they never managed to gain wide-reaching or strong popular support.

These examples make apparent the radicals' insistent efforts in favor of social causes and disadvantaged groups; but they also strengthen the impression that the battles they fought ended, in most cases, with poor results. Many of their political initiatives were violently attacked by the dominant elite or were ignored. These unfortunate outcomes, of course, were not due to a conspiracy against them. However, we should not refuse to acknowledge what was also evident: because of what their proposals implied or sought to achieve, radicals were seen as a serious threat to the established order, at least from the dominant elite's viewpoint. Because of this, the governing groups decided

---

[206] Quoted in Rodríguez Albarracín et al. (1988), pp. 256–259.

to protect the status quo with all their might. At the beginning of the independence process, and fearing that the new societies would fall in the hands of radical groups – a fear that was reinforced by the leading role of the latter during the revolutionary period – the reactions of the dominant classes were usually very violent. The same happened during the 1850s, after the revolutionary movement that stunned first Europe and soon afterward America. At that moment, the dominant groups again postponed their own internal, serious differences and worked together against what they described as threats of anarchy and social chaos. In effect, in countries like Chile, Peru, and Mexico, the divided elite began to act together for the first time. Valencia Villa made reference to this phenomenon in his analysis of Colombian political life:

> The moral of this part of our history is that, five or six years after their foundation, the ruling parties began to overcome their differences and constituted a coalition in order to confront their common external enemy that put at risk their control over the state and civil society.... When they are alone, without competitors both to the right and to the left, traditional parties fight with each other.... However, when they are not alone any more, when they realize that there are rivals outside the system or when they recognize that the popular movement is beyond control, they get together and constitute a common front in order to ensure the survival of the state.[207]

The dominant groups fought against the populist forces sometimes with brute force and sometimes – and these are the most interesting situations for this study – through the creation of new institutions aimed at reducing the political influence of their enemies. In this sense, the persistent threat of a radicalization of society helps us understand why the Americans created some of their institutions as well as why they *did not create or rejected* some other mechanisms.

For example, in the United States, because of the populists' pressures, Federalists took the need to limit congress very seriously, as it was the institution that, to all appearances, incorporated the popular will. They designed a brilliant and complex system of checks and balances, aimed at "moderating" the decision-making process. For the same reasons, they did not approve or simply rejected other proposals that promised to transform the representatives into mere advocates of the majority forces – typically, the right to instruct the

---

[207] Valencia Villa (1987), pp. 133–134.

representatives or the right to recall. Through the machinery they set in motion, Federalists changed the way in which social conflicts were usually solved. Until the enactment of the federal constitution, most social conflicts were solved through state legislatures that were closely connected to the people's demands – seemingly, the old institutional system was too biased in favor of the majority groups. After the arrival of the new institutions, however, the game began to be played in a different way, and its outcomes also changed.

The situation was not the same in Latin America. In this part of the hemisphere, social conflicts tended to take place "outside" political institutions. Because of this, the dispute between conservatives and populists took different and often more violent forms. If conservative groups turned their attention to political institutions, it was because they wanted to strengthen the powers of the executive and, therefore, prevent the risks of anarchy and chaos that they associated with the radicals' claims. In this sense, the threat of radicalism also appears as an important factor in Latin America when explaining the institutional development of the region.

One can reasonably associate some theoretical and practical problems with radicalism. Many of these problems suggest that the radicals' defense of egalitarian ideas was not totally consistent.[208] The radicals' position was vulnerable because of the way they approached the idea of "general will." Clearly, the idea that the "voice of the people" is equivalent to "the voice of God" or that the "voice of the people" can never err was very fragile. Theoretically, it is difficult to associate the opinion of a circumstantial majority with moral rectitude. But even if we accept Rousseau's proposition and *define* a correct decision as the decision that resulted from the "general will," we would still be in trouble. The distance that separated the actual practice of most political systems and the Rousseauean ideal that many Latin American constitutions seemed to accept was enormous. At that time, the majority of the people did not take part in the decision-making process in any meaningful way. Also, the radicals' insistence in equating the decisions of poorly representative legislatures with the "general will" generated obvious resistance among their opponents. Probably these problems explain why even many radical liberals promptly abandoned Rousseau's example and adopted, in its place, the teachings of the more moderate Benjamin

---

[208] To state this, however, does not imply that it is not possible to find better – more sophisticated or less vulnerable – forms of radicalism.

Constant, a defender of strong property rights and significant privileges for property owners.

If we pay attention to the details of those political systems, we find still worse problems. In many cases, legislatures depended on the executive's will, selfish representatives, and nonoperative controls and checks. These features helped to strengthen the idea that the will of the people had little in common with the idealized "voice of God." Undoubtedly, many of the problems that characterized Latin American parliaments ratified the populists' claims: the so-called radical bodies were virtually unrepresentative, and the people had enormous difficulties in checking the way these bodies functioned. However, the fact that the representative body was so inefficient, corrupt, and dependent, combined with the theoretical problems of radicalism, worked together to weaken the populists' claims.

Even worse, many radicals showed a strong disdain for all those mechanisms that could improve, refine, or clarify the will of the people. Because radicals assumed the existence of something like a predefined and unquestionable majority will, they were not attracted to such mechanisms. Rousseau himself had favored these types of assumptions when he took the view that political discussion, like any attempt to change the opinions of the people, could only vitiate or "corrupt" the "general will."[209] This analysis was also influential in Latin America, at least among Rousseau's disciples. His followers depreciated, like Rousseau, the value of political deliberation, assuming a reified idea of the "general will." The Argentinean Moreno, for example, argued that "the clash of opinions could engulf in darkness" the sacred principles of justice.[210] Not surprisingly, many of the defenders of radical politics rejected the need to control the "excesses" of the popular will: they simply did not understand this idea of "excess."

Their defense of a "strict" separation of powers represents an interesting example of the "luminous" and "dark" sides of their institutional proposals. Given their desire to preserve the radical features of the political system, they reasonably resisted the adoption of mechanisms that could distort or undermine the popular will. In this battle, however, many of them began to defend another, unreasonable claim, which stated that popular will required no controls, given that, as Rayón asserted, the majority never erred. Obviously, once again, the enemies of radicalism found in these criteria an excellent

---

[209] Rousseau (1984); Manin (1987).
[210] Quoted in Shumway (1993), p. 29.

opportunity for exposing the unattractiveness of the populists' position. And they never missed these opportunities.

Even if we chose to ignore their enemies' ill-intentioned arguments, we have to admit that the populists' favorite institutional framework included many vulnerable aspects. For example, few of them took seriously the sound idea that unicameral parliaments or strongly radical systems might favor the adoption of decisions too quickly or without proper reflection. Against these proposals, their opponents reasonably suggested using the new institutions in order to promote "more sedate reflection," to force the representatives to think their initiatives over twice before adopting a final decision. In a polemic with Jefferson, Washington brilliantly justified bicameralism in those terms.[211] Undoubtedly, Washington, like many of his colleagues, had good things to say in favor of their proposals.

The radicals' defense of decentralization had problems, too. To some of their opponents, a strongly decentralized political system impaired the possibility of coordinating decisions at a national level. This criticism was very important, and also very successful, during the postrevolutionary period in the United States. At that time, most of the people understood that the Articles of Confederation, the loose interstate agreement that was dominant before the enactment of the federal constitution, was totally contrary to the national interest. Once again, many of the critics of the articles were ill-intentioned. What they wanted, in fact, was to put an end to what they described as a period of pure radicalism or "mobocracy."[212] However, it is also true that many of these critics of radicalism were affirming something important, namely, the need to establish a national authority and to take the coordination problems that divided the nation seriously. In addition, decentralization also often meant the arbitrary rule of the minority, be it a rich elite or a powerful caudillo. The radicals' defense of democracy, then, also appeared to many to be a defense of political discretion.

Many of the problems that they confronted in their approach to questions of institutional design, the abusive criticisms of their opponents, the violence used against their most refined proposals, and the fact that the dominant institutions always tended to work against the

---

[211] Seemingly, the story went like this. Jefferson asked Washington why it was necessary to establish a senate. Washington replied by asking: "Why do you pour coffee into your saucer?" And Jefferson answered: "To cool it." "Well," Washington continued, "we pour legislation into the Senatorial saucer to cool it." See Elster (1993), p. 21.

[212] Benjamín Rush, letter to Charles Lee, Oct. 24, 1779. See in Butterfield (1951), p. 244.

majority principle created a certain aversion to institutional issues among many radicals. In addition, many radicals, and Latin American ones in particular, realized that the main decisions on matters of institutional design always remained in the hands of a self-interested elite, which was completely distanced from the demands of radicals. Worst of all, the populists recognized the abuses carried out by their opponents in the name of democracy as they observed the tragic fact that the people often voted against their own interests. Their picture of democracy and constitutionalism could not be poorer. Why, then, waste so much energy and resources on something so detached from reality? Why defend or attack institutions that would never improve the life of the most disadvantaged? For decades, this way of thinking was dominant among many radicals and contributed to separating them from an important area of theoretical reflection. Also, it contributed to favoring, among many of them, an irresponsible approach to democracy that, in the end, not only eroded their credibility but also debilitated their egalitarian commitments.

In addition, many radicals were reasonably criticized because of the way in which they approached the issue of individual rights. Radicals were suspicious of rights for both practical and theoretical reasons. On the one hand, as we know, the most ardent defenders of rights seemed to do so simply in order to protect their own interests, particularly to protect their property. Because of this, many radicals developed an unattractive practice: they associated the defense of rights with the defense of class interests and therefore with a goal that they simply wanted to reject. On the other hand, many radicals *were determined to* confront the idea of making autonomous choices about plans of life, arguing that individual decisions had to be at the service of collective decisions. When some Anti-Federalists like Richard Lee or revolutionary leaders like José Morelos defended the imposition of certain models of virtue, they were not dishonoring the populists' ideology: to the contrary, they were consistently contributing to it. They recognized, in fact, what many radical theoreticians had concluded before – namely, that self-government required a rather homogeneous society, and that this ideal was not totally compatible with full personal autonomy. Finally, it is also true that, at a theoretical level, there is an almost inescapable tension between majority will and individual rights and that any option chosen in this respect would turn out to be problematic. It is clear, then, that we are confronting a serious philosophical question regarding the possibility of defending simultaneously self-government and individual freedom. No matter what particular answer we give to these problems, however, the sense is that the populists' egalitarianism appears at this point to be seriously compromised. Radicals tended to be too hasty both in dismissing the idea of individual autonomy and in accepting the superiority of the popular will. By doing this, they abandoned their favored principle of equality: that the opinion of each person no longer counted as much as the opinion of the rest. The majority interests seemed supreme and even capable of suppressing the interests of the few, whatever they were.

Chapter Two
Conservatism: The Moral Cement of Society

The Endless Influence of Conservatism

I define the conservative model of constitutionalism by two of its main features, political elitism and moral perfectionism. This conception, which played an important role in the U.S. constitutional debates, was enormously influential in Latin America during the nineteenth century. Its presence was particularly important after 1815, once the initial enthusiasm of the revolutionaries had disappeared. During the first few years after the revolution, many radicals thought it was possible to completely reconstruct the American communities, destroying with one stroke all the remnants of the past. This dream, however, proved to be impossible to achieve. Not surprisingly, with the first difficulties of the independence revolutions, conservatives became, once again, the leading political force in the continent and remained so during the following decades. At the end of the 1840s and the beginning of the 1850s, though, the conservative model was seriously challenged because of the growing importance of the democratic and revolutionary movements that originated in Europe and immediately spread over most of Latin America. During that period, conservatives lost part of their control: democracy was no longer the utopian dream of a few confused revolutionaries but a strong and widely supported social demand. Conservatives learned a lot from this experience, which forced them to find a way to adjust their political discourse, something they did, again, with renewed success.

Clearly, the combination of political authoritarianism and moral perfectionism that they promoted did not represent an ideological novelty. In fact, conservative ideology largely preceded the revolutionary movements: at the time of independence, this ideology already had profound roots in America. We must recall, for example, that the

British colonists, who came to America to escape from the religious persecution that they suffered in England, did not transform their suffering into tolerant practices. On the contrary, they tended to reproduce these intolerant practices in the new continent, using the coercive powers at their disposal against new dissidents. Thus, for example, the colonists obliged all the members of their communities to attend church and take part in religious activities as a prerequisite for having a stake in the new societies. The dissidents suffered, again, from ruthless physical punishment, imprisonment, and exile. For Milton Konvtiz, for example, "the Virginia colony banished Puritan clergymen, Quakers, and Catholic priests. The Puritans at Plymouth gave the suffrage only to orthodox believers and legislated against Quakers. At Massachusetts Bay the voting privilege was given only to church members (there was only one church); the church and clergymen were supported by taxes, and church attendance was compulsory. The Puritans at New Haven conformed to this theocratic pattern."[1]

In Spanish America, the link between religion and political violence – the union between the Cross and the sword – was even more important than in the United States. At that time, the Spanish elite assumed that religious faith required the support of military force as a condition for its expansion.[2] Spanish military forces therefore came into America after reaching an agreement with the church: the church would recognize the legitimacy of their conquests on the condition that Americans were converted to Catholicism. Faith and force were once more close allies.

As we know, the Spanish established their empire in America for a few centuries and during that time the church grew in both political and economic power. Most important, during that period there was no alternative ideological conception to that of Catholicism, and Catholic priests monopolized all educational matters in the new continent. Not surprisingly, then, as José Luis Romero argued, "most of the men who promoted the insurgent movements, even the most 'Jacobin,' and most of the documents they produced, emphatically declared their Catholic faith."[3]

Given the hegemony of the Catholic faith, we can understand the commotion provoked by the new revolutionary ideas, which put into question the material, legal, and ideological privileges of the church.

[1] Konvitz (1957), p. 18.
[2] See Bethell (1985a), vol. 1, p. 511.
[3] J. L. Romero and Romero (1977), p. xxvi.

These new ideas questioned the privileges of the minority of the "rich and well born," who were closely associated with the interests of the church, and also the legitimacy of the Spanish authorities.

The conservative groups that appeared after the independence revolution tried to preserve and recover a world that seemed to be falling apart. But their mission did not merely consist of turning back the hands of the clock: they had a complete program that they wanted to advance; they had clear principles, clear ends, and strong commitments.

Moral Perfectionism: Preventing the Loosening of Moral Bonds

Conservatism, in accordance with the definition that we are going to use, assumes that there are certain objectively valuable "conceptions of the good" and that these conceptions have to prevail socially, independent of the people's opinion. In accordance with this view, what is "good" for someone is defined separately from his or her own preferences. Individuals must organize their life in accordance with what the "enlightened" authorities assume is the best way of life. Those who recognize what are the best conceptions of "the good" have the responsibility for defending and enforcing it. Because of this belief, conservatives normally justify the use of the state's coercive powers in defense of their preferred view. In their opinion, the use of the coercive powers of the state is simply necessary in order to honor the correct moral values and favor the common good. If one ensures that every person lives a decent life, they assumed, one favors the creation of a more decent community.[4] Without a common religion, as Juan Egaña argued, one could not have an adequate government. Moral conservatives seek, therefore, to commit the state to a particular moral program: here, moral autonomy and free choice play a secondary, opaque role in the definition of each person's moral life.

As we can see, radical and conservative views represent very different, and opposing, conceptions. While the former relies heavily on the opinions of the people, the latter assumes the need for "doing the right thing" and defining what is "right," with complete independence from the people's opinions. For the authoritarian Diego Portales, for example, it was necessary to adopt "a strong, centralizing power, formed

---

[4] For John Rawls, a conservative position is that which assumes that both the main institutions of society and the duties and obligations of the people must "maximize the products of human excellence, in arts, science and culture." Rawls (1971), p. 325. Also see Nino (1991).

by men of virtue and patriotism." Only in this way, he believed, would it be possible to "set the citizens on the straight path of order and virtue."[5] Usually, conservative policies do not support majority views; on the contrary, they seek to improve or directly replace those views.[6] In most cases, conservatism came in combination with the defense of religion, and the promotion of religion came together with the support for strong political powers, which were supposed to protect those sacred values. The highly conservative president of Ecuador, Gabriel García Moreno, clarified this view at the time of assuming the presidency of his country in 1869. In his inaugural speech, he explicitly admitted that his power would be directly committed to defend a particular conception of "the good," the Catholic creed, and that he would combat all those who wanted to put limits on his "mission." All his political opponents were thus suddenly transformed into enemies of the nation. As he put it, *"The first [goal of my power] will be that of harmonizing our political institutions with our religious beliefs; and the second will be that of investing our public authorities with the forces required to resist the assaults of anarchy."*[7] This claim remains one of the clearest expressions of conservatism in the region.

These extremely conservative attitudes were not simply a characteristic of arbitrary Latin American leaders. In the United States, for example, the adoption of a seemingly tolerant national constitution did not put an end to strong religious intolerance at the state level. By 1789, only Virginia and Rhode Island had adopted a system of complete religious freedom. Meanwhile "tax support of religion was found in Massachusetts, [for] Congregational churches; New Hampshire, Protestant churches; Connecticut, Christian churches; South Carolina, Protestant churches; and Maryland, Christian churches. In New York, Catholics were excluded from citizenship. In New Jersey and North Carolina only Protestants and in Delaware only Christians could hold public office. In Georgia, only Protestants could be members of the legislature. Pennsylvania required a belief in God, and only Christians could vote and hold public office."[8]

---

[5] Portales (1937), p. 177.
[6] Notwithstanding this, conservatives resorted to a plurality of arguments in defense of their position, one of them being, occasionally, a democratic argument. Clearly, after years of indoctrination and persecution of dissidents, many of these communities shared a common religious background. Conservatives then demanded the use of the coercive powers of the state in defense of what they assumed to be, and many times actually was, the dominant belief. Curiously, they used this "democratic" argument even when it was incompatible with their elitist assumptions.
[7] Quoted in L. A. Romero (1978), p. 115.
[8] Konvitz (1957), pp. 28–29.

Conservatives conceived of society as an organism with its own life, which was independent from the life of individuals. The preservation of their ideal community was much more important than the preservation of the life and choices of each of its members. Most of all, conservatives were interested in keeping what they described as the "shared moral principles" that gave life to the community. "Democracy cannot subsist," asserted the Colombian Sergio Arboleda, "in those places where the moral sentiments are not deeply rooted in the people's hearts." In his opinion, religion was "the basis that is required in order to shape the feelings [of the people]." Without it, he concluded, the only result would be "chaos."[9]

The coercive powers of the state came to guard the "moral basis" of the community against those aimed at undermining them. A state that abandoned this role was one that guaranteed the disintegration of society. A state that attacked or did not properly defend the "moral basis" of society would also implicitly be allowing the destruction of society: without its "moral basis" intact, society would simply fall apart. Conservatives claimed that "the loosening of moral bonds is often the first stage of disintegration."[10] An adequate state had to prevent the erosion of the moral foundations of the community and to use its force against its aggressors if necessary. That was, in the end, what the "sacred texts" taught Catholics when they referred to the experiences of the cities of Sodom and Gomorra: the relaxation of the moral parameters of society came together with the collapse of the entire society.[11]

Conservatives assumed the need to preserve the most basic fundamental values "uncontaminated": these values, they believed, were always threatened by foreign forces opposed to the dominant local traditions. The Paraguayan president José Gaspar Rodríguez de Francia, a conservative, though not a Catholic himself, carried this concept to its extreme. As he told one of his colleagues, "You know what the policy I promoted in Paraguay has been; you know that I tried to keep Paraguay completely separated from all other Latin American countries, uncontaminated by that malicious and restless spirit of

---

[9] Rodríguez Albarracín et al. (1988), p. 280. He also stated: "Suppress morality or, to state it better, suppress religion, and industries and the sciences will evolve into nothing. Only the powerful voice of faith will be able to rescue them." Ibid., p. 57. In similar terms, Juan Egaña argued that "religion is the main axis...not only of the people's morality but also of the national character, their habits and their attachment to civil institutions." See Silva Castro (1969), p. 81.

[10] Devlin (1959), pp. 14–15.

[11] Lord Devlin, in a polemic with H. L. A. Hart, popularized this defense of the conservative position.

anarchism and revolution which has infected most other nations."[12] The effect of regional disintegration and isolation, he believed, would be a more stable future for his country; it would be protected from the threatening menace of social disruption.[13]

From the point of view of American conservatives, the new ideas that favored the establishment of the popular will over "divine" authorities constituted the main source of immorality and degradation. Among these disruptive ideologies, the most feared were the ones that came from the French revolutionary world. Conservatives assumed that these ideas were responsible for the popular unrest that first provoked the revolutionary movements and then continued with attacks upon the church. The period of "terror" in postrevolutionary France or the sanguinary black revolution in Haiti, both promoted under the ideals of "liberty, equality, and fraternity," constituted two clear illustrations of their worries. Both situations brought with them dramatic social consequences and ruthless violence, and in both cases the interests of the church were challenged. Sergio Arboleda stated that "all the incidents of our revolution originated in one and the same principle and were aimed at achieving one and the same goal: its principle, the anti-Catholic French revolution; its goal, the destruction of the moral feelings of the masses."[14]

In New Granada, Mariano Ospina Rodríguez and José Eusebio Caro, two strong critics of French revolutionary thought, led the defense of the conservative position. Ospina exposed the main features of this conservative view in a statement he made in the national congress in 1842 in which he examined the recent history of his country. He denounced the "political doctrines of the French philosophers" as being responsible for the national crisis. These doctrines, he asserted, had promoted a "wild anti-Christian movement." Moreover, Ospina argued that even the so-called Guerra de los Supremos, one of the worst wars in Colombian history, had been the product of these "Jacobin tendencies" and "anarchist impulses."[15] The conservative policies that they promoted during the 1840s were all clearly marked by this same bias. In Peru, the cleric Bartolomé Herrera was the most important figure

---

[12] Quoted in J. L. Romero (1970), p. 68.
[13] For Mariano Ospira, "the Sacred Texts are the only things that can help us to correct the depraved popular instincts." Another famous conservative of his time, Julio Arboleda, argued in the same direction that "the administrative and political experience of the Church and the clergy are the only stable forces capable of preventing anarchy in American societies, where religious faith is the only unifying factor." See Zavaleta Arias (1994), p. 57.
[14] Quoted in Rodríguez Albarracín et al. (1988), p. 278.
[15] See González González (1977), pp. 176–177.

in the fight against French ideologies.[16] In one of his most notable sermons, Herrera attacked the Rousseauean proposals, claiming that "the power and the people have become the slaves of what is called the will of the people. The power and the people have become slaves of the will of demagogues."[17] The Argentinean Juan Ignacio Gorriti, a remarkable representative of local conservative thought after the independence revolution, dedicated a great deal of his *Reflexiones* to criticizing Rousseau. "Human societies," he argued, "are based on the solid and indestructible natural law" and not on any kind of "social compact."[18] We find similar opinions in the writings of Father Francisco de Paula Castañeda, another influential figure of the time.[19]

In the United States, the situation was not substantially different. Most conservatives associated the new revolutionary ideas with the social unrest that characterized the period following independence. John Adams, for example, associated the revolutionary events in France with popular uprisings such as Shays's Rebellion, an episode that had a profound impact on the delegates to the federal convention.[20] Later on, as the president of the country, he would enact the infamous Alien and Sedition Acts, mainly directed against the propagandists of French revolutionary ideas. Similarly, Alexander Hamilton referred to the French Revolution as a "great monster" that "confounds and levels everything."

---

[16] Herrera, who was born in 1808, became a cleric in 1834. For the Peruvian historian Jorge Basadre, he was the person who revitalized political discussion in his country during the nineteenth century (in particular, after the proclamation of his famous 1846 sermon). He was the head of the conservative College of San Carlos, which monopolized the education of young intellectuals for many years, until the creation of the more liberal College of Guadalupe, under the auspices of Domingo Elías and Nicolás Rodrigo. Significantly, one of the most important intellectuals whom he confronted during this period was Pedro Gálvez, a former student of his who became the head of the College of Guadalupe.

[17] Bartolomé Herrera pronounced this sermon in the Te Deum celebrated at the anniversary of Peruvian independence in the College of San Carlos (1846). See J. L. Romero and Romero (1977), pp. 136, 138. Peru, he continued, has become "the prey of the...malevolent and anti-social mistakes publicized by the French Revolution." Ibid.

[18] See this opinion, which belongs to his *Reflexiones sobre las causas morales de las convulsiones interiores de los nuevos estados americanos y examen de los medios eficaces para combatirlos*, in Chiaramonte (1997), p. 529. In Gorriti's view, Rousseau committed serious theoretical mistakes. "From a false precedent," he argued, "he deduces an absurd conclusion...he believes that men can get together in order to sign a compact that is totally prejudicial to their own interests." But that was absurd, he concluded, because "the eternal natural law forbids men to hurt themselves, even when they were determined to do so." Ibid.

[19] See, for example, Lewin (1971), p. 99.

[20] See, for example, Pendleton Grimes (1983), p. 144.

By rejecting the French revolutionary theories, conservatives were also rejecting the defense of individual autonomy. In particular, conservatives were not sympathetic to the egalitarian conception of autonomy assumed by their opponents, which said that the will of each was equally valuable. The conservatives favored a dramatically different view, which said that it was possible to replace the autonomous will of the people by the heteronomous will of a few. For them, the issue was not what the people wanted to do but what they were supposed to do. In Latin America, and particularly in countries like New Granada or Ecuador, and through the influence they exercised over educational matters, the Jesuits played a fundamental role in disciplining the new generations.[21]

In their criticisms of the more populist ideologies, conservatives began to define a complete theoretical universe with its own terminology, a theoretical universe as complete and as rich as that of their opponents. While the populists made reference to the "sovereignty of the people," the "universal principles," the "moral equality of the people," the "general will," the importance of "reason," "the rights of men," and the "social contract," conservatives made reference to the countries' "traditions," "customs," and "habits." They emphasized the need for being "realists" and objected to their opponents' fascination with new abstract theories: "abstract theories," said Simón Bolívar, "create the pernicious idea of unlimited freedom."[22] They defended the importance of "practical knowledge" and the "permanent values" of the community, which they opposed to the "imported" and "universal values" that the revolutionaries claimed to defend. For Mariano Ospina, for example, Colombia had to leave behind the "exotic" foreign ideas that had shaped its institutions for so many years: it was impossible to reconstruct the country through the use of strange ideas, which came, he argued, from French publicists.[23] Conservatives of all types shared and propagandized this view throughout the nineteenth century.[24]

---

[21] See, for example, J. L. Romero (1970).
[22] Bolívar (1951), vol. 1, p. 191.
[23] González González (1997), p. 186. Bolívar argued that "it is essential that a government mold itself, so to speak, to the nature of the circumstances, the times, and the men that comprise it. If these factors are prosperity and peace, the government should be mild and protecting; but if they are turbulence and disaster, it should be stern and arm itself with a firmness that matches the dangers, without regard for laws or constitutions until happiness and peace have been re-established." Bolívar (1951), vol. 1, p. 21.
[24] Vanorden Shaw (1930), p. 132. Similarly, Bolívar stated that "we were given philosophers for leaders, philanthropy for legislation, dialectic for tactics, and sophistry for soldiers. Through such a distortion of principles, the social order was thoroughly

The famous Argentinean caudillo, Juan Manuel de Rosas, summarized many of these ideas in his criticisms of what had been, in his opinion, the dominant ideology of the country: the ideology of the Enlightenment.[25] "This ideology," he asserted, "has provoked excitement in the souls of the people and fostered clashes among their different interests. It has propagated immorality and intrigues, dividing society so much that it is now impossible to find the bonds that hold the people together." Its dissolving effects, he continued, went so far that they even broke "the most sacred ties and, thus, those associated with religion, which was the only force that could re-create all the other ties."[26] Following on from these beliefs, Lucas Alamán emphasized the importance of using the coercive powers of the state in defense of Catholic religion: this was, he concluded, "the only common bond that held all Mexicans together; all the others have been destroyed."[27]

Opposing the rationalist tendencies that they associated with the imported views, the conservatives began to defend a form of irrationalism and traditionalism: they proposed to replace the study of the "great theories" by the study of the past, of history, and of the communities' own culture. The absurd promises of the Enlightenment

shaken, and from that time on the state made giant strides toward its general dissolution, which, indeed, shortly came to pass." Bolívar (1951), vol. 1, p. 19. Also, for example, the Chilean conservatives adopted as the guiding principle of the constitutional convention of 1833, the following: "that the constitution be revised with complete abstraction from theoretic principles in order to adjust it perfectly to the present cultural and economic state and to the actual needs of society."

[25] Rosas ruled the province of Buenos Aires almost without interruption between 1829 and 1852, hence gaining enormous influence over the entire national territory. Rosas's administration was politically authoritarian and morally conservative. During his period of power, Rosas ruled without limits, combining a nationalist or "nativist" ideology with an "agrarian" rhetoric (Myers, 1995, 60). The local legislature conceded him the "sum of the public power," an extraordinary concession of political power, which the 1853 constitution would forbid and consider a "betrayal" of the nation. Rosas violently suppressed all opposition, by closing newspapers and ordering his enemies to be killed or sent into exile. With the support of the military, his secret police forces (the *mazorca*), and the church, he imposed a policy of "political terror." The repressive policies that he advanced in the name of "virtue" and "republican" ideals included not only the imposition of exemplary punishments but also the surveillance of all public events, the suppression of all feast days, the prohibition of carnivals, and the imposition of official clothing for all public officers and, eventually, for the whole population. His confrontation with foreign countries (mostly England and France), the intense activity of his opponents in exile, and the increasing economic problems of his regime contributed to bringing an end to his rule. His forces were defeated militarily at the battle of "Caseros" by forces commanded by General Justo José de Urquiza, in 1852.

[26] Quoted in J. L. Romero (1970), p. 74.

[27] Alamán (1997), in a letter to General Santa Anna written in 1853.

had to be abandoned, they said, in order to rediscover the ideas that belonged to their own countries.

Conservatives were particularly hostile to the prevalent conception of rights. In contrast with what most of their opponents asserted, they believed that individuals' claims were subordinated to those of their society and no fundamental interests existed beyond those necessary for the subsistence of their community.[28] The idea that society had to protect certain fundamental individual interests through the adoption of a bill of rights was seen as a "ridiculous claim."[29] In Miguel Antonio Caro's opinion, "if man has the right to think and say whatever he wants, then he has the right to do whatever he wants. Absolute freedom of thought and expression come, then, with the diffusion of vices, with frenzy, and with crime."[30] In a familiar vein, Bolívar made reference to the "exaggerated maxims of the rights of men" that he believed allowed each person to act as he wished, "breaking thus the social compact and bringing the nations into anarchy."[31]

Each of the essential features of this view had been clearly anticipated and carefully developed by European conservatives and reactionaries like Edmund Burke in England, Friedrich von Gentz and Wilhelm von Humboldt in Germany, and Joseph de Maistre and Louis Bonald in France. All of them were deeply affected ideologically and often personally by the French Revolution and led a theoretical crusade against its influence. All of them defended traditionalism, localism, and moral perfectionism, and they all denounced the presence of strange and abstract theories. Some years later, a new cohort of reactionary thinkers, which included, for example, the noted Spaniards Juan Donoso Cortés and Jaime Balmes, would continue to develop the early work of that generation.

Burke had proposed a particular interpretation of the British Revolution of 1688 in order to expose all the evils that emerged from the French Revolution. In his opinion, the French Revolution represented the synthesis of all possible political mistakes: its followers failed to respect the traditions of their country and acted as if they could begin a new era from scratch. They expropriated church property, violating at the same time the rights of property and the sanctity of religion; defied the old order; and destroyed all hierarchies. For Burke, the revolutionaries had created a new constitution that

---

[28] See Dolbeare (1969), p. 18.
[29] Miguel Antonio Caro, quoted in L. A. Romero (1978), p. 69.
[30] Ibid.
[31] Bolívar (1976), vol. 1, p. 12.

ignored the habits and customs of the people, invoked and propagandized a meaningless principle of popular sovereignty, and made the people believe that the earth belonged to them.[32] Burke had many readers in both the United States and Latin America. In Mexico, Lucas Alamán, a fascinated follower of Burke's ideas, argued, for example, that Burke's "prophetic reflections on the French Revolution" anticipated the disastrous "conflicts that we have seen in Mexico and in foreign countries." "The new social movements," he said, came to replace the "tyranny of one" with the "infinitely more inadmissible tyranny of the many."[33]

The German Friedrich von Gentz emphasized, with Burke, the need to defend the traditional values of society. These values, he believed, had been challenged and ruined at the end of the eighteenth century. Events such as the French Revolution had broken the delicate equilibrium that existed between reason and history, and it was time to reconstruct that relationship. A close friend of Gentz, von Humbolt, also criticized the new revolutionary episode for its egalitarian features and, in particular, its dire attacks on private property. Like Burke, von Humbolt also ridiculed the aim of establishing a new constitution: individuals were simply unable to model society as they pleased.

The French reactionary Joseph de Maistre also believed that men could create nothing. The only thing that legislators could do was to recognize the customs of society and try to adapt them to their history and traditions. Constitutions, in that sense, were condemned to failure if they did not admit this simple fact and aimed at creating a new, different order. More ridiculous still, in his opinion, were the "Declarations of Rights," based on unsupported abstractions and supposedly universal claims. The real antonym of "legal," he claimed, was not "arbitrary" but "concrete."[34] Developing a way of thinking that would become very popular in Latin America, de Maistre called for the restoration of the ancient order, one that, he assumed, was realistic, adequately hierarchical, and normally well organized. The return to monarchy, he argued, would not imply more than to "destroy destruction."

Louis de Bonald, a colleague and admirer of de Maistre, carried the thoughts of his master still further. He also refuted the human pretension of creating a new order through a new constitution and described that attempt as an offense to nature. In his opinion, nature

---

[32] See Burke (1960); Cone (1957).
[33] Alamán (1997), pp. 168, 171.
[34] See Holmes (1993), chap. 1.

was the only existing "legislative power," and men had to respect it: they should try to follow the natural order of things instead of subverting it. Like Bonald, de Maistre also called for the restoration of the ancient order, something that, in his opinion, required the integration of men into society and the reeducation of the new generations in the principles of social order. The Chilean conservatives – and, in particular, Mariano Egaña – closely followed the teachings of Bonald and de Maistre. Bartolomé Herrera, the most important figure in nineteenth-century reactionary thought in Peru, and, later, José María Pando also followed the views of the French reactionaries. Herrera, like the Colombian Miguel Antonio Caro, found inspiration in the ideas of Donoso Cortés as well.

By the 1850s, theorists like Donoso Cortés had recovered the reactionary line of thinking promoted by the early critics of the French Revolution. Like them, Donoso also campaigned for achieving order and reestablishing authority and, in particular, for reestablishing the authority of the church. Catholicism was, in his opinion, the only true doctrine, and politics needed to be based on truth.[35] Reason, by contrast, was deceptive and political discussion useless: deliberation could bring out nothing if it was not nourished by the truth, and the truth belonged only to the Catholic religion. Donoso thus helped to develop the *antirationalist* trend already present in his predecessors: liberty was seen as the creator of terror, philosophy as an offense to religion, and abstractions as a promise of antirealism. Not surprisingly, too, Donoso Cortés defended the power of the wise and the imposition of the truth by coercive means, even by a dictatorial power.

Now, although it was very common in both Latin America and the United States to use the coercive powers of the state to persecute and imprison dissenters, this was not the conservatives' exclusive strategy. They also advanced their conservative ideas, for example, by providing privileges (i.e., additional resources) to a particular religion, by supporting or censoring certain opinions, and by taking strict control of the educational system. Thus, typically, some of the most important discussions in the United States after the independence revolution related to the possibility of financing religion through taxes collected by the state. In Latin America, also, some of the most fundamental debates had to do with the organization of the educational programs. Ospina Rodriguez's reform proposals represent an interesting example in this respect. An enormously influential figure in his country

---

[35] I learned about Donoso Cortés's views through the writings of Agustín José Menéndez.

during the 1840s, Ospina's main interest seemed to be that of reforming the Colombian educational system. His plan, written in collaboration with the Jesuits, came to replace the one established by General Francisco Santander in 1826, a plan that seemed to be a tribute to Jeremy Bentham, who was Santander's favorite philosopher. His colleague Sergio Arboleda shared this view and asserted that moral education was the only thing that could save the Colombian people.[36] The Colombian Constitution of 1886 openly proclaimed, "Public education shall be organized and directed in accordance with the Catholic Religion" (art. 41). Something similar happened in Ecuador, where García Moreno put the church directly in charge of all educational matters.[37]

Even though it is true that in most cases moral perfectionism came together with the imposition of religious values, we should not assume there is a necessary connection between conservatism and religion. A conservative state is not one that enforces the values of a particular religion but one that enforces the values that it considers adequate, be they of religious origin or not. Of course, in Latin America, almost all conservative theorists propounded the principles of Catholicism. However, there were also many exceptions: many significant leaders reproved and punished indolence, gambling, and alcoholism because they believed that these were vicious behaviors that had to be eradicated from the new countries. Bolívar represents an extraordinary example, in this sense, given that he promoted, at least for many years, religious tolerance and at the same time the imposition of strict moral values. In Bolívar's opinion, it was absolutely necessary to "regenerate" American citizens – something that required the use of the coercive apparatus of the state – in order to consolidate the independence movements. In his view, neither philosophy, which offered too many conflicting ideas, nor religion, which was too benevolent toward the malevolent, could be in charge of this regenerative task.[38] A parallel case is that of the Paraguayan president Gaspar Rodríguez de Francia, who developed a conservative and authoritarian policy while being himself, or so he claimed, a devoted disciple of French radical philosophers. In fact, Francia had a hostile policy toward the church and its representatives and promoted this attitude through the use of that radical philosophy.[39]

---

[36] Rodríguez Albaracín et al. (1988), p. 280.
[37] Gálvez (1945).
[38] Ibid, in a letter to José Rafael Arboleda, June 15, 1823.
[39] See J. L. Romero (1970).

Political Elitism: The Impossibility of Democracy in a Society "Full of Vices"

The analysis so far advanced already allows us to recognize the elitist character of conservative positions. As the philosopher Thomas Scanlon maintains, conservative theories have a "strong tendency towards elitism" because they put "a greater emphasis on the needs and interests" of a few against the needs and interests of others.[40] Conservatism therefore combines an ontological position that says that there are certain objectively valuable conceptions of the good life with an elitist epistemological position that maintains that the majority of the people are not adequately prepared to "discover" those valuable conceptions of the good life.

Edmund Burke's views exemplify this combination of political elitism with moral perfectionism. Like many theorists of his time, he assumed the existence of certain unquestionable political truths, the ontological position, while he supported the elitist view that only a few could recognize these political truths. Burke used a clear metaphor in order to illustrate his position. To him, political representatives were like good doctors. A doctor, he argued, needed to know the views of the patients, who had to tell him what problems or symptoms they had; however, the doctor would be a poor one if he consulted his patients in trying to find a cure for their illnesses. The good doctor knows the best cure for the patient: to adopt the patient's viewpoint instead would represent a totally irresponsible act. In Burke's opinion, the relationship between the representatives and the people followed a similar parameter. The voters did not know the "right" political solutions but had to have a say in the decision-making process: they had to communicate the symptoms of their illnesses to their doctors. In politics, too, only the select few are able to comprehend and take care of the interests of the majority: they are the ones who are guided by their judgment and not, like most people, merely by their opinions.

In America, most conservatives found it uncomfortably problematic to openly adopt such an extreme position, which meant questioning one of the most fundamental ideas of the time, namely, the idea that people were born "free and equal." However, many conservatives challenged even that basic principle, affirming, for example, that the most distinguishing human feature was not the equality of all but, on the contrary, the subordination of all to tradition and other heteronomous sources of power. John Calhoun put it very clearly: "Instead of

---

[40] Scanlon (1975), p. 171.

being born free and equal, [men] are born subject, not only to parental authority, but to laws and institutions of the country where born, and under whose protection they draw their first breath."[41] In a similar vein, John Adams suggested that "the Creator" had established physical and intellectual inequalities among people, from which it was possible to derive and justify other inequalities.[42] "By the law of nature," Adams asserted, "all men are men, and not angels, men, and not lions, men, and not whales, men, and not eagles, that is, they are all of the same species; and this is the most that the equality of nature amounts to. But man differs by nature from man, almost as much as man from beast.... A physical inequality, an intellectual inequality, of the most serious kind, is established unchangeably by the Author of nature; and society has a right to establish any other inequalities it may judge necessary for its good."[43]

Most conservatives, however, adopted a more indirect view in order to support similar conclusions. Thus, for example, Alexander Hamilton justified his political elitism through a particular reading of the philosopher John Locke. Locke seemed to subscribe to an ontological thesis that said that there were certain invariable "primary

---

[41] Rossiter (1982), p. 120.
[42] With independence, John Adams emerged as one of the leading and most articulate conservative thinkers. His many works, which included, for example, his well-known "Thoughts on Power;" "Discourses on Davila," or "Defense of the Constitutions of the United States," had an obvious impact on the generation that wrote the U.S. Constitution. John Calhoun followed Adams's example and espoused conservative and anti-egalitarian positions. Reproducing, as Adams did, the teachings of Burke's philosophy, he supported the value of traditions and the dominant status quo: each person, like each sector of society, should simply adapt to the place that "the Creator" had reserved for them (Rossiter 1982). Fisher Ames, Edwing Goldkin, William Sunner, Brook Adams, Joseph Story, Daniel Webster, and Paul Moore were other important defenders of this politically conservative and anti-egalitarian trend.
[43] Ibid., p. 112. Defending his belief in a natural aristocracy, he stated: "God Almighty has decreed in the creation of human nature an eternal aristocracy among men. The world is, always has been, and ever will be governed by it. Few men will deny that there is a natural aristocracy of virtues and talents in every nation and in every party, in every city and village." Ibid. In a similar vein, John Calhoun argued that "as individuals differ greatly from each other, in intelligence, sagacity, energy, perseverance, skill, habits of industry and economy, physical power, position and opportunity, the necessary effect of leaving all free to exert themselves to better their condition, must be a corresponding inequality between those who may possess these qualities and advantages in a high degree, and those who may be deficient in them.... It is, indeed, this inequality of condition between the front and the rear ranks in the march of progress which gives so strong an impulse to the former to maintain their position, and to the latter to press forward into their files. This gives to progress its greatest impulse. To force the front rank back to the rear into line with the front, by the interposition of the government, would put an end to the impulse, and effectively arrest the march of progress." Ibid., p. 121.

truths" and an epistemological thesis that maintained that these truths were "self-evident." Hamilton somewhat modified Locke's view by asserting that these truths were not so easily accessible. In *Federalist* 31, for example, he stated: "In disquisitions of every kind, there are certain primary truths, or first principles, upon which all subsequent reasonings must depend. These contain internal evidence which, antecedent to all reflection or combination, commands the assent of the mind. Where it produces not this effect, it must proceed either from some defect or disorder in the organs of perception, or from the influence of some strong interest, or passion, or prejudice." Naturally, Hamilton was trying to say that majority groups, which, as Federalists assumed, were normally motivated by irrationality, interest, and prejudice (see, notably, *Federalist* 10), were not able to recognize the fundamental primary truths without denying the basic equality of their members. In this way, Hamilton was giving foundation to an "epistemological elitism" shared by most Federalists.[44]

In Latin America, many conservative politicians simply rejected the equality principle. The Peruvian Bartolomé Herrera espoused one of the most extreme versions of this view, asserting that people had neither the capacities nor the right to create laws.[45] Like Hamilton, they argued for the existence of severe inequalities between different people without denying the basic principle of human equality. Simón Bolívar, for example, explicitly asserted that "all men are born with equal rights." However, he immediately added, "it does not follow that all men are born equally gifted to attain every rank. All men should practice virtue, but not all do; all ought to be courageous, but not all are; all should possess talents, but not everyone does. Herein are the real distinctions, which can be observed among individuals in even the most liberally constituted society. If the principle of political equality is generally recognized, so also must be the principle of physical and moral inequality."[46]

This political elitism was strictly reinforced after the independence revolutions: at that time, conservative leaders discovered the actual implications of encouraging political participation. In the United States, the people's activism at a local level had brought, in the conservatives'

---

[44] See an excellent analysis of this view in White (1987). More radical authors, such as Thomas Jefferson, read John Locke in a completely different manner. In effect, Jefferson interpreted Locke through the reading of a different philosopher, Jean-Jacques Burlamaqui, who said that any person, through his common sense, could have access to the most important political truths. Ibid.
[45] See Pajuelo (1965).
[46] Bolívar (1951), vol. 1, p. 182.

view, excessive pressures on the legislative branch and had caused the adoption of hasty and unreflective decisions. The disrespect for legal norms, the violation of property rights, the release of paper money, and the mistreatment of minority groups were, to conservatives, the expected results of the majority's intervention in politics.

In Latin America, too, many political leaders became immediately disillusioned by the first popular mobilizations produced in their countries and began to campaign against them. In Venezuela, Juan Boves's cruel counterrevolutionary movement, one that was accompanied by wide popular support, triggered strong antipopular sentiments in leaders like Bolívar, who feared a "looming 'pardocracy' (rule by the dark-skinned)."[47] In Mexico, the riot of the Parián market in 1828, which took place when Vicente Guerrero seized control of the government, provoked profound unrest in the upper classes. General Anastasio Bustamante's elitist description of these events constitutes an interesting example of this view: "I have never seen men who were so fierce and who could provoke such horror; most of them were naked or half naked, dressed in rags; they looked more like devils than soldiers, and even from a few yards' distance it was obvious that they were assassins, executioners and bandits who wanted to use their guns incessantly, provoking the peaceful citizens."[48] These types of events were reproduced in most other countries in Latin America – for example, in Bolivia, after the populist General Manuel Isidoro Belzu assumed national power;[49] or in Peru, after the revolution that took the conservative Jose Rufino Echenique from power.[50] These testimonies reflect, in addition, a typical attitude among conservatives: they tended to describe all episodes of social unrest as democratic events and the circumstantial violent expressions of the disadvantaged group as the paradigmatic expressions of "the people."[51]

---

[47] Safford (1985), p. 376. See also Bosch (1980), p. 127. Bolívar made reference to the "passions," the "fanaticism," and the "excitement" that were affecting large groups of people in his country.

[48] Fowler (1966), p. 115. And also: "The whole city was in a commotion, those people who believed that they were no longer safe in their own homes thought, in contrast, that they were safe in their friends' houses, where they moved to, carrying their possessions and personal effects, anything that was valuable; the streets were like anthills in which people came and went, and yet, the same risks could probably be found there; above all in the main streets, you could see armed soldiers continuously shouting 'get down, get down off the pavements,' afraid that they could be attacked from the sides." Ibid.

[49] Lora (1967), p. 369.

[50] Gootenberg (1993), p. 60.

[51] It is interesting to examine, for example, Mariano Ospina's analysis of the political situation in other Latin American countries. He referred, thus, to the "clumsy and

Reacting to what they described as mass popular movements, conservatives promoted peculiar representative systems where the elected and the electors were greatly distanced, and where the latter had basically no chance of imposing their will upon that of the former. Democracy, and universal suffrage in particular, became the object of their sharpest attacks. In the most extreme cases, they openly proposed to install monarchies headed by European princes, a tendency that became apparent in Argentina and Chile by the end of the 1810s.

In the United States, John Adams attacked the radical model of politics promoted by activists like Thomas Paine because, he believed, it gave no attention to the interests of property owners. Adams strongly rejected the idea of a "simple democracy," which Paine seemed to favor. "We may appeal to every page of history we have hitherto turned over," he argued, "for proofs irrefragable, that the people, when they have been unchecked, have been as unjust, tyrannical, brutal, barbarous and cruel as any king or senate possessed of uncontrollable power." He feared not only the possibility of radical excesses: in his opinion, majority rule directly and necessarily implied the violation of minority rights. "The majority," he asserted, "has eternally and without one exception usurped the rights of the minority."[52] Without directly defending an aristocratic government, both Federalists and Anti-Federalists criticized democracy, a system that they characterized as "the worst of all political evils."[53] In Elbridge Gerry's opinion, the evils the nation was suffering from derived from the excesses of democracy – "the turbulence and follies of democracy," as he described it.[54] Edmund Randolph shared these opinions, adding that the "democratic parts of [the existing] Constitutions" represented the most serious danger to any proper political system.[55] George Mason also expressed his strong objections to democracy and popular suffrage.[56] Luther Martin, too, opposed the idea of consulting the people

---

ruinous governments in Central America, Buenos Aires [Rosas's government] and that of Belzu in Bolivia." These governments, he argued, were like government of José Hilario López in Colombia: they used to talk about "democracy," "equality," and "the republic," while they executed their oppressive plans. Ospina denied, thus, the important differences that separated each of these governments from the others, as well as their inherent "democratic deficit." See González González (1997). p. 184.

[52] Rossiter (1982), p. 112.
[53] E. Gerry, quoted in Horwitz (1979), p. 74.
[54] Gerry also asserted that he was against popular elections because the people were "uninformed and would be misled by a few designing men" (Farrand, 1937, vol. 2, p. 57).
[55] Ibid., vol. 1, p. 27.
[56] Ibid., vol. 2, p. 78.

of the states directly, warning against "the danger of commotion from a resort to the people."[57]

In Latin America, we find many similar opinions. For Bolívar, for example, "the popular elections held by the simple people of the country and by the scheming inhabitants of the city add a further obstacle to our practice of federation, because the former are so ignorant that they cast their votes mechanically and the latter so ambitious that they convert everything into factions."[58] His fellow countryman Juan Antonio Páez, who would control the political life of Venezuela for decades, used the most violent terms for criticizing electoral practices. In his opinion, nothing could follow from the adoption of free and universal suffrage: "the disobeying of laws, the offense and resistance to political authorities, anarchy,...unrestrained ambitions, unchecked passions."[59]

In Chile, the very influential Diego Portales proclaimed that democracy was "an absurdity in countries like those of America, which are full of vices, and whose citizens completely lack the virtue necessary for a true *Republic*."[60] Mariano Egaña, one of the main intellectuals behind Chile's famously authoritarian constitution of 1833, wrote in a similar vein to his father, Juan: "This democracy, father, is the greatest enemy of America; it will cause her many disasters more, and eventually bring her down to total ruin."[61] He proposed to adopt a system of "liberty without democracy."[62]

Remarkably, in Argentina, right after the end of Rosas's rule, conservatives were still actively pushing for the adoption of antidemocratic measures. One of the most lucid theorists among them, Félix Frías,[63] an admirer of Chile's authoritarian experience, proposed a political program that suggested appointing a strong political authority again to discipline the lower classes and to impose the Catholic

---

[57] Ibid., p. 476.
[58] See Bolívar (1951), vol. 1, p. 22. He continued: "Venezuela never witnessed a free and proper election and the government was placed in the hands of men who were either inept, immoral, or opposed to the cause of independence. Party spirit determined everything and, consequently, caused us more disorganization than the circumstances themselves." Ibid.
[59] Quoted in L. A. Romero (1978), p. 13.
[60] Portales (1937), p. 177.
[61] He continued: "Federations, insurrections, conspiracies, continual anxieties which discourage trade, industry and the diffusion of useful knowledge; in fact, as many crimes and nonsenses as have been committed from Texas to Chiloé, all of them are the effects of this democratic fury which is the greatest scourge of nations without experience, without correct political notions." Quoted in Collier (1967), pp. 335–336.
[62] Ibid., p. 337.
[63] Halperín Donghi (1995), pp. 24–27.

religion through the coercive apparatus of the state. The main motto of his program was "order under the shadow and protection of the Holy Cross."[64] For Frías, the strong president had to "approve vigorous laws that repressed all excesses" and that would allow him to reconstruct an authority "discredited by a long period...of tyrannical abuses and a fanatic liberalism."[65] In his proposed authority, "the aristocracy of the most talented" would have to rule under "the terror of the law."[66]

Juan García del Río, who collaborated with the influential intellectual Andrés Bello on many journalistic projects, was the author of the famous *Meditaciones Colombianas*, in which he criticized democratic extremism, proposed a confrontation with anarchy and despotism to guarantee the security and property of the people, and suggested the adoption of a monarchical system.[67] In his opinion, frequent elections were a source of serious political evils. Particularly so, he said, when the people "have no virtues and general knowledge and are almost insensitive to the advantages of a free constitution, indifferent to public affairs, ignorant about their rights and duties, and inclined to persist in a situation of ignorance and degradation."[68]

Conservatives were also, in general, distrustful of federalist powers. They associated federalism with internal disorder and with the impossibility of coordinating common efforts and of defining a "national" policy. Bolívar, for example, maintained that, "although [the federalist system was] the most perfect and the most capable of providing for human happiness in society," it was, nevertheless, "the most contrary to the interests of our infant states. Generally speaking, our fellow-citizens are not yet able to exercise their rights themselves in the fullest measure, because they lack the political virtues

---

[64] Frías (1995), p. 157. He stated that "civil and political law will not be respected until the moral law becomes ingrained in every person's conscience, and given that we are still far from this situation, it is necessary that the authority, that is, the executor of the law, became armed, in order to make those who do not know or do not want to obey the law, afraid, and liberty compatible with the present state of our civilization and our habits." Ibid.

[65] Ibid., p. 155.

[66] Ibid., p. 157.

[67] Similarly, Sergio Arboleda stressed the importance of defying the projects of agrarian reform presented in his country and ensuring maximum guarantees for private property. Arboleda, a strong critic of the idea of equality, "the horrible monster with the mouth of a lion," proposed the preservation of a "complete inequality" as a guarantee of order and harmony. Like the Argentinean writer Domingo Faustino Sarmiento, he also viewed his society as the scenario of a fight between two different elements: "civilization" and "barbarism." See Herrera Soto (1982), chap. 8.

[68] García del Río (1945), p. 134.

that characterize true republicans."[69] In addition, conservatives assumed that the adoption of federalism implied leaving minorities unprotected, at the mercy of the unrestrained passions of the majority. These types of ideas were particularly common during the U.S. founding period, when many conservatives assumed that their main objective was to restrain and moderate the increasing presence of local authorities. In Latin America, too, most conservative thinkers rejected what Andrés Bello described as a "federalist fever," which seemed able only to generate turmoil and internal revolts.[70]

Through these types of considerations, conservatives were turning the assumptions and main claims advanced by the populist groups upside down. In effect, the latter considered the political activism of the masses as a necessary condition in order to adopt adequate or just decisions. Many of them defined correct decisions as decisions that resulted from majority rule. In contrast with this position, conservatives believed that any increase in the political participation of the people tended to impoverish rather than enrich the public life of the community. Moreover, popular intervention in politics appeared to be a direct obstacle to the adoption of just decisions: the less the people "interfered" with the decisions of their representatives, the greater the chances of selecting the correct policies.

What we have, in the end, is a fundamentally different conception, which assumed that "just" or "adequate" decisions were recognized through an *elitist process of monological reflection* – that is, a process by which a few well-educated men decided in the name of all the others. In other words, the conservatives assumed that all processes of collective reflection and, in particular, processes that included the participation of large numbers of people negatively affected the chances of making the right decisions. Their analyses were always biased against the role of mass, popular meetings. "Are not popular assemblies frequently subject to the impulses of rage, resentment, jealousy, avarice, and of other irregular and violent propensities?" Hamilton wondered. "Is it not well known that their determinations are often governed by a few individuals, in whom they place confidence, and are, of course, liable to be tinctured by the passions and views of those individuals?"[71]

---

[69] Bolívar (1951), vol. 1, p. 21. Similarly, he asserted that the federal system was "over-perfect." It demanded "political virtues and talents far superior to our own." Ibid., p. 118.
[70] Bello (1997), p. 258.
[71] *Federalist* 6. In line with this view, Nathaniel Ghorum made reference to "the insensibility to character produced by participation of numbers, in dishonorable measures,

The first political proposals that they advanced were obviously opposed to the populists' proposals. They were aimed at concentrating power and strengthening the authority of those in power. They wanted a centralized power capable of putting an end to the two main conflicts mentioned earlier: first, the national authority should have the means for preventing "internal disorders," so common after the independence revolution; and, second, the national authority should be able to make political decisions without interference from the popular sectors, without any serious obstacle. Portales presented an excellent picture of this view. In his opinion, "The *Republic* is the system we must adopt; but do you know how I conceive it for these countries? A strong, centralizing Power, whose members are genuine examples of virtue and patriotism, to thus set the citizens on the straight path of order and virtue. When they have attained a degree of morality, then we can have a completely liberal sort of Power, free and full of ideals, in which all the citizens can take part."[72]

The Constitution

The primary attitude of conservatives toward the constitution was one of distrust. To enact a constitution, they believed, implied accepting their opponents' favorite game. Their opponents, in effect, got excited talking about "social pacts" and "contracts" that would supposedly produce a radical reconstruction of society. Some of these opponents also insisted on the idea of personal autonomy, assuming that the Magna Carta would ensure the people's control over their own lives. For conservatives, these claims were absurdities: they showed a complete disregard for the profound traditions of each nation and implied a direct challenge to the divine authority.

---

and of the length to which a public body may carry wickedness and cabal." In his opinion, "public bodies feel no personal responsibility and give full play to intrigue and cabal" (Farrand, 1937, vol. 2, p. 42). In a related way, Elbridge Gerry mentioned the "great number of bad men of various descriptions" who commonly characterized popular bodies. For him, the people at large, in their elections, were usually "uninformed" and "misled by a few designing men" (ibid., vol. 1, p. 181, and vol. 2, p. 57).

[72] Portales (1937), p. 177. Mariano Egaña gave a more precise version of the same view. In his opinion, the required government needed "sufficient authority to give an impulse to the administration, to suppress the aspirations of the revolutionaries, and to punish the insolence of certain incendiary writers who involve the national prestige in their calumnies....If authority fails in its duties, it ought to be attacked with positive documents, in a direct way, and not by poetic jokes which take away its quality of majesty. A government without majesty will collect nothing but scorn." Quoted in Collier (1967), p. 341.

Second, they disliked constitutions because these documents were normally aimed at establishing strict limits on governmental power, an aim that conservatives rejected outright. In their opinion, the new authorities' main mission was that of reestablishing social order, and in that case the presence of constitutional limitations represented an intolerable obstacle. The famous Peruvian president Ramón Castilla nicely summarized this view when explaining his actions to congress in 1849: "The first of my constitutional functions is the preservation of internal order; but the same constitution obliges me to respect the rights of the citizen. In my own conscience...the simultaneous fulfillment of both duties would be impossible. The former, the preservation of internal order, could not be accomplished by the existing authority [under the constitution], without some measures to check the enemies of that order in a manner more stringent than was provided for by laws. Ought I to have sacrificed the internal peace of the country for the constitutional rights of a few individuals?"[73] In sum, from the conservatives' viewpoint, legal norms, as promoted by radicals and extremists, were generally useless: either they limited those who could reestablish legal order, or they failed to set limits against those who wanted to destroy social order.

Third, the very process of calling a constitutional convention and writing a constitution was full of risks. On the one hand, this initiative normally triggered social expectations that were very difficult to satisfy. On the other, it was always possible that the delegates would use their popular legitimacy to challenge the existing authorities, which promised renewed social and political unrest. Finally, the enactment of a constitution represented a very serious enterprise, one that, they assumed, could easily attract the most irresponsible politicians: the constitution was partly about the creation and distribution of power.

These arguments nourished the conservatives' aversion to constitutions. The first American experiments in this matter simply reinforced their suspicions. In the United States, the dominant elite severely attacked the process of "radical constitutionalism," which appeared right after the independence revolution. Most of the constitutions adopted during that period, they assumed, were offensive to the ideal of having an organized society. These documents, they said, simply allowed the people to give legal authority to their most inappropriate claims. In Latin America, too, conservatives were harsh in their analysis of "revolutionary" constitutions. In fact, it is remarkable

---

[73] Quoted in Werlich (1978), p. 80.

how much importance they attributed to these documents and how strongly they disagreed with their contents.[74] In Bolívar's opinion, the first Constitution of Venezuela, a document that did not last more than a few weeks, was the main cause of the political disasters that followed its adoption. Lucas Alamán had similarly strong words to say about the Mexican Constitution of 1824, as did the Chilean Andrés Bello about Chile's Constitution of 1828, or General Agustin Gamarra about the Peruvian Constitution of 1828. The three of them maintained certain common ideas and manifested certain common fears: they all thought that the rejected constitutions, through their promotion of federalism and their disregard for political order, opened the doors to anarchy.

Because of these negative experiences, some of the conservatives resisted or undervalued constitutionalism. One of the most typical cases, in this respect, was that of the Argentinean caudillo Juan Manuel de Rosas, who indefinitely delayed the demands for a new constitution, which were so important for his supporters. In his opinion, society was simply not prepared to carry out such a significant endeavor. In his famous *Carta de la Hacienda de Figueroa*, he stated that, in order to create a new constitution, it was first necessary to reestablish political order, at both the national and local levels. After the country achieved "peace and tranquillity," he predicted, the different states would naturally get together, recognize their common interests, and establish a common legal order.[75] The Chilean Diego Portales shared Rosas's skepticism regarding the value of these legal documents. Even though he finally accepted the constitutional program advanced by Mariano Egaña, he expressed a strongly negative view of constitutionalism. In Chile, he argued, the laws were totally senseless: they brought nothing but "anarchy": "In sum, to follow the opinion of the jurist Egaña, confronting a threat to overthrow authority, the Power ought to cross its arms, unless the suspect was caught in the act.... With the men of the law one cannot come to an understanding; and if it's that way, what [expletive] purpose do Constitutions and papers serve, if they are incapable of providing a remedy to an evil that is known to exist.... In Chile the law doesn't serve for anything but to produce anarchy, the lack of sanctions, licentiousness, eternal law suits.... If I, for example, imprison an individual who is

---

[74] Bolívar (1951), vol. 1, p. 23. Francisco Miranda refused to sign the 1811 constitution, asserting that the document was not compatible with the "people's uses and habits." With Bolívar, he also thought that its approval put at risk the whole independence project. See Gil Fortoul (1909), pp. 237–238.
[75] See Romero J. L. and Romero (1978), pp. 240–241.

conspiring, I violate the law: Damned law, then, if it does not allow the Power to proceed freely in the opportune moment."[76]

In spite of these criticisms, however, sooner or later conservatives recognized that the battle against the constitution was lost: it was impossible not to play the game of constitutionalism. Once the conservatives had accepted playing it, they looked to Europe for inspiration. Three experiences, in particular, attracted their attention: the Cadiz Constitution of 1812, the Napoleonic consular constitutions of 1799 and 1802, and the British Constitution.

In the United States, particularly during the "framing period," it was difficult to defend the British institutional model: the fight for independence was still too close in time, and any reference to the British example was therefore impolitic. However, that constitutional model clearly had an impact on many of the most important U.S. constitutional theorists and in many of the proposals that they advanced. Conservative Whiggery was actually fascinated with that constitution, which seemingly favored the establishment of a stable political order. One of the strongest defenders of the British constitutional model and its idea of a mixed constitution was John Adams. He developed his view on the topic in many writings, in which he argued in favor of representative rather than participatory political systems, questioned the idea of political equality, supported the assignment of a special role for property owners within the decision-making process, and commented on the importance of civic virtues in the new societies.[77] Alexander Hamilton, too, was an admirer of the British legal order, which allowed him to justify many of his more elitist proposals, such as his promotion of indirect elections or his hidden desire to transform the president into a monarch. For him, the president should be elected in third-level elections in order to suppress any possible sympathy between the executive and the people and also to reaffirm the executive's total independence. In addition, it is not difficult to find connections between Federalists' proposals for a system of "checks and balances" and the British mixed constitution: both, in a way, reserved a fixed place for the "different orders of society."[78] As we examine later, the Americans also wanted to use the different branches of power as a device for achieving social and political integration.[79]

[76] Quoted in Safford (1985), pp. 370–371.
[77] See, for example, Howard (1990), chap. 6.
[78] See, for example, ibid.
[79] Most of the Federalists assumed that society was fundamentally divided into two social groups, the majority and the minority, the rich and the poor, the creditors and

The Constitution

In Latin America, the British model was at least as influential as it was in the United States. In this case, however, its defenders did not feel the need for disguising the intellectual inspiration of their proposals. This model again appeared to be a wonderful example of how to restrict the voice of majority groups and maintain or reestablish the social order. The British, in fact, reserved to the "commons" a particular place in the constitution, but one that was strictly checked by the other two fundamental "parts of society": the monarchy and the upper classes. This idea turned out to be very attractive for Latin American conservatives. Thinkers such as Mariano Ospina, Lucas Alamán, Mariano Egaña, and Andrés Bello reflected their admiration of this model in the particular institutional proposals they campaigned for.

Bolívar, too, was deeply marked by this example during the first few years of his intellectual development, a period that includes his influential "Letters from Jamaica" of 1815 and his famous "Discourse from Angostura" of 1819. From that model, he adopted the proposal for a powerful executive and a conservative senate. "No matter how closely we study the composition of the English executive power," he said, "we can find nothing to prevent its being judged as the most perfect model for a kingdom, for an aristocracy, or for a democracy. Give Venezuela such an executive power in the person of a president chosen by the people or their representatives, and you will have taken a great step toward national happiness."[80] Bolívar also argued that the hereditary senate could become the "soul" of the republic, an institution capable of resisting all institutional catastrophes.[81]

After some time, however, Bolívar abandoned this initial source of inspiration and followed the example of the Napoleonic constitutions, although he never admitted it. This latter influence was reflected, for example, in the constitutional document that he wrote for Bolivia in 1826: this created a president for life with the power to designate his

---

the debtors, and they wanted to give an institutional place to both these groups. The lower house would be the main platform for the majority group and the senate for the minority. Arguing against this position, see, for example, Manin (1997).

[80] Bolívar (1951), vol. 1, pp. 187–188.

[81] Bolívar's concerns with stabilizing institutions and "neutral" powers seemed to derive from the influence of Constant, who was at the time closely read by both liberals and conservatives. For Frank Safford, "Constant conceived of the constitutional monarch as a neutral balance wheel, moderating conflicts among the executive, the representative and the judicial powers. Bolívar followed this scheme both in distinguishing the president (constitutional monarch) and the actions of his ministers and in placing moderating power in the hands of the censors [the "Moral Power"]. This Constantian conception of a moderating power was also found in the Mexican centralist constitution of 1836, known as the Seven Laws." Safford (1985), p. 367.

115

vice-president and his successor, interrupted the standing tradition of a tripartite structure of power, and strictly reduced the power of the municipalities. Given Bolívar's enormous influence over the development of Latin America's constitutionalism, these models also became highly influential in the constitutional life of other Latin American countries. General Andrés Santa Cruz proposed a constitution of this type for the confederation that he presided over between Peru and Bolivia. General Juan José Flores in Ecuador and the Mexican conservatives in 1836 also favored this model.[82]

The Cadiz Constitution was also very important in Latin America, in particular during the first half of the century. The document created by the Spanish Junta Central was received with fervor in the American colonies at the critical moment when the king of Spain, Fernando VII, was Napoleon's hostage, among other reasons because of the constitution's open attitude toward the region.[83] The constitution exercised a broad influence in the region, which does not imply that its influence was decisive. Two factors help explain the particular success of this model: the document was complete, well organized, and very accessible to the Americans; and it had an ambiguous character, which worked in its favor and also explains why its content attracted both progressives and conservatives. In effect, the constitution recognized the authority of the king and granted him significant legislative and veto powers, yet limited his capacities more than ever before.[84] Because of this, most Latin Americans looked to it in search of inspiration: the conservatives read the support of a strong authority into its text, while progressives saw the creation of new limits in the document.[85]

---

[82] Safford (1985); p. 366, Ayala (1995a).
[83] This new policy toward America, however, was mostly forced by two particular circumstances: America was giving important economic support to Spain at that time; and the Spanish felt forced to compensate for the benefits that, in terms of political representation, the French governor José I offered the Spanish colonies, through the Bayona Constitution of 1808. See M. Rodríguez (1978).
[84] Conservatives found in this model an additional and fundamental attraction: the Cadiz Constitution established the Catholic religion as the only official religion, with no tolerance toward any other faith. This feature, incorporated in article 12 of that document, undoubtedly represented the most important legacy of this model in Latin America's constitutions. Garófano and de Páramo (1983), p. 46. Also M. Rodríguez (1978).
[85] Both the Mexican Constitution of Apatzingán and the Venezuelan Constitution of 1811, for example, two fairly radical documents, took the Cadiz Constitution as a fundamental antecedent. The popular leader Zavala admitted the enormous interest he had in the model, as did the jurist Joaquín de Mora, who collaborated with the Argentinean reformer Bernardino Rivadavia and wrote the federalist Chilean Constitution of 1828. The same happened with the Peruvian constitutions of 1823 and

Conservative Constitutions and the Structure of Power: "A Single Well-Directed Man"

If we take into account the different features of conservative constitutionalism examined so far, especially its promotion of political elitism and moral perfectionism, we can argue that many Latin American constitutions followed the conservative pattern.

Political elitism was usually translated into the language of the constitution as a proposal for concentrating authority in one person or group. This usually implied reinforcement of the powers of the president, as recommended, for example, by Louis de Bonald. In effect, a critic of Montesquieu's doctrine of the separation of powers, Bonald argued that the division and equilibrium of powers were mere appearance: only obedience mattered, and obedience implied only one source of power.

Among the many powers that conservatives wanted to concentrate in the hands of the president, we usually find some of the following: the possibility of intervening in the political affairs of the states; broad powers of veto; broad legislative capacities and, sometimes, the possibility of directly dissolving congress; the judicial power of giving pardons or amnesties; a decisive role in the selection of judges and ambassadors; capacities for dealing with other nations; a discretionary capacity for designating and removing ministers; control over the armed forces; and the capacity to declare war and sign peace treaties. In addition, conservatives wanted to ensure a long mandate for the president, allow reelection, make him not accountable for the acts of his administration, give him "extraordinary powers" during "internal or external crises," and authorize him to declare a state of siege.

The conservatives' confidence in the presidential capacities was related, among other things, with their certainty about the president's independence of judgment. This is also why they wanted the president to be sufficiently isolated from popular pressures: independence of judgment would be the result of the manner of his election (normally, by indirect election) and his long mandate. More important, their confidence in the president related to the single-person character of this position and the qualities they associated with those who might occupy it. As we have shown, conservatives assumed that good

1828, the Uruguayan Constitution of 1830, and New Granada's documents of 1830 and 1832. At the same time, however, many conservative theorists closely followed the Cadiz Constitution. The Cúcuta Constitution of 1821, the Chilean Constitution of 1822, Argentina's authoritarian Estatuto Provisional of 1815, the Venezuelan Constitution of 1830, and the Bolivian Constitution of 1826 were all influenced by it.

decisions were the result of a process of individual rather than collective reflection. Alexander Hamilton clearly supported this view when, in *Federalist* 76, he asserted that "a single well-directed man with a single understanding cannot be distracted by that diversity of views, feelings and interests, which frequently distract and warp the resolutions of a collective body." Significantly, Hamilton was stressing that the diversity of viewpoints that characterizes collective bodies prevented the achievement of adequate decisions. Diversity, he assumed, hindered the chances of careful reasoning and made it more difficult to think about the interests of the nation: it forced public officers to defend mere partial interests at the expense of the common good.[86] The president would, in this way, be capable of giving the people the "time and opportunity for more cool and calm reflection" as opposed to "every sudden breeze of passion."[87]

In addition, a strong president promised a more stable and well-ordered nation, as well as the proper custody of the nation's "most sacred values." Arguably, the most emphatic and significant promotion of the strong president in Latin America came from Simón Bolívar.[88] Bolívar had been deeply shocked by Venezuela's 1811 constitution, which, among other things, provided for a tripartite executive. In the speech he delivered in Angostura, at the inauguration

[86] Because of similar assumptions, many Federalists supported the idea of vesting the executive in a single individual. In this way, they believed, "he would be responsible to the whole, and would be impartial to its interests" (Butler, in Farrand, 1937, vol. 1, p. 88). In addition, the way in which they organized the election of the president resulted from this view. The Framers organized the election of the executive through an "electoral college" as a way to secure "circumstances favorable to deliberation." That is, they assumed that a collective discussion by the people at large would hinder, rather than enrich, the outcome. It would prevent, rather than favor, impartiality.
[87] *Federalist* 71. In Hamilton's opinion, the "courage and magnanimity" of great men saved their communities from terrible perils.
[88] In 1826 Bolívar's view was heavily influenced by the French Consular Constitution. Following the example of the Napoleonic constitutions, Bolívar then proposed a president appointed for life, not accountable for the acts of his government, and endowed with the power to designate his successor and his vice-president (whom he could remove at will). The president was also the chief of the armed forces, which he could mobilize when he deemed it necessary. The "Libertador" presented this view before the Bolivian Congress during the inauguration of the constitutional convention, which ended with the adoption of the 1826 Bolivarian Constitution. In his speech, Bolívar also proposed the adoption of a fourth branch of power, the "Moral Power," which would be in charge of overseeing the moral life of the citizens of the country. The 1826 Bolivian Constitution closely followed Bolívar's teaching, although it did not adopt his suggested fourth branch of power. However, it lasted for a very short time and was repudiated by the Colombians when Bolívar tried to enforce it in the neighboring country. In addition, European intellectuals such as Benjamin Constant objected to Bolívar's proposal, which they found too authoritarian. See, for example, Aguilar Rivera (2000), p. 193.

of the second national congress of Venezuela, he stated: "Let us put aside the triumvirate which holds the executive power and center it in a president. We must grant him sufficient authority to enable him to continue the struggle against the obstacles inherent in our recent situation, our present state of war, and every variety of foe, foreign and domestic, whom we must battle for some time to come."[89] Later on, in his message to the Congress of Bolivia in 1826, he elaborated on a proposal he had supported throughout his life, that of a life-term, nonaccountable president. He argued for this idea by stating: "The President of the Republic, in our Constitution, becomes the sun which, fixed in its orbit, imparts life to the universe. This supreme authority must be perpetual, for in non-hierarchical systems, more than in others, a fixed point is needed about which leaders and citizens, men and affairs can revolve. 'Give me a point where I may stand,' said an ancient sage, 'and I will move the earth.' For Bolivia this point is the life-term President."[90]

Supporting the constitutional program that he presented in Peru in 1860 – his highest achievement as a constitutional theorist – the cleric Bartolomé Herrera also made reference to these goals.[91] He maintained that it was necessary to adopt "an authority capable of enforcing God's precepts. An authority that directs the will of the people and defines what must be done or not done, in accordance with the natural law. To do this is to command. But the sovereign does not oblige because he commands: he commands because he acts in accordance with natural law. His authority is not absolute. He is nothing but a minister of God who acts for the good of others...we have a moral duty to obey a legitimate power which acts in accordance with natural law."[92] His constitutional program, then, proposed the creation of a president who could be indefinitely reelected and had the capacity to close and dissolve congress at will. In addition, the president, who enjoyed the right to appoint most public officers, could obtain the power of suspending most individual guarantees.

---

[89] Bolívar (1951), vol. 1, p. 190.
[90] Ibid., vol. 2, p. 598.
[91] Herrera's proposed constitution included, among other things, a powerful president, who could be indefinitely reelected, and an extremely conservative senate, consisting of, for example, members of the clergy and the military. In this proposal, the president was also able to freely appoint and remove judicial officers and to suspend individual rights with the approval of the senate. In addition, his proposal made citizenship dependent on the individual's intellectual capacities and their possession of property, which left soldiers, servants, and the poor without political rights.
[92] Quoted in Paz Soldán (1943), p. 110.

The Chilean Constitution of 1833, which, with little modification, remained in force until 1925, was also very favorable to presidential authority.[93] The president was allowed two consecutive five-year terms. He was also endowed with significant emergency powers, which implied the suspension of the constitution and of most civil rights. If congress was in recess, which it usually was at that time, the president could decree states of siege in the provinces, subject to later congressional approval. During these crises, the president could even declare martial law in any part of the republic with the consent of the council of state.[94] In addition, the president enjoyed broad powers of veto and the right to appoint most senior officers directly. He could be judged on his actions during office only after the conclusion of his second mandate, if reelected, which in practice implied that he would become practically nonaccountable.

In Latin America, the Chilean Constitution was the first to create a provision for the state of siege, which was later adopted in the Argentinean Constitution of 1853, the Bolivian Constitution of 1861, the Ecuadorian Constitution of 1869, and the Colombian Constitution of 1886. Andrés Bello, one of the most important intellectual

---

[93] In his "Voto Particular," during the 1833 constitutional convention, Mariano Egaña, with the help of his father, Juan, developed a complete constitutional proposal, which closely followed Juan's program of 1823. It established the Catholic religion as the official religion of the country; proposed suppressing a disposition of the 1828 constitution, which maintained that people could not be persecuted or disturbed because of their personal opinions; and reintroduced the ultraconservative institution of the "Senadores visitadores" (in charge of controlling citizens' personal morality). The senators were obligated to visit the different regions of the country, inquiring about people's personal lives and exercising their powers of censorship. Galdames (1925), p. 893. In addition, the program guaranteed extraordinary powers to the president; authorized his indefinite reelection; allowed him to dissolve the legislature almost at his personal discretion; granted him strong powers of veto (the deputies could not discuss the program again until the following year, and only if they achieved a two-thirds majority); gave him powers to elect and remove state governors and the main local authorities at will; and made him politically nonaccountable. In the end, Egaña's "Voto" was partially rejected and partially approved. It was not followed with regard to his proposed senate or some of the powers he gave to the executive (e.g., indefinite reelection). His ideas were followed, however, in many significant clauses. The new constitution made the president nonaccountable, authorized him to declare a state of siege, and gave him extraordinary powers and absolute powers of veto. In addition, and again as in Egaña's proposal, it accepted the inclusion of the Catholic religion as the only religion of the country (prohibiting the public practice of all other creeds) and approved the restrictions he suggested with regard to people's basic rights. Manuel José Gandarillas, the great liberal of the convention, could not prevent the conservatives from adopting their favored proposals, including, for example, strict limitations on political rights, which excluded the illiterate and the poor.
[94] See Vanorden Shaw (1930), pp. 118–119.

authorities in nineteenth-century Chile, and also one of the authors of the new constitution, justified these powers, asserting the need for putting limits on the factional conflicts that divided his country.[95] Because of the political stability that it seemingly favored, the 1833 constitution became famous and influential throughout the region. García Moreno, for example, tried to follow its example in Ecuador. In fact, the Ecuadorian Constitution of 1869 re-created the most authoritarian aspects of the Chilean document. In this way, for example, the Ecuadorian Constitution authorized the president to create a "martial court" to prosecute those who took part in revolutionary movements. In these critical times, the president was also authorized to order the search of private houses, arrest people, or prohibit assemblies.[96]

The model of a strong executive was also adopted in most Bolivian constitutions, from the one written by Bolívar in 1826 to those of 1831, 1834, 1843, and 1851. In Colombia, the failed projects of 1826, 1828, and 1830, all inspired by Bolívar's ideas, such as the important constitution of 1843 written under the influence of extreme conservatives Caro and Ospina or that of 1886, represented the most important examples of this constitutional model. In Peru, the constitutions of 1826 and 1839, which allowed the delegation of "all the necessary powers" to the president in cases of crisis, and that of 1860 also represented significant efforts to strengthen the authority of the executive. These constitutions were reacting against the first constitutions of the country, which had tried to strictly limit the powers of the president.[97] In Argentina, different unsuccessful constitutional programs, such as those of 1815 and 1817, may also be described as conservative. However, the country's best example of a conservative regime is that led by Juan Manuel de Rosas, who ruled the powerful province of Buenos Aires during the period 1829 to 1852. During most of this time, Rosas was vested with the "sum of the public powers."

[95] See Brewer-Carías (1982), p. 142.
[96] Even the Argentinean liberals Domingo Sarmiento and Juan Bautista Alberdi, who, like many others, came to know the Chilean Constitution during their exile in that country, were fascinated with this model, which promised order and political stability. Alberdi argued, in this respect, that "both the Egañas Juan and his son Mariano] are strong with regard to theology and legislation." And he continued: "They deserve the respect and gratitude of the Chilean people because of the role they play in the country's institutional organization." See Pérez Guilhou (1984), p. 26.
[97] The 1839 Constitution of Huancayo would be in force for twelve long years. Aimed at "avoiding the horrors of anarchy," the new document strengthened the powers of the president, suppressed the existent municipalities, weakened the legislature, and subordinated the judiciary to the authority of the executive. Both individual and political rights were also severely restricted (Paz Soldán 1943).

In addition, as a way of improving the chances of (re)establishing social order, many Latin American constitutions expanded the role of the armed forces, which, in all cases, were commanded by the president of the country. Constitutions such as those adopted in Colombia in 1832 and 1834, in Ecuador in 1830, 1835, 1845, 1851, and 1852, and in Peru in 1828, 1834, 1856, 1860, and 1867 delegated to the armed forces the responsibility for maintaining the internal order of the country. Other constitutions, such as those of Bolivia in 1839 and 1851, Peru in 1834, Venezuela in 1864, and most of those adopted in Ecuador after 1845, gave the armed forces a more indirect participation in internal affairs. In these situations, the armed forces were in charge of making sure that no laws were adopted because of mere "popular pressures."[98]

In all these cases, the strengthening of the executive power, and the consequent strengthening of military power, implied the necessity for a centralized political organization. In most cases, though not in Argentina's, the idea of a strong president within a federalist regime appeared as an oxymoron. For conservatives, the president had to have the power to enforce his will throughout the entire country. Because his authority had to be consistently applied everywhere, the possibility of his decisions being checked and perhaps challenged by local legislatures or local caudillos remained unacceptable.

The conservatives' battle for centralism was one of the most important for which they fought during the nineteenth century. It always occupied a significant place in both their speeches and their actions.

In Chile, conservatives faulted the federalist constitution of 1828 for what they described as the chaos and anarchy that appeared at the end of the decade. For Bello, for example, the 1828 constitution had given so much power to the local authorities that it had actually transformed the presidency into an organ without authority.[99]

The fight against federalism was also of primary importance among Mexican conservatives. Lucas Alamán defined federalism as the "most powerful and destructive instrument imaginable."[100] Alamán was part of General Bustamante's authoritarian and centralist regime, which controlled the nation after violently ending Guerrero's federalist crusade. General Santa Anna also fervently advanced the antifederalist banner. Santa Anna was, among many other things,

---

[98] See Loveman (1993), pp. 399–400.
[99] For Bello, the situation at the state level was unbearable. Political disorder was the rule and the majorities managed to impose their will on all occasions. The rights of minority groups were ignored or violated. Bello (1997), p. 258.
[100] Fithiam Stevens (1991), pp. 31–32.

responsible for reforming the only moderately federalist 1824 constitution, which had become the symbol of a (more) decentralized country. The most important legal instrument that he promoted, the Siete Leyes, sanctioned in 1836, decisively favored the centralists' cause and the church.[101] Once again in power in 1843, Santa Anna promoted new constitutional reform, aimed at developing even further the centralist aims of the Siete Leyes. During his fifth presidential mandate, which began in 1853, Santa Anna retained Lucas Alamán as one of his main advisers. Federalist forces, however, would dramatically interrupt his reformist plan.

In Argentina, all the important constitutional documents enacted during the first part of the century were clearly centralist. The constitution of 1819 was strongly so, which provoked a reaction from the caudillos in the provinces and, in the end, resulted in the Cepeda war, which fragmented the country for years. The constitution of 1826, which tried to undo the mistakes of the former document, also resulted in an unsuccessful outcome for the federalists: its final content was still too centralist, in spite of the efforts made by a few delegates, such as General Manuel Dorrego, to give it a clearly federalist twist. Only in 1853, with the acceptance of the 1853 constitution and the fall of Rosas, did the country begin seriously to develop a federalist commitment.

In Venezuela, Bolívar made enormous efforts to advance the centralist cause. He promoted it through all his constitutional initiatives and argued against federalism in many of his letters and most important speeches. Displeased by resistance to his centralist proposals,

---

[101] Among other things, the "Seven Laws," created through the political pressure of Santa Anna and the intellectual influence of Alamán, provided for an indirectly elected and powerful executive, organized the judicial system, and crafted a "Supreme Conservative Power" with ample political power. Among other powers, the "Supreme Conservative Power" was allowed to control the constitutionality of the laws (it could even invalidate the decisions of the supreme court or suspend it if it improperly interfered with other powers) and also to remove the president in case of physical or moral incapacity. See, for example, Barrón 2001. A council of state, composed of members of the military, the church, and the wealthiest sectors of society, was in charge of advising the president. For the famous Mexican jurist Emilio Rabassa, the "Seven Laws" created the basis for "oligarchic constitutionalism," while the new "Bases" laid the foundation for "constitutional despotism" (Rabassa, 1991, p. 127; see also Aguilar Rivera, 2001). Returned as president of the country in 1841, and always suspicious of the "Supreme Conservative Power," Santa Anna promoted the enactment of a new constitution. The new document, the "Bases Orgánicas de 1843," suppressed the "Supreme Conservative Power"; provided for Catholicism as the official religion of the country; restricted individual rights, which could simply be suspended by the decision of congress; strictly limited political rights; created a strong executive and a very conservative senate; and insisted on a centralist type of structure.

he claimed: "Federation may be the system most favored by the people...they do not want monarchy, or a life-term president, or, most emphatically, an aristocracy, so why do they not hurl themselves outright into the tempestuous, rolling sea of anarchy?"[102] The Venezuelan Constitution of 1830, with which José Antonio Páez ruled the country for decades, adopted a "center-federalist" form of government, which was in fact a direct reaction against the federalist impulses of the 1811 constitution.[103] The struggle for and against centralism dominated the country during the century and became increasingly dramatic after the 1850s. In 1857 President José Ruperto Monagas sanctioned a strongly centralist constitution, in which local *diputaciones* were suppressed and the president was authorized to select and remove the main local authorities at will.[104]

The 1857 constitution, the most centralist in the history of Venezuela, was promptly replaced in 1858 with a new one, more favorable to the federalist ideal. However, the seeds of discord were already planted and the Federal War exploded soon after its approval. In that context, the influential political leader Fermín Toro made a famous speech in defense of a more centralized political organization. On that occasion, Toro revealed the elitist assumptions shared by most of those who promoted centralist ideals:

> Men have not enough intelligence for deciding by themselves, for enlightening themselves, for progressing, for acknowledging their rights and interests; and it is impossible for them to have a clear idea of the political constitution. Because of this, we see many electoral processes where the proprietors simply drag the people as if they were animals, and these people have to decide the destiny of the country through the designation of the new authorities. It is impossible, then, to accept pure federalism, thus characterized. A federalist

---

[102] Bolívar (1951), vol. 2, p. 734. Against the Colombians, he stated that "they had better divide Colombia rather than subject her to a ruinous federation void of every social principle and guarantee....I foresee certain destruction, unless the government is given enormous power, capable of shifting the anarchy which will raise its thousand and one seditious heads...federation will be Colombia's grave." Letter to General Páez, Jan. 1828. Ibid., pp. 672–674.

[103] See Boulton (1976); Pino Iturrieta (1991); Picón Salas (1953).

[104] At a time of profound social unrest, a significant representative of the conservative view, Juan Vicente González, declared that the press was "teaching the people to undermine their authorities [and] hate the government." Liberal journalists, he added, were defending criminals and fostering social anarchy (Pino Iturrieta 1991, p. 353). Another influential conservative, Cecilio Acosta, shared González's view and denounced the growing "abuses of liberty, which imply its death." Acosta directly advocated establishing a system of censorship (for a favorable analysis of his view, see Picón Salas, 1953).

power presupposes intelligence, morality, independence and good will. A great deal of patriotism in the majority, in the great number of society.[105]

In this speech, Toro was simply repeating what was, at that time, the conservatives' viewpoint on the topic: federalism was unacceptable because most people, they assumed, were not actually prepared to participate in politics. The people, they believed, were not totally free: they depended, economically as much as psychologically, on other people. The federalist alternative, then, was unacceptable because it implied an increase in the power of those with fewer intellectual capacities.

Both the conservatives' objections to federalism and their support of a strong executive pointed in the same direction: their distrust of majority rule. The most extreme defenders of this view directly supported aristocratic forms of power or at least a power especially sensitive to the interests of the so-called aristocracy. Consequently, we find many references to the power of the "wise," something that Donoso Cortés demanded in Spain, as did his disciple Herrera in Peru. While Herrera supported rule by the "aristocracy of intelligence," his compatriot José María Pando considered an "imperious necessity" the creation of a "perpetual aristocracy." The Chilean Juan Egaña also maintained that the best government was one that reserved a significant role for the aristocracy. In a letter of 1828, he noted that "in Rome, England, and other states where aristocracy is mixed with democracy, men who are distinguished by their civic virtue always come from the nobility."[106] In Mexico, this was also the view of influential people such as Mariano Paredes y Arrillaga. Similarly, in the United States many supported the adoption of an aristocratic government, as many others promoted institutions such as the senate, assuming that its members would be representatives of the national aristocracy. In the opinion of some U.S. conservatives, the senators constituted "a portion of enlightened citizens" whose virtues "might reasonably interpose against impetuous councils."[107] Perfectionists assumed senators would belong to "the wealth of the Nation" and ensure "the rights of property." Hamilton, too, justified the senate as a way of "protecting the rights of property against the spirit of democracy."[108]

---

[105] Toro (1954), p. 85.
[106] Quoted in Collier (1967), p. 277.
[107] Madison, in Farrand (1937), vol. 1, p. 422.
[108] Ibid., vol. 3, p. 498. In a similar vein, Mason asserted that one of the most important objectives of the senate was that of "secur[ing] the rights of property." Ibid., vol. 1,

Obviously, most of them showed a serious distrust of popular legislatures. This view was widely held, for example, within the U.S. federal convention. In that context, Gouverneur Morris stated that "public liberty [is] in greater danger from legislative usurpation [and poor laws] than from any other source."[109] "However the legislative power may be formed," he claimed, "it will, if disposed, be able to ruin the country."[110] James Wilson and Rufus King had exactly the same viewpoint.[111] Edmund Randolph, too, made references to "the passionate proceedings to which numerous assemblies are liable" and criticized the powers of the lower house."[112] George Mason supported very similar criteria, pointing out the dangerous tendencies that distinguished the functioning of the lower house. He emphasized that "it must be expected frequently to pass unjust and pernicious laws."[113] In agreement with these opinions, Elbridge Gerry argued that the legislature "might ruin the country [by exercising its power] partially, improving one and damaging another part of it."[114]

Conservative constitutions tried to dilute the popular will by different means. In some cases, they simply did not include a legislature. The Chilean Constitution of 1818, for example, designed under the influence of General Bernardo O'Higgins, contained no popular elected legislative body.[115] Similarly, in the Argentinean Estatuto de

p. 428. See also Davie, ibid., p. 542; Baldwin, ibid., p. 470; Pinckney, ibid., vol. 3, p. 110; and Madison, vol. 1, p. 562. In Latin America, Bolívar, who, like Hamilton, proposed life appointments for the senators, also justified "his senate" as a body aimed at tempering "absolute democracy." "The function of my senate," he said, "is to temper absolute democracy and to adjust the format of an absolute government to that of more moderate institutions; for today it is an accepted principle of politics that an absolutely democratic government is as tyrannical as any despot; hence only a hybrid government can be free. How would you have me temper democracy, except with an aristocratic institution?" See Bolívar (1951), vol. 1, p. 227.

[109] Farrand (1937), vol. 2, p. 76.
[110] Ibid., p. 307. For Morris, the first branch had to be strictly checked because of its "precipitation, changeability, and excesses." The lower house, he believed, had "a propensity...to legislate too much, to enter into programs with paper money and similar expedients."
[111] See Wilson, ibid., pp. 300–301, and Rufus King, ibid., p. 198.
[112] Ibid., p. 51.
[113] Ibid., p. 78.
[114] Ibid., p. 307.
[115] During O'Higgins's mandate, two important constitutional documents were approved, one in 1818 and the other in 1822. The first, partially based on Argentina's Estatuto Provisional of 1815, created a "legal dictatorship," with a powerful president who had the right to appoint both political and judicial officers. The second, written by O'Higgins favorite, José Antonio Rodríguez Aldea, is presently known as the first significant constitutional document in Chile's history. It established a tripartite division of power, a powerful president, and a senate that included representatives of the main interest groups in the country.

1815, in which the Chilean document found inspiration, there was only one article referring to the legislature, delaying its implementation until the meeting of a new general congress.

Other strategies with the same objective, that is, to diminish the capacity of the popular assembly, included the reform of the electoral system to restrict the popular character of the administration even further; the creation of a conservative second legislative assembly; a reduction in the number of popular representatives; and a reduction in the frequency of its meetings. Thus, for example, the Ecuadorian Constitution of 1843 proclaimed that congress could hold its meetings only after four-year periods, while a five-member senate in collaboration with the executive would take care of the legislative decisions of the country for the rest of the time. Similarly, the Peruvian Constitutions of 1839 and 1860 proclaimed that congressmen could come together only after two-year periods.

Within this context, the senate was always called upon to play a fundamental role: it had to control the "ambitions" and "excesses" of the popular assembly. The requirements of advanced age and wealth, usually established as preconditions for becoming a senator, as well as the way they were elected (usually through indirect elections and with the extension of their mandate some years beyond that of the members of the popular assembly), seemingly ensured the capacity and decency of its members. In addition, their long tenure apparently ensured their "firmness and independence,"[116] distinguishing them from the "fluctuations and cabals" expected from members of the house.[117] Indirect elections would supposedly help them to avoid the "rivalry and incidents of discontent resulting from election by districts."[118] Their small number permitted them to proceed "with more coolness, with more system, and with more wisdom, than the popular assembly."[119] Their more "mature" character was believed to guarantee their having a "greater extent of information and stability of character."[120] In this way, conservatives justified the significant powers they reserved for the senate: they included, for example, its

---

[116] Randolph, in Farrand (1937), vol. 1, p. 218.
[117] Madison, ibid., vol. 3, p. 337.
[118] Pinckney, ibid., vol. 1, p. 155.
[119] Madison, ibid., p. 427. He also stated that if you enlarge the size of the senate, "you [will] communicate to them the vices they are meant to correct." Ibid., p. 151. Similarly, Mason stressed the "danger of making the senate too numerous" (ibid., vol. 4, p. 15), and Randolph maintained that the senate should be "much smaller than the [lower house]" in order to be "exempt from the passionate proceedings to which numerous assemblies are liable." Ibid., vol. 1, p. 51.
[120] See *Federalist* 62.

privileged role in the election of judicial officials and ambassadors, its decisive participation in the impeachment of public officers, and its treaty powers, making reference both to the confidence they had in the qualities of the senators and to their distrust of the popular assembly. Hamilton was particularly explicit in this sense, attributing to the senators and the president an "accurate and comprehensive knowledge of foreign politics; a steady and systematic adherence to the same views; a nice and uniform sensibility to national character, decision, secrecy and dispatch; [virtues that are] incompatible with the genius of a body so variable and so numerous [as the House of Representatives]."[121]

Bolívar, who, in 1819, proposed the creation of a hereditary senate, considered that the high qualifications required for becoming a senator could not be left to "the outcome of elections." He then suggested educating them "in an atmosphere of enlightened education." Only then would the senate become "the fundamental basis of the legislative authority, and therefore the foundation of the entire government." In addition, Bolívar assumed that such a senate would "serve as a counterweight to both executive and people; and as a neutral power it will weaken the mutual attacks of these two eternal rivals."[122] Juan Egaña, too, saw in the senate a "conservative institution" based on the "moral force" of its members. This moral force, he believed, would allow them to resist both the assaults of the president and the violence of popular passions.[123]

Finally, conservatives reserved a significant role for the judiciary. Because of the qualities required of its members, the institution seemed a proper safeguard for certain fundamental values and interests. In effect, given the high educational standards required for becoming a judge, and their indirect election, the conservatives were certain that only a few well-established people would have access to these positions. In this sense, it is not surprising that they reserved for them some extraordinary powers, such as that of declaring a law void. The U.S. Constitution, the most advanced of all the American

---

[121] See *Federalist* 75.
[122] See Bolívar (1951), vol. 1, p. 186. "The liberators of Venezuela" were also "entitled to occupy forever a high rank in the Republic" and, for that reason, they would also form part of the senate. In his opinion, then "[no] inducement could corrupt a legislative body invested with the highest honors, dependent only upon itself, having no fear of the people, independent of the government, and dedicated solely to the repression of all evil principles and to the advancement of every good principle, a legislative body which would be deeply concerned with the maintenance of society, for it would share the consequences." Ibid., p. 187.
[123] Quoted in J. L. Romero and Romero (1978), p. 163.

constitutions with regard to the judiciary, did not include this power in its text. However, it is also true that most members of the convention assumed, at that time, that this right was actually incorporated into the text.[124] In fact, some members of the convention put forward a clear justification for this power; they did so even more openly during the first national congress, where they discussed, among other things, the famous judiciary act. Clearly, judicial review was not, and is not today, easy to defend. (Why should it be acceptable that undemocratically elected judges should be able to invalidate a decision made by the people's representatives? How could anyone defend such a possibility within a republican or democratic society?) Anticipating objections to this practice, which still surround contemporary discussions on the power of judges, Hamilton wrote his famous *Federalist* 78, in which he provided a persuasive defense of the institution and practice of judicial review. In his opinion, judges could not be accused of acting against democracy when they declared a law unconstitutional. They could perfectly well annul a "democratic" law, for example, in order to protect the "even more democratic" will of the people expressed in the constitution. He did not accept, however, that through their interpretative powers the judges could directly define or re-create the content of the constitution and not simply enforce its commands. Because of this, judges could invalidate a law not *because* it openly contradicted the constitution but because *they were persuaded that it contradicted the constitution*, because they came to believe so. Not surprisingly, the judge who first declared a law unconstitutional was the extreme conservative John Marshall, a close ally of Hamilton and ex-president John Adams, in the famous case *Marbury v. Madison*.[125]

In Latin America, most leaders agreed upon the need to deal with the problems inherited from the former Spanish judicial system. Bolívar, for example, made reference to inadequate laws from "that welter of Spanish legislation which, like time itself, was collected from all ages and from all men, whether the works of the sane or of the demented, whether the creations of brilliant or of extravagant minds, and whether gathered from monuments of human thought or human caprice." For this reason, he asserted that "[this] judicial compendium, a monster of ten thousand heads" was "the most subtle punishment" that "Heaven" could have inflicted upon America. Although many Latin American political leaders recognized the need

---

[124] See Beard (1962; 1941).
[125] There are innumerable works to read on the topic. See, for example, Friedman (2002; 2009) or Kramer (2005).

for changing the Spanish system, they did not dedicate too much energy to the reorganization of the judicial system. The differences we find in this aspect from what happened in the United States probably have to do with the extraordinary powers they reserved to the president and the fact that nobody seriously disputed the elitist composition of the judiciary. Most important, Latin American conservatives did not see the legislatures as the main threatening force. The challenge, in this case, seemed to come fundamentally from "outside" the institutional system. For that reason, they wanted more than anything else to grant "emergency powers" to the president. From their viewpoint, the main source of conflict resided in the unchecked popular masses and not, as in the United States, in the unchecked legislatures.

Rights: "To Form Customs and National Character"

For conservatives, it was never easy to deal with the question of rights. They never felt comfortable with the bill of rights, either because they considered it unnecessary or because they believed that it would create too many dangerous expectations. Hamilton made both these points in *Federalist* 84. In his opinion, the proposed constitution was sufficient and included, implicitly among its clauses, many references to the demanded rights. In addition, he maintained that a bill of rights "would even be dangerous." The bill "would contain various exceptions to powers not granted; and, on this very account, would afford a flexible pretext to claim more than were granted." Bolívar seemed more clearly concerned with this second view, something that moved him to refer to the "exaggerated precepts of the rights of man," which, in the end, "disrupt[ed] social contracts and reduce[d] nations to anarchy."[126]

In spite of these reactions, and given the pressures on them to enact a bill of rights, conservatives accepted the need to include at least a few rights in their constitution. In most of these cases, however, they made it clear that the new rights were not absolute but, on the contrary, subordinate to other more fundamental values. Rights, then, were not seen as *unconditional*: they depended on and had to serve other more important interests. Conservatives assumed the existence of an external and generally divine moral scale, whose principles were intrinsically valuable and which the state should always protect

---

[126] Bolívar presented this view, for example, in his early "Manifiesto de Cartagena," of 1812.

and promote: the ultimate aim of education should be "to form customs and national character."[127] The defense and cultivation of these values, they assumed, guaranteed both personal and social order, while their violation threatened it. Using the "moral basis" argument, they argued that an attack upon, or an ineffectual defense of, the moral foundations of the country would lead to the debasement of the entire society. Because of these assumptions, then, individual rights were acceptable only insofar as they could be accommodated to those higher or more important external claims.

Juan Egaña – undoubtedly one of the most important representatives of constitutional conservatism in the region – provides us, again, with an excellent example of this view.[128] His project shows the importance he attributed to certain external moral values (Catholicism, in this case) and the subordinate role he reserved for individual rights. In his view, even the seemingly most fundamental liberties were seen as merely instrumental: their enjoyment depended on a calculus of costs and benefits, where religion appeared as the unit of measurement. He asserted, for example: "It is a mistake to allow every type of insult and calumny, to allow attacks upon the most sacred and inviolable principles of morality and religion, with the expectation of punishing its authors later.... *The sum of the evils produced by a free press on religion, morality, the mutual concordance among individuals and even the exterior credit of the nation is much greater than the goods it produces.*"[129] He added: "It is true that a man does not sacrifice the domain of his thoughts to the social pact; but he *has* sacrificed the domain of his external actions, for these can influence order and public morality, and society has the right to make them conform to

---

[127] Egaña, quoted in Collier (1967), p. 275.
[128] Egaña was born in Peru, although he lived all his adult life in Chile, where he acquired a reputation for his legal skills. His influential work was a first and fundamental step in the writing of Chile's first "Declaración de Derechos." Actually, this document consisted of the enumeration of political principles that included, for example, the concepts that the people of Chile were in charge of the internal government and the external affairs of the country and that they had established the Catholic religion as the country's only religion. He also wrote an early constitutional program in 1811 (which began with Rousseauean words, included a list of restricted rights, divided power into three branches, and established both a centralist government and a very strong executive authority). His main legal creation, however, was the constitution of 1823 and its additional moral code.
[129] Egaña (1969), pp. 84–85 (emphasis added). "In my own republic," he added, "I would only allow liberty of the press for those older than forty; but young people's works would always be subject to revision.... In all nations we find age requirements for becoming a senator, and advisor, a director of morality, religion, or education: why, then, should we allow the most corrupt and thoughtless to...teach and address themselves to the whole nation?" Ibid.

the state's system of political organization."[130] According to this view, in his proposed institutional system the only unrestrained activity was that of thinking. "Speech and writing," on the other hand, were open to regulation; "they belong to political jurisdiction," he argued, "since they can so greatly influence the domestic and social order."[131] These public expressions, he insisted, should not offend the "mysteries, dogmas, religious discipline, and the morality generally approved by the Catholic Church."[132] All written material, then, was to be subject to the preliminary "advice of good men," who would inform the writer of all the censurable elements which appeared in his work.[133] In addition, Egaña's constitution declared the Catholic religion to be the official religion of the country and seriously restricted the public practice of other beliefs.

In Gabriel García Moreno's model, too, the Catholic religion was declared the official faith of the country, "with the exclusion" of all others.[134] In accordance with article 9 of the 1869 constitution, the state was, again, obliged to use its coercive powers in order to protect Catholicism and ensure its public respect. Individual rights were also based on respect for its external values: article 2 of the constitution proclaimed that "the expression of thoughts" would be totally free from preliminary censorship as long as these expressions respected "religion, morality, and decency."[135] García Moreno justified the restrictions on a free press included in the new constitution, asserting that "the demagogic press, unbridled as never before, insults our religion and our chastity, calls for revolutionary passions and favors anarchy."[136] The church played a fundamental role in this structure,

---

[130] Collier (1967), p. 271.
[131] Ibid.
[132] Ibid. For Egaña, the right to freedom of the press would be recognized as long as it "contribu[ted] to the formation of morality and good habits; to the examining and discovering of all useful objects...; to expressing in a properly grounded way the civic virtues and defects of public authorities; to honest and decorous pleasures." See Donoso (1967), pp. 136–137.
[133] Donoso (1967), pp. 228–229. In his opinion, the morality approved by the church could not be challenged by anyone: it was "delirious" of anyone to try to question it. Ibid.
[134] As the president of Ecuador, García Moreno made clear that he was determined "to moralize the country," to put an end to the battle of "good against evil," and to do so through the "energetic and efficient repression of crime" and the "religious education of the new generations" (Castillo D' Imperio, 1998, p. 48). He ruled the country as he had first promised: he did not care much about the legal limits of his mandate, enforced the Catholic religion with the help of state violence, and reestablished political order by means of repressive measures.
[135] See Efrén Reyes (1942); Castillo D'Imperio (1998); and Borja y Borja (1951).
[136] Efrén Reyes (1942), p. 113.

given that, in accordance with a decree of December 1871, a group of its members had to check the morality of all materials before they were printed, including privately owned material that offended the church's morality. All questionable writings were then burned in a public ceremony. In a similar way, the constitution recognized the people's right to association as long as they "respected religion, morality, and public order" (art. 109). Moreover, the document explicitly established that these associations would be "under the authorities' surveillance."

Similarly, in this respect, article 16 of the Colombian Constitution of 1843 proclaimed that "the Apostolic Roman Catholic religion" was "the only faith supported and maintained by the Republic." The Colombian Constitution of 1886 went even further. It recognized Catholicism as "the religion of the Nation," proclaimed that all public authorities were required to "protect it and cause it to be respected as an essential element of the social order" (art. 38), and commanded that public education be organized and directed in accordance with the precepts of the Catholic Church.[137]

Other significant constitutions of the time, such as those of Argentina in 1853 and Mexico in 1857, were not written exclusively by conservatives. In these constitutions' final approach to individual rights, however, the influence of a conservative way of thinking was also evident. The progressive delegates who controlled the Mexican constitutional convention, for example, did not manage to obtain one of their main demands: religious tolerance. They simply succeeded, in the end, in preventing the establishment of religious *in*tolerance.

---

[137] The 1886 constitution was defined by Miguel Antonio Caro as "the best model of a conservative Constitution in the world" (Ocampo López 1990, p. 73). The constitution tried to put an end to the federalist era inaugurated by the constitution of 1832, which was blamed for the crisis of the "Supremos." The new constitution strengthened the president's authority and provided for the complete subordination of local authorities to the national government: the president, for example, could now appoint and remove governors at will. Ospina was also the man responsible for the profound educational reforms adopted during those years. Using these reforms, conservatives aimed to extirpate the influences of utilitarian thinkers who had been dominant at both schools and universities since Santander's administration. By that time, Rafael Núñez had assumed the presidency of Colombia, with the goal of "restoring" political authority in the country. The most important legal expression of the administration was, undoubtedly, this influential constitution of 1886, which was written mainly by Miguel Antonio Caro (Arango 2001; Sierra Mejía 2002). The document represented a strong reaction to the then prevalent and liberal constitution of 1863, distinguished by its anticlericalism and federalism. The new document, among other things, provided for a strong president, declared the Catholic religion to be the official religion of the country, and weakened both individual rights and the power of local authorities.

In Argentina, the more open-minded delegates had to confront a large group of conservatives. In this case, the conservatives were particularly strong because they knew that, in the end, all the delegates shared a common religious view. Their demands were extraordinary. During the debates they claimed, for example, that all employment, both public and private, should be open only to Catholics and that Catholicism should be the official faith and receive official support. Their arguments were both vigorous and offensive: they talked about the risks posed by pluralism, both to the internal structure of families and to the social life of the state, and they made reference to the evils of having Jewish or Muslim officers. "What could happen to us," claimed the delegate Pedro Ferré, "if a Jew or a Mohammedan occupied the presidency of the republic?"[138] "How could a judge give due protection to the Catholic religion without being a Catholic?" asked Manuel Leiva. [139] Returning to the "moral basis" argument, the delegate Pedro Zenteno, too, stated that "dividing our opinions and our religious feelings [freedom of worship] could drive us once again to the horrible anarchy we have just been through, caused by a diversity of opinions and political systems, which, unfortunately, have divided the Argentinean Republic, creating discord and civil strife among its members." In his opinion, the state could not and should not be indifferent to the diffusion of false and pernicious ideas that threatened public order. The affirmation of "one single sentiment, one single opinion and one political system" would be, rather, the best contribution to peace.[140] In the end, the Argentinean conservatives could not achieve many of their own most extremist demands; they obtained, however, important concessions to their claims. For example, in accordance with article 2 of the constitution, Catholicism was given a particular status, above that of other faiths. In addition, the constitution established the requirement of being Catholic as a condition for becoming the president of the country, granted respect for

---

[138] For Zenteno, too, freedom of religion tended to create unacceptable crises within the family: "It could happen that one day, your child, seeking support in the Constitution, could tell his parents: 'I do not want to follow your religion, the one that you accept and taught me. I want to be Jewish, or Mohammedan, or Protestant, using the liberties that the laws of the country give me.'" Ibarra (1993), p. 509.
[139] Ibid., p. 524. "Otherwise," he argued, "religions will become weaker, a general demoralization will develop, and later on we will have indifference to everything, which is even worse than a false belief, politically speaking." Ibid.
[140] Ibid., p. 508. Similarly, Ferré made reference to the risks of a caudillo who, taking advantage of the people's distress (a distress seemingly motivated by lack of protection for the Catholic religion), would defy the entire country, again under the motto "religion or death." This, he anticipated, would bring the government and the same constitution to an end. Ibid., p. 512.

"private actions" only as long as they did not offend God and "public morality," and demanded the conversion of Native American people to Catholicism.[141] In the end, if the Argentinean representatives did not go further in their conservative decisions, this was because, as they declared, they assumed that, in a fervent Catholic country like theirs, the strong hand of the state was not particularly necessary.

The conservatives' restrictive view on rights becomes apparent not only when examining legal texts. In most cases, their willingness to remove or dismiss certain fundamental rights became even clearer through the repressive politics that they promoted. By these decisions, they showed that they were ready to immediately restrict certain basic liberties in defense of their favorite moral values or in the name of social order.

One remarkable expression of this attitude appeared in the United States, when conservative president John Adams promoted the previously mentioned Alien and Sedition Acts.[142] Under the guise of defensive laws protecting national interests, Adams clearly repressed the activities of his political opponents. Using the first of these laws, the Alien Act, the president could deport those foreigners who put the internal order of the country at risk. The Alien Enemies Act authorized the deportation of foreigners from an enemy country and also the limitation of their rights, in case they remained. Finally, the Sedition Act provided for strict limitations on the press and authorized sanctions on those who conspired against the United States or published "malicious" information against the authorities. Even though parts of these laws were never implemented, they still allowed those in power to censor the press and imprison many of their opponents – among them, four of the five main editors of the Republican newspapers.[143]

In Argentina, the popular caudillo Juan Manuel de Rosas tried to reestablish political order and political stability through repressive measures, including the suppression of the most fundamental liberties. In fact, Rosas created a personal armed group, the *mazorca*, a group that President Manuel Isidoro Belzu, for example, re-created in Bolivia during this time to help him carry out numerous, cruel massacres. Together with the military and the church, the *mazorca* became one of the key factors in explaining Rosas's long stay in office.

---

[141] Curiously, even the most open-minded Argentinean delegates, such as José Benjamin Gorostiaga, enthusiastically defended the need for converting the Native Americans to Catholicism. Later on, he asserted, they could opt for another faith.
[142] See, for example, Spinrad (1970).
[143] Hentoff (1980), p. 83.

Of course, the use of severe violence was common during these years and particularly common under conservative administrations. In Latin America, we find many other examples of these authoritarian practices, such as that of General Flores or García Moreno in Ecuador,[144] Portales in Chile, Rodríguez de Francia in Paraguay, and Santa Anna in Mexico. Most of them assumed, as General O'Higgins commented to his Argentinean colleague José de San Martín, that the people needed "a big stick": "they are very revolutionary," he argued, "but nobody will joke when the whip cracks."[145]

The Regeneration of American Citizens

For conservatives, one of their fundamental missions was that of "regenerating" American citizens. An improvement in the moral qualities of the population promised very important consequences, both for the private life of each individual and for the public life of the community. By honoring the official religion, individuals would become at peace with themselves, while the community would also achieve social harmony: the status quo, in a way, would remain unchanged. Not surprisingly, then, a coalition of the richest part of the community, the church and the armed forces, always supported conservative proposals.

In a famous letter addressed to Santa Anna in 1853, Lucas Alamán offered a crude expression of this position. He argued that "property-owning citizens, the clergy and all those who desire what is best for their nation" all believed in the following principles:

1) that the Church and its privileges should be respected and protected, for the Catholic faith was the only tie left that united the Mexican people; 2) that any anti-clerical and anti-Catholic publications should be censored; 3) that the government needed to be strong, even though he stressed that it was important that it was subjected to certain "principles and responsibilities" in order that it did not abuse its power; 4) that the federation should be dismantled and replaced with a centralist system; 5) that any form of popular representative system based on elections should be eradicated for the time being; 6) that the army needed to be large, albeit suitable to times of peace; 7) that the army could be supplemented by militias made up of property-owning

---

[144] Flores's constitution of 1843 was known as the "Charter of Slavery." Notably, García Moreno's constitution of 1869, which followed the 1833 Chilean Constitution, became known as the "Black Charter of Slavery to the Vatican."
[145] Collier (1967), p. 241.

citizens, like those which had been formed under the colony; and 8) that Santa Anna, because of his energy, was the ideal person to lead this political proposal.[146]

Alamán was probably right in his portrayal of the ideology of the dominant sectors, which he understood well at that time.

Conservatives went far beyond their obsession with the extraordinary powers of the president. The constitution, they assumed, could also define the principles that should distinguish future public decisions: their favored principles could then receive the strongest legal support.

In some very important but also rather unusual cases, conservatives saw the constitution as a means of directly controlling the moral life of the community. According to this view, the constitution had to offer precise instructions regarding what values to honor and by which means. The most extraordinary example, in this respect, comes from Juan Egaña's legal proposals: Egaña was blindly confident in the transforming powers of legal instruments. These, he believed, should prescribe habits, exercises, duties, public activities, rites, and pleasures that "would transform laws into customs and customs into civic and moral virtues."[147] Thus, he proposed creating institutions, first a Tribunal de Censura and later a "Conservative Senate," that had not only the power of veto over all legislation but also the duty of guarding the moral behavior of the population.[148]

The "Conservative Senate," consisting of nine members, was in charge of the "mores and morals of the nation."[149] Some of its members had the obligation to visit, every year, the three provinces of the state, in order to examine "the righteous acts of the citizens, their morality, their civic activities and their religiosity." As guardians of morals, these senators carried a register in which they recorded the citizens' behavior. The senators had to promote the adoption of punishments and rewards for both sinful and virtuous citizens.

After the enactment of the 1823 constitution, these dispositions were more precisely defined in a group of laws also written by Egaña. He gave a particularly detailed account of his views in a moral code: it

---

[146] Fowler (1966), pp. 83–84.
[147] See Silva Castro (1969), p. 81.
[148] In his opinion, there were two main ways to foster civic virtues: "Transform laws into customs and customs into civic and moral virtues; and secondly, give prizes and honors for beneficial actions, public opinion being the only judge of these. In each state, elders or magistrates will evaluate [the good actions] and the people will reward one or more [of the selected cases]." Ibid., p. 87.
[149] Galdames (1925), p. 703.

represented, in his opinion, the best and most thoughtful expression of his lifelong theoretical reflections on morality. Although ultimately it was not sanctioned, the moral code deserves close attention, as it is an excellent example of an extreme conservative position.

The first part of the code was dedicated to religion and the need for protecting it. It regulated, for example, the way in which people were to celebrate the church's public festivities, as well as relationships between individuals and their confessors. In the second part, the code analyzed the family, its composition, and the interrelationships of its members. In this respect, it provided for strict sanctions on behavior such as ingratitude, vanity, denigration, or the abandonment of one's parents. The third part was concerned with education, which played a central role in Egaña's program. The code also regulated the use of alcohol, provided for strict parameters to follow in private and public ceremonies, and created prizes for the best citizens. "In our own times," he lamented, "there are no triumphs, Olympic games, civic crowns... we do not live under the sway of opinion and enthusiasm for national glory."[150] Egaña proposed, in addition, four major civic holidays, when virtues were to be celebrated and the deserving recognized. The first holiday was to be dedicated to national prosperity, the second to filial love, the third to agriculture and the arts, and the final one to the great national heroes. Moreover, the code demanded the creation of a new journal, the *Mercurio Cívico*, which would be published by the senate and be dedicated to questions of morality and civic virtue.

The moral code had a particular section devoted to arts and paid special attention to popular music. It defined, for example, the appropriate music to be used on different occasions: in public ceremonies, music had to be "majestic, simple and moving, in order to elevate and penetrate each person's heart." Moreover, Egaña's code regulated national dances, which, he argued, had to evoke the nation's triumphs and its patriotic accomplishments as well as the victory of virtue over vice. "No dramatic spectacle will be permitted which does not foment virtues," he asserted. The code proclaimed, in addition, a prohibition on circulating pamphlets and leaflets without the previous authorization of a group of censors. Finally, it insisted that each individual carry an identity document, without which they could be deemed an indolent or "unknown" person – something that authorized the local authorities to directly expel them from their jurisdiction. The code

---

[150] Collier (1967), p. 269. See his Moral Code, title X, in Egaña (1836).

included strict sanctions against those citizens who "created political parties and frankly displayed their opinions, or those who gathered in public places."[151] In accordance with its dispositions, the worst crimes were to be punished by garroting, at grandiose ceremonies. Other offenses, which included gambling, drunkenness, dueling, atheism, and satire, were also strictly penalized.[152]

In sum, the moral code created the strongest possible connection between the state and the moral education of the community. In its passion for detail and strict sanctions against the most trivial misbehavior, Egaña showed both his fanaticism and the extraordinary scope of his views.

Probably inspired by Egaña's proposal,[153] Bolívar promoted a secular version of Egaña's moral code. In order to advance this ideal, Bolívar created a new institution, which he annexed to the traditional three branches of power, and which he sometimes called the "Moral Power" of the nation. Bolívar made reference to this body in his famous "Letter from Jamaica" and at the Angostura Congress of 1819. In his Jamaica letter, he maintained that the new institution's main responsibilities were the design of educational plans, the promotion or restriction of written materials, and the promotion and protection of civic virtue. The new institution would consist of two chambers: the first, the oral chamber, would be in charge of publishing statistical tables with the existing virtues and vices, as well as comparative lists of the most virtuous and distinguished people in the nation. The second, the educational chamber, would control the moral and physical education of children, until the age of twelve.

In Bolívar's opinion, the new power was necessary in order to supply, through punishments and rewards, what religion and philosophy could no longer supply to society. "Religion," he argued, "has her thousand indulgences for the wicked, and philosophy offers many diverse systems, each favoring some particular vice. The one has binding laws and fixed tribunals; the other has only exponents with no codes or enforcement agencies empowered by political institutions." The "Moral Power," he believed, would be able to mediate "between these two extremes," authorized "both by fundamental laws and by the overwhelming force of public opinion."[154]

---

[151] Egaña (1836), title XII.
[152] See Collier (1967), p. 268. See his Moral Code, title XIII, in Egaña (1836).
[153] See Collier (1967), p. 279.
[154] Thus, in a letter to José Rafael Arboleda, June 15, 1823. There, Bolívar thanked Arboleda for his (rather isolated) support for this new branch of power. See Bolívar (1951), vol. 1, p. 382.

The new institution would consist of forty members, appointed for life and selected by congress from parents who paid special attention to their children's education and developed their public virtues in a suitable manner. In his view, members of the new institution had to "safeguard morality, the sciences, the arts, education, and the press." His program established that the new power would be mainly concerned with "moral and political works, newspapers and all other reading materials." The members of the new chamber, in addition, had to guard against ingratitude toward and mistreatment of parents, husbands, the elderly, teachers, magistrates, and virtuous citizens, as well as dealing with problems of breach of promise, indifference to public tragedies, and disgraceful conduct of relatives and friends.[155] The censors could "condemn to eternal opprobrium arch criminals and usurpers of the sovereign authority. They [could] bestow public honors upon citizens who have distinguished themselves by their probity and public service. The sceptre of glory," he concluded, "has been placed in their hands, for which reason the censors must possess integrity and conduct above reproach.... To these high priests of the laws I have entrusted the preservation of our sacred tablets, as it is for them to denounce the violators of these laws."[156]

In adopting this institution, Bolívar showed how much he cared about the moral development of the citizens as well as the importance he assigned to the public enforcement of a certain morality. Bolívar assumed that he, and the educated elite that accompanied him, practiced virtues that most people ignored. In the same way that Egaña's moral code was a complete failure, Bolívar's "Moral Power" was a fiasco. Bolívar defended its creation in all the constitutions he wrote; in fact, no other institution seemed to play such an important role among his proposals; but it was approved only once, in Bolivia, and for a very short time.

[155] See ibid., p. 192. He clarified, however, that the jurisdiction of the tribunal "should be effective with respect to education and enlightenment, but advisory only with regard to penalties and punishments." Notwithstanding, he also asserted that "its annals or registers containing its acts and deliberations, which will, in effect, record the ethical precepts and the actions of citizens, should be the public books of virtue and vice." These books," he added, "would be consulted [for guidance] by the people in elections, by the magistrates in their decisions, and by the judges in rendering verdicts." Ibid.
[156] Ibid., vol. 2, p. 598. Revealing the main source of his inspiration he argued that "[the] censors exercise a political and moral power not unlike that of the Aeropagus of Athens and the censors of Rome. They are the prosecuting attorneys against the government in defense of the Constitution and popular rights, to see that these are strictly observed. Under their aegis has been placed the power of national judgement, which is to decide whether or not the administration of the executive is satisfactory." Ibid.

The Ecuadorian president García Moreno is another important example of extreme Latin American conservatism. However, his case is partially different from those we have examined thus far, because García Moreno managed to implement and enforce his moralizing plan for many years. In order to carry out his ideas, the "theocratic" president frequently resorted to the coercive apparatus of the state. In his work, García Moreno was assisted by a large group of spies, who were in charge of controlling the most private aspects of each person's life. The president was proud of the system that he enforced because it allowed him to control all possible excesses. "I am alert," he maintained; "I have a system of spies and inspire fear [in my enemies]."[157] Thus, he imposed strict penalties on those denounced by his agents, without much attention to the rights of the accused and to questions of due process, in general. The constitution he promoted in 1869 came to legitimize his view and, thus, the consecration of the Ecuadorian state to Catholicism. In a public speech that he made defending his document, García Moreno objected to the "modern civilization created by Catholicism," which was losing its character and distancing itself from religious principles. This degeneration, he asserted, was the "illness of the century."[158] As a conservative, García Moreno prohibited different cultural expressions, including the theater, and provided for strict punishments for all those who lived a "licentious life." Concubines, for example, were imprisoned or deported and drunks were prosecuted and penalized.[159]

These cases do not simply represent stories about picturesque characters. In fact, many of the decisions that Bolívar, Egaña, or García Moreno adopted had enormous influence over their countries, as well as over other cultures.

Private Property and Political Rights: The Realm of the Wealthy

Conservatives, like radicals, were highly concerned with the need for securing certain basic preconditions as necessary requirements for having a good government. The two groups, however, had a very different understanding of these preconditions. The radicals proposed the expansion of political rights, to ensure a broader political participation, and favored changes in society's distribution of wealth,

---

[157] Carrión (1959), p. 437.
[158] Romero S. L. and Romero (1978), p. 115.
[159] Gálvez (1945).

to guarantee a more egalitarian economic structure. Conservatives concentrated their attention on two opposing proposals: they assumed that in order to preserve the basic values of the community it was necessary to ensure greater protections to the landowners and to limit the access of the masses to the political sphere, two intimately related objectives.

Conservatives, in fact, believed that the protection of property was required to secure the interests of the nation. As Blackstone had maintained long before, only the great landowners were effectively committed to the interests of the country: they not only had "a will of their own" but had a real stake in the nation's destiny.[160] Many other conservatives, however, associated wealth with intellectual capacity and therefore wanted to reserve a significant role for the wealthy in the political affairs of the community. Gordon Wood, for example, has shown that this was a very common view in the United States during the founding period – most conservatives considered that wealth, power, and intelligence went together.[161] The privileged defense of property rights promised an improvement in the rationality of the entire decision-making process.

The senate, as the mouthpiece of the "main interests" of the country and the voice of those who had "a stake in society," appeared to be an excellent institutional tool for articulating these elitist assumptions. General Paredes y Arrillaga openly recognized, in a letter to Santa Anna, written in 1842, that the "affluent classes are to politics what generals are to war."[162] In a similar vein, Lucas Alamán proposed in 1834 the creation of a senate that included, among its members, representation of "rustic, urban, industrial, and agricultural property (38 deputies); mining interests (14 deputies); liberal professions (14 deputies); the magistrature (10 deputies); literary professions (14 deputies); manufacturing industries (14 deputies); the public administration (10 deputies); the clergy (20 deputies); and the military (20 deputies)."[163]

Alamán sought to represent and guarantee the protection of these interests by reserving, especially for landed interests, a fixed place in the constitution. "It is necessary," he argued, "that proprietors, and in particular landholders...have a direct influence in legislation." Landed interests represented "the most stable [interest] and [that which was] most closely linked to the prosperity of the nation."[164]

[160] Blackstone (1844).
[161] Wood (1969).
[162] Fowler (1966), p. 72.
[163] See A. Lira's prologue in Alamán (1997), p. 53.
[164] Ibid., pp. 187–192.

Alamán also objected to attempts aimed at dividing the two chambers without ensuring in each of them different interests and suggested complementing such a proposal with another limiting the right of suffrage to property holders only.[165]

In line with Alamán's proposals, Bartolomé Herrera suggested the creation of a senate composed of the clergy, the military, scientists, representatives of the administration, landowners, mining and commercial interests, and the judiciary. The Argentinean Constitution of 1819 also included representatives of the church, the military, and the university as members of the senate. The Chilean Constitution of 1822, written by the intellectual José Antonio Rodríguez Aldea for General O'Higgins, created an unusual senate composed of members of the court, representatives elected by the chamber of deputies, former "supreme directors," ministers of state, bishops with jurisdictions within the territory, a magistrate of the supreme court of appeals named by that tribunal itself, three army officers appointed by the executive, the directorial delegate of the place where the congress met, a doctor of each university chosen by the faculty, and two businessmen and two agriculturists possessing capital of at least thirty thousand pesos, named by the chamber of deputies.[166] In the constitutions designed by both Juan and Mariano Egaña, we also find proposals of this type.

In addition, conservatives assumed that by limiting the people's participation in politics they could prevent the adoption of wrongful decisions, that is, decisions motivated by ignorance, envy, or hate. They also believed that the masses were too vulnerable to the action of demagogues or the bribery of a few and, because of this, susceptible to unacceptable outcomes. They felt that nobody needed more protection than the rich: they were a minority and the object of envy and hate. At the same time, they were absolutely necessary for the country's survival.

The idea of establishing strict restrictions on political rights was a common one even within the U.S. constitutional convention in 1787. In effect, in this case many of the delegates talked about the importance of establishing property qualifications as a prerequisite for obtaining the right to vote or in order to be elected. During the debates, one of the strongest defenders of property qualifications was John Dickinson, who stated that freeholders were "the best guardians of liberty; and the restriction of [political rights] to them...a necessary

[165] Ibid.
[166] Vanorden Shaw (1930), p. 93.

143

defense against the dangerous influence of those multitudes without property and without principle."[167] Gouverneur Morris also defended this principle against those who contended that the idea of a freeholder would not only be unpopular but also very difficult to define in practice: "The ignorant and the dependent cannot [be trusted] with the public interest."[168] John Mercer, from Maryland, supported these proposals on the basis of his belief that "the people cannot know and judge of the characters of the candidates."[169] In the end, these extreme proposals were rejected, but, notwithstanding, political rights were established in different measures at both the national and local levels.

In Latin America, too, many constitutions strictly limited the possibility of either becoming a citizen or having full political rights, or both. Among the conditions required, we find those of age, property, and literacy. According to Frank Safford, "Distrust of the political capacity of the mass of the people was reflected in the property qualifications established in almost all of the centralist constitutions of the 1820s and 1830s."[170] In some extreme cases, the constitutions even included the requirement of having certain "civic merit" in order to become a citizen, as happened in some of Bolívar's initiatives, or in the Chilean Constitution of 1833. In this latter case, "civic merit" depended on the previous fulfillment of one of the twenty-one conditions described in the constitution, all related to some particular service to the country. Among them were teaching; the improvement of a rural estate; legitimate fatherhood of more than six children; the study of medicine; free service in improving roads, hospitals, asylums, and public buildings; assistance for beggars, paupers, and the lame and halt; and encouraging the diffusion of religion and morals.[171] For this constitution, "the qualification of persons eligible for high offices was determined by the supreme director, the senate and the departmental councilors, who verified the fitness of from one to three persons for each vacancy."[172] The Venezuelan centralists objected to the extension of political rights even during the famous "Convención de Valencia." There, Pedro Gual argued that universal suffrage was a "luxury" and an "exaggeration." Miguel Maya asserted that the poor should not vote but be allowed to give only a vote of confidence; Prebendo Machado

[167] Farrand (1937), vol. 2, p. 202.
[168] Ibid., p. 203.
[169] Ibid., p. 205.
[170] Safford (1985), p. 363.
[171] Vanorden Shaw (1930), p. 102.
[172] Ibid., pp. 101–102.

stated that the illiterate and the poor should not be able to vote; the delegate Bartolomé Herrera maintained that the people were "ignorant" and an easy object of manipulation; and Hilaríon Antich justified the restriction of political rights because of the moral degradation that the country had suffered in former years.[173]

Moreover, most conservative constitutions dedicated a few articles to establishing under what conditions people would lose their citizenship or political rights, including, for example, the habit of gambling or "habitual drunkenness." In order to become a citizen of the country, Colombia's Constitution of 1843 proclaimed that one had to be at least twenty-one years old, own real estate or possess a certain amount of money, pay taxes, and be able to both read and write. The Colombian Constitution of 1886 provided for the suspension of the rights of citizenship in the case of "notorious mental derangement," because of a judicial order, in the case of habitual drunkenness, or when charges were pending in a criminal matter and a warrant of arrest had been issued. The Mexican Constitution of 1836 permitted the suspension of citizenship if one was a domestic servant, had been criminally prosecuted, or was illiterate. In addition, it sanctioned loss of citizenship in many other cases, including, for example, that of being indolent or lacking a "decent way of living."

Bartolomé Herrera was involved in two famous political disputes on these topics with two progressive political thinkers of his time, Benito Laso and Pedro Gálvez. During the first dispute, which included more than twelve articles written by Laso and eleven responses from Herrera, the cleric defended both the need for limiting the political rights of the people and the importance of concentrating the decision-making process in the hands of a few. In his opinion, those who ignored "eternal truths" were guided solely by their passions and caprices.[174] During the second dispute, held at the National Parliament, Herrera argued the importance of denying voting rights to illiterate Indians and "mestizos," given their "natural incapacity."[175] Herrera reflected this view, in addition, in his famous 1860 constitutional proposal; he linked the holding of citizenship with having intellectual capacity and being the owner of property. These requirements, which, in practice, affected most rural workers, servants, soldiers, and "indolents," implied for a majority of people the actual loss of their civil liberties.[176]

---

[173] See Gabaldón (1987), pp. 302–306.
[174] He said: "They wanted to recognize an absolute sovereignty in the will of the people, when God said that only he is the Lord." See L. A. Romero (1978), p. 142.
[175] Basadre (1949), p. 226.
[176] See Pajuelo (1965), p. 21.

In Ecuador, the authoritarian 1869 constitution went beyond all other conservative constitutions of the time. It proclaimed that one should be Catholic in order to become a citizen and considered affiliation to a society prohibited by the church to be a reason for losing citizenship.

Conservatism and Constitutionalism in the Americas: A Balance

In spite of the disputable nature of most of their proposals, conservatives made some important contributions to America's political life. Conservatives were particularly concerned with matters of order and political stability, two topics of primary importance after the independence revolutions. Undoubtedly, Americans had to discuss these problems; but when it was important to do so, they did not seem prepared to say anything very meaningful in dealing with them.

Many revolutionaries, and many radicals among them, simply dismissed these concerns, assuming that independence would bring with it the resolution of most social problems. Of course, this belief was false. Even worse, what usually happened was that independence revolutions were immediately followed by periods of economic crisis and political turmoil. Revolutions were economically very costly, and a new political order was difficult to stabilize. In addition, the populists' political actions and proposals were very problematic. Both their theories and practices created problems in terms of political stability, even if their goals were perfectly fair and justifiable. Radicals defended active popular participation in politics, which undoubtedly threatened the fragile order following independence. In addition, they sometimes encouraged counterinstitutional actions, such as rebellion against the courts, again affecting the establishment of a new order. Challenging them, conservatives insisted on the idea of order. They believed that political institutions should be capable of perpetuating their own stability. Of course, the methods they suggested for stabilizing the country were, to say the least, very controversial. However, the problem they posed for the political agenda was fundamental and one that their main adversaries did not take as seriously as they should have. More egalitarian thinkers simply disregarded the importance of this issue and eroded the basis of their own success in this way.

In addition, conservatives, more than any other group, insisted on the idea of maintaining the traditions and customs of the country. They acted in the name of "political realism," accusing their opponents of being too idealistic. Many of their opponents seemed to assume that the simple introduction of a few new ideas would have a fundamental and immediate impact on the life of the new countries. These activists possibly attributed too much importance to the impact of revolutionary ideas on the eventually successful independence struggles; they may have deduced that foreign political models would also provoke sudden and immediate changes in people's minds. But, in the end, these activists were also too naive and unsophisticated in their analysis. It was one thing to destroy an old and discredited political order and quite another to construct a new one. Revolutionaries seemed to believe that any change in the legal norms could bring a substantial change in the people's culture. Even worse, they sometimes seemed to believe that it was possible to introduce populist legal and political changes, no matter what the shape of the political culture into which they were introduced. In this sense, the conservatives' call for realism was not absurd. They taught their opponents not to put so much weight on theories or so much faith in the power of ideas. Conservatives taught their opponents to pay attention to the particular and the local: the most exciting egalitarian project could fail dramatically in the absence of certain basic social conditions, such as the existence of strong bonds of solidarity and a strong sense of identification among community members. Again, in this case, one has to admit that conservatives were touching a fundamental chord, even if one dislikes the melody that they were trying to play.

Finally, we should mention another very important contribution they made, an *unintentional consequence* of their work. In effect, conservatives helped to develop two fundamental political notions: the idea of minorities and the idea of rights. The conservatives' contribution mainly originated from a more specific concern, namely, with the fate of the "rich and well born." They wanted to protect *this* specific minority and *one* particular right, the right to property. The interests of this specific minority were identified, then, as the interests of *the* minorities.[177] Their support of a more or less unrestricted right to

---

[177] Hamilton was very clear in this respect. See, for example, Farrand (1937), vol. 1, p. 299. Madison had an identical approach to the concept of minorities. This approach, for example, became apparent in some of his references to the senate and its members. Thus, for example, he argued that the senate was an institution which aimed to "protect the minority of the opulent against the majority." Ibid., p. 431. This statement did not constitute an isolated opinion within his broader political conception. On the contrary, it represented a characteristic expression of his viewpoint. Typically, Madison employed terms such as "the rich," "creditors," "property owners," and "the minority" as related and interchangeable. In the same way, he used the idea of "the poor," "debtors," "those who are without property," and the concept of "the majority" as synonyms. There are good illustrations, in this respect, in *Federalist* 10, in his significant paper "Vices of the Political System," in many other speeches at the federal convention, and in the letters he wrote during

private property was presented as a support of *rights*, in general.[178] Conservatives were, as usual, very clear in their strategy. Even when they simply tried to abuse others using seemingly harmless and attractive concepts such as rights and minorities, they actually contributed to increasing their strength. They used time and resources to support certain fundamental political concepts, concepts that grew by themselves and finally escaped from the conservatives' control.

Although conservatives made some significant contributions, they created difficulties for the development of political institutions in America. In the first place, the way in which they abused the concepts of minorities and rights was prejudicial throughout America and, in particular, in Latin America. The fact that the same politicians who spent so much time talking about the importance of rights and the evils of oppression simultaneously ignored the mass violations of individual and group rights that occurred in America was undoubtedly detrimental to the survival of these key notions. We could say the same regarding their indifference toward poverty and huge inequalities. In the United States, at least, there were other political groups that, for different reasons, dealt more seriously with these questions and managed to rescue these fundamental concepts from their discredited position. In Latin America, however, the development of these concepts was more problematic. Many began to wonder why they should be concerned about rights if they only served to benefit a few. Why participate in any process of legal reform if the fate of the majority was always the same? Why care about institutions if, in the end, they always worked in favor of the same minority?

More significantly, many conservatives attacked the very notion of basic equality, which said that all people were born equal. Accordingly, they also promoted restrictive political systems that prevented the participation of the majority of the population. Their main political proposals were elitist: they wanted to concentrate the decision-making process in the hands of a few and, in many cases, succeeded in their

---

and after the convention. See "Vices of the Political System of the United States," Apr. 1787, Rutland and Rachal (1975), vol. 9, p. 355. See also his speeches of June 4 and 6, 1787 (ibid.); and his letters to Jefferson, Oct. 24, 1787 (ibid., vol. 10, p. 213) and Oct. 15, 1788 (ibid., vol. 11, p. 287).

[178] Robert Dahl supports this understanding of Madison's approach to the concept of minorities in the analysis of what he calls "Madisonian democracy." For Dahl, "the Madisonian style of argument provided a satisfying, persuasive, and protective ideology for the minorities of wealth, status, and power who distrusted and feared their bitter enemies, the artisans and farmers of inferior wealth, status, and power, who they thought constituted the 'popular majority.'" See Dahl (1963), p. 31. In contrast with this view, see Beer (1993), p. 281.

efforts. In this sense, we could argue that they consistently fought to erode the strength of egalitarian ideals. In the end, the force of the egalitarian principle, which said that all people were equally endowed with reason, proved irresistible. A page was turned in the history of Western society. No theory or politician could deny the force of that principle. Conservatives therefore found it more and more difficult to maintain their anti-egalitarian drive, at least in its original form. They either began to accept the force of certain egalitarian principles or found other more indirect routes to achieve their fundamental goals, such as electoral fraud, so popular in Latin America throughout the nineteenth century. Very slowly, then, conservatives began to change the main basis of their arguments. They began to point, for example, to the majority's lack of "technical capacities" or to the practical impossibility of holding adequate debates within large bodies. They therefore did not have to focus on the inequalities that separated people or on their incapacity for deliberation. This line of thinking is still popular within conservative groups and openly defended in public discussions. The discussion, however, seems blocked at this stage of the argument: in the end, conservatives and their opponents differ on their main epistemic assumptions, and there is no clear way out of that. Conservatives, in effect, insist on the idea that a debate among a few well-prepared people represents the best means for adopting or "discovering" correct decisions. Their opponents, however, tend to insist on a different view, maintaining that a public debate, open to the participation of all those potentially affected, tends to be better in terms of making correct or impartial public decisions. Although the philosophical point in question is difficult to resolve, it is important to remember that democratic societies are normally based on the values of the latter and not on those promoted by conservatives.

Finally, conservatives assumed that only a few know how to live and act, that most people just do not see what is good for them, and that the former have to force the latter into the right path. Their opponents, of course, attacked the conservative assumptions in different ways. These opponents supported tolerance and a respect for autonomous individual choices. They asserted that, with regard to personal matters, the use of coercion was not only not useful but also self-defeating, as the Mexican José Mata argued in the 1857 constitutional convention. They suggested a principle of equal treatment and reciprocity, as Pedro Moncayo did when he proposed not mistreating dissidents in order not to be mistreated by them after a change in power.[179] They

[179] Trujillo (1993), p. 121.

maintained, as did a few of the Argentinean delegates to the 1853 constitutional convention, that the legislature was simply not competent to deal with questions of personal faith, given that it was not a religious institution. They invoked Christian piety. They even appealed to the economic needs of the country, as most Latin Americans did, when they promoted religious tolerance. The argument went, How will we attract new immigrants if we do not respect their faith? The conservatives argued that the religion they supported was practiced by the majority of the country. They maintained that political order and social peace were prerequisites for any desired policy. They asserted that the immigrants who wanted to come to the country would come in any case, regardless of the state's attitude toward religion. What seems clear, in any case, is that the development of conservative ideas greatly affected the development of egalitarian ideas in America. Undoubtedly, in this sense, they must take an important share of the responsibility for the persistence of profound social, political, and economic inequalities in the continent.

The Conservative Legacy

Given the strength of some of their arguments and, above all, the political and legal force they held in support of their proposals, conservatives exercised an enormous influence over the development of American constitutionalism. In this sense, it should be stressed, they achieved an influence that radicals never managed. While the latter were normally ignored, defeated, or repressed, conservatives were able to advance their ideas from a privileged position.

The influence of conservatism becomes apparent when we focus, for example, on the role which most Latin American constitutions (or state constitutions in the United States) reserved for religion. In the first Latin American documents, this commitment to a particular religion appeared in its most extreme form: many constitutions, for example, declared an official faith, "without any tolerance" for others. Eventually, these initial declarations changed and the constitutions admitted the possibility of exercising alternative faiths in private; later they accepted religious tolerance. In spite of this, however, conservative pressures made it impossible to separate the church and the state as required in the U.S. national constitution. In many cases, then, Latin American constitutions reserved the most important public positions for Catholics (e.g., the presidency of the country, in the Argentinean Constitution of 1853); granted special constitutional status to Catholics; and, whenever possible, subordinated other fundamental liberties to the demand for respect of Catholicism.

With regard to the structure of government, the conservatives' influence was, once again, enormously important. It was partly because of their pressures that Latin American constitutions created such strong executive powers. The conservatives usually supported presidents with long terms of office, ample powers of veto, and "emergency" and extraordinary powers. In addition, they usually favored the presidents' powers to declare a *state of siege*, an expansion of his legislative and judicial capacities, and discretionary powers for designing his cabinet. Many of these proposals, which gave rise to a strong presidentialist system, still distinguish many Latin American constitutions and had a fundamental impact on the development of regional political life.

Today in both the United States and Latin America we still find powerful senates, which, in some cases, have "aristocratic" components, representing (as, perhaps, in the United States) the wealthiest part of society. One may still wonder, in this respect, whether senates, organized as they are, contribute to enhancing public discussion or to distorting it. The pressure from conservatives is also important to our understanding of the role and ample powers granted to the judiciary in most of the new nations. The powers that they gave to the judges, we must recall, included the right to have the "last say," even against the will of congress, in all constitutional cases – that is, in effect, in every important case.

The influence of conservatism also helps to explain the existence of weak legislatures, or the "distance" that still characterizes the relationship between representatives and the people in most representative systems. This influence also helps us understand the lack of means to foster popular participation in politics and the absence of adequate forums for promoting a reasonable public debate.

Latin American conservatives managed, in addition, to ensure that the church and the military had a special role within emerging institutional systems. Looking for arguments in favor of these proposals, they immediately found support in the political traditions of the region, characterized, for centuries, by the long-standing influence of these two groups. Undoubtedly, the activity of these groups turned out to be fundamental to their main purposes: they wanted to diffuse certain definitions of "the good" and to prevent any reactions against the order that they helped to establish. In some cases, conservatives reserved a particular institutional place for some of the members of these two groups. Thus, for example, in the constitutional proposals of Egaña in Chile, Lucas Alamán in Mexico, Bartolomé Herrera in Peru, or even in the 1819 Argentinean Constitution, we find special seats in the senate reserved for representatives of both the armed forces and the church. In other cases, conservatives included members of these groups in new, specially formed institutions, such as advisory councils. Finally, in many other situations, they used the constitution as a way to legitimize the influence of these groups, for example, by reserving a fundamental role for the military in the preservation of the national order.

Examining the conservatives' influence, it is difficult not to maintain that, in the end, they managed to impair the life of the American people. For example, their active campaign against fundamental individual rights certainly did not improve the lives of a majority of people in the region. In Latin America, in particular, their theoretical influence played a significant role in the actual justification of nondemocratic regimes or in a more general "devaluation" of the bill of rights. In addition, their influence on the distribution of political powers resulted in strong presidents and weak legislatures, which nourished a "poor" institutional dynamic.[180] Within these "hyperpresidential" systems, which were very common in Latin American countries, presidents began to concentrate the decision-making authority in their own hands, creating high expectations of their individual performance and "personalizing" the entire political system. Within such a context, political instability is often more frequent, given that the real or perceived failure of the president tends to represent a failure of the entire institutional system symbolized by his figure alone. The sad experience of Latin American countries, in this respect, only reinforces these fears.

---

[180] See, for example, among many others, the works of Linz and Valenzuela (1994); Nino (1997); O'Donnell, Schmitter, and Whitehead (1986); Przeworski (1991).

Chapter Three
Liberalism: Between Tyranny and Anarchy

The Sovereignty of the Individual

Liberal theory had a decisive influence on the development of American constitutionalism. Compared with the radical and conservative alternatives, it soon appeared an attractive option. In order to achieve this privileged position, liberals insisted on demonstrating the differences that separated their view from the two main alternatives present at that time. In some cases, they pointed to the past and highlighted the social violence and the political authoritarianism that distinguished the postrevolutionary years: liberalism, they promised, would prevent these situations from happening again. On other occasions, they simply announced the consequences that seemed to follow on from the adoption of rival positions.

Liberals were clever enough to identify the alternative conceptions with their most extreme and unacceptable features and to present their own conception as an ideal mediating position. The chief expression of this view was that which asserted the need for preventing the evils of tyranny and anarchy. Liberals such as James Madison argued that it was necessary to adopt a completely new set of institutions in order to ensure peace and social progress. The influential Mexican José María Mora also made reference to the importance of preventing both the absolutism of the despot and the tyranny of the majority.[1] The Argentinean caudillo Justo José de Urquiza, the politician mainly responsible for the enactment of the 1853 constitution, demanded the adoption of "a Constitution that made impossible both anarchy and despotism."[2]

---
[1] Jorrín and Martz (1970), p. 91.
[2] "Both monsters, he added, have engulfed us. One has covered us with blood; the other, with blood and shame." Quoted in J. L. Romero (1969), p. 152.

Even when both terms "tyranny" and "anarchy" were given different meanings on different occasions, the first was normally reserved to refer to the "arbitrary government of one," whereas the second was normally used to describe the "government of many." In Latin America and the United States, the notion of tyranny was often used to describe the absolutist political regimes that preceded the independence revolutions. North Americans, in addition, used the idea of "anarchy" to describe the chaotic period that followed the independence revolution and dominated the nation while the seemingly inefficient "Articles of Confederation" were in play. Many Latin American liberals, also, used the idea of "anarchy" to describe the regime of abuses that, in their opinion, characterized those regimes controlled by popular caudillos.

Liberals promised that, if they were in power, these two horrifying alternatives would come to an end. They would prevent the discretionary use of power and the tendency to use the legislature as a mere instrument in the arbitrary hands of majority groups. In addition, their government would put an end to the "moral dictatorship" that certain groups, particularly Catholic groups, wanted to impose on the entire society. Translating those claims into institutional terms, we could say that liberals proposed to ensure both the *equilibrium of powers* that their opponents destroyed or were unable to guarantee and certain basic *rights* that the opposition did not recognize or simply dismissed.

Although liberals had to confront radical and conservative tendencies in both the United States and Latin America, one should also recognize the important differences that existed between these two contexts. In effect, during the founding period in the United States, liberals encountered serious institutional opposition from radical groups. In Latin America, on the other hand, radicalism had almost no institutional power, whereas the conservatives had achieved enormous influence at all institutional levels.

In the United States, the more liberal tendencies increased their influence following the grave institutional crisis that came immediately after the independence revolution. During that period, principally between 1776 and 1786, the political situation was distinguished by a lack of a common government capable of coordinating efforts among the different states and strong enough to put an end to the frequent social conflicts that characterized these years. This was a time of intense political activism at the state level and of strong local legislatures. In the Federalists' view, this situation generated unfair outcomes; political decisions tended to favor just one particular group, the debtors – that is, the majority of society. In one of the most brilliant analyses of the time, published shortly before the federal convention in 1787, Madison made a clear reference to this problem. Aimed at examining the *Vices of the Political System*, the Virginian mentioned the numerous defects that affected the dominant institutional organization. Among them, he mentioned the states' lack of respect for federal authorities, the absence of laws for preventing political violence, and the frequent violations of national laws and international agreements. Most of all, though, Madison stressed the vices that derived from the "multiplicity," "mutability," and "injustice" of laws approved at the state level.[3] That is to say, in the analysis of one of the most lucid and influential thinkers of the time, the activism of state legislatures appeared to be the main source of existing social problems. In Madison's view, the representatives of the people were too obedient to the will of their constituency: they acted as mere agents of their voters.

In Latin America, the situation was entirely different. Within this context, nobody really cared what state legislatures did; nobody could realistically assume that the representatives were too close to the people. The "threat" of radicalism appeared because its enemies *anticipated* what radicals could do if they controlled the institutional machinery. But the fact is that the defenders of majority rule almost never controlled the national or local institutions. The place of the radicals was fundamentally extra-institutional: they wanted to occupy positions to implement a radical set of measures but never achieved such power.

On the contrary, conservatives achieved an enormous political influence over Latin America by actually controlling key institutions within the legal structure of the new nations. In this endeavor, the church and the military, two groups that already had a strong presence within the dominant institutional organization, usually helped them. As a result, in Latin America the conservative alliance represented, at least for long periods, the main institutional opposition to liberalism.[4] In contrast with what happened in the United States,

---

[3] Rachal (1975), vol. 9, pp. 345–358.
[4] The alliance represented, in Murillo Toro's view, "the same party that supported the King of Spain [during the colonial period]." Quoted in Torres Almeida (1984), p. 65. As the Ecuadorian Pedro Moncayo described them, they conceived of "liberty as the hurricane or anarchy, and the law as a source of rebellion and civil war." "Militarism," he argued, "...is the heir of despotism and inquisition, the defender of torments, grief and all the iniquities denounced and combated in 1810.... Supported by the clerical aristocracy and the bankers, they have been persecuting freedom of the press." See Villamarín (1993), p. 50.

Latin American liberals had to counter a group that supported the concentration of power and not its diffusion, as radicals wanted, and promised to limit the liberties that they most valued. These differences between events in Latin America and the United States help to explain what distinguishes the U.S. Constitution from most liberal Latin American constitutions. In both contexts, however, the liberals' response was made in the name of the individual.

As a theoretical starting point, liberals, in contrast with most conservatives, adopted the egalitarian principle that all individuals were born equal and equally endowed with reason. In their opinion, political institutions had to favor the well-being of individuals and be organized according to their actions and decisions. They also rejected the possibility of organizing the political life of the community in accordance with or in honor of any "divine" extrahuman authority. They rejected, too, the radicals' proposal of using coercion in the name of a particular majority or against any particular minority. Each person, they assumed, was important and deserved the respect of public authorities, regardless of their particular convictions or whether they belonged to the most numerous group of society.

Liberals defended the autonomy of each person, which they identified with each person's right to choose freely and develop his or her preferred way of life. This right had to be protected even when the programs of the few did not coincide or were incompatible with the conception of good preferred by the majority, or when they generated aversion in others. Liberals defended all ways of life as long as their development did not seriously harm other people's lives. They defended the equal right of each to decide and to act in ways that did not affect third parties. They assumed, as John Stuart Mill put it, that "over himself, over his own body and mind, the individual is sovereign."[5] Of course, it is not easy to define what causes a relevant harm in others and, therefore, to discriminate between what conduct should be permitted and what prevented through the use of the iron hand of the state. Nevertheless, most liberals tried to reflect that liberal principle, with varying degrees of success, in the constitutional texts that they proposed.

Juan Bautista Alberdi, an active intellectual, made an explicit and influential defense of liberalism. In his opinion, his country, Argentina, was in crisis because it lacked "the apparition and predominance of *individualism*, that is, of the liberty of men."[6] A free society was one

---
[5] Mill (1956), p. 13.
[6] Alberdi (1920), vol. 9.2, pp. 155–156.

that tried to honor its members by ensuring not only their freedom but also their general well-being. In the end, he assumed, a properly organized society should rely on the choices and initiatives of its members. Allowing the development of these choices, the development of the entire nation would also be encouraged. For Alberdi, "contemporary societies have progressed thanks to their *individuals*.... The growth of modern nations does not result from the freedoms of the Nation but from individual freedoms. Because of the latter, men have been able to achieve... their own personal grandeur, an elemental factor in the grandeur of the really important and free nations."[7]

Liberals' concluded that nothing was as dangerous for personal freedom as the coercive powers of the state and its coercive apparatus. Given the scope and permanence of its power and its indisputable strength, the state always appeared as the dark cloud in the liberals' dream. Not surprisingly, liberals directed most of their efforts to the task of limiting the state: only a state with very limited functions and strictly controlled by independent agencies seemed compatible with the freedom of individuals.

Liberals basically had two strategies for restricting the movements of the state. The first was to "shield" individuals by establishing "barriers of protection" around each of them. The second was to operate on the state's political apparatus itself in order to hinder its movements, making it more "heavy" and slow.

Moral Neutrality: A Wall of Separation

In order to ensure individuals' interests, liberals tried to "shield" individuals' lives. They wanted, as Jefferson graphically stated, to build a *wall of separation* between individuals and the state.[8] Granted, the

---

[7] Ibid.
[8] He wrote: "Believing with you that religion is a matter which lies solely between man and his God, that he owes account to none other for his faith or his worship, that the legislative powers of government reach actions only, and not opinions, I contemplate with sovereign reverence that act of the whole American people which declared that their legislature should 'make no law respecting an establishment of religion, or prohibiting the free exercise thereof,' therefore building a wall of separation between church and State.... Adhering to its expression of the supreme will of the nation on behalf of the rights of conscience, I shall see with sincere satisfaction the progress of those sentiments which tend to restore to man all his natural rights, convinced he has no natural right in opposition to his social duties." Letter to the Danbury Baptist Association, Jan. 1, 1802, in Jefferson (1999), p. 397. Reproducing ideas similar to those of J. S. Mill, he stated, "Difference of opinion is advantageous in religion.... Is uniformity attainable?... What has been the effect of coercion? To make one half of the world fools, and the other half hypocrites.... Reason and persuasion are the only practicable instruments." Jefferson (1984), p. 286.

image of a wall of separation was primarily used to refer to the need for preventing the use of state coercion in religious matters. However, that image helps us to see the liberals' general approach to the issue of the coercive powers of the state. In the end, liberals wanted to build a wall of separation that protected each person from the arbitrary imposition of *any* conception of the good, a wall that kept the iron hand of the state away from the people's beliefs.

The image of the wall makes an interesting starting point when we examine some of the key ideas normally associated with this view: individualism; the defense of tolerance; the commitment to a "neutral," secular state; the distinction between the "public" and "private" spheres; the concern with the idea of rights; the promotion of a "countermajoritarian" institutional procedure; and the bias against the powerful state.

The model proposed by liberals was that of the tolerant state, one that allowed individuals to live according to the principles they chose. This state allowed each person to adopt and promote his or her ideology and allowed each person to cultivate the talents and ideals he or she preferred. Today, we tend to describe this type of state as the "neutral" state. In spite of the difficulties that exist for giving a precise content to that concept, the *neutrality principle* that liberals defended would basically say that the state should not take sides in favor of any particular conception of the good. The state should not use its coercive powers in favor of or against any view of the good. As long as individuals do not interfere excessively with the lives of others, neither should the state.

Perhaps the best example we find in America of the adoption of this neutrality principle is the one from the United States. There, many liberals developed a sustained crusade against the establishment of a religion, first at a local and then at a national level. They wanted to prevent the state from using its force and its resources in favor of a particular faith. James Madison was, once again, a key figure in this movement toward neutrality, which recognized a fundamental antecedent in the work of Roger Williams in Rhode Island.[9] Madison, in collaboration with George Mason, wrote the first "Declaration of

---

[9] During the colonial period, Roger Williams was obliged to escape to Rhode Island because of the religious persecution he suffered. He settled in the city of Providence, where he fostered the celebration of a municipal compact that proclaimed that the will of the majority would be respected only with regard to civilian questions. Later on, the authorities of Providence, in alliance with those of other neighbor cities, wrote a document that proclaimed, in its preamble, that all men could follow the dictate of their consciences and honor their own god.

Rights," which came to guarantee complete religious freedom to all Virginians. Every person, they argued, had an equal right to follow his conscience in religious matters. However, politicians like Patrick Henry, an important representative of what we describe as radicalism, opposed that declaration. Henry proposed supporting the different Christian churches through taxation, arguing that the decline of religion would imply a decline of morals. Against his proposal, Madison argued that the state lacked the authority to demand those payments. Moreover, he asserted that the absence of a prevalent and protected religion would not necessarily imply the moral decay of society. This disgraceful situation could come about, for example, because of inadequate and unjust laws or the lack of a good educational system, but not as the product of a "neutral" state.[10] Trying to give theoretical foundation to his views, Madison also wrote his well-known paper "Memorial and Remonstrance against Religious Assessments." In this document, supported by numerous adherents, he asserted the importance of blocking Henry's initiative, which appeared to be the first step toward the establishment of a religion. As Konvitz asserted, Madison feared that "the removal of some stones from the new wall of separation of church and state in Virginia might lead to the collapse of the wall and to state support of religion in general."[11] Madison's successful campaign contributed, in addition, to the success of Jefferson's Bill for Establishing Religious Freedom in Virginia.[12] This was probably the first law in the world enacting complete religious freedom.

There are many factors that may help us to understand the partial success of the principle of neutrality in the United States. First, many of the new colonists suffered from religious persecution, either in their country of origin or in the United States, so they all knew the dangers of establishing a nonneutral state. Second, religions were many and varied in the United States, so none could claim to be the fundamental and deeply rooted religion of the entire country, as would happen in Latin America. In addition, it is also worth mentioning that the new immigrants brought with them new theories propounded by Locke, Montesquieu, and Voltaire, which certainly contributed to building

---

[10] Konvitz (1957), p. 22.
[11] Ibid., p. 24.
[12] The bill, finally approved in 1786, proclaimed that "no man shall be compelled to frequent or support any religious worship, place or ministry whatsoever, nor shall be enforced, restrained, molested, or burthened in his body or goods, nor shall otherwise suffer on account of his religious opinions or belief; but that all men shall be free to profess, and by argument to maintain, their opinion in matters of religion, and that the same shall in no wise diminish, enlarge or affect their civil capacities."

an intellectual consensus in favor of tolerance. In the end, the important issue is that the 1787 constitution, through the First Amendment, prohibited the U.S. Congress from establishing a particular religion or preventing any person from freely exercising his own faith, an event that marked the history of the United States deeply.[13]

In Latin America, as in the United States, tensions between the church and national authorities largely transcended the independence revolutions. In fact, many of the most important disputes that characterized Latin American politics during the nineteenth century had a religious source: Should the church maintain the *fueros*, the judicial privileges, that it has? Should the church keep the extraordinary amount of land that it acquired during the colonial period? Should it be possible to tax the citizenry to support Catholicism? Should the clergy continue to control education, as it had done for the last four hundred years? Could the support of Catholicism imply the restriction of fundamental rights?

The influence of the Catholic Church in Latin American societies was extraordinarily important for centuries.[14] In addition, and throughout those years, no other faith challenged the supremacy of Catholicism, and no other ideology limited its monopoly and influence in educational matters. In spite of this, or maybe because of it, in the first era of independence (1810–1825) the power of the church began to decline. The new "enlightened" ideas, which fascinated most of the revolutionaries, were not particularly favorable to the power of the church. In addition, the church was closely associated with Spanish power, which seriously affected its authority and prestige. At the time, even the most reactionary political leaders rejected, and managed to promptly abolish, the Inquisition and reaffirmed their rights over the church, such as the right to appoint to the higher ecclesiastical offices, the rights of the *patronato*. However,

---

[13] The First Amendment of the U.S. Constitution reads as follows: "Congress shall make no law respecting an establishment of religion, or prohibiting the free exercise thereof; or abridging the freedom of the press; or the right of the people peaceably to assemble, and to petition the Government for a redress of grievances." Granted, the liberal group was not mainly responsible for the creation of the First Amendment, but its previous work in favor of religious tolerance justifies the fact that, sometime after its enactment, the amendment became the symbol of liberalism.

[14] During the whole colonial period, the church undoubtedly played a primary role in the organization of the "new" societies, in close alliance with public authorities. Only during the Bourbon period, and through some of the reforms that it proposed, did this strong alliance moderate some of its policies. The Bourbons favored a more decentralized political organization, adopted a more tolerant policy toward Native Americans, and to some extent reduced the legal and economic privileges of the church.

the tensions between the interests of the church and the needs and demands of the new governments were multiple: the number of properties in the hands of the church, its wealth, and its judicial privileges generated new animosities against the religious authorities.[15] And the latter did not respond pacifically – according to Leslie Bethell, the church "reacted not by intellectual debate, for which it was ill prepared, but by appeal to the state to suppress the enemies of religion."[16]

The most significant rupture between the state and the church appeared in a second, later period (1845–1870) distinguished by a stronger liberalism and also a stronger defense of fundamental individual freedoms. During this era, disputes about the scope of the church's power were more intense and frequently the cause of violent social conflicts. Normally, liberals played a leading role in these confrontations. At that time, for example, the Ecuadorian deputy Pedro Moncayo promoted the adoption of more "neutralist" policies: "It is necessary...not to confuse religion with politics [because] the object of the first is eternal happiness and the object of the second to attain social happiness....a political assembly [should not] extend its powers beyond the limits necessary for achieving the formal and material well-being of the people."[17] In Peru, the famous priest Francisco de Paula González Vigil made a valuable contribution to the liberal cause, writing a six-volume book on the need for separating the church from the state.[18] As a member of parliament, González Vigil, violently criticized by Bartolomé Herrera and also by other progressive thinkers such as Francisco Xavier Luna Pizarro, campaigned for many liberal initiatives,[19] including

---

[15] There is a clear parallel between this situation and that of the armed forces. Not surprisingly, liberals needed to confront both.
[16] Bethell (1985b), p. 231.
[17] Trujillo (1993), p. 121.
[18] Francisco de Paula González Vigil represents one of the most emblematic and interesting figures of Peruvian liberalism during the nineteenth century. He consistently defended the liberal ideal and combated authoritarianism. In this respect, González Vigil gained national reputation after a speech he gave in November 1832, in which he accused President Agustin Gamarra of going beyond his powers and in this way violating the national constitution.
[19] Against him, Bartolomé Herrera claimed that "Peru, free from the Spanish authorities, is still the servant of the Lord, and only in this servitude can it find real liberty." González Vigil proclaimed the need for separating the church from activities that did not belong to its jurisdiction and ridiculed Herrera's claims. In his opinion, the liberties that Herrera defended were those of "the prison and the sepulchres." In addition, the liberal priest defied Herrera's assertion that the people were not prepared to participate in politics. Herrera considered that what González Vigil was espousing was "close to the socialism of Proudhon." "Lock yourself up in your library and don't

proposals for limiting the properties of the church and for abolishing the death penalty.[20]

The Peruvian priest was not alone in his crusade. For example, the Mexican José María Mora, one of the founders of the best liberal traditions in Mexico, defended state neutrality and also the limitation of the church's privileges. In Argentina, too, the bishop of Catamarca, Fray Mamerto Esquiú, played a decisive role in securing the enactment of the new constitution of 1853;[21] at a moment when most religious authorities were boycotting the document, Esquiú made a famous speech in its favor: "Obey the Constitution.... Without obedience there is no law, without law there is no fatherland and no real freedom; there are only passions, anarchy, dissolution, war, and evils."[22] This fight for religious neutrality continued throughout the century. Liberals had to confront influential people like Pedro Goyena, who believed that the word "neutrality" was "only a euphemism, used in order avoid a more direct, genuine, precise and terrible word: atheism!"[23]

Liberals' promotion of religious neutrality was soon translated into a different and broader claim, one prohibiting any kind of state intervention against an individual's personal convictions. For liberals, individuals should be able to enjoy their "privacy," a "space" free from public interference. The "private" sphere appeared, therefore, as a sacred and intangible area where each individual was the absolute sovereign. On the other hand, in the "public" sphere, state action was allowed in principle. From then on, liberals were concerned with how to establish, keep, and justify strict limits on the state – limits that separated what the state could justifiably do from what it could not do. They became experts in "the art of separation."[24]

In the end, what liberals were doing was defending an *antiperfectionist* view: they believed that, in all personal matters, individuals should be allowed to decide what they wanted to do freely. Consequently, they denied the conservative claim that objectively

---

come to disturb the tranquility of our students or to take the country into religious anarchy." See González Marín (1961), pp. 180–185. See also Ballon Lozada (1986).

[20] The Chilean Lastarria, who defended, in his country, very similar proposals, praised González Vigil's work in a letter to the Argentinean Bartolomé Mitre. To Lastarria, the Peruvian liberal priest had performed an outstanding achievement in indicating how to distinguish between secular and religious tasks. See Varona (1973), p. 42.

[21] Argentina's new constitution ratified and partially modified what came to be known as article 19, which represented a strong commitment to the principle of state neutrality (see Sampay 1975).

[22] J. L. Romero (1969), p. 154.

[23] Quoted in Botana and Gallo (1997), p. 203.

[24] See, for example, Larmore (1987); Walzer (1984).

"better" conceptions of the good exist, which people should pursue in order to have a good life. In their opinion, each person was in charge of deciding what was good or bad for him or her. There were no objective ways of life to be enforced by the use of the state's coercion. Every person, they assumed, should be considered equally able to decide what was good or bad and should freely decide how to shape his or her own future.

This concern with the autonomy of individuals distinguishes liberals from both radicals and conservatives, who, though for different reasons, proposed a certain kind of moral perfectionism, one that called for the use of the coercive powers of the state regarding "personal" matters. Both groups campaigned for the demolition of the liberal wall of separation.

Political Neutrality: The Procedural View

Liberals knew that it was not enough to merely sanction a bill of rights in order to protect people's autonomy. They soon realized that it was also necessary to act upon the state's internal structure: its organs and its innate mechanisms. Most of all, liberals recognized the importance of preventing two possible institutional outcomes, namely, the accumulation of powers in the hands of one person and the discretionary use of majority rule.

For them, public power had to be exercised according to individuals' preferences: the state had to be fully respectful of the people's choices. The Colombian intellectual Florentino González, author of three fundamental constitutional programs in his country, argued that this was the feature that distinguished, and should always distinguish, American politics from European politics. "In America the main principle says that political institutions must be based on the liberty and sovereignty of individuals. The community has no rights but to do what is necessary for the liberal cause. In Europe, on the other hand, the main principle is that government can sacrifice individuals in the name of the community. Socialists build their system upon the European principle... true democrats build theirs upon the American one.... In America individuality and in Europe the community. Here we have two banners; here we have the two conflicts."[25]

In the end, these two visions, one more liberal, the other more radical, had at least one thing in common: a contractualist foundation. Both views, in effect, assumed that the main reason for respecting

[25] Quoted in Molina (1973), p. 86.

public authority was that it originated in an agreement among the people. Both views therefore rejected the pre-Enlightenment idea that the community had to be organized in accordance with the will of a "divine," extrahuman authority. Liberals, however, did not accept radicals' claim of the primacy of the community over each of its individual members. In order to respect individual freedom, one had to free each person from all possible oppressions, including the oppression of the community's majority.

A free and respectful society, liberals assumed, should allow each person to develop his or her own personal projects as far as they wanted, insofar as they respected other people's rights. A free society, they said, should not "imprison" its citizens with regulations that impaired the possibility of their reaching agreements with others or pursuing their own programs. On the contrary, it should create public procedures that made it possible for its members to live according to their own desires and preferences. Michael Sandel, for example, defers to this view of a "procedural" position, saying that, for liberals, "[since] people disagree about the best way to live, government should not affirm in law any particular vision of the good life. Instead, it should provide a framework of rights that respects individuals as free and independent beings, capable of choosing their own values and ends. Since this liberalism asserts the priority of fair procedures over particular ends, the public life it informs might be called the procedural republic."[26] To organize the life of a community from a proceduralist perspective means to reject what we may call a "substantivist" position. The community, liberals assert, should not impose its "substantive" views on what is a good economic, political, social, or cultural life. The life of the community should always be open to the different initiatives of its members. Its particular "contents" should, in the end, be defined *spontaneously* – that is, in accordance with the autonomous choices of its members. Its shape should be that decided by its members, through the formal or informal contracts that they formed between themselves. The Colombian intellectual José María Samper canonically synthesized these ideas in his famous *Ensayo sobre las revoluciones políticas y la condición social de las repúblicas colombianas*. There, Samper asserted that in modern societies *spontaneous* processes favored balanced results. In defending this "social spontaneity," he defended liberalism, which he defined as an *individualist, anticollectivist,* and *antistate* position.[27]

---

[26] See, for example, Sandel (1996), p. 4. See also C. Taylor (1989), pp. 172, 178.
[27] Samper believed that "the Northern races have the spirit and traditions of individualism, liberty and personal initiative. In those societies the state appears as a

In his view, it is necessary to legislate as little as possible and to renounce the mania of regulation and imitation. In old societies, where interests are complicated and have deep roots, the regulation of social life is not justifiable, although understandable. In new societies, however, which are exuberant and unruly, regulations mean stagnation. Hispanic-Colombian rulers have an obsession about ruling in a European way, copying their systems, which are not suitable for the New World. This has produced the most absurd of all contrasts – regulations in a democracy, two ideas that are mutually exclusive. If what we want is to have stability, liberty, and progress in Hispanic-Colombia, what we need is public officers who adopt the practice of regulating as little as possible, trusting in the good sense of the people and the logic of freedom; they should make efforts to simplify situations, suppressing all artificial questions whose only purpose is our mutual embarrassment.[28]

Samper's view helps to clarify the outlines of the liberal position. His defense of spontaneity, like his fears of an interventionist state, implied an anticollectivist position and, in the end, an antimajoritarian one. For liberals, the presence of a strong majority group always carried with it the possibility of having this group "capture" the state, using the state's powers for its own benefit. Who could prevent the majority from doing so? Who could avoid this risk, when an oppressive majority already existed?

Many Latin American liberals were afraid of having to face such a situation. In the United States, however, liberals actually confronted that dreadful possibility. In many different states, in fact, the majority group managed to control the decision-making process and use the state's apparatus at will. James Madison gave an excellent explanation of liberals' fears in *Federalist* 10: "If a faction consists of less than a majority, relief is supplied by the republican principle, which enables the majority to defeat its sinister views by regular vote. It may clog the administration, it may convulse society; but it will be unable to execute and mask its violence under the forms of the Constitution. When a majority is included in a faction, the form of popular government, in fact, enables it to sacrifice to its ruling passion or interest

---

consequence, and not as a cause, as a guarantee of the law, and not as its source, as an aggregation of forces, and not as the only force. Therefore, we find the habits of calculation, creation and individual effort. Our Latin races, by contrast, substitute calculation with passions, individual effort by improvisation, individual action by the action of the masses, the rights of all detailed in every one by a collective right that engulfs it all." See Jaramillo Uribe (1964), p. 50.

[28] Samper (1881), pp. 486–488.

both the public good and the rights of other citizens. To ensure the public good and private rights against the danger of such a faction, and at the same time to preserve the spirit and the form of popular government, is then the great object to which our inquiries are directed." At this time, the main point of liberals' theoretical reflections, and of their constitutional discussions, was to define how to limit the majority will. By limiting it, they assumed, they would prevent the "colonization" of the state and ensure individuals' liberty. This proposal was therefore consistent with their concerns for each person's life: liberals wanted to strictly control the behavior of popular majorities because they wanted to protect minority groups.

Now, the goal of protecting minorities is undoubtedly legitimate and worthy, though it may also turn out to be too costly. In effect, liberals' concern with minority rights may result in a weak democratic system – that is, a democracy where the majority group is deactivated, unable to fulfill even its most harmless plans. Clearly, we need to prevent excesses and avoid the enforcement of merely irrational decisions, but how much are we prepared to lose in order to avoid the impulsive decisions of a particular majority? The liberal project, at this point, may sound curious: it is both blindly confident about individual choices and decisions and blindly unconfident about collective choices and decisions.

Once again, liberals' asymmetric reactions may be easily explained. On the one hand, they are not so much concerned with individuals' actions because the latter are not as threatening as collective actions, in that a majority may easily take control over the entire decision-making process. On the other hand, liberals know that a collective deliberation may be affected by problems that are not normally present in the isolated deliberation of an individual. For example, large groups may face serious time constraints that prevent each person from presenting his or her viewpoints; large groups may be easily controlled by demagogues; and so on.

These are good reasons justifying the introduction of certain distinctions when dealing with individual and collective decisions. However, this approach still has some problems. The fact is that, in America, the previously mentioned reasons were only partially used. If liberals tried to disable majority groups, this was because of other less interesting and less justifiable assumptions related to the irrationality of majorities. They believed that majorities had an unbridled tendency to adopt irrational decisions. "Has it been found that bodies of men act with more rectitude or greater disinterestedness than individuals?" asked Hamilton. His answer was that "the opposite of this has been inferred by all accurate observers of the conduct of mankind."[29] "The people," he concluded, "collectively from their number and from their dispersed situation cannot be regulated in their movements by that systematic spirit of cabal and intrigue."[30] Hamilton's opinion was widely shared by most of the U.S. "founding fathers."

In the end, the countermajoritarian bias of liberalism was reflected in the adoption of antimajoritarian institutions, namely, institutions that retained an opaque role for popular majorities within the decision-making process. Their defense of proceduralism implied a defense of institutions that were hostile toward both collective meetings and collective discussions.

From the Sovereignty of the People to the Sovereignty of Reason

Throughout all of America, liberals were required to confront political forces that represented the past and called for a more traditional form of political organization. In the United States, however, the independence revolution seemed to solidify a widely shared social agreement: none of the dominant forces wanted to recreate any form of authoritarianism where an external power, such as the British monarchy, defined the internal political organization of the country. There was, so to speak, a "republican agreement." The presence of this agreement does not mean that in the United States there were no conservative forces after the revolution. These forces were undoubtedly present and influential. However, their demands also had a limit regarding what could be expected from the new societies. The situation was different in Latin America, where the same republican game seemed to be at risk: the institutions inherited from Spain had not incorporated most of the population, and most political conflicts, even after the independence revolutions, seemed to take place fundamentally "outside" the existing institutional structure. The alternative of subverting the entire republican project was attractive to many and supported by large parts of the population that felt no personal commitments to the creation and preservation of the dominant institutional framework.

In Latin America, the need for articulating an anti-authoritarian discourse became particularly strong during the first few years of independence. At that time, many conservatives openly defended

[29] *Federalist* 5.
[30] *Federalist* 76.

authoritarian or quasi-authoritarian proposals as a way of both restraining the impact of new revolutionary ideas and definitively consolidating independence. Typically, the two greatest military leaders of the independence struggle, San Martín and Bolívar, supported monarchical alternatives. Even when some liberals, in despair after the independence crisis, also found those alternatives attractive, most rejected them and heroically fought against all types of authoritarianism. Most Colombian liberals – Vicente Azuero, Ezequiel Rojas, or Florentino González, among them – assumed the difficult task of confronting Bolívar and his political proposals.[31] Many Ecuadorian liberals, led by Colonel Francisco Hall, offered their lives for the anti-authoritarian cause shortly after the independence revolution.[32] The Peruvian liberals,[33] led by José Faustino Sanchéz Carrión and Francisco Luna Pizarro, carried out a remarkable battle against the creation of a monarchical or quasi-monarchical political structure.[34]

This reaction was necessary again in the middle of the century, when Latin American conservatives attempted to restore antiliberal values, following the "restoration" period that was taking place in

---

[31] González regretted having recognized Bolívar's authoritarianism so late: "Since it became apparent that [Bolívar's efforts] were not directed at establishing a Republic and a Democracy... our fascination [with his figure] turned into horror toward the ambitious person who had frustrated all our expectations and wanted to use for his personal advantage everything that the people had done for their right to selfgovernment. His death caused no pain to our people. The only people who lamented it were those who had favored his [authoritarian] plans." F. González (1975), p. 182. José María Samper referred to Bolívar as the representative of "monarchy, colony, and barbarism." Rodríguez Albarracín et al. (1988), p. 238.

[32] Hall was an English colonel, a disciple of Jeremy Bentham who had traveled to America, encouraged by Simón Bolívar. Once he arrived, Hall participated, with General Antonio Sucre, in many battles in favor of the independence cause (the famous battle of Pichincha, among them). Founder of the famous Sociedad el Quiteño Libre, Hall organized the newspaper with the same name (later directed by Pedro Moncayo), which, in its defense of liberal principles, strongly confronted Bolívar's authoritarianism and Flores's arbitrary regime (Ayala, 1993). Fearing the intellectual capacities and political skills of his opponents, Flores commanded the assassination of Hall and more than one hundred of Hall's allies in October 1833. See Villamarín (1993).

[33] A first generation of Peruvian liberals, led by Luna Pizarro, Sánchez Carrión, Francisco Vigil, and Benito Laso, among others, had a profound impact on the early institutional developments of the country. Many of Peru's first constitutions, those enacted in 1823, 1828, and 1834, reflected their liberal views, particularly regarding the position of the executive.

[34] Both political leaders, however, betrayed the liberal cause a few years after they had ardently fought for its advancement. In effect, Sánchez Carrión began to collaborate with Bolívar's dictatorship after his splendid defense of liberalism in the constitutional convention of 1823. Similarly, and as the archbishop of Lima, Luna Pizarro became the main enemy of González Vigil, who was at the time the main representative of the liberal cause.

many European countries. Then, once again, many liberal groups led a decisive battle against authoritarianism. As examples, we could offer the lucid criticisms against Rosas's regime that the so-called Generación de 1837 advanced from its exile; the achievements of the radical liberals in Colombia against the conservative forces that controlled the country after the war of the Supremos; the solitary fight of people like Pedro Moncayo in Ecuador; the provocative and courageous pages of the first liberal newspapers in Venezuela; and the fragile but consistent fight of Chilean liberals, like Victorino Lastarria, against decades of authoritarianism.

Because of their confrontation with authoritarian forces, Latin American liberals began to develop certain fundamental ideas, decisive for republican and democratic causes. First of all, they began to argue against the persistence of all legal privileges, such as those that had favored the military and the church for centuries. In Argentina, Mexico, and Colombia, these early and intense fights decisively shaped the political life of their communities, at least during the first half of the century. Similarly, they campaigned for the adoption of strict limits and controls within the political system, particularly those aimed at restricting the power of the executive body. Moreover, these fights strengthened their commitments to federalism: the atomization of power appeared to be an excellent means for avoiding the prevalent authoritarian tendencies.

When we examine the relationship between liberal and conservative forces we find not only disagreements but also much in common between the two; they both shared certain fears (e.g., an unbridled majority) and cherished certain values (e.g., property rights). What is most important, they both seemed to share certain elitist attitudes regarding the capacities of majority groups. In the United States, however, liberals were extremely careful on this topic and tried not to repeat in public some of the judgments they made behind the closed doors of the constitutional convention. In Latin America, the strong public presence of conservative leaders and the limited role played by popular majorities at an institutional level to some extent helped liberals to be more open about their final assumptions. In Latin America, therefore, more obviously than in the United States, many of them used openly elitist arguments that clearly contradicted some of their liberal and egalitarian principles. One of the most interesting and influential cases in this respect is that of Argentina's liberals.

In effect, most of the members of the Generación del 1837 assumed that the people were not well prepared to assume a fundamental role in politics. In order to give some substance to their claim, they distinguished between the *sovereignty of reason* and the *sovereignty of the people*. In their opinion, the continual discussions on sovereignty were confusing, because the advocates of self-government did not recognize that it was not the time to affirm the complete sovereignty of the masses. Domingo Sarmiento provides us with an excellent example of this position. In Argentina, Sarmiento symbolized then, and still does today, the image of the "good educator," the person who dedicated most of his life to creating a strong educational system. In this sense, like many liberals, Sarmiento assumed that the people could improve their intellectual capacities and deserved the opportunity to do so. However, Sarmiento's passion for education had to do with, among other things, his conviction that the people were actually ignorant. In his time, he assumed, it was irresponsible to act as if the people were fully capable of participating in the discussion of the public affairs of the community. The will of the nation, he argued, "is only expressed through the reason of educated men, and this is what is called national reason....We are democrats with regard to the establishment of liberty in favor of national reason [but we oppose the] national will." He concluded that "wherever the masses, the national majorities, have the will and the means for expressing its will we will have...the affirmation of a popular caudillo representing the instincts and beliefs of the numeric majority [acting against the desires of the educated minority]."[35] In this way, Sarmiento both objected to French democratic and egalitarian ideas and defended a representative democracy led by the educated minority.[36] In saying so, Sarmiento continued and strengthened a way of thinking fundamentally developed by two other noteworthy members of the same group: Esteban Echeverría and Juan Bautista Alberdi.[37] What they all claimed was not the union of the sword and the Cross, as conservatives claimed, but rather the union of the sword and intelligence.[38]

Thus, in his "Dogma Socialista" Echeverría had famously asserted that "the sovereignty of the people is absolute when it has reason as its norm. Only collective reason is sovereign, and not the collective will. The will is blind, capricious, irrational: the will only has wants; the reason, instead, examines, balances, decides."[39] Democracy, he

---

[35] See Pérez Guilhou (1989), pp. 56–57.
[36] "The colonial system, he believed, has habituated the U.S. to expect everything from the constitutional authorities." The new representative system had to favor, instead, the free initiatives of the people. Pérez Guilhou (1984), p. 158.
[37] See, for example, Svampa (1994), chap. 2; Corblit, Gallo, and O'Connell (1965).
[38] Terán (2008), p. 99.
[39] Echeverría (1915).

said, was not "the absolute despotism of the masses or the majorities, but the regime of reason."[40] Similarly, Alberdi stated that "liberty does not simply reside in the will but also in the intelligence...that is why sovereignty belongs to the intelligence. The people are sovereign when they are intelligent."[41] Alberdi believed that the majority of the people were incapable of governing themselves: "Suffrage by the multitude where the multitude is incapable of it...can produce no other practical result than placing the country's government in the hands of...those who are best at getting votes through coercion or trickery....Any country governed by the ignorant multitude...unfailingly has at its head tricksters and masters of intrigue."[42] In Mexico, the extraordinary liberal thinker José María Mora espoused similar ideas.[43] Inspired by Benjamin Constant, Mora was a systematic critic of majoritarism,[44] arguing that "national sovereignty is the sum of individual sovereignties....It cannot be communicated in itself." He denounced the evil consequences of fostering radical equality and objected to proposals that favored an unrestricted democracy. He defended the establishment of strict limits upon the legislative power: the failing of this, he said, would cause "all the evils suffered

---

[40] Echeverría assumed that sovereignty was the "greatest and most solemn act of reason of a free people." Therefore, all those who were unable "to discern between what is right and what is wrong" should be prevented from taking part in the elections. The "ignorant people," he believed, had no opinion of their own and were ready to compromise the liberties of the country or accept the suggestions of ill-intentioned people. Ibid., pp. 185–186.

[41] In his "Fragmento para el estudio del derecho." See also Pérez Guilhou (1984), p. 84.

[42] Quoted in Shunway (1993), pp. 150–151. Also, he stated that "to elect is to discern and to deliberate [but the ignorant] cannot discern...misery cannot deliberate, it sells itself. To take away suffrage from the hands of ignorance and indigence is to ensure its purity and [its success]." Alberdi (1886), vol. 5, p. 66. And he asked: "[Can't you restrict the suffrage] because demagoguery taught you to exploit [this situation]? Then, do not suppress it but create different degrees and applications: let some people elect the legislators and let the others elect the municipal authorities." Ibid.

[43] Educated in a religious and conservative environment, Mora became a professor of theology and participated in politics as an adviser of Vice-President Valentin Gómez Farías, who fulfilled presidential duties during General Santa Anna's long absences from power. Inspired by both Montesquieu and Benjamin Constant, Mora gave solid theoretical foundations to early Mexican liberalism. He fought against Agustin de Iturbide's discretionary powers, criticized Bolívar's, and also strongly opposed the privileges of both the church and the military. In the same way that he resisted despotism and authoritarianism, Mora, like most liberals, denounced the risk associated with the more radical and egalitarian political conceptions. He believed that the country was not ready for a classic type of democracy and, following Benjamín Constant's teachings, recommended instead the model of a democracy of proprietors.

[44] For Constant's ideas on the representative system, see Roldán (2002).

during the last fifty years by the peoples [of Europe] who have adopted the representative system."[45] Popular passions, he believed, tended to turn majoritarian bodies into "passive bodies" subject to "the will of a small number of factious charlatans and adventurers."[46] We find similar opinions among the advanced Colombian liberals of the 1850s, particularly among the so-called *gólgotas*,[47] and among the Chileans of the time. In Latin America, therefore, liberals obstructed, rather than favored, the advancement of more progressive and democratic ideas.

The Economy: The Politics of Laissez Faire

The model of institutional organization proposed by liberals was fundamentally coherent. According to our previous analysis, they conceived of the state as the main threat to individual freedoms and used all their energy to reduce it to its minimal expression. Freedom was seen as the necessary consequence of an absent state: the lesser the role of the state, the greater the room for freedom. In order to limit the influence of the state, liberals argued for the protection of individuals' rights and the creation of strict controls over the different branches of power. In this way, they assumed, factious leaders occupying public positions would find it very difficult to impose their malicious and oppressive projects. As James Madison said in *Federalist* 10, these types of measures made "[a] rage for paper money, for an abolition of debts, for an equal division of property, or for any other improper or wicked project...less apt to pervade the whole body of the Union."

In their approach to economic issues, liberals simply extended these ideas. Once again, they assumed that state interventionism was the source of most evils. In order to respect people's liberties, it was necessary to allow them to choose freely and carry out their economic initiatives. The parallel they established between the moral, the legal, and the economic order seemed irreproachable; the state,

---

[45] See Hale (1986), pp. 86–87.
[46] Ibid., p. 100.
[47] José Florentino González, for example, claimed "we want, then, an enlightened democracy, where intelligence and property lead the destiny of the country; we do not want a barbarous democracy where proletarians and the ignorant [make public happiness impossible] and bring confusion and disorder....the class of the poor and the ignorant should be raised to the level of the enlightened and rich; but intelligence and wealth should not be destroyed in order to equalize [these two classes]....this would be to aim for degradation instead of perfection. We will, then, be opposed to the leveling doctrines, which in their demands for liberty and equality try to nullify intelligence, knowledge and wealth, so as to [equalize] all in a common disgrace." Quoted in Molina (1973), p. 59.

they assumed, had to be neutral regarding the people's different conceptions of the good and their different preferences. It should impose no conception of the good life upon the people, as it should impose no economic regulations. By contrast, it was necessary to simply organize a framework that allowed each person to pursue his initiatives. Individuals' preferences had to prevail and occupy the place of the state's preferences. *The personal life of each person should depend on autonomous choices as the public life of the community should depend on the particular initiatives and agreements of the people.* Any state intervention against these individual options was then seen as an unacceptable irruption into the life of the people, only capable of distorting the free will of the citizenry.

The former criteria tell us something about the "invisible hand principle," advanced by Adam Smith and adopted by most liberals in postrevolutionary America. According to this view, state intervention in the economic sphere was deemed not only morally reproachable but also impractical. The Argentinean Domingo Sarmiento argued that "the power and strength of a nation depend on the [moral capacity] and intellect of the individuals that compose it."[48] The protection of each individual's freedom was therefore not only just but also necessary for the growth of the country. In fact, liberals assumed that self-interested agreements negotiated by different individuals would actually make this growth possible.

Many liberals, both in the United States and in Latin America, defended this view, which contradicted the independent economic policies that were most common before independence. These were characterized by regulations and monopolies, which certainly did not favor the development of the colonies. Liberals opposed monopolies as much as they opposed communally held Native American lands or the concentration of land in the hands of the church, which obstructed the free circulation of land. While the "invisible hand," the absent state, promised growth, prosperity, progress, and liberty, monopolies or immobilized resources represented scarcity for most and benefits for only a few. Not surprisingly, then, we find throughout all the American countries testimonies of distinguished liberals defending the state's abstinence in the economic field.

An interesting example of this view, developed in the first half of the century, is that of Bernardino Rivadavia in Argentina.[49] First,

[48] Quoted in Halperín Donghi (1975), p. 244.
[49] Rivadavia spent many years in Europe, from 1812 (when he was removed as secretary of the Primer Triunivirato) until the 1820s. In Europe he was in close contact with Jeremy Bentham and other significant intellectuals of the time. Bentham would

as a minister of Martín Rodríguez's government (in 1821) and, after February 1826, as the president of the republic, Rivadavia tried to radically modernize society. An extreme liberal, he put forward the idea that each person should assume responsibility for his own life. In line with this assumption, he not only tried to ensure basic individual liberties but also opened up the economy of the country. He fostered foreign inversions and immigration, reduced the privileges of the church, and tried to mobilize the land previously owned by Native Americans through the so-called law of *enfiteusis*.[50] He also obtained a substantial loan from the British company Baring Brothers and tried to enlarge the labor market (often by, arguably, unorthodox liberal methods).[51] At the same time, in New Granada, Vice-President Francisco de Paula Santander advanced another important set of economic policies that, with some significant exceptions, can also be classified as favorable to economic liberalism. Like Rivadavia, Santander also tried to favor the "free initiatives of individuals." In this sense, for example, he decided not to use the state's resources in favor of agricultural or mining projects; their success, he assumed, had to depend on the efforts and wealth of individuals' initiatives.[52] In addition, he suppressed internal tolls and other taxes that threatened these personal efforts. He combated the system of *gremios*, which he assumed opposed the principle of laissez faire; abolished the state's system of assistance toward the poor; and promoted the division of Native Americans' communal land. For Bushnell, Santander's government assumed that its role was that of creating the most favorable conditions for the development of private enterprises; within that favorable context, each individual should then strive for his own development, in accordance with his own preferences.[53] In spite of this, though, and like Rivadavia, he combined his orthodox economic liberalism with other unorthodox programs.[54] In Ecuador, President

later praise Rivadavia's public initiatives, although he would distance himself after his unsuccessful experience as president. See Gallo (1998).

[50] Originally, the idea of the law was to give land for long-term use, while the state remained its proprietor. However, the state's inability to collect the established duties, the fact that there existed no limits on the quantity of land to be distributed to each, and the manipulation of some speculators transformed the law into a means of concentrating property in the hands of a few.

[51] For Halperín Donghi, Rivadavia's economic liberalism found a sudden discontinuity in this area: his laws against the "lazy" and the "vicious," aimed at introducing them into the labor market, were harsh and intolerant. See Halperín Donghi (1975), pp. 350–351.

[52] See Bushnell (1954), p. 154.

[53] Ibid., p. 192.

[54] Like Rivadavia, he also forced the "lazy" to enter the labor market and kept certain areas of the economy under state protection (e.g., tobacco).

Vicente Rocafuerte, who had been a brilliant leader in opposition and an excellent advocate of liberalism, combined a strong authoritarian government with economic liberalism. In his opinion, it was necessary to "remove all the obstacles that prevented the free circulation of industrial and agricultural products," abolishing all types of monopolies and privileges.[55]

Since the late 1840s, Florentino González had been an active defender of laissez faire doctrines in New Granada. Curiously, González began to advance his liberal economic program as minister of finance for General Tomás Mosquera, one of the most authoritarian rulers of the first half of the century. González had arrived from England in 1846 and was well acquainted with extreme liberal views for organizing the economy.[56] His economic plan, at the time, included the abolition of the tobacco monopoly, a decision strongly resisted by Santander during his mandate, and an important 25 percent reduction in duties. Arguably, these radicalized measures helped liberalize the entire Mosquera regime.[57] However, they also seriously affected the domestic artisans, who then became the main group supporting José Hilario López's ascendance. Once in power, López forgot his supporters and followed González's economic plan even more closely. López enacted a radical set of measures that promoted both political and economic freedom. Among many others, they included the end of the Native American common lands, the total abolition of slavery,[58]

---

[55] See Ayala (1995b), vol. 7, p. 174. Vicente Rocafuerte was a significant figure within Ecuadorian liberalism. He had lived many years outside his country and studied history and law. In Mexico during the 1820s, he was a leader of the liberal opposition. When he returned to Ecuador, he defended and tried to import the U.S. federalist and liberal system to his country. In doing so, he also became an active political opponent of Flores, particularly after he was elected to congress. President of the country some years later, he promoted economic liberalism, which he combined with harsh political repression. By this time, his early political liberalism as well as his promotion of federalism had vanished.

[56] In Gonzalez's opinion, the only way to escape from the contemporary economic crisis was through the creation of wealth. The growth of "big interests" that came together with the creation of wealth represented a gift for the government. On the one hand, their need for order and public peace would force these interests to ally with the government. On the other hand, the rebellious poor would also be forced to respect these interests, given their need for securing their own subsistence. See Molina (1973), pp. 56–57. José María Samper's brother, Miguel, supported, with González, a rather elitist liberal view, primarily directed at protecting the rich and well-off. His writings include, for example, an important exchange between him and Murillo Toro, who sharply criticized his defense of laissez faire.

[57] Bushnell (1993), p. 99.

[58] For Bushnell, "Underlying the measures on slaves and Native Americans was a concerted effort to eliminate restrictions on free movement and allocation of property and labor." Ibid., p. 107.

the elimination of most tax burdens, and the elimination of academic degree requirements to enter the professions.

In Peru, a remarkable group of well-educated liberals, which included, among others, José Simón Tejada, Fernando Casós, and Silva Santisteban, campaigned for economic liberalism as a way of preserving freedom and improving the well-being of the lower classes.[59] Similarly, José María Químper showed the continuities that existed between the liberal objections to the privileges of the church and the military and the objections to labor unions and the state's regulations of the economy. Químper also criticized those who, "abolishing freedom in the name of labor...tried to resuscitate the old system of...worker associations...with one variance...equality of salaries: absurd equality! [They believe that] production should be paralyzed and distribution equalized." In his opinion, nothing could help the growth of work opportunities but "freedom and [the pursuit of] personal interest."[60] We find similar convictions in many other leaders such as General Carlos Soublette in Venezuela, where the promotion of economic liberalism was in the hands of conservative groups, or General José María Linares in Bolivia.

In Argentina, Alberdi defended free trade in some of his most important works, such as *Bases*, the text that he prepared before the constitutional convention of 1853.[61] During his more liberal period, he argued for laissez faire policies, which he began to espouse after encountering the writings of Herbert Spencer and Adam Smith. "All the cooperation the state should give to [our growth should consist of] creating a safe context where life, property, industry, and peace are guaranteed."[62] In all other tasks, he anticipated, the state was

---

[59] In his work *Emancipación de la Industria,* Tejada defended the need for providing the poor with the possibility of obtaining their sustenance independently from the government. This freedom would allow each person to pursue his own projects and would favor public life. A world of employed workers would be a peaceful and progressive world because "the industrious, occupied man does not want war or upheavals. We should not prevent that possibility by establishing limitations and regulations....Industry, is a terrible social power when hampered and a fundamental social power when respected and protected. Occupation is the main foundation of order." See Leguía (1939), p. 137. Also, in criticizing the political activism of Peruvian artisans, he stated that "if artisans could not fully accept free markets and free trade...they had no one but themselves to blame for their poor political performance." Quoted in Gootenberg (1993), p. 135.

[60] Químper (1948), pp. 67–68.

[61] He also argued in favor of protectionism in some of his previous writings, such as in his "Fragmento Preliminar," and in some of his late works.

[62] "Private initiatives have done a great deal, and a great deal of good, as Spencer [stated]....[They have] fertilized our soils and built our cities, discovered and exploited mines, created routes, opened channels." He claimed that the actions of

condemned to fail. On those occasions, he argued, the state acted "as an ignorant"; it could only impair, instead of favor, the interests of the country.[63]

Alberdi represented a fairly extreme, but not totally unusual, position among liberals. In one of his most famous and remarkable defenses of freedom, he made a sharp distinction between civil and political freedoms and asserted that the state should "distribute" them in a different way. Political liberties, which included the right to vote, should be restrictively distributed. "I do not share [the fanatic and inexperienced position] that it is necessary to freely distribute political freedom."[64] Most people, he assumed, were not able to use these freedoms properly. By contrast, "economic freedoms" had to be distributed unrestrictedly among "natives and foreigners." These civic freedoms included freedoms such as those to "buy, sell, work, navigate, trade, travel, and undertake any industry."[65] These freedoms, he assumed, would help bring new people to the country and, therefore, enrich and civilize it. Political liberties, on the other hand, were neither necessary nor demanded by foreigners, who looked only for their well-being and for peace and dignity for their families. In addition, political liberties became, in the hands of locals, "the instrument of ambition and unrest."[66]

According to these views, the actions of the state and those of the individual appeared to be guided by different and opposing principles, which were incompatible. Acting alone, individuals seemed capable

---

the state, and never those of the individuals, brought poverty to the country. Alberdi (1920), vol. 6, p. 159. In similar terms, the Peruvian Tejada objected to the public authority that "pretended to know it all and, for that reason, pretended to decide it all: it prescribed the selection of raw materials, prohibited certain procedures, fixed the quality of our products, its form...its color....The state was the merchant who traded tobacco, salt, coffee, sugar, snow, cards, explosives, paper...the exclusive manager of banks, channels, bridges, routes, mines and everything else. Its regulations...defined the laws of offer and supply while economic law was silent." Tejada (1947).

[63] "The state intervenes everywhere, everything is done because of its initiatives....The state becomes the producer, the constructor, the entrepreneur, the banker, the merchant, the editor and, therefore, is distracted from its essential and only mission, which is that of protecting the individuals against all internal and external aggressions." Alberdi (1920), vol. 6, p. 157. He added that "individual liberty...is the main and most immediate basis of all [the] progress, all [the] improvements and all the conquests of civilization....But the most terrible rival of...civilized countries is the omnipotent and all-powerful fatherland, personified in omnipotent and all-powerful Governments, that do not [want that freedom] because it is the most sacred limit to its omnipotence." Ibid., pp. 170–171.

[64] See his "Sistema Económico y Rentístico," in ibid., vol. 14, pp. 64–65.
[65] Ibid.
[66] Ibid.

177

of achievements that the state, which in a way could give force to collective demands, tended only to destroy. Asserting this view, liberals reaffirmed their confidence in the individual and their distrust of the state and of collective actions in general. "Societies that await benefits from the hands of Government," said Alberdi, "await something that is contrary to its nature. Because of the nature of things," he added, "each man is in charge...of his own well-being and progress."[67] As Vicente Rocafuerte argued during his liberal years, it was necessary to put an end to all state monopolies that appeared in the political, religious, or economic spheres.[68] Arduously promoted by liberals during the first half of the century, Manchesterian economic principles would become prevalent within the dominant elite (composed of both liberals and conservatives) by the middle of the century.

Constitutionalism

Most American constitutions still reflect the enormous impact of liberal thinking. After the colonial period, in both the United States and Latin America, liberal ideas were the most important, and they replaced the political authoritarianism and moral perfectionism of the previous years. Yet the liberals' quest was only partly successful. Although liberals were able to change many constitutions, they did not manage to immediately reverse the dominant traditions, as most of them desired and many others expected. In addition, liberals could not put in motion and stabilize their preferred "institutional machine," at least in most cases. In America, the only really successful experience of a liberal constitution is the U.S. Constitution. In most other cases, what we have is either very liberal but also short-lived constitutions or interesting liberal projects that, after passing through the constitutional convention, evolved into liberal-conservative projects.

In contrast to what happened in Latin America, delegates in the United States were forced to abandon their more conservative aspirations. The states were too strong to be ignored, and they were not going to accept any initiative from the central authorities that came to concentrate political power in the hands of a few. They wanted federalism, a decentralized political system, and demanded additional rights that allowed them to create an indestructible fence against the central state's interventionism. In addition, the local states were

---

[67] Ibid., p. 139. "When, in those societies, the people...need to improve the public interest, they look at each other, they look for each other, they gather together, they discuss and reach an agreement, they work by themselves." Ibid., p. 139.
[68] Rocafuerte (1960).

sufficiently well organized to back their demands. They had been constructing their power base for many years and had strong political institutions that supported their arguments.

Of course, the success of North American liberalism was not simply due to the difficulties faced by the most conservative. Liberals had some extraordinary figures on their side, such as James Madison, who knew how to deal with the political climate of the period. They knew, for example, that even though the states were too strong, a majority of the people was hostile toward their more populist demands. The period following independence had been chaotic enough to result in the idea of adopting a loose national agreement or to defend still quite uncontrolled legislatures. The system of "checks and balances," which was then proposed, fitted in perfectly with these different and competing pressures.

In Latin America, after the declaration of independence, liberals were also strengthened by the presence of many talented characters, but the social and political situation dominant at the time made things difficult for them and their institutional projects. External conditions were unfavorable: because the Spanish wanted to reconquer their territories by force, liberals were hardly able to advocate a system of balanced and strictly controlled powers. Internal conditions were also difficult. In many cases, the new countries lacked a well-organized set of political institutions but had wealthy elites or powerful military leaders who challenged new institutional projects aimed at establishing political controls and securing equality before the law. Because of this, the numerous liberal initiatives we find both before and after the 1850s could not prosper as they did in the United States.

The Argentinean Rivadavia represented, perhaps, the most interesting example of a liberal reformer. A close disciple of the revolutionary Jeremy Bentham, he introduced numerous reforms, including a new constitution, property reform, the creation of the University of Buenos Aires, universal suffrage, and a new economic policy. His proposals were ambitious and far-reaching. However, Rivadavia never had the chance to put them into practice for long, as he was forced out of office before his term was up.

The case of Santander, in New Granada, has some similarities with that of Rivadavia. Santander was also an imaginative and active reformer, admired Bentham's work, and occupied significant public positions at different times during the first decades of the nineteenth century. Even though he managed to stay in power for longer periods than Rivadavia, he also had to confront the unrelenting pressures of conservative forces during his mandate. In addition, many of his initiatives were reversed when he finally lost power in the 1840s, when the moderates took control of the state's apparatus.

During these initial years, the Peruvians were even less successful in their reformist plans, but they managed to approve different constitutional texts that to some degree restricted the extent of the president's authority, an important objective at a time when there were so many voices clamoring for a strong executive. The Chilean liberals were weaker than their neighbors: the more conservative groups appeared to control the whole political arena, leaving little space for liberal initiatives. In the late 1820s, a breeze of federalism let them enact the quite liberal constitution of 1828. Shortly after, however, the conservatives regained political control of the country and maintained it for several decades. The case of Mexico was rather strange; the strength of the conservative forces was, in this case, exceptionally important. However, we still find interesting liberal initiatives and important liberal thinkers, such as José María Mora.

After the 1850s, external threats had basically disappeared, making the case for monarchism or political authoritarianism much less plausible. However, many Latin American countries had already suffered, and put an end to, violently conservative experiences that they did not want to repeat anymore. This was clearly the case of Argentina, after the terrible period of Rosism, and of Mexico, after the chaotic years of General Santa Anna. Not surprisingly, both the Argentineans and the Mexicans managed to enact at that time liberal constitutions (the Argentineans in 1853, the Mexicans in 1857), which were clearly written with an eye to the authoritarian past.

The Chilean liberals passed through a somewhat similar experience of conservatism, although by the beginning of the 1860s the political scenario was also favorable to the introduction of liberal reforms. In New Granada, liberals regained power at the end of the 1840s, managed to enact extremely liberal constitutions, but were seriously defeated during the 1880s. Finally, the Colombians began the new century with a very conservative government and conservative constitution.

Rights: The Fight against All Privileges

The previous analysis may help us achieve a better understanding of the constitutional proposals of liberalism. In our analysis, liberals wanted to ensure respect for individuals' rights; promote federalism; make the representatives more independent; limit the strength of popular organs; restrict the powers of the executive; strengthen the organisms of control, and the judiciary in particular; and establish an adequate system of checks and balances.

The enactment of a bill of rights represented one of the most paradigmatic liberal creations. The list of rights came to ensure the protection of the people's most basic rights: they were the "bricks" that gave shape and strength to the liberal "wall of separation." As the notable Victorino Lastarria claimed, "The state has for its object the respect of the rights of the individual: there is the limit of its action."[69]

Individual rights functioned, therefore, like "trump cards"[70] through which each individual was able to defy and defeat all collective claims. Through the defense of individual rights, liberals asserted their basic assumption that each person was worthy of respect, regardless of whether the majority or the dominant group rejected or disliked his or her own personal project. Each person had to count as an individual. In the opinion of liberals, no person should be sacrificed in the name of another person or group or entity. In this way, liberals differentiated their program from those defended by radicals and conservatives. Only liberals saw rights as categorical, absolute, and unconditional. Rights were in their view inviolable: they did not depend on other values. Radicals and conservatives, instead, accepted rights only insofar as their acceptance helped them to ensure social order or did not interfere with the majority's position, the dominant faith, or the so-called common good.

Liberals defended the enactment of a bill of rights as a way of preventing what both alternative views proposed or accepted, namely, the adoption of conservative policies. If society were ruled by governors with authoritarian tendencies, rights should serve to put limits to their arbitrary impulses: they should allow the people to continue criticizing them, enjoy their property, and worship their own God. The same should happen if the majorities governed. Colombian liberal Ezequiel Rojas argued that "in those societies where majorities govern it is essential to [organize the political powers] in a way that prevents their tyranny and arbitrariness, or reduces those tendencies, which are so common in all human entities that want to impose their will and have the means for doing so."[71]

Of course, the likelihood of survival of these bills of rights was, particularly in Latin American, very poor. Once they got into power, the new governments would modify the existing rules in order to act

---

[69] Quoted in García Calderón (1918), p. 238. See also Cruz (1980).
[70] Dworkin (1977).
[71] See Jaramillo Uribe (1964), pp. 165–666.

181

with more freedom, look for support for their oppressive plans in the judiciary, or simply find legal subterfuges that allowed them to act as they wished and without serious legitimacy questions. Even in spite of these events, however, we may still recognize the enormous political and symbolic importance of rights in all America. These lists of rights represented, after they were first adopted, limits to the state's actions. They won general respect and general approval; even the "enemies" of rights used the rhetoric of rights.

The bill of rights implied, among other things, the idea that all individuals were born free and equal. This seemingly simple claim was in fact a revolutionary one. At the time, it implied a direct confrontation with the privileges enjoyed by the church and the military. Liberals confronted these two groups, assuming that they were receiving privileges that were denied to most other individuals. Their fight against privileges showed their particular concern with the establishment of *legal equality* among all citizens. For that reason, the fact that army officers or members of the church received special legal protections and public benefits represented an insult to the idea of equality; no reason existed to give them what was denied to others. This same bias explains liberals' hostility toward class or racial privileges. In contrast with the benefits resulting from such privileges, they asserted that nobody had to receive better or worse public treatment because of the name he carried or the color of his skin. They confronted not only the privileges of groups such as the church or the military but also those "advantages" seemingly enjoyed by the Native Americans. This explains, for example, liberals' hostility toward the existence of communal and indivisible lands in the hands of Native Americans. In the end, liberals believed that the life of each person should exclusively depend on the choices made by each and not on facts that were totally out of the individual's control. Each individual should remain free to achieve what he wanted through his talents and efforts.

The Venezuelan Constitution of 1811 not only abolished the existing *fueros* but also proclaimed legal equality between all races. Another very early and significant attempt at establishing legal equality appeared in Argentina, through the work of the Asamblea del año XIII. The assembly discussed three different constitutional projects and recommended numerous reforms aimed at securing basic freedoms and legal equality. These reforms included, among other things, a law of free birth;[72] the abolition of the *mitas* and *yanaconazgos*,

---

[72] The law was supplemented by a Reglamento para la educación y ejercicio de los libertos, which proclaimed that male children of slave mothers remained under the

through which Native Americans were forced to work on behalf of state, church, or private citizens; and the suppression of all titles of nobility. The new measures also prohibited the use of instruments of torture, abolished the Inquisition, and accepted the public expression of faiths other than Catholicism. Through its work, the assembly made a fundamental contribution to the abolition of all types of privilege, individual or collective, and of monopolies.

In Colombia, the adoption of legal equality became one of the fundamental issues in the discussion between liberals and conservatives. Vice-President Santander undoubtedly favored this fight for legal equality, partly because of his devout "Benthamism." Utilitarianism recommended the abolition of all privileges; the maximization of each individual's happiness was incompatible with the persistence of artificial distinctions and therefore with the still vast powers of the church. Santander's reformist policies were also reflected in the adoption of the "Plan of Studies of Gran Colombia," which favored the diffusion of utilitarian ideas through the educational system, triggering a severe confrontation between the government and the church. Over the following years, Santander's crusade in favor of utilitarianism was developed by his disciples. A long polemic between Ezequiel Rojas and Miguel Angel Caro appeared to be the best example of this confrontation that separated utilitarians from conservatives.[73] The constitutions of 1853, 1858, and 1863 also largely contributed to enforcing the individual's commitment to liberal principles.

In Mexico, these disputes were even more intense. In particular, during the first half of the century both José Mora and Vice-President Valentín Gómez Farías, sometimes even in spite of themselves, made a substantial contribution to this fight against privilege. Mora criticized the privileges of the church not only because of his utilitarian philosophy but also after his analyses of the national economy: most of the country's property was stagnant or unused because it was in the hands of the church. In addition, the church's advantages contradicted the 1824 constitution, while its overwhelming influence over the educational system blocked the circulation of new ideas. Mora argued for similar ideas in his analysis of the military's advantages:[74] Mora

---

tutelage of the mother's owner until age twenty and female children until sixteen or married. After this age, they would become fully free.

[73] Caro wrote five "open letters" criticizing Rojas and denouncing the moral degradation that had followed from the enforcement of utilitarian theories. Utilitarian education, in his opinion, transformed Christian students into arrogant and disrespectful people. G. Rodríguez (1970), p. 121.

[74] Also, Mora was one of Bolívar's most ardent critics. He asserted the Latin Americans had been fighting not for their independence but for their liberty and that they would

recognized, for example, that a large army would absorb too many people, who would then be unable to contribute to the development of the country.[75] A large army, in addition, constituted a source of permanent disputes, something that obviously contradicted Mexico's need for peace and institutional stability.[76] While in power, Gómez Farías tried to enforce some of these criteria. He made significant efforts to restrict the power of the military and reduce the number of its members. However, President Santa Anna, who had left Gómez Farías in control of the presidency, did not accept these initiatives and assumed power again in order to put a definite end to these reforms.

By the mid-1850s most Latin American countries had effectively abolished slavery and titles of nobility. However, the struggle to establish legal equality was still at a very early stage. In particular, the church and the military continued to enjoy benefits, such as the *fueros*, that were prohibited to all other groups. In Mexico, the fight against these persistent privileges was even more intense than in other countries, given the wealth and the number of privileges accumulated by these two groups. One of the most notable efforts at ending these privileges came after Santa Anna's definitive defeat. At that time, two progressive laws named after their authors, the Ley Juárez and the Ley Lerdo, appeared to challenge directly the prevailing privileges. The Ley Juárez, sanctioned during Juan Alvarez's transitional government, suppressed the civil *fueros* of the military and the church and opened up the possibility of renouncing the religious *fueros* in the case of common crimes.[77]

The laws caused such great agitation that, in the end, Juan Alvarez was forced to resign from his position and Benito Juárez to abandon his law. Ignacio Comonfort, who, by this time, had developed excellent connections with both the military and the church, occupied Alvarez's position. In spite of this, Comonfort could not prevent the enactment of the Ley Lerdo, which was closely linked to the Juárez

---

achieve too little if they replaced Spanish dominion with the oppression of Bolívar. In addition, he was a severe critic of Iturbide and his extreme powers. See Mora (1963), p. 624.

[75] The Uruguayan liberal José Ellauri battled for the exclusion of military officers from the senate. In his opinion, the presence of these officers in the representative body could both undermine the civic liberties of the people and impair the balance of power. See Pivel Devoto (1955).

[76] See, for example, Fowler (1966), pp. 189–209.

[77] Leader of the "Ayutla Revolution" that put an end to the long centralist regime of Santa Anna, Alvarez was surrounded by a significant group of *liberales puros* or radical liberals, such as Guillermo Prieto, Melchor Ocampo, Benito Juárez, and Miguel Lerdo.

law. Sebastián Lerdo de Tejada, a radical liberal who had participated in Santa Anna's last cabinet, promoted this law as a way of mobilizing and redistributing the church's unused property. For liberals, the church was perniciously obstructing the free circulation of property, so the Ley Lerdo established that the church had to sell all its urban and rural properties to its tenants at a price that was accessible to them. If necessary, the state would sell these lands through a public auction. Set up like this, the law did not expropriate or confiscate the church's lands, which at one point even the moderate Mora had demanded. In fact, the enforcement of the law promised to keep the church's wealth intact, because the whole proceeds of these transactions would fall into the hands of the church.[78] The church, however, decided not to comply with the law, arguing that it was impossible to communicate this law to Rome and to respect at the same time the schedule fixed by the government. The difficulties of enforcing the law forced Lerdo to advance even more radical reforms. Comonfort, though, decided not to accept more of these initiatives. After the president disapproved of his policies, Lerdo resigned his position, accusing Comonfort of being too "mild and conciliatory."[79]

The 1857 Mexican constitutional convention and the Argentinean convention of 1853 are two excellent examples of the battle that liberals had to fight in order to ensure religious tolerance. In both cases, the more liberal delegates found support in some ardent but still "neutralist" Catholics, who accepted the need for separating the state and the church. In Mexico, the delegate Francisco Zarco, one of the most important figures at the convention, rejected the establishment of the Catholic religion, asserting, in contrast to his personal beliefs, that the role assumed by the Mexican church during all those

[78] Lerdo defended the law as a way of mobilizing the wealth of the country, encouraging the development of new industries, and increasing the number of taxable individuals. See Blázquez (1978).
[79] Under the pressure of the military and the church, Comonfort decided to suspend the constitution. But it was already too late: the new concession was not enough, and Comonfort himself was forced to leave his position shortly afterward. Confronting the illegal forces that had overthrown the government, Benito Juárez, the last president of the supreme court, proclaimed that the "legal" and constitutional government was alive and represented by himself. Some of his early colleagues, Melchor Ocampo, Guillermo Prieto, and Manuel Ruiz among them, joined forces with Juárez, who then established a provisional government in Veracruz and defied the de facto forces that controlled the capital. These were the first days of a long battle led by Juárez, trying to restore the constitution to its rightful place. Finally, after ten years of resistance, Juárez proclaimed the victory of the liberal forces in 1867 and restored the full legality of the constitution. The 1857 constitution remained in force until 1913, with only a few, albeit important, changes promoted by Juárez himself.

185

years had been unacceptable. He claimed that "it has denaturalized Christ's religion because it has declared itself the enemy of freedom; it has accumulated wealth impoverishing the country; it has deceived the people...it has defended privileges and money, disregarding the truths of Catholicism."[80] In Argentina, delegate José Benjamin Gorostiaga proposed to ensure absolute religious freedom, denying the constitutional convention's right to interfere in religious matters: "Congress is not an Ecumenical Council," which explained why the deputies should not decide questions related to Catholic "dogma." Active Catholic members of the assembly, like Benjamin Lavaysse, also contributed to the liberal fight for ensuring a greater degree of state neutrality. Neither Mexican nor Argentinean liberals were completely satisfied in their demands after the sanction of their respective constitutions. In Mexico, liberals had to content themselves with preventing the establishment of "religious intolerance." In Argentina, the constitution included the right to freedom of religion (art. 14) but also reserved a privileged role for Catholicism. Article 2 of the constitution, in fact, declared the state's constitutional obligation to "support" the Catholic faith, an obligation that has still not received a clear legal interpretation.

Colombian liberals were somewhat more successful in this respect. During his term of government, President José Hilario López promoted freedom and prepared the field for the enactment of the 1853 constitution, one of the most advanced liberal documents of the time. The 1863 constitution carried the liberal proposals of the previous document still further, allowing the state to supervise all matters concerning religion, prohibiting it from using its powers to collect contributions for the church, and preventing religious communities from acquiring property.[81] Moreover, the constitution reestablished the right to divorce and civil marriages and banned the name of God from its text.[82]

In Chile, the struggle for religious neutrality was also important within the liberals' political agenda. However, it is also true that Chilean liberals had more problems than those in neighboring

---

[80] For Zevada (1972), pp. 38–39.
[81] Therefore, in accordance with articles 6 and 23 of the constitution.
[82] In a detailed report presented to the convention, deputies Justo Arozamena, and Salvador Camacho justified the need for separating the church from the state, asserting that the alliance between the two had been dreadful, both for Catholicism and for liberty. Catholicism, they argued, has been "corrupted in contact with mundane interests, and governments have used enormous powers that have transformed them into repressive ones. This sacrilegious alliance has engendered two terrifying monsters: Inquisition and Jesuitism." Correa (1937), pp. 232–234.

The Fight against All Privileges

countries defending state neutrality. By the end of the century, liberals had a good opportunity for promoting their views in the revision of article 5 of the Chilean Constitution of 1833, which stated that Catholicism was the official faith of the country and prohibited public worship by other cults. This debate did not result in the modification of the constitution but was still fundamental to the cause of liberal tolerance in the country. In Ecuador, Vicente Rocafuerte appeared as the most influential defender of religious tolerance and the separation of church and the state during his years in opposition. In addition, the liberal Pedro Carbo, fought for a more tolerant policy toward non-Catholics during the famous constitutional convention held in Cuenca in 1845. His tolerant proposals, however, obtained support only from rather isolated delegates, such as Pedro Moncayo, within an assembly largely composed of ardent Catholics.[83]

The liberals' campaign for legal equality and religious neutrality represented only one part of their fight to affirm basic individual freedoms such as the freedom of the press, freedom of association, freedom of education, and the establishment of jury trials. Among the numerous liberals who argued for the affirmation of these basic rights was the Mexican José María Mora. A first important demonstration of Mora's commitments to basic freedoms appeared in his criticisms of the 1824 Mexican Constitution. Mora criticized the document in particular because it established religious intolerance, which, in his opinion, introduced an unacceptable "transaction" into the core of the constitution. In order to repair this grave mistake, he proposed adopting a liberal "program" that combined his two most fundamental aims: the consecration of an "absolute freedom of opinion" and the "suspension of all repressive laws" against the press.[84] Mora's support of the freedom to "think, speak, and write" reproduced in both its rigor and its depth John Stuart Mill's defense of these basic liberties. In his famous writings, Mora recognized that there would always be and should always be mistaken views, which would have negative consequences. However, he argued that prohibitions were not the means of remedying such evils but that "free circulation of ideas as well as the contrast that results from their opposition is the only thing that can rectify opinions." He made the point that "if any authority had the power to regulate [that circulation of ideas] he would immediately

---

[83] Notably, the same Carbo argued, after he had presented his proposal, that "nobody attacked religion, nor wanted to do it within such a Catholic community. If one had intended to do so, the laws would have been there to limit and punish him." Ayala (1995a), p. 88.

[84] See De la Madrid Hurtado (1982), pp. 146–148.

abuse that power." Nobody, he believed, was well positioned to prohibit others' mistakes; and nobody, especially not the government, was exempt from committing mistakes.[85]

The Argentinean Bernardino Rivadavia also occupies a fundamental place among liberals who campaigned for individual rights. From his multiple public positions, Rivadavia promoted an ample reformist program that favored both wider religious freedom and freedom of the press. However, in the same way that Mora was forced to abandon his country, Rivadavia became disenchanted with the antiliberal doctrines that became prevalent in Mexico and abandoned his proposal under pressure from the "federalist," in this case the more conservative, groups. In Chile, the 1828 constitution also introduced some changes aimed at mitigating some of the defects of the previous conservative constitution of 1823. Curiously, one of its main authors was a Spanish intellectual, José Joaquín de Mora, who had worked with Bernardino Rivadavia for some years.[86] The new constitution, for liberals, "contains all the precautions which the most ardent friends of liberty long for to calm the fears which the exercise of power might inspire in them."[87] Based on French revolutionary documents, the Mexican Constitution of 1824, the Cádiz Constitution of 1812, and especially José Infante's previous federalist program for reforming the Chilean Constitution, the document proposed by Mora obtained final approval in 1828. The constitution included certain inviolable rights, such as the right to petition, the right to a free press, and the right to property and security. Its enactment was followed by a liberal free press law, also written by Mora, approved in December 1828.

In Peru, the fight for basic freedoms was fundamentally in the hands of liberals and, particularly, in the hands of the "second generation of liberals," which included, among others, the brothers Gálvez, Ureta, and Benjamín Cisneros and Ricardo Palma. Greatly influenced by

---

[85] See his "Discurso sobre la libertad de pensar, hablar y escribir," in Mora (1963). In his opinion, the best and safest means for achieving the truth was through free reflection and the revision of others' ideas. There was nobody wise enough to acknowledge and discuss all serious matters alone. For that reason, he argued, "in all matters, but particularly in those related to the government, it is necessary to receive help from others." That help would be unavailable, however, without providing a strong protection to the freedoms of speech and press, or preventing criticisms against certain opinions. Therefore, he concluded, "government should neither prohibit nor provide protection to any doctrine: its only function is to comply with and enforce the laws." Ibid.

[86] Rivadavia had met Mora in Europe and invited him to work with him in Argentina. Mora began working with Rivadavia, then moved to Santiago and then to Bolivia, where he also worked with the highest political authorities.

[87] See Hale (1968), p. 321.

the revolutionary events that took place in Europe in 1848, the group systematically worked for the expansion of liberties and individual rights. They promoted these commitments through associations, such as the well-known Club Progresista;[88] newspapers like *El Progreso*; and educational institutions such as Colegio de Guadalupe, which had been directed by Pedro Gálvez since 1850. Among other things, the Peruvian liberals were responsible for the enactment of two famous constitutions, in 1856 and 1867. Significantly, the delegates who wrote the first of these constitutions were elected, for the first time, through the use of universal and direct suffrage. Its members, mostly liberals, tried to reverse the conservative constitutional framework elaborated in Huancayo. In this way, they reduced the state's obligations toward the church; partially suppressed the legal rights of the church to collect *diezmos*; recognized for the first time the rights of association and petition; favored political decentralization; and defended popular suffrage, abolishing by this means the system of electoral colleges. At the convention, the most extreme liberals advocated the reduction or direct elimination of the armed forces;[89] the suppression of the death penalty, which they obtained; and an absolute freedom of religion, which they did not manage to ensure.

This progressive convention seemed to strengthen the liberal character of the new government, which had already abolished slavery and the Indians' tribute. However, President Ramón Castilla never trusted the constitutional assembly and boycotted it from the very beginning.[90] His confrontation with the radical liberals came to a head when the delegates reduced the president's military powers and passed some restrictions on the interests of the church and the military. Then, and after two years of disputes, Castilla brutally dissolved the convention and in 1860 replaced the constitution with a new one.[91] In 1867 liberals managed to enact a new constitution, which partially

---

[88] Among others, Francisco Quirós, Pedro Gálvez, and José Sevilla were members of the Club Progresista. This institution represents one of the most important forerunners of the Peruvian Liberal Party.

[89] In addition, the convention suppressed an article from the Huancayo Constitution aimed at guaranteeing military discipline.

[90] Castilla became particularly uncomfortable with the extension of the convention's sessions and its inefficiency. After eight months, his delegates completely abandoned it.

[91] In his speech, he presented his objections to the document and predicted that its application would cause public disturbances. Soon afterward, several military leaders began to mobilize against the government, and Castilla took advantage of this situation and put an end to the constitutional assembly. In addition, he sent some of his enemies into exile and closed some hostile newspapers. The romance between Castilla and the liberals had concluded. See, for example, Pike (1967).

reproduced the 1856 text and partially went beyond that document. It proclaimed complete freedom of education, which implied restricting the normally dominant role of the church in this matter. In addition, and even when it kept a special place for the Catholic religion, it undermined the aim of the 1856 constitution, which obliged the state to protect the church "through all means."[92] However, the new constitution was as unsuccessful as the previous one: it had lasted only four months when a military coup finished off the liberals' endeavor.

At the same time, in Venezuela liberal ideas began to have a greater influence at a constitutional level. In particular, this influence was reflected in the 1858 and 1864 constitutions. The first, for example, included a long list of individual rights. In addition, it provided for a jury system for criminal cases and expanded the very limited political rights. The constitution, however, remained basically unimplemented, given the dramatic events of the so-called Federal War, which affected the country during those years. The federal forces finally achieved a victory in 1863. Shortly afterward, they called for a new constitutional convention and enacted the 1864 constitution. The new constitution provided for free education, universal suffrage, and some other new rights such as the right to petition. In addition, it ensured procedural guarantees, proclaimed legal equality among the citizens, replaced the national military with "civilian militias," and abolished the death penalty. The 1864 constitution was enormously influential and defined, for many decades, the basic legal structure of the country.

The fight to gain new rights reached its highest point in New Granada, where the liberal group of *gólgotas* pushed the executive to incorporate numerous rights in the constitution as a way of blocking the conservatives' return to power. The *gólgotas* were a group of extreme liberals, very much influenced by the "Manchesterian" liberal school, and, with the so-called *draconian*s, one of the two main sectors that promoted José Hilario López when he came to power in New Granada during the 1850s.[93] The liberal 1858 constitution went so far as to include the people's right to "traffic in arms and munitions"

---

[92] Paz Soldán (1943), p. 262.
[93] The *gólgotas* received that name after the speech made by one of its members, which invoked the "tears of the martyr of Gólgota." The *gólgotas* had opposed the clerical forces of General Pedro Alcantara Herrán and were now campaigning against the death penalty. The *draconianos,* however, favored this measure. The latter worked in close alliance with the military and the artisans, two groups in a poor relationship with the *gólgotas,*who defended radical economic liberalism. The *draconians* aligned, among its members, relevant political figures such as Obando, Azuero, and other activists who wanted revenge after the repression they suffered at the hands of

(art. 11.4) and the right to "express thoughts in print without any responsibility whatsoever" (art. 56.4).[94] The constitution of 1863 not only abolished the death penalty and adopted "habeas corpus" but also carried some of the radical rights adopted by the previous constitution still further. For example, it protected the "freedom to possess arms and munitions and to engage in the commerce thereof in time of peace" against violation by both the national government and the state government (art. 125.15). It also extended the unlimited freedom of press incorporated in the constitution of 1853 to an unlimited freedom of speech (art. 15.6 and 7).

Liberals also played an important role in the defense of a broader suffrage. On the basis of the principle of autonomy, which proclaimed that the life of each person had to be the result of his or her choices and, sometimes, his or her utilitarian philosophy, many liberals defended a broadening of political rights as a precondition for achieving general well-being. Rivadavia, for example, a disciple of Jeremy Bentham, promoted a curious but still significant law of universal suffrage.[95] Peruvian liberals also approved a law securing universal suffrage in 1828. This law even favored the political participation of illiterates, servants, or foreigners who had served in the national military, groups that were always excluded from the electoral process. However, disappointed with its effects, the same liberals put an end to this initiative in 1834 after the adoption of a new constitution.[96] Colombian liberals proposed some broadening of political rights in their constitutional projects of 1828 and 1832 under the influence of Vicente Azuero. In Venezuela, liberals included a constitutional

---

presidents Herrán and Mosquera. (For that reason, too, they defended the adoption of the death penalty. See, for example, Zavaleta Arias, 1994.)

[94] Article 11 gives a good idea of the extreme liberalism of the *gólgotas*. The article prohibited the state from alienating to foreign powers any part of the territory, from authorizing slavery, from interfering with religious matters, from impeding traffic in arms and munitions, from imposing levies on foreign commerce, from imposing any duties on national bodies or public functionaries, from levying taxes on articles to be consumed in another state, from levying taxes upon the effects or property of the confederation, from subjecting the inhabitants of another state or their property to any burdens, and from levying or collecting duties or taxes on produce or goods subject to national taxation.

[95] Halperín Donghi, among others, described the actual limits of this law, which distinguished between "active" and "passive" voters: given the political apathy of most people and the discouragement of political participation, Rivadavia managed to manipulate most elections. In particular, Rivadavia tried to control the polls through the mobilization of the troops, which allowed him to greatly increase the influence of the government's forces in the final results. The political decisions, therefore, continued to reside in the hands of a small elite. Halperín Donghi (1975), pp. 360–363.

[96] The constitution of 1856 would finally restore universal suffrage.

protection of universal suffrage only in 1858. In Ecuador, the constitution of 1861 also granted this right for the first time.

The liberals' commitment to broader suffrage did not necessarily imply a commitment to active citizenship. Liberals tried to discourage the people's intense participation in politics because they wanted to protect each person's initiatives and because they did not trust majority groups. In this sense, what the North American liberals did is a good example of what happened in all the American countries. For right or wrong reasons, the North Americans rejected the establishment of strict limits on political rights, but at the same time they did all they could to discourage popular participation in politics. Therefore, the enactment of the federal constitution was followed by an "intense and massive" reaction "against conventions," a reaction that ended in a successful campaign for "replac[ing] the traditional town meeting...with a mayor and a representative council."[97] By the mid-1780s these changes were almost completed, although in cities like Boston and Philadelphia the defenders of the town meeting model managed to delay the reformists' attempts and denounced the undemocratic principles that guided the conservatives' proposals.[98] For the latter, the public assemblies were unnecessary and too conflictive within a republican organization. When the national constitution was enacted, most states had definitely abandoned their earlier form of communal organization. For R. Brunhouse, "times had changed. Men of wealth, social prestige, and respectability were coming to the front."[99]

In Latin America, the story was basically the same. In Argentina, for example, Rivadavia combined the approval of his important law of universal suffrage with another that abolished the *cabildos*, the most "popular" institution of the time, which, to Rivadavia, was superfluous within the new representative system. In a familiar vein, the writers of the 1853 constitution made clear that they did not want to foster any kind of public participation.[100] In addition, they included in article 22 of the text an explicit statement that the people had no right to deliberate or to rule except through their representatives, and those who believed themselves to be representatives of the people and

---

[97] Patterson (1981), pp. 50–52.
[98] See Brunhouse (1942), pp. 220–21. The newspapers, for example, denounced the principles as "aristocratic polic[ies]...in a manner repugnant to the genius and spirit of our constitution." *Pennsylvania Packet* (Philadelphia), Aug. 23, 1786.
[99] Brunhouse (1942), pp. 220–21.
[100] Curiously, the preface differed from the one that served as its model, the preface of the U.S. Constitution, in one important detail: it does not speak in the name of the people ("We the people...") but in the name of the representatives of the people ("We, the representatives of the people...").

petitioned in their name would be charged with sedition. We have already examined the skeptical attitude of Argentine liberals toward political participation. They did not even want the presence of poor people in the popular branch of government: as Sarmiento argued, "When we say people, we understand noteworthy, active, intelligent people; a governing class. We are decent people, belonging to a patrician class. For that reason, in our legislature one should not see gauchos, black or poor people. We are decent people; that is to say, patriotic people."[101]

Similarly, the Colombian leader Santander discouraged the "frequent meetings of the people," which he deemed too risky, and he showed no inclination to broaden the people's participation in politics. He also denied the people's right to select their governors and mayors and was always hostile toward the power of municipalities. Vetoing a law that favored the election of local authorities by the people, he said that "very famous politicians" had asserted that active popular participation was bad for the health of the country and that it was absurd to make the election of local authorities more democratic than those of national authorities. "One day," he argued, "some perverse men [elected as local authorities] may use the purity of those elections in order to lead the country to chaos." Local *cabildos* were, in his opinion, "indifferent to the public good" and "unable to promote it."[102] The Mexican José María Mora, following Constant more than Bentham for this purpose, proposed to limit suffrage only to property holders, because in his opinion only they enjoyed the independence necessary to elect or be elected. Objecting to those who supported a broader popular participation in politics, he stated: "We are convinced that this exaggerated equality, understood literally, has spread among us a seedbed of errors and an abundant source of misfortunes."[103]

This strong bias against political participation may be explained by a particular concern with the protection of private property. The right to private property always appeared in the liberals' agenda as one of the most sacred, or as *the* most sacred, right when it came to discussing such matters. Clearly, liberals' strong commitment to property rights creates ample space for agreement between liberals and conservatives: they both took the support of property rights as one of their priorities. Although both groups took opposing positions in many other debates – for example, regarding the status of

---

[101] Quoted in Shunway (1993), p. 151.
[102] See Bushnell (1954).
[103] Quoted in Hale (1968), p. 96.

the church and the military or the importance of other fundamental rights – they always came together on this issue. In addition, they both recognized that mass assemblies constituted a serious threat to social peace and, particularly, to their most favored right. They both assumed that popular meetings tended to end with the adoption of irrational decisions, prejudicial to the interests of the country. Good examples of this latent convergence between the two views include the fascination of many liberals, especially Argentineans, with Egaña's very authoritarian constitutional model; the proclivity of many U.S. Federalists toward the creation of an "aristocratic branch" of power; and Mora's proposal for concentrating political decisions in the hands of property owners.

The Organization of Power: A System of Checks and Balances

At the time of proposing how to organize the political structure of society, liberals showed both their agreements and disagreements with the conservatives' position. Joining with them, they proposed to establish strict limits against "the tyranny of the many," and opposing them, they suggested strictly limiting the authority of the president and ensuring an "equilibrium of powers."

First of all, most liberals recognized the need for controlling the ambitious decisions of the majority group. The majority, they assumed, was normally aiming to appropriate the state apparatus in order to serve its own interests, overcoming any obstacles it found in its way. In that sense, what happened in the United States during the years that preceded the federal convention is particularly telling about the evolution of their political views and institutional recommendations. For U.S. liberals, legislative chaos and social violence distinguished the first years following the declaration of independence. The problems that developed then were so profound that they demanded the complete institutional reorganization of the country. Three ideas that became apparent after that institutional crisis related to political participation, the relationship between representatives and the people, and the connections between the different branches of power of the government.

According to the first idea, the citizenry had enormous difficulties in deliberating in a peaceful and well-organized way. Because of that problem, majoritarian assemblies tended to produce unjust or self-interested laws. In their opinion, the preconstitutional experience of "town meetings" demonstrated that, when the people assembled together, they tended to approve the direst and most violent measures, without any concern for minority rights. The reasons for this phenomenon were numerous. On the one hand, mass meetings seemed incompatible with the possibility of presenting arguments in an appropriate way. In those contexts, it was difficult to discuss in a reasoned way and carefully elaborate and refine any argument; confusion tended to prevail. The larger the number of people participating in the meeting, it seemed, the smaller the chance of discussing matters properly. On the other hand, the same conditions that made public dialogue difficult seemed to be particularly suitable for the emergence of agitators and demagogues. In those contexts, in effect, the louder and more "seductive" voices always seemed to be preferred. Madison opened his most important paper, *Federalist* 10, by making reference to the problems originated by popular governments. "The instability, injustice, and confusion introduced into the public councils, have, in truth, been the mortal diseases under which popular governments have everywhere perished," he argued. "In those contexts," demagogues "inflamed [parties] with mutual animosity, and rendered them much more disposed to vex and oppress each other than to co-operate... the most frivolous and fanciful distinctions have been sufficient to kindle their unfriendly passions and excite their most violent conflicts."

For liberals, in mass meetings public rationality had almost no place; it was displaced by self-interested arguments or with *irrationality*. If self-interest seemed to be the main motivational factor in each person's life, passions seemed to be the fuel of large groups. Moved by these passions and other regrettable impulses, these groups tended to evolve into *factions*, that is, groups that acted against the interest of the nation and the rights of other individuals.[104] Liberals did not consider these disgraceful consequences occasional. Indeed, they believed that they were the *necessary* result of majoritarian politics. Moreover, people like Madison began to elaborate a theory that irrational decisions and oppressive outcomes were the necessary products of mass deliberative meetings. In *Federalist* 55, Madison summarized this view, shared by most federalists, in a general law that stated "*in all very numerous assemblies, of whatever characters composed, passion never fails to wrest the scepter from reason.*"

---

[104] In accordance with Madison's famous definition, a faction was "a number of citizens, whether amounting to a majority or minority of the whole, who are united and activated by some common impulse of passion, or of interest, adverse to the rights of other citizens, or to the permanent and aggregate interests of the community."

The second idea to appear during the preconstitutional period referred to the relationship between the representatives and the people. It said that when the two groups were "too close" to each other, as had seemingly happened during the preconstitutional period, then the representatives tended to become more partial in their decisions. This result occurred not only because of the difficulties in reasoning properly in mass meetings but also because of the pressures of the majority. Under the intense pressures that came from the will of their electors, the representatives had little chance of deliberating freely. They could not change their minds in the face of a new idea or a better argument: they had to stick to the people's mandates. The British conservative Edmund Burke had supported the same idea many years before in his famous argument with Henry Cruger in Bristol. At that time, Burke argued that parliament should be the "deliberative assembly of one nation" and not "ambassadors from different and hostile interests, which interests each must maintain, as an agent and advocate, against other agents and advocates."[105] Most liberals seemed to share this view, which suggested that representatives tended to become "blind" because of the majority pressures and, therefore, ready to adopt partial decisions, usually against the interests of the few. In the United States, this conclusion was shared by most Federalists after different "waves" of "papermoney" releases: state legislatures had become, in their opinion, the mere tool of the irrationality of the majorities. Nonindependent representatives, they believed, could not help but take partial, prejudiced, locallyoriented decisions.

The third idea that developed after the revolutionary period in the United States was closely linked to the other two and concerned the relations established among different branches of power. In this case, liberals made reference to the risk of having a particular branch of power trying to replace or displace others. In particular, they suggested that local legislatures had frequently demonstrated their tendency to encroach on the judges' or the executive's jurisdiction. Events such as those which took place on Rhode Island during those years simply confirmed their worst fears. There, the local legislature, disappointed by a supreme court decision, asked the judges to "give their immediate attendance at the assembly to assign the reasons and grounds of their [unacceptable decision]."[106] This situation was immediately reproduced in other localities.[107] All these dramatic

---

[105] See Ross et al. (1979), p. 116.
[106] See Bates (1967), pp. 134–135.
[107] In North Carolina, for example, a legislative commission accused the judiciary of disregarding the authority of a law that attempted to equalize the legislative acts

cases confirmed their initial suspicions: the legislature, as the most popular branch of government, always tended to act too fast and too partially, invading the jurisdiction of other powers and impairing the rights of minority groups.

Taking into account these three lessons from history, liberals developed three basic institutional proposals that would become fundamental to the evolution of modern constitutionalism. First, they defended the need to limit the people's mass and direct participation in public matters. This was based on the assumption that popular bodies would act merely out of irrationality or self-interest. Second, they proposed to increase the existing distance between the representatives and the people, making the former more "independent" and autonomous in their choices. Third, they established a system of "mutual controls" or "checks and balances," aimed at preventing the invasion of one branch of power into the affairs of others.

Individualists also tried to reduce the influence of civic assemblies or "town meetings." They wanted the representatives to adopt their decisions freely, without significant pressures. They began to defend a "principle of separation" or "distinction"[108] between the representatives and the people, which put an end to the populist assumption that representatives had to share the interests of their electors in order to be able to act as their advocates. This view of the representative system was clearly opposed to that held by radicals, who viewed it as an "evil" or "second best" option, given the impossibility of establishing a "pure" democratic system. In contrast with this view, liberals assumed that representation was a "first option," a *necessary* alternative, in order to refine the quality of public decisions and, therefore, prevent the unacceptable consequences of alternative systems.

In the famous article *Federalist* 10, Madison presented an excellent example of this view, in its defense of both the "principle of distinction" and the representative system as a "first" or desired option. By the middle of that paper, in effect, Madison had demonstrated the

---

and the constitutional mandates. The legislative accusation proceeded, but finally the representatives decided not to sanction the judges, something that most people assumed would happen. New Hampshire's legislature also attempted to sanction some members of the judiciary after the judges attacked the validity of one of their approved statutes. Again, the legislature formed a commission in charge of examining the cases and the behavior of the judiciary. However, the commission found the judges guilty of no fault and decided, as in the previous case, to exonerate the magistrates. In the state of New York, on the other hand, the legislature did manage to accuse and condemn the judiciary, although its delegates decided, in the end, not to replace the members of the tribunal.

[108] See, in this respect, Manin (1997).

advantages of the "republican" representative system in comparison with direct democracy. He wanted to show, in fact, the disadvantages of the more participatory systems that prevailed at state level before the adoption of the federal constitution. In comparing these two types of regime, Madison claimed that a representative system "refines and enlarges the public's views, by filtering them through the medium of a chosen body of citizens, whose wisdom may best discern the true interests of their country, and whose patriotism and love of justice will be least likely to sacrifice it to temporary or partial considerations." Through the adoption of this system, "it may well happen that the public voice, mediated by the representatives of the people, will be more consonant to the public good than if mediated by the people themselves, convened for that purpose."

The idea of a system of checks and balances, the key to the U.S. Constitution and later to many others in Latin America constitutions, came to reinforce the first solution, the election of a specific representative system. The system of "checks and balances" was a direct reaction to the radical system of "strict" separation of powers that, seemingly, left too much power in the hands of the most popular branch of power. In contrast with this view, liberals wanted not only to divide power, which radicals accepted and conservatives frequently rejected, but also to allow each branch of power to defend itself against the possible attacks of the others. For *Federalist* 51, it was evident that "the best security against a gradual concentration of several powers in the same department" was that of "giving to those who administer each department the necessary constitutional means and personal motives to resist encroachments of others." In particular, liberals asserted, as seen in the case of Rhode Island, that the legislature, as the most powerful branch of government, would always be tempted to invade the others. For that reason, obviously, they concentrated most of their controlling devices on the activities of the U.S. Congress. They also organized *countermajoritarian* institutions – that is, institutions capable of weakening the authority of the majorities, institutions that, in fact, took away from majority groups the main and final "say." Since then, this "last institutional say" has been in the hands of the judiciary, an organism that does not directly depend on the majority will.

Through these means, liberals in the United States tried to remedy what they recognized as the main defects of the prevalent institutional organization. In a way, the institutional system that they proposed represented a direct answer to the model of radical constitutionalism seemingly practiced in a majority of states. Of course, at the same time we find other issues and fears that motivated the choices of the then dominant groups – that is, to make tyranny impossible and to avoid the fragmentation of the country – but these do not undermine the previous assertion. The federal constitution of 1787 was the legal response that liberals prepared against the challenge posed by the radical constitutions enacted in 1776.

Because of these types of assumptions, liberals put forward many different proposals aimed at limiting the activism of majoritarian groups in the U.S. Congress. For that purpose, they suggested measures such as extending the representatives' mandates and even authorized their immediate reelection. Through these initial measures, liberals confronted some of the radicals' most important institutional proposals, such as annual or frequent elections and mandatory rotation. Radicals had defended these proposals as a way of strengthening the relationship between the people and their representatives, preventing the formation of political elites, and of favoring the participation of more diverse people as public officers. Liberals, however, supported the opposite position as a way of separating the electors from the elected, favoring the adoption of more stable policies, fostering the emergence of a more experienced group of politicians, and avoiding the existence of permanent pressures upon their actions. For similar reasons, liberals sometimes proposed the adoption of indirect elections; the creation of small, rather than large, deliberative bodies; and the design of large electoral districts. Finally, liberals objected to and rejected, when necessary, all political means that could subordinate the will of the representatives to the will of the people. In particular, they rejected the right to "instruct" the representatives, which was normally accompanied by the right to "recall" them.

In the United States, these measures were fully discussed at the Federal convention. At that opportunity, federalists defended indirect elections, which, they assumed, "render[ed] the choice[es] more judicious"[109] and favored the choice of people "more likely to correspond with the sense of the community."[110] They also argued for the

---

[109] Madison, in Farrand (1937), vol. 3. p. 330. Gerry also rejected direct elections for choosing the executive because the people, he argued, "are uninformed, and would be misled by a few designing men" (ibid., vol. 2, p. 57).

[110] Ibid., vol. 1, p. 359. For Rutledge, "an election by the Legislature would be more refined than an election immediately by the people: and would be more likely to correspond with the sense of the whole community. If this Convention had been chosen by the people in districts it is not to be supposed that such suitable characters would have been preferred." Ibid.

existence of a correlation between the small size of the institutions and the quality of its decisions. Typically, they considered that "smallness" represented a necessary condition for providing "more coolness," "more system," and "more wisdom" to the political debates.[111] They proposed long terms of office in order to provide "firmness and independence" to the body of representatives[112] and to motivate people "of the first weight" to participate in the government.[113] They also suggested the creation of "large districts," assuming that they were "manifestly favorable to the election of persons of general respectability, and of probable attachments to the rights of property, over competitors depending on the personal solicitations practicable in a contracted theater."[114] And they quickly rejected the right to instruct and recall the representatives because, they believed, this would transform the elected into mere "mouthpieces" of the electors.[115]

In Argentina, too, the Asamblea del año XIII had the opportunity to quickly discuss and reject the demands of the representatives of the Banda Oriental, who arrived at the assembly with very detailed instructions – namely, that "in the Constitutional Assembly [the deputies of the Banda Oriental] will not act as Deputies of the Nation, but as representatives of this state."[116] On the contrary, they approved a decision that maintained that "deputies of the United Provinces are deputies of the Nation, in general...and they are not able to work [under instructions] in any circumstances."[117] At that time, Carlos María de Alvear led the majority group and, following Burke's ideas, asserted that "when the General Assembly is formed...the Deputies of the people become the deputies of the Nation."[118] The same debate took place during the constitutional convention of 1826, where Manuel Antonio Castro, as the head of the constitutional commission, declared that, once they arrived at the convention, "the deputies do not belong any more to the province that has appointed them, but to the nation."[119] Castro's view was refuted by some delegates from the "interior," such as Deán Funes and Juan José Paso. For

---

[111] Madison, in ibid., p. 151.
[112] Ibid., p. 152.
[113] See Madison, in ibid., p. 220.
[114] See his opinion in "Note to His Speech on the Right of Suffrage," ibid., vol. 3, p. 454. As Bernard Manin explained, Federalists assumed that large electoral districts would favor the selection of the "natural aristocracy." Manin (1997), p. 163.
[115] See, in this sense, Sunstein (1993), chap. 1.
[116] Chiaramonte (1999), p. 112.
[117] Quoted in Busaniche (1965), p. 336.
[118] Chiaramonte (1999), p. 112.
[119] Ibid., p. 113.

Paso, "in the Congress we still do not have a nation: what we find are men who belong to different provinces, and who came with the idea of establishing a nation."[120]

Liberals also proposed the establishment of strict controls over congress and, particularly, over "the most democratic branch of government," the lower house.[121] This branch, they assumed, was the most powerful of all branches and, because of it, the most dangerous. This view was clearly reflected in Madison's significant article "Vices of the Political System," where he described the problems that characterized unrestrained legislatures. For Madison, decisions made by congresses tended to be unfair because these bodies were so large that it was difficult to have reasonable discussions; they also were of popular composition and, therefore, were normally driven by irrational impulses. In addition, the deputies were frequently subject to new elections, something that motivated them to try to "please" their electors. In his opinion, from majoritarian bodies one could expect nothing but "numerous," "mutable," and "unjust" laws. In Latin America, most liberals seemed to share this view. José María Mora, for example, was strongly biased against the legislature. The lack of strong controls over this body, he assumed, was "what caused all the evils suffered during the last fifty years by the peoples [of Europe] who have adopted the representative system." In his opinion, the

[120] Ibid., p. 114. Also, see Chiaramonte (1997).
[121] As Wood claims, writing about the development of state constitutionalism in the United States, "Instead of draining all power from the governors and placing it in the legislatures, particularly in the lower houses, as the early state constitutions had done, [the] later constitutions strengthened the executives, senates, and judiciaries. The Massachusetts constitution of 1780 especially seemed to many to have recaptured some of the best characteristics of the English constitutional balance, which had been forgotten during the popular enthusiasm of 1776." Wood (2002), p. 143. In addition, in these new constitutions, "popular legislatures were reduced in size and their authority curbed. Senates or upper houses were instituted where they did not exist, as in Pennsylvania, Georgia, and Vermont. In states where senates did exist, they were made more stable through longer terms and higher property qualifications for their members. The governors were freed from their dependence on the legislatures and given the central responsibility for government. And judges became independent guardians of the constitutions. By 1790, Pennsylvania, South Carolina, and Georgia had reformed their constitutions along these conservative lines. New Hampshire, Delaware, and Vermont soon followed in the early 1790s." Ibid., p. 144. Finally, North Americans began to fight to make the constitution "immune from legislative encroachment": until then, some states "simply declared their constitutions to be fundamental; others required a special majority or successive acts of the legislature for amending the constitution. But none of these measures proved effective against repeated legislative encroachments." For that reason, they began to emphasize the importance of having a special convention for creating the constitution. Ibid., pp. 144–145. By that time, in addition, the regular army was strengthened at the expense of the militia. Ibid., p. 146.

source of these evils resided "not in the depositary of power [but] in the power itself."[122] In Colombia, the influential José María Samper maintained that "nothing [was] so dangerous as the domination of numbers, which normally overcome intelligence and virtue." Given this assumption, he became "an open enemy of...the prevalence of legislative bodies, which Jacobins distinguish as sovereign bodies." Also, and for the same reason, he suggested adopting all the necessary "precautions," which included "not only a wise, unobjectionable division of powers" but also "limitations on suffrage" and particular "securities in favor of minority groups." These means, he argued, could help ensure the independence of the government and prevent the "tyranny" and "irresponsibility" of majority groups.[123] As an extreme expression of these beliefs, the Argentine Constitution of 1819, promoted by the radical liberal Bernardino Rivadavia, included an aristocratic senate and it did not openly declare its republicanism, which at the time was reasonably interpreted as an invitation to monarchical government.

The organization of the judicial system also occupied an important place within liberals' constitutional proposals. In both the United States and Latin America, liberals recognized a fundamental ally in the judges and, because of that, reserved significant functions for this branch of power. Mexico's Mora asserted that, "in a wisely constituted nation which has adopted for its government the representative system, the effective independence of the judicial power is the complement to the fundamental laws and the guarantee of public liberties."[124] Their confidence in the judgment of the magistrates stemmed from different sources. First, judges were "technically" well prepared. Second, because of the manner of their appointment and their stability, they were not dependent on the will of any group. As Madison claimed in *Federalist* 49, judges were "by the mode of their appointment, as well as by the nature and permanency of it...far too removed from the people to share much in their prepossessions." Third, the small number of its members (e.g., in a court of appeals or a supreme court) favored the deliberative process among its members. All these conditions, it seems, favored the adoption of impartial decisions.[125]

---

[122] Hale (1968), p. 86.
[123] Samper (1881), pp. 486–488. Samper asserted that it was obvious that, in France, the "democratic spirit, always exaggerated by the passion of equality, alternatively forced the French towards two possible abysses," that of communism and popular envy and that of socialism. Ibid.
[124] Quoted in Hale (1968), p. 93.
[125] However, one should note that in Latin America the courts never managed to become totally independent from political power. See, for example, Verner (1984).

Directly or indirectly, most liberals defended the right of the judicial power to decide the validity of all laws. That is, they defended the judges' right to have the last word regarding the constitutionality of democratically enacted legislation. Of course, theoretically speaking at least, politicians could always persist with their projects and initiatives, even when judges decided to invalidate them. However, it is also true that the judges could always persevere with their opinions and block the enforcement of certain laws.[126] In this way, liberal constitutions implicitly recognized the superiority of the judicial branch over others. In their favored democratic system, it is not the majority but, in fact, a peculiar minority that was authorized to have the "final" institutional word. In the end, this conclusion reflected the particular epistemic position of liberalism: they rejected both the radicals' view that impartiality was linked to the opinion of the multitude[127] and the conservative position that associated "right" decisions with those that reflected the "natural order" of things.

Judicial review, together with bicameralism and the powers of veto left in the hands of the executive, gave shape to the so-called system of checks and balances. The benefits of this system seem apparent. It forced the legislators to consider their decisions twice, improving the decision-making process; it ensured a special protection to minority groups; it forced each of the different sectors of society to anticipate and evaluate the decisions of the others; it favored the possibility of having "multiple eyes" looking at the same problem; and it made it very difficult for any group of self-interested representatives to simply impose their oppressive decisions upon the others. As Madison clearly explained in *Federalist* 51, the proposed device provided the members of the different branches of power with the "necessary

---

This fact, which distinguishes the judicial organization in Latin American countries from that in the United States, is the product of many different factors. Among them, many emphasize the different legal cultures of these two regions – namely, the "civil law" system in Latin America, and the "common law" system in the United States. See, for example, Rosen (1990). I believe, though, that these differences have been overemphasized.

[126] We already know that most constitutions did not openly incorporate the system of "judicial review," here under discussion. However, we also know that this power was usually recognized as "implicit" in the text of the constitution. This was, for example, the case in the United States, until Judge John Marshall made that situation explicit in his famous ruling in *Marbury v. Madison*.

[127] For this reason, also, some liberals showed no confidence in the jury system. José María Mora, for example, adopted an extreme position in this sense, arguing the need for forming juries of property holders only. "Only this group of citizens," he argued, "is truly independent and can inspire confidence in both the legislator and the rest of the nation." See Hale (1968), p. 95.

constitutional means, and personal motives," to resist the oppressive attempts of others. This solution, he argued, was based on a "reflection on human nature":[128] given the impossibility of disregarding the people's self-interest, the political system had to be prepared to counteract its worse consequences. As Madison put it, "ambition must be made to counteract ambition." Organized this way, the political institutions would allow them to prevent their most feared nightmare: the possibility of having an unchecked majority trying to implement its will through legal means.

If the main task of liberals was that of limiting the excesses of the majority group, the second was that of limiting the potential abuses of the executive. In order to achieve this second goal, they suggested adopting many different devices. For example, they proposed to limit the president's term of mandate; to prevent his reelection; to restrict his powers of veto or to facilitate congress's capacities for overcoming it; and to restrict or eliminate the executive's extraordinary or exceptional powers, so frequently used in Latin America. Colombian liberals made extraordinary efforts to limit the powers and ambitions of Bolívar. Santander, for example, kindly and ironically suggested to Bolívar that his constitutional proposals were compatible with the authority of a king or an emperor. Similarly, General José María Córdoba rebelled against Bolívar and rejected his institutional proposals. In these proposals, he argued, "everything is for life, everything tends to create a monarchy under the clothes of a [republican] presidency." In his opinion, a president appointed for life and politically unaccountable represented nothing less than a "monarch," endowed with powers that even kings lacked.[129]

Vicente Azuero also objected to Bolívar's constitutional proposals, asserting that the executive power that it created was stronger than that of the French and British monarchs. Bolívar's proposal, he argued, would invariably degenerate into despotism.[130] Vicente Azuero and Florentino González also argued against Bolívar's authoritarian proposals. In *La razón de mi voto*, which is recognized as the first important political declaration of Colombian liberalism,

---

[128] "If men were angels," wrote Madison in *Federalist* 51, "no government would be necessary. If angels were to govern men, neither external nor internal controls on government would be necessary. In a government which is to be administered by men over men, the great difficulty lies in this: you must first enable the government to control the governed; and in the next place oblige it to control itself."
[129] Morales Benítez (1997), pp. 27, 182, 189.
[130] Ibid., pp. 166–171. He exclaimed: "Que Bolívar sea grande, pero que Colombia sea libre!" Ibid., p. 161.

Ezequiel Rojas suggested the adoption of vast legal reforms. These included strong support for the rule of law; a proposal for adopting a truly representative system; his promotion of an efficient administration; and, fundamentally, a claim for adopting a limited executive, subordinated to the will of congress.[131] The antipresidentialist bias of Colombian liberals reached its pinnacle during the famous Río Negro Convention, which enacted the 1863 constitution. The new constitution limited the term of the president's mandate to just two years, allowed congress to overcome his veto by a simple majority, and delegated to the senate the power to appoint all high military and civil public officers, a power that conservative constitutions normally reserved for the president.[132] For José María Samper, "it reserved such a preponderant and dangerous authority to Congress...that the Executive appeared as a mere agent of the Legislature."[133] The 1863 constitution, which was notably stable for its time, lasting twenty-three years, inaugurated a period of more than two decades of liberal governments in New Granada. It also reaffirmed and radicalized the federal organization of the country. For Ramón Correa, this was the victorious principle: "the individual against the state, concretizing, therefore, Spencer's utopia and the states against the Nation."[134]

In Argentina, after the experience of Rosas's government, liberals decided not only to eliminate the possibility of presidential reelection but also to prohibit any delegation of extraordinary powers. In fact, article 29 of the 1853 constitution establishes that the delegation of "extraordinary powers" or "the sum of the public powers" will always be considered void. Even more strongly, it says that those who consented to that delegation or offered those powers would be considered to be "betrayers of the country." In Peru, also, liberals advocated the establishment of strict limits upon the authority of the president. The first three constitutions, those of 1823, 1828, and 1834, were fundamentally aimed at reducing the risk of a monarchical government, like the one suggested by General San Martín. The commission charged with writing the 1823 document, which was deemed the most "Rousseauean" of the three, asserted the need for "ensuring

---

[131] The article was published on July 16, 1848, in the newspaper *El Aviso*.
[132] During the debates, three clear factions emerged: one that represented the interests of the military and, therefore, of Mosquera; a second, composed of moderate liberals; and a third, more moderate, which mediated between the first two. The virtual absence of conservative groups, among the present factions, favored the creation of this very liberal document.
[133] Rivadaneira Vargas (1978), p. 128.
[134] Correa (1937), p. 295.

political liberty, a problem that cannot be solved by delegating too many powers to the Executive Power, which is the most dangerous [of the three branches] because it controls the military and the purse."[135] José Fanstino Sánchez Carrión proposed and defended the adoption of a three-headed executive, which would make it more difficult for it to advance any oppressive project because "three cannot get together to oppress." "A government by one," he argued, "was better if the people had to be treated as beasts, but if one wanted to defend liberty, then the presence of a single president represented the undesirable threat of tyranny."[136] At that time, Francisco Xavier de Luna Pizarro, who was the head of the first constitutional congress, claimed that "just to hear the word president scares me."[137] He was also the delegate who most strongly promoted the creation of very weak executives during the constitutional conventions of 1828 and 1834. In Uruguay during the debates of the 1830 constitution, a group of liberals led by José Ellauri tried to limit the powers of the executive, establishing the impossibility of removing a minister during his first year in power and the impossibility of extending his mandate beyond four years. Although this idea was strongly attacked during the convention, the proposal was considered necessary to restrict the scope of the executive's powers.[138] The liberal leader Bernardo Bello, founder of the Partido Blanco, continued this anti-authoritarian battle. In both his speeches and his political decisions, he repudiated the legacy of Rivera, Bolívar, Santa Cruz, and Napoleón. "These are names that irritate me," he said.[139]

In Ecuador, liberal deputies led a difficult fight against President Juan José Flores. This confrontation, which became particularly acute when liberals decided to deny Flores the concession of extraordinary powers, ended with an unsuccessful popular rebellion against the government. In this dispute, Vicente Rocafuerte played an active role, as a result of which he, among others, was expelled from the country and many others lost their lives. After decades of fruitless

---

[135] Basadre (1949), vol. 2, p. 267.
[136] Basadre (1949), vol. 1, p. 12.
[137] Pizarro had led the opposition to Bolívar's proposed constitution of 1826.
[138] What is important, argued Ellauri, is whether the minister has fulfilled his task or not. If the former, then one should protect those who acted properly. If the latter, then it should be no surprise that the constitution provided for legal means for removing someone. Bauzá (1887), pp. 320–321. The liberals, always concerned with the abuses of power, were defeated in this proposal but, notwithstanding, they obtained another significant victory: they included a prohibition on military officers becoming members of the parliament.
[139] Pivel Devoto (1951), p. 8.

opposition, liberals gained some strength during the 1840s and came to control the new constitutional convention assembled in 1845. Aimed at putting an end to long years of authoritarianism, liberals restricted the powers of the president and limited his term of mandate to only four years. The anti-authoritarian position was then led by Pedro Moncayo, one of the most remarkable representatives of the liberal camp,[140] and Gabriel García Moreno, who would soon become the president of the country and develop a highly conservative government. In Venezuela, during the 1840s, Antonio Leocadio Guzmán led a strong movement aimed at promoting political pluralism after decades of a conservative military regime. Guzmán's movement, which would give birth to the Liberal Party, was supported by numerous liberal associations and a strong and active press.[141] In 1845 he wrote a famous article in which he stressed the importance of opening the political arena to new parties with new and different political programs.[142] The article summarized the views of many Venezuelans who were tired of José Antonio Páez's authoritarian regime. Guzmán and his allies decided to participate in the next electoral contest and adopted a motto demanding "freedom-popular-sovereignty-progress-equality-alternation-constitution."[143] In some ways, Guzmán's initiative was not successful; it inaugurated a period of violence, which, among other things, included the prosecution and imprisonment of many liberals, Guzmán among them.[144] However, the movement that he launched symbolized the end of Páez's era and the coming of a new one in which conservative groups were no longer the hegemonic force of the country.

---

[140] Moncayo dedicated his life to criticizing authoritarianism. First, he fought against Bolívar and President Flores, who were, in his opinion, simply two cruel dictators. Villamarín (1993), p. 49. Later on, he led a persistent fight against President García Moreno. He and Eloy Alfaro were the two heroes of liberty against García Moreno's "theocracy" (they were, as they were called, "the pen and the sword"). Most of the time, Moncayo presented his ideas through the press, first through *El Quiteño Libre* and then through *La Linterna Mágica* or *El Progresista*. See, for example, Ayala (1993).

[141] At that time, in effect, the press seemed significantly lively. In a short period of time, many diverse newspapers appeared, including, for example, the well-known *El Venezolano*, *El Republicano*, *El Observador*, and *El Patriota*.

[142] This was the *Memoria que presenta la reunión liberal de Caracas a todos los hombres y círculos liberales de Venezuela*, which he wrote with Juan Manuel García and Manuel María Echandía, among others. See, for example, Quintero (1992).

[143] Boulton (1976), p. 86.

[144] Guzmán was condemned to death but then pardoned and freed by Monagas's government, which seemed to act in accordance with the supreme court. Significantly, after a short while Monagas appointed Guzmán first as his minister and then as his vice-president. See Bamko (1990).

In Chile, in 1858 José Victorino Lastarria dedicated one of his most important writings to objecting to the 1833 constitution, particularly the extraordinary powers that it delegated to the president.[145] In addition, accompanied by Federico Errázuriz, Lastarria proposed a radical reform of the national constitution. He suggested electing the president through indirect elections, prohibiting reelections, restricting the constitution's functions, and adding a bill of rights to the charter. A few years later Errázuriz would become the president of his country and promote a change in the constitution. These reforms included, among others, one for restricting the powers of the executive.[146]

Liberalism and Constitutionalism in the Americas: A Balance

What can we say about the influence of liberalism over matters of constitutional design? First of all, we should recognize that liberals had a defining influence in both the United States and Latin America. In the United States, they represented the main force behind the constitutional document of 1787. They designed most of the critical features of the constitution, such as the system of checks and balances or the strong federalist system. The U.S. Constitution, in turn, had an enormous influence over Latin America: even today, the majority of the constitutional documents in the region somehow echo the North American constitution. Its influence has even reached Europe, where institutional procedures such as judicial review seem to be more popular every day.

In Latin America, however, liberals had serious difficulties in guaranteeing stability to their programs. The Chilean Constitution of 1828, the only good example of a liberal constitution during the entire nineteenth century in Chile, was immediately removed and replaced

---

[145] José Victorino Lastarria probably represented the best of the so-called 1842 generation of young liberals. Creator of the Literary Society of Santiago, he was elected deputy in 1843 and presented multiple legislative proposals aimed at reducing the authoritarian features of the existing constitution. His book *La Constitución Política de la República de Chile Comentada* remains an excellent critique of the 1833 document. In this book, he deemed the Chilean Constitution to be totally inadequate to the time. The executive power, he wrote, was able to subordinate the other branches to its authority. In addition, its declaration of rights was insufficient. At the same time, another similarly critical analysis of the 1833 constitution was published by Carrasco Albano (*Comentario sobre la Constitución política de 1833*).
[146] See, for example, Donoso (1967).

with another in 1833. In Peru, the constitutions of 1823, 1828, 1834, 1856, and 1867 were all short-lived documents. In Colombia, documents such as those of 1832 and 1853 could not form the basis of a solid liberal tradition. The constitutions that immediately followed the 1853 charter developed some of its most interesting features but were finally replaced with the fundamental and very conservative document of 1886. In Venezuela, after the very short-lived project of 1811, liberals had enormous problems in regaining influence over constitutional matters.

The legacy of liberalism to the history of constitutionalism seems enormous. Liberals taught us to fear the power of the state. A powerful state, they strongly maintained, would always threaten individual liberties: liberals showed us that those who control the coercive apparatus of the state will continuously try to abuse it. They showed us that, given the poor personal qualities of human beings, it is necessary to establish strict controls over those who occupy public positions. In this sense, they have decisively fought to limit the dangerous proposals of their enemies, reducing the power of both majority institutions and the executive. In the United States, they played a fundamental role in the fight against an unrestrained congress, and in Latin America they were fundamentally important in the fight against quasi-monarchical executives. In addition, liberals left to posterity the influential system of checks and balances, aimed at securing a proper internal balance between the different branches of power. Despite the criticisms we could make of this system, both its normative foundations and its practical functioning, we must admit that it exercised a tremendous influence over the development of modern democracies. Through this and other institutions, liberals have helped many generations to counteract the tyranny of "one" and the tyranny of "the many."

In their attempts to reduce the risk of abuses of power, most American liberals campaigned for the atomization of the decision-making power, specifically, through federalism. Federalism seems to have many interesting characteristics. It seems to lessen the distance between the decision makers and those affected by the decisions at stake. It seems to favor the adoption of more "genuinely" popular decisions, namely, decisions that are not distorted by state bureaucrats. In sum, it promises to diminish the risk of another tyranny – the tyranny of central power over local powers.

Another creation of U.S. liberals, that of judicial review, largely transcended the barriers of their country and extended to most Western countries. This institution, which was actually born in 1801, although it was arguably implicit in the original U.S. Constitution, contributed to strengthening the idea that democracy is not only about majority will but also about how to protect individual rights.[147] Even when they were not the only actors in this battle for securing individual rights, liberals played a major role in diffusing the fundamental idea that each person is endowed with rights that deserve public protection. Nowadays, in fact, we tend to associate the idea of rights with the growth of liberalism, which recognizes many causes – that liberals were "born" fighting against religious despotism, that they took seriously the idea of the "neutral" state, and that they were always particularly concerned with the life of each individual person.

In conclusion, it is impossible to deny the important role played by liberals in the whole of America and to obscure the significance of their legacy. Most current American constitutions are still based on the model that they promoted.

Having said this, it is also important to stress other more problematic elements that we can associate with the influence of liberalism. In the first place, one could say that liberals have been incoherent in their actual works. Many of them, for example, wrote important pieces and made valuable speeches against state interventionism, while defending the participation of the state in order to make it possible to consolidate or strengthen their proposals. Many liberals, therefore, called on the state to "discipline" the workers (e.g., establishing the mandatory recruitment of the "lazy"); to discourage the "social" measures advanced by the "private" sector;[148] or to simply control the most dynamic sector of the economy, which promised the creation of more resources.

Of course, one could reasonably argue that the incoherence of some self-proclaimed liberals says nothing about the value of liberalism (even less so when we are discussing only "ideal models" with which to examine nonideal practices). However, the frequency of these contradictions is still surprising. These problems perhaps are the symptom of a more serious problem, namely, that liberals demand the presence of a "neutral" state, assuming a very peculiar conception of "neutrality," one that implies only a *certain* type of state passivity. In this view, liberals would favor only a *less* active role for the state in certain areas, and only after they had achieved a certain desired state of affairs.

---

[147] See, among many others, Dworkin (1996).
[148] See, for example, Halperín Donghi (1975), p. 359.

More generally, liberals seem undisturbed by the tremendous difficulty of defining what a situation of "full" state neutrality is. What always happens is that, in one way or another, by action or by omission, the public power supports a particular state of affairs. The situation that liberals assume to be "natural," such as a state free of public interventions, is also the product of state interventionism. We could ask liberals why one should consider, as was the case in Latin America, that the state has the duty to maintain a certain prevalent distribution of land unchanged, one that resulted from violent or unjustified appropriations. And why should one accept, as most liberals in America did, that the freed slaves should "naturally" restart their lives without sufficient resources, when for so long they had been prevented from obtaining them "naturally"? And why should one accept it as "natural" that the most advantaged groups of society used their advantages in order to appropriate the "new" available land? And why should one consider it as "natural" that the state did not provide any particular protection to the Native Americans after liberals deprived them of their common lands?

Liberals never made sufficient efforts to demonstrate that there were good reasons for considering "natural" the distributive state of affairs that they defended. They simply assumed the state of affairs that they most valued as "neutral" or given. Moreover, from this unjustified starting point they reached an additional conclusion, that the "neutral" or "natural" state of affairs was one that should be free, or almost free, of modifications. That is, they assumed that the state had a duty not to interfere, or, in other words, it had to protect a certain state of affairs. In those cases, they assumed, the state should not remedy or put limits on the undesirable consequences, even by liberals' standards, that could derive from that state of affairs.

Liberals, in this sense, did not want to recognize that the state was not being "neutral" but, on the contrary, was actively taking sides in favor of certain groups, through its actions and omissions. The state, for example, was actively supporting slavery in the United States, through both its actions and omissions. In addition, it was being partial when it allowed the concentration of property in a few hands, as happened, for example, during the López regime in New Granada; or after the enactment of the Ley de Enfiteusis in Argentina; or when it left the nonproprietors defenseless before those who owned large properties, as happened in most countries. In these cases, just a few examples among hundreds, the indifference of the state represented a kind of unjustified "blindness" that benefited only a small section of society, the group that, for reasons beyond its own responsibility, occupied a favored position within society.[149]

Contrary to what seems to be the presumptions of liberal constitutionalism, the state may be deemed responsible for a just or unjust dominant social situation. It is the state that prevents or allows these situations. Because of that, it should always provide reasons for what it does or does not do. It should justify each of the steps it takes.

Moreover, liberals have not considered fundamentally relevant those interventions made by the state when it creates and gives support to the police forces, when it enacts and enforces property laws, or when it protects through its coercive apparatus the existing distribution of lands. This intense state activism is described as the mere organization of the "natural order of things." Curiously, when it comes to defending these interventions, liberals no longer consider the state to be "ignorant" or a terrible threat, as Alberdi or Samper used to consider it. Liberals believe it is perfectly coherent, on the one hand, to reject any labor law, on the assumption that the state should not interfere with the private decisions of citizens, and, at the same time, to intervene in order to protect the existing distribution of property. They think it is coherent to reject state economic interventionism, alleging the risk of its abuses, but to defend its use of criminal law, in order to prevent violations of property law. That is, they fear the state in some cases but not in others.

In addition, liberals defend an unjustifiably biased view: they identify the state as being responsible for certain actual or potential evils that could perfectly well derive from other sources, for example, from the action of other particular individuals. Of course, to say this is not to affirm that the state should not be feared or controlled. Rather, what is suggested here is that it may be necessary to control all those individuals or groups that could cause harm to individuals. Clearly, one could reasonably say that there is no worse threat than that from the state, given the fact that the state has the "legitimate" control of coercion and numerous oppressive means under its control. However, it is difficult to defend this view when we examine the eighteenth or nineteenth century, periods when particular groups had an enormous capacity for imposing their will upon that of others.

Similarly, we could reproach liberals for being illogical: they have normally demanded respect for individuals' autonomous will while disregarding what we could call the "conditions for adopting autonomous decisions." If liberals really valued free individual choices, one

---

[149] See, for example, Holmes and Sunstein (1999).

could maintain, they should be more concerned about the conditions that make those free choices possible. To state this does not mean to say that one should aim at achieving "perfectly free" choices, or that one should try to recognize what are the "real" interests of each person. However, these reflections should move liberals to worry about certain particularly difficult situations. People who have spent most of their lives in conditions of slavery, for example, or who have been arbitrarily deprived of all their possessions are obviously in no condition to make good autonomous choices, for reasons clearly beyond their control. The state, then, becomes partly responsible for these difficult situations when it allows certain groups, for example, former slaves or Native Americans, to become povertystricken after being freed or after arbitrarily being deprived of their communal properties. When the state allows these situations to happen, as it did in both the United States and Latin America, it undermines the ideal of autonomy that it invokes in other situations, in order to justify the role it plays.

Finally, we should also mention other types of contradiction that affect liberal views. Those who defend this approach do not seem totally consistent in their support of "agreements between consenting adults." The confidence they have in individual will, which differentiates them from their more conservative colleagues, suddenly evolves into distrust in the case of majority will. Of course, any appeal to majority will has to confront difficulties that we do not find when we simply take individual will into account. For example, as Madison wrote in reply to Thomas Jefferson's arguments, any call to the majority will may trigger "passions" that may obscure rather than enlighten the decision-making process. In addition, it is always difficult to properly "read" the majority will: what did the people want to say when they voted in favor of this or that decision and against that other? Finally, it is also true that majoritarian decisions may be directly opposed to certain fundamental individual interests that liberals want to preserve at any cost.

Now, if liberals were really worried about majority passions, or about the difficulties they found in properly "reading" the majority will, they could explore the use of other institutional means, better prepared for acknowledging the popular will. They could propose more frequent and specifically oriented elections; they could propose the creation of public forums aimed at improving public dialogue; they could find the means for promptly removing those public officers whom the people reject. Moreover, they could try to defend individual fundamental interests without endangering all majority decisions, as they normally do, when they defend judicial review. However, liberals tend to criticize and reject these kinds of means. They support, instead, the adoption of other instruments that make it still more difficult to "refine" the public views that do not help the people themselves to think more calmly and adopt public decisions. Their promotion of large mandates, indirect elections, or weak congresses certainly does not contribute to a better understanding of the voice of the people. In addition, their distrust of open assemblies and their fear of popular discussion do not foster a mature public dialogue.

In the end, the liberal approach, in actual practice, seems to be based on controversial elitist assumptions that fair or impartial decisions are better ensured through the debates of a small and enlightened or a technically efficient minority, one that includes the supreme court. This assumption, I believe, is at least arguable when we try to defend a democratic system that is normally based on opposing assumptions. We tend to support democracy, in effect, because we assume the majority is already well prepared to adopt fundamental political decisions. If this were not the case, we should deny this last statement openly, as did many significant intellectual liberals, such as Alberdi, Echeverría, and Sarmiento.

Chapter Four
The Quest for Equality

Ulysses' Disloyalty

The constitutional models adopted in most American countries, I believe, dishonored the egalitarian ideals that were present at the beginning of the revolutions of independence. Most people became engaged in, or enthusiastic about, those independence struggles because of the egalitarian promises associated with the revolutionary movements.[1] They believed in the importance of collective self-government and wanted to prevent foreign societies from deciding how locals should live and how they should organize their political institutions. They believed that all the members of society had to have an equal and decisive say in the collective affairs of their community. They believed in the value of personal equality, in the idea that all men are created equal and that all are endowed with a "moral sense," as Jefferson put it.[2] They assumed that all had the same inalienable rights, an idea that they first learned from the French revolutionaries and which was pushed forward by their political leaders. As Wood claims, "The Revolution shattered traditional structures of authority, and common people increasingly discovered that they no longer had to accept the old distinctions that had separated them from the upper ranks of the gentry. Ordinary farmers, tradesmen, and artisans began to think they were as good as any gentleman and that they actually counted for something in the movements of events. Not only were the

---

[1] This does not imply that other values were not present during the revolutionary period, particularly the value of freedom. For a discussion about the ideal of equality and its dimension, see Dworkin (1977); Kymlicka (1991).

[2] Jefferson said that "man was endowed with a sense of right and wrong.... This sense is as much a part of his nature as the sense of hearing, seeing, feeling; it is the true foundation of morality.... The moral sense, or conscience, is as much a part of man as his leg or arm." Quoted in Schleifer (1991), p. 180.

215

people being equated with God, but half-literate plowmen were being told even by aristocrats like Thomas Jefferson that they had as much common or moral sense as learned professors."[3]

The very first line of the U.S. Declaration of Independence explicitly incorporated these egalitarian beliefs, which we also find in the first revolutionary constitutions in Latin America. That is to say, *the commitment to equality can be deemed the essence of America's social contract.*[4] However, as it evolved, American constitutionalism helped to erode those egalitarian ideals and not to strengthen them. American constitutionalism, rather than developing their potential, impaired, at least in part, those egalitarian aims.

I assume that equality has different dimensions and that it has not been discredited in all of them. I distinguish, at least, between a personal and a collective dimension, the first requiring an equal respect for each person's way of life and the second requiring respect for the majority will. To respect both those dimensions, in addition, requires ensuring certain social preconditions. Taking into account these assumptions, I would say that most constitutions in America tried, although not always successfully, to guarantee respect for each person's beliefs but failed to guarantee collective self-government and to ensure its preconditions. These constitutions, then, undermined the idea that all people were and should remain equally capable of participating in politics.[5] They dishonored the egalitarian principle that said that "all citizens, whatever their economic or social position, must be sufficiently equal in the sense that all have a fair opportunity to hold public office and to affect the outcome of elections."[6] Liberals did not facilitate but rather hindered the majority's capacity to form, express, and enforce its opinions. To put it another way, they helped the disloyal Ulysses to tie the hands of his sailors.[7]

---

[3] Wood (2002), p. 131.
[4] Ronald Dworkin interprets the U.S. Constitution as a document fundamentally committed to the idea of equality. See, for example, Dworkin (1985).
[5] One could wonder then: so what? Well, this would not be a problem if we did not still care about these egalitarian ideals. I believe, however, that these egalitarian ideals still matter and that they are implicit in the commitments we normally assume and express when we defend democratic politics.
[6] See Rawls (2001), p. 149.
[7] I use this metaphor only to manifest my skepticism regarding certain contemporary and rather optimistic views about constitutionalism. See, for example, the works included in Elster (1993). An interesting and more balanced analysis of these issues is in Elster (2000). In this new work, Elster's view on constitutionalism is certainly more skeptical than the one he presented in his earlier works, where he analyzed the potentialities and limits of individual and collective rationality. See Elster (1989; 1993).

The Unfulfilled Promise of Radicalism

Within the history of American constitutionalism, radicalism frequently seemed to be the most feared phantom. Both liberals and conservatives confronted radicals and depicted their real or imagined proposals as the worst of all possible evils.

In spite of the fact that most political leaders saw radicalism as their main opponent, radicals never achieved much influence within the constitutional life of their respective communities. Radicals were virtually absent from the U.S. constitutional convention. It is true that, in their support for local interests and political decentralization, as well as in their opposition to concentrated authority, many Anti-Federalists represented some of the radicals' most fundamental claims. However, it is also true that Anti-Federalists were not, in general, democratic leaders but, on the contrary, leaders who repudiated democracy and deprecated the will of the people. The radicals' absence from the constitutional convention does not mean, though, that they did not play an important role during that foundational period. In fact, most of the delegates at the convention anticipated a strong opposition to the constitution at the local level, where, they assumed, radicals exercised an important influence. Although radicals were not the main political voices at state level, they certainly exercised some influence over the population through their speeches and writings, and gained some support among people normally open to their democratic proposals.

In Latin America, the influence of radicalism was even shallower than in the United States. To start with, radicals were normally absent from the constitutional assemblies. In addition, within the fragile institutional structure that existed within those countries, radicals never gained, as they did in the United States, significant influence. Of course, the radicals' weakness at an institutional level has its counterpart: radicals were quite influential outside the existing institutions, that is, they played an important role at an extra-institutional level. Whereas in the United States, radicals, through their institutional influence, kept a certain capacity of *veto* over the way in which the new political institutions were designed, in Latin America, they basically lacked these powers.[8]

---

[8] This difference may help us to explain, for example, the lack of commitment showed, for a long time, by most Latin American radicals toward the political institutions: they never perceived these institutions as interesting and useful for developing their projects.

Despite these differences between the United States and Latin America, though, the final balance is fundamentally the same. In both contexts, radicals were feared, but they lacked an effective presence at constitutional conventions. The new constitutions did not properly reflect their views and demands. Most American constitutions came to *prevent* the influence of radicalism, by making it more difficult for radical groups either to gain political power or to carry out their projects. Most new constitutions, therefore, created a strong separation between the representatives and the people, burning most of the bridges still existing between them; they deactivated popular participation and strengthened the role of countermajoritarian devices.

When we recognize the weak presence of radicalism in the American constitutional assemblies, another broader question becomes dominant: what explains the absence or extraordinary brevity of radical movements during the period under examination? It is worth considering the following examples. The Venezuelan Constitution of 1811 – deemed, at its time, to be a radical constitution given the power it transferred to the congress, its federalist features, and its Rousseauean phraseology – was soon displaced and replaced by a dictatorial government. In the Banda Oriental, the democratic and federalist experience of the early years of independence promptly disappeared, and Artigas was forced to abandon politics. Artigas's legacy was important for posterity, but nobody seriously tried to develop his democratic proposals and his egalitarian concerns. In Mexico, Hidalgo and Morelos, leaders of the first independence movements of the country, were both savagely killed. The federalist government of Guerrero, a figure who tried to follow Hidalgo's policies, did not last more than two years in power. Even before that time, two of the main allies of the government, Minister Lorenzo Zavala and the American ambassador Joel Poinsett, were forced to leave their positions under the accusation of being too radical. Another of Hidalgo's followers, Juan Alvarez, also left his position as president of the country at a very early stage. His government, mostly formed by *liberales puros*, lasted only a few months and its most radical member, Melchor Ocampo, kept his position for only fifteen days.

In Argentina, Mariano Moreno, the most extremist (which does not necessarily mean the most radical) revolutionary leader of the time, died in 1811 after only one year of intense political activity. Moreno died, or according to many was killed, while he was leaving the country, disappointed with the way in which the revolutionary movement was evolving. A very interesting federalist political leader, Mariano Dorrego, was killed a few years later, when he was beginning to develop a political life that promised to be extraordinary. In Chile, the egalitarian Sociedad de la Igualdad carried out intense political activity, which, notably, did not last even one year: the Sociedad was dissolved and most of its prominent members were sent into exile or arrested. Similarly, in Ecuador, the Sociedad el Quiteño Libre was suddenly aborted. Governmental forces killed many of its most important members, the noted Francisco Hall among them. In Colombia, many radicals played a fundamental role in José Hilario López's electoral victory: they contributed to ensuring that triumph through a dense net of "Democratic Societies." However, once in power, López ignored the demands of their supporters and promoted an economic program that fundamentally harmed the interests of the artisans. In addition, Murillo Toro, probably the most brilliant representative of Colombia's radical liberalism, was soon obliged to resign from Lopez's cabinet. His proposals for a reform in the organization of property, proposals that he would not readopt in his subsequent years in politics, seemed to be too radical for this government.

Perhaps one should consider all these situations as merely isolated events. Perhaps one should not bring them together, suggesting, as I am, that there was a common thread connecting them. However, it would still be true that that enumeration summarizes the most important radical experiences in the region. The tragic and abrupt end of most of them says something about the difficulties that radicals found, during the foundation years of constitutionalism, in giving political life and ensuring stability to their proposals.

The difficulties faced by radicals may be attributed to a diversity of causes: the hostility that the radicals' proposals generated within a homogeneous political class; the fact that some of their most important goals were directly opposed to the interests of the most sensible and most privileged groups in society (the group of "creditors" in the United States, the church and the military in Latin America); the difficulty that their leaders had in articulating a socially attractive and easily understandable discourse; or, perhaps, simply the internal defects of their proposals. In any case, what is clear is that radicals could not impose their own views of how to institutionally reorganize new societies and faced serious institutional and extra-institutional difficulties in advancing their proposals.

There did result, however, one curious set of alliances, not so unusual in American history – namely, the alliance between radical and conservative forces. This alliance acquired a certain importance at that time and continued to exist, after the end of the nineteenth century, even when the two forces fought each other on so many occasions. In order to explain this peculiar alliance, references to opportunistic motives are only partially helpful. I think that our previous analysis provides us with a better explanation for this curious combination. According to our description of the two groups, and in spite of their differences, some significant coincidences did exist between radicalism and conservatism. For example, both were hostile to individualist ideals – that is, antiliberal. Both radicals and conservatives distrusted the democratic formalism and commitment to the rule of law that distinguished liberal positions. More significantly, both strongly rejected the ideal of state neutrality, which they considered an ideal not only impossible to sustain in practice but also undesirable. For conservatives, neutrality implied a denial of their main goal, namely, that of sustaining a certain conception of "the good" through the coercive apparatus of the state. For radicals, it implied a dismissal of their commitment to majority rule: they wondered why they should prevent majorities from publicly defending their own beliefs.

In his excellent study of Juan Manuel de Rosas's regime, Jorge Myers makes an interesting point: "The habits of morality and personal self-control that were underlying the new order...could deserve either a Christian or a republican reading: the Christian virtue offered a social cement at least as powerful as the republican *virtus*."[9] The two groups representing conservatism and radicalism could join forces not only for opportunistic reasons but also, and more importantly, because significant coincidences did exist between them. Therefore, their strong opposition regarding the political organization of society was sometimes overcome by their partial coincidences regarding the role of the state. They normally wanted different things, or the same thing for different reasons – for example, one might defend the Catholic religion as the right faith, the other as the faith of the majority. But they had a common enemy, and that was sometimes enough for them to make an alliance.

Liberalism: Stabilizing Its Own Program

One of the most salient events in the constitutional history of the region has to do with the marked influence of liberalism over the shaping of its basic institutional structure. The importance of this conception may be acknowledged in the main features of the most fundamental constitutions then adopted. For example, we can mention the federal

[9] Myers (1995), p. 85.

Liberalism: Stabilizing Its Own Program

structure promoted by these constitutions; their bill of rights; or the entire system of checks and balances, with its bicameral congress, the veto powers of the president, and judicial review. In addition, we perceive the influence of liberalism in the hostility that many fundamental protagonists of the time manifested toward the state. The state's abstinence, which they supported, was normally justified as a way of ensuring the strictest respect for individual rights. In addition, liberals said that abstinence would favor the free choices of individuals.

Of course, this does not imply that liberals were always equally successful in America. Rather, the liberal-individualist project prospered in the United States[10] to some extent, while it could not create the basis of its own stability in Latin America.[11] In part because of external pressures and in part through their own fault, Latin American liberals frequently needed the help of conservative forces in order to guarantee the political stability they could not ensure alone.[12] Conservatives appeared to be the great providers of political stability in a continent usually affected by political turmoil.[13] This successful alliance between liberals and conservatives – successful, that is, in terms of political stability – brought with it the gradual corrosion of the liberal program. Liberals began to open the door to decisions they used to reject on principle. These changes become apparent when we examine their tendency to defend more concentrated political systems, especially those systems with a strong executive power, capable of suspending fundamental rights and guarantees, intervening in the internal affairs of local states, or taking part in the legislative activity of the community. Additional changes are reflected in the liberals' gradual tendency to defend conservative policies, for example, giving special status to the Catholic Church.

---

[10] We should admit that the stability that liberals ensured for their project in the United States was also bought at a high price, a price that included, for example, the postponement of the discussion of slavery.
[11] See also, in this respect, Aguilar Rivera (2000).
[12] The fact that conservatism was particularly successful in Latin America does not imply that it was not also very successful and influential in the United States. In fact, conservatives played a fundamental role during the constitutional debates in that country and never ceased to play an important role in its political life. However, it is also true that, in this case, liberals managed to restrain their pressures to adopt more conservative or authoritarian policies. In this sense, one could affirm that U.S. liberals managed to preserve a political system fundamentally loyal to their ideals.
[13] We should think not only of the stability they sometimes provided to the liberal programs but also of the stability they ensured for their own proposals. Recall, in this sense, the experiences of Páez in Venezuela, Rosas in Argentina, Francia or López in Paraguay, García Moreno in Ecuador, and the forty years of severe conservatism in Chile.

221

By getting closer to the conservatives and more sensitive to their demands, liberals obtained political oxygen and managed to strengthen their own programs. At the same time, however, this attitude turned out to be harmful to their own interests. In effect, given the fundamental incompatibility between the liberal and conservative projects, their own political mistakes, the voracity of their main ally, or simply the enormous fragility of the societies they had to govern, liberals found it extremely difficult to sustain their plans in the long run. In Latin America, at least, after each electoral victory liberals tended at first to evolve gradually into conservatives and finally became engulfed by their powerful ally.

In spite of this, liberals played a key role in the institutional development of new societies, both in the United States and in Latin America. They were probably more successful in the fight to design new institutions than in ruling their societies.

This at least partial success of liberalism, predominant in the United States and highly influential in Latin America, has several explanations. Liberals were quick to situate themselves between their two main rivals, conservatives and radicals. Seemingly, from this intermediate position they were able to satisfy at least part of the claims of all the different groups in society. Liberals were also successful in showing themselves capable of avoiding the extremism of both their opponents. They were skillful, in addition, in presenting their rivals' views in their extreme, less acceptable forms. Their axiom, "neither anarchy nor tyranny," summarized their quest perfectly and attracted genuine republican spirits, who were numerous during the period under examination. Most people, in fact, could easily imagine what could emerge from the abuses of "one" and the oppression of the many. Neither conservatives nor radicals, liberals reasonably claimed, were capable of putting an end to the disorder and violence that affected the new nations. Exploiting the weaknesses of their opponents, liberals began to defend the ideal of the state's neutrality and political *equilibrium*. Liberals promised moderation and the establishment of limits to power.

Liberals not only successfully exploited the differences that distinguished them from their opponents. They also appealed skillfully to the consensus they had with these opponents, whenever they found it necessary to do so. For example, liberals and radicals worked together when confronting the dictatorial threats that menaced their countries. In Latin America, they fought together against the unjustifiable privileges of the church and the military. Moreover, they commonly defended the egalitarian principle that all people were born equal. In this sense, they affirmed the primacy of the individual over the traditions and habits of the societies in which they lived, the final primacy of human reason. These particular coincidences were fundamental in fostering contingent alliances between the two and helped them to confront conservative forces. However, the links between liberals and conservatives were still more profound and fruitful.

Liberals, Conservatives, and Political Inequality

The main Latin American constitutions after the 1850s represented a mixture of liberal and conservative features. In fact, we clearly find this gradual convergence between liberals and conservatives in the Chilean *fusión* (a political alliance between the two groups), which appeared in the second half of the nineteenth century; in Argentina, through the constitution of 1853; in Peru, through the (modified) constitution of 1860; in Colombia, with the end of a radical-liberal period of constitutionalism and the ascendance to power of President Rafael Nuñez; in Mexico, after dramatic constitutional events; and in Venezuela, after the end of the federalist wars. This circumstance may sound surprising, given the great divergence between these two views. Undoubtedly, liberals and conservatives espoused totally opposing views with regard to matters of personal morality. The former believed that each person should be in charge of his or her own life, whereas the latter assumed that the right conception of "the good" had to prevail, no matter what each person chose to do. In fact, this issue is the cause of many of the most important wars and political struggles in Latin America.

How do we explain, then, the convergence between liberal and conservative forces? As the Argentinean writer J. L. Borges could have said, these two forces joined together not from love but from fear. In effect, they both recognized that they would be worse off with anarchy or the unconstrained dominance of popular majorities. In that sense, they found that it was better to leave their differences behind than to perish because of a radical victory.

There was an important space for cooperation between the two forces: the differences that separated them with regard to matters of personal morality were compensated for by the consensus they had regarding matters of public morality. This overlapping consensus was grounded on multiple and varying reasons. First, conservatives strongly rejected radicalism because they assumed that an active popular majority could prevent or constantly threaten the promotion of their favored conception of "the good." Second, many conservatives assumed that a vast majority of the population was unable to participate in politics. Similarly, many liberals assumed a proper decision-making process required quiet and sedate reflection, which active popular assemblies unequivocally tended to undermine. Radicalism was, therefore, not only unacceptable but also inconvenient. In addition, many liberals believed that the ideals of individual autonomy and collective self-government were in permanent tension and that, in the end, the former had to prevail over the latter. They primarily wanted to protect the life and plans of each individual against the desires of a dictator or the preferences of the majority. A final point, and probably the most important one, was that conservatives and liberals shared certain basic economic concerns (even when they often defended these concerns for different reasons). Both groups strongly defended property rights. Both of them assumed that it was necessary to create very firm barriers against the arbitrary usurpations of a majority of propertyless people. All these factors favored a convergence between liberals and conservatives: by deactivating or neutralizing the growing impact of popular majorities, they would both advance some of their most cherished proposals. To do so, it was necessary to weaken the forces of radical groups and their advocates. Through their combined efforts, liberals and conservatives designed an institutional system that had a number of features.

First, they rejected direct democracy and proposed, in its place, a representative system that was based on a profound distinction between the people and their representatives. The representatives were not supposed to be the advocates of the people but the quasi-independent guardians of their interests.[14] In a similar vein, they discouraged public assemblies and town meetings and proposed to replace them with "a corporate form whereby the towns could be governed by mayors and councils."[15]

Second, they weakened the links that existed, or could exist, between representatives and the people, leaving the latter in control of very rigid institutional tools only. For radicals, periodic elections, usually the only significant institutional powers remaining in the hands of the people, were problematic in at least two different ways. On the one hand, they implied rejecting annual elections and, thus, short-term mandates; this aspect they valued highly. On the other hand, they did not allow the development of a proper connection between the people and their representatives. How could the

---

[14] A discussion of these issues is in Urbinati (2000).
[15] Jensen (1967), pp. 118–121.

people tell their representatives, through elections, that they wanted to support proposal A but not B? How could they applaud their representatives for advancing proposal X and, at the same time, punish them for advancing Y? For radicals, popular suffrage seemed to be an acceptable but problematic starting point: in the absence of other political instruments, it promised to be a very difficult time for popular majorities.

Third, liberals and conservatives put too much weight on internal controls and, particularly, on a questionable set of such controls. In some cases, they were used to ensure that all the main sectors of society had an institutional say. Liberals also commonly pursued this goal, characteristic in conservative or mixed constitutions. Typically, the senate or the other branches of power selected by indirect election came to represent the voice of the wealthy or property owners, while the lower house represented those without property. Arguably, this result could ensure that no one sector of society would oppress any other. However, the price that was paid for this purpose was exorbitant, at least in democratic terms: majority rule was directly replaced by another system, which gave the so-called minority an equal voice. These criteria find another expression in the promotion of counter-majoritarian controls, such as judicial review. Notably, through the adoption of judicial review, liberals and conservatives left the last institutional say in the hands of a group not elected by the people and not directly accountable to them. Democracy, as a system fundamentally based on majority rule, was seriously challenged.[16]

Finally, the new institutional system tried to ensure all the previously mentioned conditions by making it very difficult for the people to modify the constitution. In most cases, constitutional reform required the support of supermajorities, which left a final power of veto in the hands of minority groups. In his "Notes on the State of Virginia," Jefferson carefully and intelligently argued against this outcome, which he considered contrary to his commitment to majority rule.

Moreover, this institutional structure was normally supported by an economic system that contributed to reproducing and creating more inequalities. The economic system favored by liberals

---

[16] There are thousands of books and articles dedicated to this point and aimed at showing that judicial review does not offend democratic values. However, after more than two hundred years of discussion, there are still no definite, convincing arguments for the compatibility between democracy and judicial review. See excellent discussions on the topic in Bickel (1962); Dworkin (1977; 1996); Ely (1980); Friedman (2002; 2009); Kramer (2005); Nino (1997); Sunstein (1993); Tushnet (1999); Waldron (1999).

was based on the assumption that each individual should be left alone: the economic structure of the country had to be created by the free and spontaneous decisions of the citizenry. Undoubtedly, in societies that were already extremely unequal, this principle implied that the decisions of a few privileged men defined the economic destiny of all the rest. If the institutional system created and reproduced political inequality, the economic system created and reproduced economic inequalities. In addition, both liberals and conservatives rejected the radicals' initiatives for fostering economic equality. They dismissed Artigas's plan for agrarian equality, ridiculed the proposals of the radical Mexicans and Venezuelans for distributing the land, and simply ignored Arcos's plan for economic fairness. They adopted in their place laws protecting the right to property and ensuring against confiscation; these included, for a long while, protections for the right to own slaves. Political inequalities, in the end, were supported by profound and growing economic inequalities.

Ultimately, liberals, either alone or with the help of conservatives, partially abandoned the principle of political equality that had often been proudly included at the start of the constitutions they promoted. As a result, they left the decision-making process in the hands of a minority of representatives who could act with independence from the people. In addition, within this political sphere the most popular branch of government appeared as the most affected: a set of countermajoritarian devices came to dilute the power of the majoritarian branch of the government. The idea that each person counted as one, the idea that the voice of one person had to receive the same attention as the voice of another, was suddenly denied. The voices of a few public officers and, among them, the voices of selected minorities acquired more importance than the voice of the people at large.

This situation seems curious: by acting in this way, we could maintain, *liberals were dishonoring the very egalitarian principle that made their view attractive.* In fact, their defense of personal morality showed their strong and significant commitment to equality: they wanted to ensure respect for each person's way of life, regardless of its particular content. They assumed that the viewpoints and preferences of each member of the community mattered equally and that the government should treat them with equal consideration. They assumed, in sum, that each person was entitled to equal concern and respect.[17] However, they did not pursue this commitment consistently. They did

---

[17] See Dworkin (1977).

not translate their defense of each person's decisions regarding their private life into a defense of the community's decisions regarding public life. We have to explore, then, two questions: Was it reasonably possible for them to act in a different way? And how should they have acted in that case? Or, to state it differently, what would a more consistent egalitarian position look like?

Political Inequalities: Were They Unavoidable?

In spite of these problems, it could be maintained that liberal, and even liberal-conservative, constitutions were to some degree egalitarian. Let us consider three such possible claims.

First, designing a political system more egalitarian than the one we have is not possible. Direct democracy, a political system that in principle seems more closely related to egalitarian political principles, was not, nor is it today, available in large, heterogeneous societies. A representative democracy, we could conclude, is the closest we can come to political equality.

This first claim faces many problems. Above all, representative democracy was not supported as a second-best or a necessary evil, as many radicals promoted it, but, on the contrary, as a first and desired choice. Liberals assumed, as Madison famously wrote in *Federalist* 10, that through a representative system "it may well happen that the public voice, pronounced by the representatives of the people, will be more consonant to the public good than if pronounced by the people themselves, convened for that purpose." The primary idea was that direct democracy was undesirable, as Madison stated clearly in the same paper; and that, given the defects that normally affected collective deliberations and, consequently, made direct democracy undesirable, the decisions of a select few could substantially improve the decisions of the majority at large. In Latin America, this view received even stronger support. The best representatives of Argentinean liberalism, for example, the members of the 1837 Generation, proposed a crude distinction between the representatives and the people, in accordance with which it was necessary to accept the *sovereignty of reason* but not the *sovereignty of the people*, an argument that openly expressed their political elitism. Liberals such as José María Samper in Colombia or José María Químper and Fernando Casós in Peru clearly shared this view. Liberals' preference for a representative system was frequently based on unjustifiable assumptions about the irrationality of popular majorities. The problem, of course, is not simply that the *arguments* that came to support the liberal-conservative system were problematic in terms of political equality but rather that the very institutions that they defended were questionable in those terms. Given their distrust of majority rule, they discouraged rather than promoted political participation, majoritarian assemblies, and popular debates.

Second, the planned institutions simply tried to prevent the evil consequences that followed from the adoption of a pure majoritarian system. The argument can be stated as follows: given that certain majoritarian procedures only help us to discover an unrefined version of the majority will, we need to adopt different refining procedures. In the end, it is arguable that the system of checks and balances, for example, helps us to refine the voice of the people, as Madison put it in *Federalist* 10, and not to disregard it.

In contrast with this view, however, we could first argue that it is not at all clear that a device such as the system of checks and balances refines the voice of the people. On the one hand, we could join some early radicals and say that it makes the decision process too complex, making it difficult to get a genuine sense of what the people, or their representatives, were really thinking regarding a certain issue. The system of checks and balances requires the intervention of too many hands, before the eventual enforcement of any law. Moreover, those who intervene in this process have very different democratic credentials, different legitimacy, and different interests. For example, some of them may have been democratically elected, whereas some of them may not. Some of them may have been selected after a recent election and for a short time, whereas others may have been occupying their position for a long time and have life tenure. Some of them may have been put in place to defend local interests, whereas others may be in office to defend national interests. In the end, it is difficult to argue that the law that emerges at the end of this complex process actually expresses a refined democratic will and not a mere patchwork of views and opposing interests.[18]

On the other hand, we should remember that during the founding period institutional alternatives already existed that were open to those sincerely committed to the refinement of majority rule. Thomas

---

[18] For example, the lower house passes an initiative, the senate partially modifies it, the house includes additional changes, the executive modifies it a little more, the congress accepts these changes, a judge says that the enacted law is partially unconstitutional, the court of appeals partially modifies that opinion. After all these changes and challenges, it is difficult to think that the initial decision has been refined and, therefore, in some way improved. It may be the case that we end up with a patchwork that nobody identifies with anymore. That is, the presence of multiple hands in the creation of a law does not necessarily imply the improvement of the law.

Paine, for example, defended some of these initiatives, as when he answered the critics of his unicameral proposal; this took seriously the aim of refining the voice of the people, without diluting the majoritarian character of the political system. The idea, of course, is not that *these* alternatives were the right ones, but rather that it is, as it was, possible to consistently promote both these aims. Liberals, on the other hand, seemed to support the first goal, the refinement of the majority view, while disregarding the importance of the second, the preservation of the law's majoritarian character.

Third, the politically inegalitarian character of the liberal-conservative system was necessary in order to prevent a profoundly inegalitarian outcome, namely, that of having the majority oppressing the minority. In contrast with this position, however, we could first say that it is not obvious that these two ideals, individual autonomy and collective self-government, necessarily collide and that one, therefore, had to prevail over the other. Second, even accepting that these two ideals are in tension, it is not clear why the protection of individual autonomy should prevail over the protection of collective self-government. Third, and assuming the need to give priority to the protection of individual autonomy, we could say that there are other instruments available to protect individual rights, without dishonoring the ideal of collective self-government.[19] In fact, just to mention one important example, mechanisms such as judicial review, the main instrument associated with the custody of individual rights, give the judiciary vast more powers than necessary to protect individual autonomy. Typically, judicial review allows the judges to have the last say in all types of political decision and not only a say in those cases that seemingly affect individual autonomy. Finally, we have a problem derived from the fact we profoundly disagree about the meaning of individual autonomy and how to protect it: Is the protection of (an unequally distributed system of) private property a necessary condition for the protection of individual autonomy, as many Americans

---

[19] For example, in order to avoid the countermajoritarian objection to the judiciary, we could prevent it from having the last institutional say but still preserve an important role for it in the protection of minority rights. One possible solution could be that judges could remand the challenged law to parliament, rather than declare it void in a particular case. In presenting this example, I simply mean to show that there are solutions that would permit the preserving of both the majoritarian features of the political system and our concern for minority rights. The Canadian "notwithstanding clause" (which allows a simple majority of the political branch of government to pass a law that is immune to the judicial scrutiny, with respect to certain parts of the constitution) represents an interesting contemporary alternative to the United States' "pure" system of judicial review. See, for example, Tushnet (1999).

simply assumed? Should the protection of individual autonomy prevent us from publicly reacting against a consumerist, individualist culture? And, in those cases, what (re)actions should be allowed or disallowed?

Egalitarianism and Politics: Recognizing the Value of Public Discussion

If political inequalities were not unavoidable, making it possible to defend a more egalitarian alternative, what would it look like? I believe that this alternative would try to promote both of the basic ideals that we have been examining so far: the ideal of *personal self-government* and the ideal of *collective self-government*. The promotion of personal self-government would be of primary importance, as a way of recognizing that each person is the best judge of his or her own interests. In other words, this principle of personal self-government implies that nobody should be sovereign over other people's lives, that each person's personal decisions are as important as those of any other. This equal respect for each person is then reproduced in the public sphere. Once again, we assume that the opinion of each person should count as much as the opinions of all the others: each counts as one and only as one. Once again, we assume that neither monarchy, aristocracy, oligarchy, nor plutocracy should prevail over the collective will.

This double compromise with personal and collective self-government implies a substantial challenge to the different views so far examined. Here, the idea is that *personal problems should be handled by each individual, and collective problems should be confronted and solved collectively.*[20] Clearly, this *egalitarian* view challenges the

---

[20] The crucial question here (as in most other theories, I would add) is how to distinguish between the personal and interpersonal or collective spheres. This is an important and enormously difficult question. The first thing I would say is that one should not define the personal sphere through a spatial conception; that is, the personal is not what happens at home, for example. If a person is abused by others, the problem becomes nonpersonal (see, e.g., Nino, 1991). The question, then, has to be: what does abuse mean? Again, the answer is very difficult, although I think that, at this point (although maybe not in other areas) Dworkin's distinction between personal and external factors may be useful. External factors concern the goods, resources, and opportunities one wants available to others (see Dworkin, 1977, p. 234). In this sense, I would say that a problem does not become a collective one because of the external factors that some person or group happens to experience (e.g., they happen to feel uncomfortable with someone else's way of life). I will leave the problem here, although there are still many things to say in order to clarify this issue.

conservative view, which seems to reject both claims. Conservatism, as we described it, disregarded the importance of both personal choices and collective choices. Conservatism represented, then, the complete denial of egalitarianism. Radicalism, instead, would partially affirm and partially deny egalitarianism. It would affirm it in its support for collective self-government, in its fight against the tyranny of the few. It would deny it in its disrespect for personal self-government and its lack of interest in each individual's personal plans. Radicals, in fact, simply accepted that majority will could prevail over personal choice. It is not well equipped to deny, for example, the value of a collective decision regarding homosexuality or the personal consumption of drugs. By contrast, it provides the terms within which these decisions could be defended. In this sense, radicalism does not take the equal value of each person's decisions seriously.

Something similar occurs with liberalism, which partially supports and partially condemns the egalitarian viewpoint. It supports it for its protection of the individual will and individual autonomy. No other theoretical viewpoint has done more for the protection of each person's lifestyle than individualism. However, liberals do not seem to take the collective will seriously: they do not trust majoritarian assemblies and collective decisions. They want to install the principle that individual decisions alone should count.

In the end, the view that became dominant in American constitutionalism partially reflects this latter view. Liberal and liberal-conservative constitutions reflect the same anticollectivist bias; they both disregard the importance of collective agreements.

On the contrary, egalitarianism aims at strengthening, rather than eliminating or weakening, the possibility of achieving popular collective agreements. By doing this, it tries to reestablish an egalitarian dimension that disappears when the collective life of the community begins to depend on the initiatives of a powerful minority. In this sense, we may add, egalitarians try to be *consistent* with their egalitarianism, to carry the partially egalitarian commitment of alternative views further. Egalitarians assume that the social life of the community should be the product of a genuine agreement among equals, an agreement in which the opinion of each individual matters, independently of the economic resources or the political abilities and connections that person may have. This would be a genuine way of showing respect for each person: a collective agreement on public issues would ensure that each person is counted as an equal. To state this is not to simply assume the importance of supporting, for example, the right of freedom of association or the right to suffrage.

What egalitarians want is not only the formal possibility of expressing a collective opinion or reaching an agreement with other citizens. Egalitarians defend the actual adoption of collective decisions on certain public questions. They are not satisfied with the possibility of having merely spontaneous agreements among people.[21] Egalitarians believe that social agreements are a public good that partly depends on the state's support. The economic life of the community, for example, would be the outcome of a collective agreement: the phenomenon that is common today, in which, in many communities, the sudden decision of a few becomes more important than the opinion of the majority, would simply never occur.

Following on from these beliefs, more egalitarian constitutional thinkers supported public discussion and active popular participation in politics. They tried to promote this participation through collective associations. "Associations are the necessity of our century," claimed Juan Montalvo. In his opinion, "Isolation, the separation between citizens, implies the triumph of despotic governments. [However,] if the oppressor has to confront a vast group of united men, then they become afraid and retreat." Despotism and anarchy, he believed, could be confronted only by the association of "all good men."[22] In this sense, egalitarians wanted to reverse the many existing initiatives that discouraged civic activism.[23] They believed that the people's active participation in associations would favor collective self-determination as well as the autonomy of each. "The spirit of association is characteristic of human beings and of civil society," argued González Vigil. Associations, he believed, helped people to think about others, to abandon individualism. They allowed people to meet with others and to integrate with them.[24] In this way, egalitarians defied those liberals who linked liberty with individual autonomy and resisted the ideal of collective self-determination. As Montalvo put it, egalitarians

---

[21] In fact, liberals affirm that they do not block the formation of these agreements. However, they usually discourage them because of their distrust of majority rule. They not only refuse to give incentives to public meetings but also raise disincentives to popular decisions through the support of countermajoritarian institutions.

[22] Montalvo presented this view in the inaugural speech of the Sociedad Republicana. See Roig (1984), p. 233.

[23] Similarly, González Vigil claimed that "associations...have...as their first and indispensable requirement...to promote and assist the general interests....it is absurd that government distrusts associations...there is no reason to discredit or forbid them....it is absurd to pretend that, in democratic governments, citizens do not get involved in politics...an extravagance...which is inconceivable." González Vigil (1948), pp. 19–21.

[24] González Vigil (1948), pp. 19–23. See also Montalvo, in Roig (1984).

believed that "liberty" was a "collective good" that had to be protected by the collective actions of the community.[25]

Clearly, one may put forward many arguments against those of the egalitarians. For example, critics may remain silent about the importance of associations or the importance of reaching collective agreements, but object to the evil consequences associated with them. Many liberals, for example, feared the presence of huge popular associations because they believed that they could easily oppress their members or the members of minority groups. Others, like the U.S. Federalists, believed that the voices of demagogues always tended to prevail in such groups. Even when it is difficult to deny that mass meetings may generate disturbances and confusions not likely to appear in smaller groups, however, one should not forget the benefits of promoting open, public discussion. This open exchange allows each person to recognize arguments he had not previously considered, to acknowledge difficulties and consider solutions not previously seen, and to obtain a better picture of the problems involved. Moreover, it can force each person to modify his preferred arguments in order to make them acceptable to others. It may also have a healthy educational effect, improving people's abilities to reason and to live alongside others. In a letter to John Adams, written in 1787, Thomas Jefferson referred to some of these benefits and criticized the secret character of the debates at the federal convention. "I am sorry," he said, "[that the federal convention] began their deliberations by so abominable a precedent as that of tying up the tongues of their members. Nothing can justify this example but the innocence of their intentions, & the ignorance of the value of public discussions." In contrast with what most Federalists believed, Jefferson deemed that the only way of adopting impartial political decisions was through an open exchange, a collective discussion among those potentially affected. Of course, to put forward this view implies subscribing to certain assumptions that many critics of egalitarianism refuted: egalitarians and nonegalitarians seem to be separated not only by political but also by basic epistemic assumptions.

In order to strengthen the egalitarian position, we should clarify that not *every* public issue needs to be discussed in public, especially when this implies that *all* those affected need to intervene in that discussion. A reasonable egalitarian conception simply needs to support the formation of public agreements every time that a matter of serious

[25] See Roig (1984), p. 217.

public concern is at work.[26] In addition, the goal of deciding most public problems collectively does not necessarily require egalitarians to resort to mass assemblies or gigantic meetings that may seriously affect the possibility of exchanging arguments. In contrast with this view, many egalitarians supported the atomization of the decision-making process, making it possible for decentralized assemblies to participate in increasingly circumscribed decisions. The town meeting experience in the United States represents a good example of how these assemblies could work.[27] In sum, egalitarians do not need to commit themselves to the implausible picture that their critics want to present of them. Moreover, egalitarians do not need to subscribe to the implausible assumption that "the voice of the people is the voice of God": their defense of majority rule does not need to imply a blind support of radicalism. In the end, to respect the will of the people does not require the enforcement of the first idea that comes to the collective mind. It may require, instead, the use of procedures to refine the voice of the people, without, at the same time, taking the final public authority away from them.[28]

Thus, reasonable limits may be put on an egalitarian constitutional model, including the frequency of collective assemblies (in order not to "tire" the public with permanent convocations for debate); their objects (as it is not necessary to discuss all existing public matters);

[26] Here we find additional problems regarding how to select these "serious matters" and how to organize the agenda of the discussion. These are significant problems, but also, in the end, the kind of problem that any political conception would usually confront. Moreover, the egalitarian position is, in this respect, particularly attractive: it fundamentally opposes the possibility of leaving these basic decisions in the hands of an elite or a bureaucracy, which most democrats need to repudiate.

[27] In fact, historians do not tend to object to these meetings in terms of their efficiency. Most of them agreed on the fact that their discussions were normally well organized and disciplined. See Gargarella (2000).

[28] One does not need to deny, however, other problems affecting collective organizations. For example, they may end up being controlled by a bureaucracy or an elite group. We should not forget that we are comparing imperfect political organizations, and our quest is to find which system minimizes certain risks and favors certain other more desirable possibilities. We suggest, in that respect, that the risk of adopting "bad" (here, "partial") decisions increases when we cannot hear the voices of those who are affected by the decisions at work. Egalitarian systems tend to diminish this undesirable risk. Moreover, one should not assume, as many liberals did, that it is almost impossible to prevent the state's abuses. When liberals defend criminal law, they do so assuming that, although the state controls all these coercive means, this does not prevent it from administering its forces with a certain care. If we accept this possibility, it is difficult to understand and justify the liberal's harsh pessimism regarding the state's intervention in the design of less intrusive (i.e., economic) norms. A final point: we should remember that less egalitarian structures, such as those which dominated America during its founding period, were not at all immune to the influence of interest groups.

their subjects (as the main potentially affected group may be just a small, decentralized group); and their procedures (as not all collective procedures for adopting decisions are equally interesting).

Egalitarianism and Rights: The Equal Value of Each Person's Opinions

The egalitarian position required organizing the political system in a different way, by changing some of the priorities that their opponents favored. But what could egalitarians say with regard to organizing and protecting the private lives of individuals?

I believe that egalitarians could advance two main points. They could emphasize that a respect for individual rights does not necessarily require the dismantling of the state, as some of their opponents seem to assume. Public institutions are not necessarily enemies of individual rights. On the contrary, they are absolutely necessary for their preservation. Without judicial institutions, individual rights may be totally unprotected; without the use of the state's coercive apparatus, they may be impossible to enforce. Our commitment to individual autonomy does not require laissez faire but, on the contrary, an active state.

Moreover, egalitarians believe that, to make each person the author of his or her own life, individuals should not suffer from burdens that they did not choose. Individuals should assume responsibility for the choices they make and not for circumstances that are beyond their control.[29] Clearly, this was not what happened to most people in America. When the slaves were freed or when the Indians were deprived of their properties, they became mere instruments of the wealthy. In most American societies, people lived in terrible conditions of exploitation, no matter how we define the idea of exploitation. Some people simply took unfair advantage of their position of privilege. In most cases, some people were better off; this was not owing to the laziness or indolence of the disadvantaged but to the existence of unjustified inequalities reproduced throughout the generations.

In cases like these, the egalitarian state needs to rescue disadvantaged groups: it does not honor the autonomy of those affected by merely breaking the chains of slavery or forced work. The state has duty to put an end to the circumstances of oppression that it has itself contributed to creating, the circumstances of oppression which it has

[29] Rawls (1971).

been enforcing for decades or centuries.[30] Liberals assumed that in order to respect individuals' autonomy, the state had to simply step back: it had to take its hands off the people's lives; it had to merely protect the negative rights of people. Egalitarians, by contrast, want the state to attack the conditions that affect the lives of individuals and groups. They do not want natural disadvantages to evolve into social disadvantages. They want the basic structure of society "to secure the citizen's freedom and independence, and continually moderate tendencies which lead, over time, to greater inequalities in social status and wealth, and in the ability to exert political influence and to take advantage of available opportunities."[31] The noted Peruvian thinker González Vigil presented an interesting approach to these difficult theoretical problems. He said:

> Given that all men are equal in their nature and in the faculties and rights that constitute their being...why is there so much inequality in the natural degrees and so many differences in society?...natural inequalities do not need justification because they are the creation of God. Social inequalities, however, are or should be based on the interests of society; that is the only reason to justify them, because no class or family could allege any rights against them....we violate our duties and we affect social order [when inequalities] do not respond to the mandate of the providence and the goals of the society in which they appear.[32]

González Vigil provided an adequate distinction between natural and nonnatural inequalities, challenging the conservative idea that each person occupies the place reserved for him or her. He also challenged the liberal view that public authorities were not guilty of these inequalities. Vigil understood, in the end, that the state was actually the creator of existing inequalities because of its actions, by forcing the "lazy" to work, censoring the press, and pursuing dissidents, as

---

[30] See Holmes and Sunstein (1999).
[31] Rawls (2001), p. 159. This view corresponds to what John Rawls has described as either a "property-owning democracy" or a "liberal-socialist" regime. In contrast with what welfare-state capitalism would imply, these conceptions would "prevent a small part of society from controlling the economy, and indirectly, political life as well." By contrast, Rawls adds, "welfare-state capitalism permits a small class to have a near monopoly of the means of production." Ibid., p. 139.
[32] González Vigil (1948), pp. 58–59. For him, the poor were not allowed to "snatch the super-abundance of property that is in the hands of the powerful; but the latter are obliged to give them at least part of that super-abundance, in order to satisfy the hunger that it creates, in order to clothe the naked and alleviate other needs. These are the conditions in which many live, in our society. Only then will the word socialism achieve its pure, rational, historical sense." Ibid.

much as by its omissions, that is, by allowing a few to take undue advantage of others' lives. Quite properly, Vigil objected to those inequalities unsupported by "law or reason." He knew how to distinguish between justified and unjustified inequalities and proposed putting an end to the latter. The distinction he made between them was absolutely relevant, because it acknowledged that some people could simply choose to live a more modest life than others. According to him, and according to the egalitarian conception presented here, chosen inequalities are not a problem: what is unacceptable is that people live a life of deprivation for reasons beyond their control.

This reflection helps us to see, in addition, that unjustified inequalities are not simply reduced to economic inequalities. Economic inequalities are particularly serious when the access to most social good depends on first having access to economic resources. But egalitarians oppose *all* social disadvantages independent of people's choice. The basic institutions of society should distribute obligations and benefits for reasons independent of skin color, gender, or social standing.

At this point, we are better prepared to analyze a fundamental concern of egalitarian policies, namely, the need for connecting individuals' self-determination with society's self-government. Clearly, this connection not only requires us to respect the right of suffrage or the right of freedom of association. In order to make both individual autonomy and collective self-government possible, a different organization of society's basic structure is necessary. The social and material conditions necessary for ensuring equal liberties for all should be taken more into account. Murillo Toro made this point in his analysis of revolutionary France in 1848, arguing that "the more direct way to absolutism is universal suffrage, when it is guaranteed as an isolated measure and without the economic reforms that it requires." In his opinion, the private and the public spheres were intimately interconnected: one could not responsibly ensure certain fundamental individual freedoms without at the same time ensuring certain basic social conditions:

> The basic question is to ensure the purity of the suffrage through the independence of the voters.... Every political reform has to [be accompanied by] an economic reform. And if we do not carry out this latter reform when we propose the former, we run the risk of not only working uselessly, but also of discrediting our work before the eyes of the people.... political forms are worth nothing if they are not accompanied by a radical reconstruction of the society.... what is the meaning

The Quest for Equality

of universal and direct suffrage...in a society where [most of the voters] have their basic needs unsatisfied and, for that reason, depend on the will of [a few]?[33]

Going beyond liberals' concerns, Murillo Toro considered that "the independence of individuals and their education" could never be obtained without previously guaranteeing the subsistence of each.[34] In a similar vein, Thomas Jefferson claimed: "There are two subjects, indeed, which I shall claim a right to further as long as I breathe; public education, and the sub-division of counties into wards."[35] Similarly, the Ecuadorian Juan Montalvo associated the establishment of a democratic system with the diffusion of public education and the egalitarian distribution of lands.[36]

These political leaders were showing, therefore, a commitment to what we could call the *social requirements* or *social preconditions* of an egalitarian system. In their view, the establishment of a new, more egalitarian society could not happen and become stable just because of the committed will of a few. This achievement required the adoption and establishment of certain preconditions, especially, they assumed, the education of the masses, a goal also supported by many liberals, along with radical economic reform.[37]

These opinions are also important because they allow us to see that the most basic egalitarian concerns are deeply associated with a concern with individual autonomy. Egalitarians do not merely promote equality as a way of ensuring certain collective goals but also as a way of honoring individual freedom. This requires them to support

[33] Murillo Toro (1979), p. 72.
[34] Ibid. Also, other radical thinkers, such as the Chilean Santiago Arcos, minimized the importance of the rights of suffrage after comparing it to certain economic rights. "The people will actively participate in the affairs of the Republic,", he claimed, "when it offers them land, cattle, work tools; when it offers to make them rich and, after that, promises to give them a share in the affairs of government....When the poor recognize that the triumph is not only a glorious event for this or that general, but a way of enforcing a political system that transforms him into a man, that enriches him, then he will be ready to risk his life in the fight." Arcos (1977), p. 147.
[35] Thus, in a letter to Joseph Cabell, Jan. 31, 1814. See Jefferson (1999), p. 197.
[36] Montalvo (1960).
[37] I believe that, in an egalitarian regime, the people should be able to solve their collective problems collectively. In this sense, they should not be prevented from discussing and eventually modifying (even) the basic conditions that make their collective self-government possible. However, this majoritarian commitment should not be "blind." It could reasonably include, for example, particular procedures in case the majority wanted to modify some of these preconditions (e.g., the majority could be required to vote on different occasions, separated by certain periods of time, before being able to modify these preconditions). See, for example, Ackerman (2000).

certain negative liberties as much as certain positive ones, like the liberty to choose and develop one's way of life. This purpose requires them, in addition, to find ways for promoting and facilitating the holding of collective discussions.

Between these two tasks, taking care of both individual and collective autonomy, there is a *continuity* that egalitarians are interested in exploring: they want to ensure both goals at the same time. *They consider that a situation in which each person's life is defined by the will of all is as bad as a situation in which collective life is defined by the will of one or a few.* If each person is the best judge of his or her own interests, that person should decide what to do with his or her life, not a heteronomous will. Democracy is seen, then, as a natural continuation of this commitment: it appears as a way of ensuring that public life is the product of the decision of all the affected citizens and not the outcome of a common will. Thomas Paine made reference to this continuity when he said: "Every generation is equal in rights to the generations which preceded it, by the same rule which says that every individual is born equal in rights with its contemporary."[38] That is, he asserted his commitment to both individual and collective equality. The Chilean Francisco Bilbao showed similar concerns, when he claimed that the Sociedad de la Igualdad would serve to "ensure each person's right to think and be as he wanted...[and] the sovereignty of the people."[39] Murillo Toro was also clear about this point: "We began by establishing...individual rights...the rights and freedoms of industry, of thought, of communication, of travel, the freedom of education, religion, and association. These rights belong to the absolute and exclusive domain of the individual, as an independent and morally free being. But given that men do not live isolated...we also have to guarantee the relationships that may be created between these different individuals."[40]

An important question is whether the majority should be completely silent with regard to individual rights. The answer would be no, for at least three different reasons. First, in order to properly honor the idea of self-government, it is at least necessary to prevent the possibility of having an internal minority or an external group making decisions in the name of the entire community. The community cannot be indifferent to its own fate. This may require both fostering the civic commitments of its members and creating political institutions that favor

---

[38] Paine (1989), p. 76.
[39] See Gazmuri (1992), p. 78.
[40] Murillo Toro (1979), p. 90.

self-government. To state this does not mean that individuals could not choose to be indifferent to the fate of others, but simply that the community should try to preserve itself as self-governing. We should not think, as many may seem to, that we should either accept political apathy or force each person to participate in politics. Between these two alternatives there is plenty of room for other options, which a self-governing community could try to implement. In addition, this community should bolster rather than undermine the idea that all its members are equals. This implies that the community could encourage respect for each person's preferences, tolerance of different conceptions of "the good," or solidarity toward the least advantaged, that is, toward those who are situated in a less-than-equal position. In this sense, to promote an egalitarian position would not imply indifference toward the way in which people choose to live.

In addition, the egalitarian position would not be neutral or indifferent to the way in which the social and cultural environment is shaped. In fact, the preferences and desires of the people are usually shaped by external influences related to an environment that they do not control. The social and cultural environment shapes its own *ideal models* of what a good person does, what beauty is, what a successful life includes. These ideal models are shaped by a complex mechanism[41] that is not under collective control. Egalitarians, I believe, would extend to this area the same recommendations they offer when they discuss the economic structure of society. Like the economy, the social and cultural environment should not be shaped by the will of a few: it should be shaped, instead, after collective agreement.[42] Clearly, a more egalitarian distribution of resources would be a necessary ingredient of the egalitarian formula, but it would still be equally important to discuss the common good and the ideal models that, accepted or not, would become dominant and shape our desires and our common beliefs.

Finally, the egalitarian position would not deny the importance of collectively discussing the scope and contents of rights. As Jeremy Waldron says, it is insulting and offensive to individuals if they are not permitted to participate in these agreements in determining the shape of the rights they will actually have. Undoubtedly, this statement raises many difficult questions, but the same happens with

---

[41] A mechanism that, in G. A. Cohen's opinion, is fueled by money and activated by greed and fear. See Cohen (2009).

[42] Writing about republicanism, Sandel maintains a similar position: the republican tradition seeks to shape a public culture of a certain kind even where doing so privileges certain conceptions of the good life over others." Sandel (1996), p. 329.

all alternative answers to the problem under discussion. We cannot accept the idea that rights are natural or self-evident entities that only a few technicians or judges can properly discern. To know what rights we have and how to interpret them, we need to have, as far as we are able, an ongoing discussion, which future generations will continue. In Waldron's view, "Those who value popular participation in politics should not value it in a spirit that stops short at the threshold of disagreements about rights... [those who fought for] the franchise [did so] because they believed that controversies about the fundamental structure of their society, such as factory and work hours legislation, property rights, free speech, police powers, temperance and campaign reform, were controversies for them to sort out, respectfully and on a basis of equality, because *they* were the people who would be affected by the outcome."[43]

Egalitarians try to remedy the worst aspects of their opponents' positions: the conservatives' disrespect for basic human equality; the liberals' disrespect for majority rule and the social conditions of autonomous choices; the radicals' difficulties in asserting individual rights over others. Egalitarians want to re-create and reinvigorate the liberal commitment along with the idea of rights and to restore the radicals' emphasis on majority rule.

The Egalitarian Constitution

I believe that many egalitarians would share some of the radicals' proposals regarding a political system. Egalitarians want, as radicals wanted, to strengthen the majoritarian features of such a system. For this reason, many of them may demand, as many U.S. radicals demanded, more direct forms of democracy or closer links between the people and their representatives. Egalitarians may support both stricter external controls over the representatives and a more fluid communication between the people and their representatives.

---

[43] Waldron (1999), pp. 15, 16. He also notes: "If on the other hand, the desire for entrenchment is motivated by a predatory view of human nature and of what people will do to one another when let loose in the arena of democratic politics, it will be difficult to explain how or why people are to be viewed as essentially bearers of rights." Ibid., p. 222. Waldron subscribes to Joel Feinberg's view of participation and respect for individuals. He says: "Perhaps [the support of] the right to participate has less to do with a certain minimum prospect of decisive impact and more to do with avoiding the insult, dishonour, or denigration that is involved when one person's views are treated as of less account than the views of others, on a matter that affects them as well as the others." Ibid., p. 238. A sophisticated discussion of these topics is in Habermas (1996).

Taking into account the existing distribution of powers, based on the division of functions among three branches, egalitarians may tend to favor a stronger popular branch. In that sense, they would oppose both a powerful executive, such as we still find in most Latin American constitutions, and the type of equilibrium that we find in the U.S. Constitution. If it is reasonable to prevent the potential abuses of each branch, it is unreasonable to do so ensuring each of them a relatively equal share of power. This policy is offensive to those who believe that the most popular branch is the most capable of recognizing and properly weighing the different viewpoints that exist among the people. If this is so, given, for example, the number and diversity of its members, then it is difficult to understand why the majority opinion should be balanced with the opinion of particular individuals or elites. The system of checks and balances that still prevails in most American constitutions tends, in fact, to reduce the importance of the popular branch. Moreover, the system seems undesirable because of the problems that radicals were quick to detect in the United States. In their opinion, the system of checks and balances was not only undesirable but also inefficient, given its tendency to produce paralysis in the decision-making process, and in view of the way it encouraged unprincipled bargaining and mutual extortion between the branches and their members.[44]

Egalitarians would probably insist, as radicals did, on the idea that even a properly composed congress could have problems accounting for the extreme diversity of interests present in society. An adequate consideration of every different existing social interest may require the use of different institutional means, capable of processing views and voices that seem, at present, absent from our public institutions. These new institutional arrangements should be able to ensure the presence of the different parts of society.[45] Egalitarians would certainly support the creation of new public forums that gave room to these still unrecognized positions. They would probably promote

---

[44] See Ackerman (2000).
[45] See, for example, Williams (1998; 2000); Phillips (1995); Kymlicka (1996). The creation of these institutions generates numerous theoretical problems: How should these groups be tailored? Who should choose them? How shall we decide which group each of us belongs to? How can we ensure that the representatives of each group actually represent the interests of that group? All these problems are undoubtedly relevant. However, the present institutional structure also seems unsatisfactory with regard to these and similar questions: Why should we assume that our representatives will represent us? How can we control them properly? How can we force them to obey our will in those questions we are most interested in? Why do so many voices still seem unrepresented?

reforms aimed at creating more room for pluralistic discussions of public issues. In the same way that the U.S. radicals pressed for giving additional weight to the demands of local states, demands that were deemed to be of primary importance, egalitarians would press today for giving particular attention to the interests of those who have problems in satisfying their basic needs.

More significantly, egalitarians would question the role that judges play in American institutional systems. What justifies an elite of legal experts having the last institutional say regarding all fundamental questions? As Jeremy Waldron put it, "You may write to the newspaper and get up a petition and organize a pressure group to lobby Parliament. But even if you succeed, beyond your wildest dreams, and orchestrate the support of a large number of like-minded men and women, and manage to prevail in the legislature, your measure may be challenged and struck down because your view of that right we have does not accord with the judges' view."[46] The fascination of contemporary jurisprudence with judicial review only reveals what Roberto Unger calls their "discomfort with democracy," which appears not just "in the ceaseless identification of restraints upon majority rule as the overriding responsibility of judges and jurists; in the consequent hypertrophy of counter-majoritarian practices and arrangements; and in the single-minded focus upon the higher judges and their selection as the most important part of democratic politics."[47]

Egalitarians may also insist on the idea that politics does not end in the interplay between the different branches of government or through periodic and distant elections. Politics should fundamentally be related to the actions of the people at large. In this sense, an egalitarian position would say, first, that "all citizens, whatever their economic or social position, must be sufficiently equal in the sense that all have a fair opportunity to hold public office and to affect the outcome of elections."[48] Second, egalitarians would emphasize the importance of external or popular controls over internal or endogenous ones.[49] Third, they would open up more opportunities for direct democracy, assuming that the political life of the community is enriched, and not

[46] Waldron (1993), p. 51.
[47] Quoted in Waldron (1999), p. 8.
[48] See Rawls (2001), p. 149.
[49] This is, for example, what Jefferson did when in his "Notes" he claimed "that whenever any two of the three branches of government shall concur in the opinion, each by the voices of two thirds of their whole number, that a convention is necessary for altering the constitution, or correcting breaches of it, a convention shall be called for the purpose." This would simply be one example of how to use external controls.

impoverished, by popular intervention in politics.[50] This commitment would imply not simply authorizing political participation but creating forums for making it possible.

Would this imply subscribing to a blind commitment to radicalism? No. Egalitarians assume that the voice of the majority, like the voice of any minority, is usually imperfect and in need of enrichment. They assume that the voice of the majority needs to be refined, but they still reject most of what their opponents say. Contrary to the conservative position, they would not use that excuse to simply replace that voice, as if something like "the voice of the wise" existed. In contrast with the liberal position, they would not want to filter that voice through the medium of a strongly independent group of representatives, even less so when assuming (as Madison did, in *Federalist* 10) that the voice of the representatives "will be more consonant to the public good than that of the people themselves, convened for that purpose." Contrary to the majoritarian opinion, they would not assume that whatever the people say is right, simply *because* it was said by the people. The voice of the majority may be refined in many different ways, which do not need to include forms of undue paternalism. For example, properly balanced debates in public forums may help all those involved to develop their own opinions. Such debates may allow us to have a more sedate reflection, while honoring the heterogeneity of conceptions of the public good present in society.

Do these popular controls over the representatives imply that the latter will become mere mouthpieces of the people? Not in my opinion, although many authors suggest so, particularly in their analysis of the right to instruct the representatives.[51] In the critics' view, popular pressures would prevent the representatives from exchanging opinions and mediating their initial preferences. In the egalitarians' view, however, the idea is that representatives might be allowed to debate and change opinions on multiple issues but not *all* of them. Representatives might be allowed to debate and modify their own views, even regarding the best means for satisfying the specific ends demanded by their constituency. They might, for example, be forced to vote in favor of the right to abortion but nevertheless be free to discuss how to implement it; at how many months, in which cases, or by which means. The idea that rights such as that to instruct the representatives do not leave room for debate is simply a dogmatic one.

---

[50] See in this respect, for example, Elkin (1987).
[51] Sunstein (1993), chap. 1. An analysis of these issues is in Przeworski, Stokes, and Manin (1999).

As a final point, I would like to add a few words about what could be the egalitarians' approach to the idea of constitutional rights. I believe that egalitarians would not simply associate rights with negative rights, as many liberals did. In the egalitarians' opinion, I believe, the protection of personal autonomy would require not only the defense of such things as personal security and physical integrity but also access to certain benefits that allow one to develop one's own chosen way of life. Second, egalitarians could reasonably argue that rights might be violated both through actions and by omissions, and by both the state and private organizations. Nobody – be it the state, a private corporation, the church, or the military – should be allowed to take unfair advantage of anyone else. Third, egalitarians may challenge the individualist foundations of the liberals' viewpoint on rights. This individualist foundation prevents liberals from providing adequate protection for the interests of groups that have been historically disadvantaged, usually by the active intervention of the state. As an example, egalitarians might defend the special rights of Indians to have fixed seats in parliament if their unequal access to politics has to do with prohibitions and barriers that had been publicly created and enforced against them. Fourth, egalitarians might have a different reading of certain basic rights, usually promoted by liberals.

Typically, the right to property would not have the sacred status that liberals assign to it. This right would always take second place to others, such as personal autonomy and collective self-government. On the other hand, rights such as freedom of expression, or political participation, might receive stronger protection.[52] Rights such as freedom of expression, of association, and of the press all need to be firmly protected in order to ensure both personal autonomy and collective self-government. As a final point, egalitarians might promote a more robust view of so-called social rights. These rights were strongly supported by some of the Mexican *liberales puros* (Ponciano Arriaga, Melchor Ocampo, Castillo Velasco, Ignacio Ramírez) or by politicians such as Murillo Toro or Manuel Madiedo in Colombia. In contrast with what would be the liberal, Madisonian view on the topic, Murillo Toro supported the idea that "landed property has always been the cause of social inequalities, the exploitation of the weak in the hands of the powerful." That was why he campaigned for the reform of the constitution, why he thought it necessary to improve the condition of the

---

[52] Note, however, the qualifications we enumerated under the heading "Egalitarianism and Rights."

poor.[53] In the egalitarians' view, I believe, the list of individual rights should be completed by a carefully chosen list of social rights.

At this stage, we may need to add a cautionary note about these issues. In contrast with what some people may think, we should not expect that, by simply adding new social or participatory rights to a liberal constitution, we might transform it into something completely different. The flexibility and sometimes promising potential of these constitutions should not make us think that they are generously open to all kinds of new progressive initiatives. In other words, the passage from a liberal model to a more egalitarian model is not an easy one, to be simply obtained by the introduction of a few cosmetic or modernizing constitutional changes. On the contrary, what seems to happen is that these modernizing changes end up being engulfed by a constitutional structure created and operated under different principles. An example may help us to understand this claim. From the end of the 1910s, in fact since the enactment of the 1917 Mexican Constitution, many American countries with liberal or liberal-conservative constitutions began to introduce significant changes into their main charters, aimed at incorporating new social rights such as the right to work, shelter, or personal protection. These new rights faced a very difficult struggle and, in many cases, became transformed into something very close to a dead letter. This outcome was hardly surprising when the new social rights were added to an institutional structure that was, to say the least, unprepared to welcome them. For example, the new rights had to be enforced by indirectly elected and, as a result, unrepresentative judges who, in a majority of cases, simply declared them "inoperative rights."[54] Perhaps something similar will happen with the new participatory rights included in many American constitutions during the 1980s and 1990s.[55] By saying this, I do not mean to say that these rights should not be incorporated into a constitutional text. I am simply stating that one should not expect magic from legal words: to create a more egalitarian political system requires much more than the introduction of a few new articles into old constitutions.

One final note. The difficulties we have in finding good examples of egalitarian initiatives, throughout early American history, may be a sign of the practical or even theoretical difficulties that exist when elaborating and properly defending such a viewpoint. Perhaps an

---

[53] Murillo Toro (1979), p. 72.
[54] An excellent discussion on the topic in Fabre (2000).
[55] Thus, in such cases as those of Argentina, Colombia, Brazil, Nicaragua, and Peru.

egalitarian program is internally inconsistent or conceptually problematic. How should we distinguish precisely, for example, between decisions that have to remain in the hands of individuals and those that have to be collectively discussed? Is it not true that the two are basically inseparable? What is the best way to distinguish or refine the popular voice? And what should be done in order to avoid the creation of mutual blockades between collective and individual initiatives? After more than two hundred years of history, egalitarians still find it difficult to define and advance their policies. Of course, there are many just and egalitarian objectives that are difficult to achieve. In this case, as in others, these difficulties do not give us a reason to abandon our worthy goals. On the contrary, they give us more reasons to defend and pursue them more firmly, with all our strengths.

Bibliography

Abramson, J. (1994). *We, the Jury: The Jury System and the Ideal of Democracy.* New York: Basic Books.
Abramson, P. (1999). *Las utopías sociales en América Latina en el siglo xix.* México: Fondo de Cultura Económica.
Acevedo, E. (1942). *Manual de Historia Uruguaya.* Montevideo: A. Monteverde y Cía.
Ackerman, B. (2000). "The New Separation of Powers." *Harvard Law Review* 113: 633–729.
Adrianzén, A. (1987). *Pensamiento político peruano.* Lima: Centro de estudio y promoción del desarrollo.
Aguilar Rivera, J. A. (2000). *En pos de la quimera. Reflexiones sobre el experimento constitucional atlántico.* México: Fondo de Cultura Económica.
(2001). *El manto liberal. Los poderes de emergencia en México, 1821–1876.* México: Universidad Nacional Autónoma de México.
(2003). "Vicente Rocafuerte, los panfletos y la invención de la república hispanoamericana, 1821–1823." Unpublished manuscript, CIDE, México.
Aguirre, E. (1986). *Valentín Gómez Farías. Hombre de dos mundos.* México: Alambra Mexicana.
Alamán, L. (1997). *Los imprescindibles.* México: Mazatlán.
Alberdi, J. B. (1886). "Elementos del Derecho Público Provincial Argentino." In *Obras Completas,* vol. 5. Buenos Aires: La Tribuna Nacional.
(1920). *Obras selectas.* 8 vols. Buenos Aires: Librería La Facultad.
(1960). *Bases y Puntos de Partida para la Organización política de la República Argentina.* Buenos Aires: Rosso.
Allen, A. L., and M. Regan, eds. (1998). *Debating Democracy's Discontent.* Oxford: Oxford University Press.
Allen, W., and L. Gordon, eds. (1985). *The Essential Antifederalist.* New York: University Press of America.
Ames, S., ed. (1983). *Work of Fisher Ames.* 2 vols. Indianapolis: Liberty Classics.
Amunátegui, M., and B. Vicuña Mackena, (1917). *La dictadura de O'Higgins.* Madrid: Biblioteca de Ayacucho.
Arango, R. (2001). "La construcción de la nacionalidad in Miguel Antonio Caro." Unpublished manuscript, Universidad Nacional de Colombia, Facultad de Ciencias Humanas, Bogotá.
Arboleda, S. (1936). *Las letras, las ciencias y las bellas artes en Colombia.* Bogotá: Biblioteca Aldeana de Colombia.

Bibliography

Arcos, S. (1977). "Carta a Francisco Bilbao." In Carlos Rama, ed., *Utopismo socialista, 1830–93*. Caracas: Biblioteca Ayacucho.
Arguedas, A. (1922). *Historia General de Bolivia, 1809–1921*. La Paz: Arnó hermanos.
Avedaño González, A. (1994). *Introducción a la historia del pensamiento colombiano*. Bogotá: Editorial Antillas.
Ayala, E., ed. (1993). *Pensamiento de Pedro Moncayo*. Quito: Corporación Editora Nacional.
Ayala, E. (1995). *Lucha política y origen de los partidos en Ecuador*. Quito: Corporación editora nacional.
—— ed. (1995b). *Nueva historia del Ecuador*. 15 vols. Quito: Ed. Grijalbo.
Aylmer, G. (1975). *The Levellers in the English Revolution*. Ithaca, N.Y.: Cornell University Press.
Bagú, S. (1971). *Mariano Moreno*. Montevideo: Biblioteca de Marcha.
Ballon Lozada, H. (1986). *Las ideas sociopolíticas en Arequipa*. Publiunsa.
Bamko, C. (1990). *Las luchas federalistas en Venezuela*. Caracas: Monte Ávila Editores Latinoamericana.
Barbagelata, A. (1957). *El constitucionalismo uruguayo a mediados del siglo xix*. México: Fundación de Cultura Universitaria.
Barrón, L. (2001). "Liberales y conservadores: Republicanismo e ideas republicanas en el siglo xix en América Latina." Paper presented at the meeting of the Latin American Studies Association, Washington, D.C.
Barros Arana, D. (1913). *Un decenio de la historia de Chile*. Vols. 1 and 2. Santiago de Chile: Institu to de Historia, Pontificia Universidad Católica de Chile.
Basadre, J. (1949). *Historia de la República del Perú*. 2 vols. Lima: Editorial Cultura Antártica.
Bates, F. (1967). *Rhode Island and the Formation of the Union*. New York: Columbia University Press.
Bauzá, F. (1887). *Estudios constitucionales*. Montevideo: A. Barreiro y Ramos.
Baylin, B. (1992). *The Ideological Origins of the American Revolution*. Cambridge: Cambridge University Press.
Bazant, J. (1977). *A Concise History of México: From Hidalgo to Cárdenas, 1805–1940*. Cambridge: Cambridge University Press.
—— (1991). "From Independence to the Liberal Republic, 1821–1867." In L. Bethell, ed., *Mexico since Independence*, pp. 1–49. Cambridge: Cambridge University Press.
Beard, C. (1941). *An Economic Interpretation of the Constitution of the United States*. New York: Free Press.
—— (1962). *The Supreme Court and the Constitution*. Englewood Cliffs, N.J.: Prentice Hall.
Beer, S. (1993). *To Make a Nation*. Cambridge, Mass.: Harvard University Press.
Belaúnde, V. (1967). *Bolívar and the Political Thought of the Spanish American Revolution*. New York: Octagon Books.
Bello, A. (1982). *Bello y la América Latina*. Carcas: Fundación La Casa de Bello.
—— (1997). *Selected Writings*. Oxford: Oxford University Press.
Benson, N. (1955). *La diputación provincial y el federalismo mexicano*. México: El Colegio de México.
Bernhard, W. (1965). *Fisher Ames, Federalist and Statesman*. Chapel Hill: University of North Carolina Press.
Bethell, L., ed. (1985). *The Cambridge History of Latin America*. 4 vols. Cambridge: Cambridge University Press.

Bibliography

Bethell, L. (1985b). "A Note on the Church and the Independence of Latin America." In L. Bethell, ed., *The Cambridge History of Latin America*, vol. 3. Cambridge: Cambridge University Press.
ed. (1994). *Mexico since Independence*. Cambridge: Cambridge University Press.
Bickel, A. (1962). *The Least Dangerous Branch*. New Haven, Conn.: Yale University Press.
Bilbao, F. (1886). *El gobierno de la libertad*. Vol. 1. Ed. Manuel Bilbao. Buenos Aires Imprenta de.
Blackstone, W. (1844). *Commentaries on the Laws of England*. 4 vols. London: E. Spettigue.
Blanchard, P. (1996). "The 'Transitional Man' in Nineteenth-Century Latin America: The Case of Domingo Elías of Perú." *Bulletin of Latin American Research* 15, no. 2: 157–176.
(1982). *The Origins of the Peruvian Labor Movement, 1883–1919*. Pittsburgh: University of Pittsburgh Press.
Blanco Acevedo, P. (1939). *Estudios constitucionales*. Montevideo.
Blanksten, G. (1951). *Ecuador: Constitutions and Caudillos*. Berkeley: University of California Press.
Blaustein, A., and J. Singler, eds. (1988). *Constitutions That Made History*. New York: Paragon House.
Blázquez, C. (1978). *Miguel Lerdo de Tejeda. Un liberal veracruzano en la política nacional*. México: El Colegio de México.
Bolívar, S. (1950). *Bolívar. Obras completas*. 3 vols. La Habana: Editorial Lex.
(1951). *Selected Writings of Bolívar*. 2 vols. New York: Colonial Press.
(1976). *Doctrina del Libertador*. Caracas: Biblioteca Ayacucho.
Borden, M. (1965). *The Antifederalist Papers*. East Lansing: Michigan State University Press.
Borja y Borja, R. (1951). *Las Constituciones del Ecuador*. Madrid: Ediciones Cultura Hispánica.
Borrego Plá, M. (1993). "La influencia de la Francia revolucionaria en México: El texto constitucional de Apatzingán." In L. Zea, coord., *América Latina ante la revolución francesa*. México: Universidad Nacional Autónoma de México.
Bosch, J. (1980). *Bolívar y la guerra social*. Santo Domingo: Editora Alfa y Omega.
Bossano, F. (1959). *Evolución del derecho constitucional ecuatoriano*. Quito: Talleres Gráficos de la Escuela Militar "Eloy Alfaro."
Botana, N. (1996). "La transformación del credo constitucional." *Estudios Sociales* (Univ. Nacional del Litoral) 11: 23–48.
(1997). *La tradición republicana. Alberdi, Sarmiento y las ideas políticas de su tiempo*. Buenos Aires: Sudamericana.
Botana, N., and E. Gallo, (1997). *De la República posible a la República verdadera*. Buenos Aires: Editorial Sudamericana.
Boulton, A., comp. (1976). *Política y economía en Venezuela*. Caracas: Fundación John Boulton.
Bravo, J. A. (2007). *Francisco Bilbao*. Providencia, Santiago: Ed. Cuarto Propio.
Brewer-Carías, A. (1982). "La concepción del Estado en la obra de Andrés Bello." In *Bello y la América Latina*, pp. 99–154. Caracas: La Casa de Bello.
(1985). *Instituciones políticas y constitucionales*. Caracas: San Cristóbal.
Brito Figueroa, F. (1973). *Historia económica y social de Venezuela*. Caracas: Universidad Central de Venezuela.
(1975). *Tiempo de Ezequiel Zamora*. Caracas: Ediciones Centauro.

Bibliography

Brooke, J. (1989). "To the Quiet People." *William and Mary Quarterly* 46, no. 3 (July): 425–462.
Brown, R. (1970). *Revolutionary Politics in Massachusetts*. Cambridge, Mass.: Harvard University Press.
Brunhouse, R. (1942). *The Counter-Revolution in Pennsylvania*. Harrisburg: Dept. of Public Instruction, Pennsylvania Historical Commission.
Burke, E. (1960). *Selected Writings*. New York: Modern Library.
Burns, B. (1980). *The Poverty of Progress; Latin America in the Nineteenth Century*. Berkeley: University of California Press.
Busaniche, J. L. (1965). *Historia Argentina*. Buenos Aires: Solar Hachette.
Bushnell, D. (1954). *El régimen de Santander en la Gran Colombia*. Bogotá: Universidad Nacional.
    (1993). *The Making of Modern Colombia: A Nation in Spite of Itself*. Berkeley: University of California Press.
Bushnell, D., and N. Macaulay (1994). *The Emergence of Latin America in the Nineteenth Century*. Oxford: Oxford University Press.
Butterfield, L., ed. (1951). *Letters of Benjamin Rush*. Princeton: Princeton University Press.
Caetano, G., and J. Rilla (1994). *Historia contemporánea del Uruguay*. Montevideo: CLAEH.
Camacho Roldán, S. (1946). *Memorias*. 2 vols. Bogotá: Biblioteca Popular de Cultura Colombiana.
Campos Harriet, F. (1977). *Historia constitucional de Chile*. Santiago: Editorial Jurídica de Chile.
Carrión, B. (1959). *García Moreno. El Santo del Patíbulo*. México: Fondo de Cultura Económica.
Castillo D' Imperio, O. (1998). *García Moreno o el orden de la piedad intolerante*. Caracas: Fundación Centro de Estudios Latinoamericanos Rómulo Gallegos.
Chávez Orozco, L. (1985). *Historia de México, 1808–1836*. México: Instituto Nacional de Estudios Históricos de la Revolución Mexicana.
Chiaramonte, J. C. (1997). *Ciudades, provincias, Estados: Orígenes de la Nación Argentina (1800–1846)*. Buenos Aires: Ariel, Biblioteca del Pensamiento Argentino.
    (1999). "Ciudadanía, soberanía y representación en la génesis del estado argentino, 1810–1852." In H. Sábato, coord., *Ciudadanía política y formación de las naciones. Perspectivas históricas de América Latina*. México: Fondo de Cultura Económica, 94–416.
Chipman, N. (1833). *Principles of Government*. Burlington: Edward Smith.
Churruca Peláez, A. (1983). *El pensamiento insurgente de Morelos*. México: Editor Porrúa.
Cohen, G. (2009). *Why Not Socialism?* Princeton: Princeton University Press.
Colautti, C. (1979). *Antecedentes de la Constitución argentina*. Buenos Aires: Abeledo Perrot.
Collier, S. (1967). *Ideas and Politics of Chilean Independence*. Cambridge: Cambridge University Press.
Collier, S., and W. Sater (1996). *A History of Chile, 1808–1994*. Cambridge: Cambridge University Press.
Colomer Viadel, A. (1993). "La revolución francesa, la independencia y el constitucionalismo en Iberoamérica. In L. Zea, coord., *América Latina ante la revolución francesa*, pp. 181–188. México: Universidad Nacional Autónoma de México.

Bibliography

Cone, C. (1957). *Burke and the Nature of Politics: The Age of the American Revolution*. Lexington: University Press of Kentucky.
(1968). *The English Jacobins: Reformers in Late 18th Century England*. New York: Scribner.
Contreras Estrada, M. (1960). *Melchor Ocampo. El agrarista de la reforma*. México: [TALLS. GRAFS. GALEZA].
Córdoba Mariño, L. (1998). *Apuntes de historia constitucional y política de Colombia*. Bogotá: Fundación Universidad de Bogotá.
Cornblit, O., E. Gallo, and A. O'Connell (1965). "La generación del 80 y su proyecto." In T. Di Tella and G. Germani, eds., *Argentina, sociedad de masas*, pp. 18–58. Buenos Aires: EUDEBA.
Correa, R. (1937). *La Convención de Río Negro*. Bogotá: Imprenta Nacional.
Cosío Villegas, D. (1957). *La Constitución de 1857 y sus críticos*. México: Ed. Hermes.
Countryman, E. (1981). *A People in Revolution*. Baltimore: Johns Hopkins University Press.
Cruz, P. (1980). *Bilbao y Lastarria*. Santiago de Chile: Editorial Difusión Chilena.
Dahl, R. (1963). *A Preface to Democratic Theory*. Chicago: University of Chicago Press.
De Armas Chitty, J. (1966). *Fermín Toro y su época*. Caracas: Instituto Nacional de Cultura Y Bellas Artes.
De Asís, A. (1954). *Bartolomé Herrera, pensador politico*. Sevilla: Escuela de estudios hispanoamericanos.
De la Madrid Hurtado, M. (1982). *Elementos de derecho constitucional*. México: Instituto de Capacitación Política.
De la Portilla, A. (1987). *Historia de la revolución de México contra la dictadura del General Santa Anna*. México: Instituto Nacional de Estudios Históricos de la Revolución, Mexicana de la Secretaria de Gobernación y Gobierno del Estado de Puebla.
De la Torre Villar, E. (1964). *La Constitución de Apatzingán y los creadores del Estado mexicano*. México: Universidad Nacional Autónoma de México.
De Mesa, J., and T. Gisbert (1965). *José Joaquín de Mora, secretario del Mariscal Andrés de Santa Cruz*. La Paz: Academia Nacional de Ciencias de Bolivia.
Demophilus (1776). *The Genuine Principles of the Ancient Anglo Saxon*. Philadelphia: Printed, and Sold, by Robert Bell, in Third-Street.
Devlin, L. (1959). *The Enforcement of Morals*. Maccabaean Lecture in Jurisprudence of the British Academy. Oxford: Oxford University Press.
Díaz y Díaz, F. (1972a). *Caudillos y Caciques*. México: El Colegio de México.
(1972b). *Santa Anna y Juan Alvarez frente a frente*. México: Secretaría de Educación Publica.
Díaz Sánchez, R. (1950). *Guzmán. Eclipse de una ambición de poder*. Caracas: Ediciones del Ministerio de Educación.
Documentos de la Conformación Institucional Argentina, 1782–1972 (1972). Buenos Aires: Poder Ejecutivo Nacional, Ministerio del Interior.
Dolbeare, K. (1969). *Directions in American Political Thought*. New York: Wiley.
Donoso, R. (1967). *Las ideas políticas en Chile*. Santiago: Facultad de Filosofía y Educación.
(1977). *Vicuña Mackenna, su vida, sus escritos y su tiempo*. Buenos Aires: Editorial Francisco de Aguirre.
Douglass, E. (1971). *Rebels and Democrats*. Chapel Hill: University of North Carolina.

Bibliography

Dworkin, R. (1977). *Taking Rights Seriously*. London: Duckworth.
  (1985). *A Matter of Principle*. Cambridge, Mass.: Harvard University Press.
  (1996). *Freedom's Law: A Moral Reading of the American Constitution*. Cambridge, Mass.: Harvard University Press.
Echeverría, E. (1915). *Dogma socialista de la Asociación de Mayo, precedido de una ojeada retrospectiva sobre el movimiento intelectual en el Plata desde el año 37*. Buenos Aires: Librería La Facultad.
Edwards Vives, A., and E. Frei Montalva (1949). *Historia de los partidos políticos chilenos*. Santiago de Chile: Editorial del Pacífico.
Efrén Reyes, O. (1940). *Historia de la República*. Quito: Imprenta Nacional.
  (1942). *Breve Historia General del Ecuador*. Quito: Talleres Gráficos del Ministerio de Gobierno.
Egaña, J. (1836). *Colección de algunos escritos políticos, morales, poéticos y filosóficos del Dr. Don Juan de Egaña*. Burdeos: Imprenta de la S.V. Laplace y Beaume.
  (1969). *Juan Egaña. Antología*. Ed. Raúl Silva Castro. Santiago de Chile: Andrés Bello.
Elkin, S. (1987). *City and Regime in the American Republic*. Chicago: University of Chicago Press.
Elster, J. (1989). *Salomonic Judgements: Studies in the Limitations of Rationality*. Cambridge: Cambridge University Press.
  ed. (1993). *Constitutionalism and Democracy*. Cambridge: Cambridge University Press.
  (2000). *Ulysses Unbound: Studies in Rationality, Precommitment, and Constraints*. Cambridge: Cambridge University Press.
Ely, J. (1980). *Democracy and Distrust*. Cambridge, Mass.: Harvard University Press.
Encina, F. (1949). *Historia de Chile*. Vols. 12 and 13. Santiago: Editorial Nascimento.
Escovar Salom, R. (1966). *Orden político e historia de Venezuela*. Caracas: Italgráfica.
  (1975). *Evolución política de Venezuela*. Caracas: Monte Ávila eds.
Estep, R. (1949). *Lorenzo de Zavala, profeta del liberalismo mexicano*. México: Lib. De Manuel Porría.
Eyzaguirre, J. (1977). *Historia de las instituciones políticas y sociales de Chile*. Santiago: Ed. Universitaria.
Fabre, C. (2000). *Social Rights under the Constitution*. Oxford: Oxford University Press.
Farrand, M., ed. (1937). *The Records of the Federal Convention of 1787*. 4 vols. New Haven, Conn.: Yale University Press.
Feinberg, J. (1984). *The Moral Limits of Criminal Law*. New York: Oxford University Press.
Fernández Cabrelli, A. (1968). *Artigas y los curas rebeldes*. Montevideo: Imprenta Norte.
Ferrero, R. (1958). *El Liberalismo Peruano*. Lima: Grace.
Fiske, J. (1916). *The Critical Period of American History*. Cambridge: Cambridge University Press.
Fithian Stevens, D. (1991). *Origins of Instability in Early Republican Mexico*. Durham: Duke University Press.
Ford, P. (1968). *Pamphlets on the Constitution of the United States*. New York: Da Capo Press.
Forner, P., ed. (1945). *The Complete Writings of Thomas Paine*. New York: Citadel Press.

Bibliography

Fowler, W. (1966). *Mexico in the Age of Proposals, 1821–1853*. Westport, Conn.: Greenwood Press.
Frega, A. (1998). "La virtud y el poder. La soberanía particular de los pueblos en el proyecto artiguista." In N. Goldman and R. Salvatore, comps., *Caudillismos Rioplatenses. Nuevas miradas a un viejo problema*, pp. 101–134. Buenos Aires: EUDEBA.
Friedman, B. (2002). "The Birth of an Academic Obsession: The History of the Countermajoritarian Difficulty, Part Five." *Yale Law Journal* 112: 153–259.
(2009). *The Will of the People*. New York: Farrar, Straus & Giroux.
Frías, F. (1995). "Necesidad de la unión y del orden de la República Argentina." In T. Halperín Dongui, *Proyecto y construcción de una nación, 1846–1880*. Buenos Aires: Ariel, Biblioteca del Pensamiento Argentino.
Frías Valenzuela, F. (1976). *Historia de Chile*. Santiago de Chile: Arnascimiento.
Gabaldón, E. (1987). *La ideología federal en la Convención de Valencia*. Caracas: Biblioteca de la Academa Nacional de la Historia.
Galdames, L. (1925). *Historia de Chile. La evolución constitucional*. Santiago de Chile: Balcells.
Galletti, A. (1972). *Historia Constitucional Argentina*. La Plata: Editora Platense.
Gallo, K. (1997). "Reformismo Liberal o Radical? La política Rivadaviana en una era de Conservadurismo Europeo, 1815–1830." Universidad Torcuato Di Tella, Working Paper no. 38.
(1998). "Un caso de utilitarismo rioplatense: la influencia del pensamiento de Bentham en Rivadavia." Universidad Torctuato Di Tella, Working Paper no. 49.
Gálvez, M. (1945). *Vida de don Gabriel García Moreno*. Madrid: Gráficas Gonzalez.
García Calderón, F. (1918). *Latin America: Its Rise and Progress*. London: Fisher Unwin .
García del Río, J. (1945). *Meditaciones colombianas*. Bogotá: Biblioteca Popular de Cultura Colombiana.
García Valdecasas, A. (1982). "Andrés Bello y el Derecho." In *Bello y la América Latina. Cuarto Congreso del Bicentenario*. Caracas: Fundación La Casa de Bello.
Gargarella, R. (1995). *Nos los representantes*. Buenos Aires: Miño y Dávila.
(1996). *La justicia frente al gobierno*. Barcelona: Ariel.
(1998). "Full Representation, Deliberation, and Impartiality." In J. Elster, ed., *Deliberative Democracy*, pp. 260–267. Cambridge: Cambridge University Press.
(2000). *The Scepter of Reason: Public Discussion and Political Radicalism in the Origins of Constitutionalism*. Dordrecht: Kluwer.
Garófano, R., and J. R. de Páramo (1983). *La Constitución Gaditana de 1812*. Cádiz: Diputación de Cádiz.
Gazmuri, G. (1992). *El "48" chileno. Igualitarios, reformistas, radicales, masones y bomberos*. Santiago de Chile: Ed. Universitaria.
Gibson, W. (1948). *The Constitutions of Colombia*. Durham: Duke University Press.
Gil Fortoul, J. (1909). *Historia Constitucional de Venezuela*. Caracas: Parra León hnos.
(1954). *Obras Completas. Historia Constitucional de Venezuela*. 3 vols. Caracas: Ministerio de Educación.
Gilmore, R. (1956). "Nueva Granada's Socialist Mirage." *Hispanic American Historical Review* 36, no. 2: 190–210.

Goldman, N., and R. Salvatore, comps. (1998). *Caudillismos Rioplatenses. Nuevas miradas a un viejo problema.* Buenos. Aires: EUDEBA.
Gómez, J. C. (1952). *Escritos.* Montevideo: Sociedad de Hombres de Letras.
González, A. (1937). *El Manifiesto de Lamas.* Montevideo: Imprenta El Siglo Ilustrado.
 (1962). *Las primeras fórmulas constitucionales en los países del Plata (1810-1814).* Montevideo: Barreiro & Ramos.
González, F. (1975). *Memorias.* Medellín: Editorial Bedout.
 (1981). *Escritos Políticos, Jurídicos y Económicos.* Bogotá: Instituto Colombiano de Cultura.
González, J. V. (1945). *El juicio del siglo, o cien años de historia argentina.* Rosario: Editorial Rosario.
González González, F. (1997). *Para leer la política: Ensayos de historia politica colombiana.* Bogotá: Política Colombiana, CINEP.
González Marín, C. (1961). *Francisco de Paula González Vigil, el precursor, el justo, el maestro.* Lima: Tall de le Escuelo de Arjes Gráficas del Polité cnico Nacional Superior José Pordo.
González Portacarrero (1987). "Conservadurismo, liberalismo, y democracia en el Perú del siglo xix." In A. Adrianzén, *Pensamiento político peruano,* pp. 87-98. Lima: Centro de estudio y promoción del desarrollo.
González Vigil, F. (1948). *Importancia de las Asociaciones. Importancia de la Eduación Popular.* Lima: Ediciones Hora del Hombre.
Gootenberg, P. (1993). "Imagining Development. Economic Ideas in Peru's 'Fictious Prosperity' of Guano, 1840-1880." In J. Love and N. Jacobsen, *Guiding the Invisible Hand: Economic Liberalism and the State in Latin America History,* pp. 263-264. New York: Praeger.
Grant, C. (1961). *Democracy in the Connecticut Frontier Town of Kent.* New York: Columbia University Press.
Grases, P. (1967). *El pensamiento constitucional hispanoamericano.* Caracas: Academia Nacional de la Historia.
Gros Espiell, H. (1956). *Las Constituciones del Uruguay.* Madrid: Ediciones Cultura Hispánica.
Gros Espiell, H., and J. Arteaga (1991). *Esquema de la evolución constitucional del Uruguay.* Montevideo: Fundación de Cultura Universitaria.
Habermas, J. (1996). *Between Facts and Norms: Contributions to a Discourse Theory on Law and Democracy.* Cambridge, Mass.: MIT Press.
Hale, C. (1968). *Mexican Liberalism in the Age of Mora, 1821-1853.* New Haven, Conn.: Yale University Press.
 (1986). "Political and Social Ideas in Latin America." In L. Bethell, ed., *The Cambridge History of Latin America,* vol. 4, chap. 10. Cambridge: Cambridge University Press.
Halperín Dongui, T. (1971). *De la revolución de la independencia a la Confederación rosista.* Buenos Aires: Poidós.
 (1972). *Revolución y guerra. Formación de una elite dirigente en la Argentina.* Buenos Aires: Siglo XXI.
 (1973). *The Aftermath of Revolution in Latin America.* New York: Harper and Row.
 (1975). *Politics, Economics and Society in Argentina during the Revolutionary Period.* Cambridge: Cambridge University Press.
 (1985) *Historia Contemporánea de América Latina.* Madrid: Alianza.
 (1993). "Liberalism in a Country Born Liberal." In J. Love and N. Jacobsen, eds., *Guiding the Invisible Hand: Economic Liberalism and the State in Latin America History,* pp. 99-416. New York: Praeger.

Bibliography

(1995). *Proyecto y construcción de una nación, 1846–1880.* Buenos Aires: Ariel, Biblioteca del Pensamiento Argentino.
Handlin, O. Y., and L. Handlin (1982). *A Restless People.* New York: Anchor Press.
Hardy Callcott, W. (1965). *Liberalism in Mexico, 1857–1929.* Hamden, Conn.: Archon Books.
Hart, H. (1988). "Moral Populism and Democracy." In *Law, Liberty and Morality,* pp. 77–83. Oxford: Oxford University Press.
Hay, C. (1979). *James Burgh, Spokesman for Reform in Hanoverian England.* New York: University Press of America.
Heise González, J. (1978). *Años de formación y aprendizaje políticos, 1810–1833.* Santiago de Chile: Editorial Universitaria.
Hentoff, N. (1980). *The First Freedom.* New York: Delacorte Press.
Henríquez, C. (1970). *Antología.* Santiago de Chile: Editorial Andrés Bello.
Herrera Luque, F. (1977). *Boves, el urogallo.* Barcelona, Venezuela: Los libros de Plon.
Herrera Soto, R. (1982). *Antología del Pensamiento Conservador en Colombia.* Bogotá: Instituto Colombiano de Cultura.
Hoffman, R., and P. Albert, eds. (1981). *Sovereign States in an Age of Uncertainty.* Charlottesville: University of Virginia Press.
Hofstader, R. (1979). "The Founding Fathers: An Age of Realism." In R. Horwitz, ed., *The Moral Foundations of the American Republic,* pp. 73–85. Charlottesville: University of Virginia Press.
Holmes, S. (1988). "Precommitment and the Paradox of Democracy." In Jon Elster and A. Hylland, eds., *Foundations of Social Choice Theory.* Cambridge: Cambridge University Press.
(1993). *The Anatomy of Antiliberalism.* Cambridge, Mass.: Harvard University Press.
Holmes, S., and C. Sunstein (1999). *The Cost of Rights: Why Liberty Depends on Taxes.* New York: Norton.
Horowitz, M. (1979). *The Transformation of American Law.* Cambridge, Mass.: Harvard University Press.
Howard, D. (1990). *The Birth of American Political Thought.* London: Mcmillan.
Hyneman, C., and D. Lutz (1983). *American Political Writing during the Founding Era.* Indianapolis: Liberty Press.
Ibarra, E. (1933). *Congreso Constituyente de 1852.* Buenos Aires: E. Frigerio ed.
Jaramillo Uribe, J. (1964). *El pensamiento colombiano en el siglo xix.* Bogotá: Editorial Temis.
(1997). *Travesías por la historia. Antología.* Bogotá: Biblioteca Presidencia de la República.
Jefferson, T. (1984). *Writings.* New York: Literary Classics of the United States.
(1999). *Political Writings.* Cambridge: Cambridge University Press.
Jensen, M. (1967). *The New Nation: A History of the United States during the Confederation.* New York: Alfred Knopf.
Jijón y Caamaño, J. (1929). *Política conservadora.* Vol. 1. Riobamba: La Buena Prensa del Chimborazo.
Jimenez Llaña-Vezga, L. (1990). *El pensamiento liberal en las constituciones colombianas.* Bogotá: Ediciones El Tiempo.
Jonson, R. (1974). *The Mexican Revolution of Ayutla.* Westport, Conn.: Greenwood Press.
Jordán de Albarracín, B. (1978). *Documentos para la historia del derecho constitucional boliviano.* La Paz: Talleres gráficos "SanAntonio."
Jorrín, M., and J. Martz (1970). *Latin American Political Thought and Ideology.* Chapel Hill: University of North Carolina Press.

Kelly, A., and W. Harbison (1948). *The American Constitution: Its Origins and Development*. New York: W. W. Norton.
Kenyon, C. (1966). *The Antifederalists*. Boston: Northeastern University Press.
Knight, B., ed. (1989). *Separation of Powers in the American Political System*. Fairfax, Va.: George Mason University Press.
Koch, A., and W. Peden, eds. (1946). *The Life and Selected Writings of Thomas Jefferson*. New York: Modern Library.
Konvitz, M. (1957). *Fundamental Liberties of a Free People: Religion Speech, Press, Assembly*. Westport, Conn.: Greenwood Press.
Kramer, L. (2005). *The People Themselves*. Oxford: Oxford University Press.
Krauze, E. (1994). *Siglo de caudillos. Biografía política de México, 1810–1910*. Barcelona: Tusquets Editores.
——— (1991). *Contemporary Political Philosophy*. Oxford: Oxford University Press.
Kymlicka, W. (1996). *Multicultural Citizenship: A Liberal Theory of Minority Rights*. Oxford: Oxford University Press.
Larmore, C. (1987). *Patterns of Moral Complexity*. Cambridge: Cambridge University Press.
Lastarria, V. (1944). *Lastarria*. Ed. E. Délano. México: Ediciones de la Secretaría de Educación Pública.
Leguía, G. (1939). *Estudios Históricos*. Santiago de Chile: Ediciones Ercilla.
Letelier, V., ed. (1901). *La gran Convención de 1831–3*. Santiago: Imprenta Cervantes.
Levaggi, A. (1991). "Las Constituciones iberoamericanas en el siglo xix." In *Historia de las Américas*, vol. 4, pp. 149–173. Ed. Navarro García. Sevilla: Universidad de Sevilla.
Levene, R. (1963). *A History of Argentina*. New York: Russell & Russell.
Lewin, B. (1971). *Mariano Moreno, su ideología y su pasión*. Buenos Aires: Ed. Libera.
——— (1980). *Rousseau en la independencia de Latinoamérica*. Buenos Aires: Depalma.
Leyes fundamentales de México (1967). México: Ed. Porrúa.
Linz, J., and A. Valenzuela (1994). *The Failure of Presidential Democracy: The Case of Latin America*. Baltimore: John Hopkins University Press.
López, J. H. (1942). *Memorias*. Bogotá: Biblioteca Popular de Cultura Colombiana.
López, V. F. (1913). *Historia de la República Argentina*. Buenos Aires: G. Kraft.
López Alves, F. (1993). "The Authoritarian Roots of Liberalism: Uruguay, 1810–1886." In J. Love and N. Jacobsen, eds., *Guiding the Invisible Hand: Economic Liberalism and the State in Latin America History*. New York: Praeger.
López Cámara, F. (1959). "Los socialistas franceses en la reforma mexicana." *Historia mexicana* 9: 269–273.
Lora, G. (1967). *Historia del movimiento obrero boliviano, 1848–1900*. La Paz: Editorial LosAmigos del Libro.
Love, J., and N. Jacobsen, eds. (1993). *Guiding the Invisible Hand: Economic Liberalism and the State in Latin America History*. New York: Praeger.
Loveman, B. (1988). *The Legacy of Hispanic Capitalism*. Oxford: Oxford University Press.
——— (1993). *The Constitution of Tyranny: Regimes of Exception in Spanish America*. Pittsburgh: University of Pittsburgh Press.
Luna Pizarro, F. (1959). *Escritos Políticos*. Lima: Univ. Nacional Mayor de San Marcos.
Lutz, D. (1988). *The Origins of American Constitutionalism*. Baton Rouge: Loussiana University Press.

Bibliography

Lynch, J. (1992). *Caudillos in Spanish America, 1800–1850*. Oxford: Clarendon Press.
Manin, B. (1987). "On Legitimacy and Political Deliberation." *Political Theory* 15, no. 3: 338–368.
McDonald Spindler, F., and N. Cook Brooks (1984). *Selections from Juan Montalvo Translated from Spanish*. Tempe: Arizona State University.
McEvoy, C. (1997). *La utopía republicana*. Lima: Pontificia Universidad Católica del Perú.
Madison, J. (1979). *The Papers of James Madison*. 7 vols. Ed. R. Rutland and W. Rachal. Chicago: University of Chicago Press.
Manin, B. (1997). *The Principles of Representative Government*. Cambridge: Cambridge University Press.
Martínez Báez, A. (1996). *Ensayos históricos*. México: Universidad Autónoma de México.
Matthews, R. (1977). *Violencia rural en Venezuela, 1840–1858*. Caracas: Ed. Monte Ávila.
Mayer, J. (1973). *Alberdi y su tiempo*. Vol. 1. Buenos Aires: Abeledo Perrot.
Mejía Zúñiga, R. (1982). *Valentín Gómez Farías, Hombre de México*. México: Fondo de Cultura Económica.
Mill, J. S. (1956). *On Liberty*. Indianapolis: Bobbs-Merrill.
Miranda, J. (1952). *Las ideas y las instituciones políticas mexicanas*. México: Instituto de Derecho Comparado.
Molina, G. (1973). *Las Ideas Liberales en Colombia, 1849–1914*. Bogotá: Colección Manuales Universitarios, Tercer Mundo.
Monguió, L. (1967). *Don José Joaquín de Mora y el Perú del 800*. Berkeley: University of California Press.
Montalvo, J. (1960). *Juan Montalvo*. Puebla: Editorial J. M.Cajica.
Moore, Barrington, Jr. (1966). *Social Origins of Dictatorship and Democracy*. Boston: Beacon Press.
Mora, J. M. (1963). *Obras sueltas*. México: Ed. Porrúa.
Morales, R. (1993). "Pedro Moncayo, fundador del periodismo de combate." In E. Ayala, ed., *Pensamiento de Pedro Moncayo*, pp. 67–96. Quito: Corporación Editora Nacional.
Morales Benítez, O., ed. (1997). *Origen, programas y tesis del liberalismo*. Bogotá: Biblioteca del liberalismo.
Moreno, M. (1937). *Escritos políticos y económicos*. Ordenados por Norberto Piñeiro. Buenos Aires: Ediciones Letias Argentinas.
Morón, G. (1963). *A History of Venezuela*. New York: Roy.
Murillo Toro, M. (1979). *Obras selectas*. Bogotá: Cámara de Representantes.
Myers, J. (1995). *Orden y virtud: el discurso republicano en el régimen rosista*. Buenos Aires: Universidad Nacional de Quilmes.
——— (1998). "La revolución en las ideas: la generación romántica de 1837 en la cultura y la política argentinas." In "Consolidación del régimen rosista, 1835–1852." In N. Goldman, ed., *Nueva Historia Argentina*, vol. 3, pp. 381–445. Buenos Aires: Sudamericana.
Negretto, G., and J. A. Aguilar Rivera (2000a). "Rethinking the Legacy of the Liberal State in Latin America: The Cases of Argentina (1853–1916) and Mexico (1857–1910)." *Journal of Latin American Studies* 32, no. 2: 361–398.
——— (2000b). "Liberalism and Emergency Powers in Latin America: Reflections on Carl Schmitt and the Theory of Constitutional Dictatorship." *Cardozo Law Review*, 21, nos. 5–6: 1797–1823.

Nevins, A. (1927). *The American States during and after the Revolution*. New York: A. M. Kelley.
Nino, C. (1991). *The Ethics of Human Rights*. Oxford: Oxford University Press.
(1997). *The Constitution of Deliberative Democracy*. New Haven, Conn.: Yale University Press.
Noriega, A. (1980). *Francisco Severo Maldonado. El Precursor*. México: Universidad Nacional Autónoma de México.
(1984). *Las ideas políticas en las declaraciones de derechos de las constituciones políticas de México*. México. Universidad Nacional Autónoma de México.
Ocampo López, J. (1990). *Qué es el liberalismo colombiano*. Bogotá: Plaza y Janés.
O'Donnell, G., P. Schmitter, and L. Whitehead (1986). *Transitions from Authoritarian Rule: Latin America*. Baltimore: John Hopkins University Press.
O'Gorman, E., ed. (1978). *Fray Servando Teresa de Mier. Ideario político*. Caracas: Biblioteca de Ayacucho.
Oropeya, A. (1985). *Evolución Constitucional de nuestra República*. Caracas: Serie Estudios.
Otero, M. (1967). *Mariano Otero. Obras*. Vol. 1. México: Editorial Porrúa.
Oyarzun, L. (1953). *El pensamiento de Lastarria*. Santiago de Chile: Editorial Jurírica de Chile.
Pagden, A. (1990). *Spanish Imperialism and the Political Imagination*. New Haven, Conn.: Yale University Press.
Paine, T. (1944). *Representative Selections*. Ed. H. Clark. New York: American Book Company.
(1989). *Political Witings*. Ed. B. Kuklick. Cambridge: Cambridge University Press.
Pajuelo, M. (1965). *Los fines de la educación necesaria en la ideología y acción educativas de Bartolomé Herrera y los Hnos. Gálvez*. Lima: s.e.
Palacios, M. (1998). "Colombian Experience with Liberalism: On the Historical Weakness of the State." In E. Posada Carbó, ed., *The Politics of Reforming the State*. London: Macmillan Press.
Paladines, C. (1990). *Sentido y trayectoria del pensamiento ecuatoriano*. Quito: Biblioteca de la revista cultura, Banco Central del Ecuador.
Parcero, M. (1969). *Lorenzo de Zavala, fuente y origen de la reforma liberal en México*. México: Instituto Nacional de Antropología e Historia Mexicana.
Park, J. (1985). *Rafael Núñez and the Politics of Colombian Regionalism, 1863–1886*. Baton Rouge: Louisiana State University Press.
Pattee, R. (1944). *García Moreno y el Ecuador de su tiempo*. México: Editorial Jus.
Patterson, S. (1981). "The Roots of Massachusetts Federalism. Conservative Politics and Political Culture before 1787." In R. Hoffmand and P. J. Albert, eds., *Sovereign States in an Age of Uncertainty*, pp. 38–39. Charlotte: University of Virginia Press.
Paz Soldán, J. (1943). *Las Constituciones del Perú*. Madrid, Ediciones Cullena Hispánica.
Peach, B. (1979). *Richard Price and the Ethical Foundations of the American Revolution*. Durham, N.C.: Duke University Press.
Pelliza, M. (1897). *Historia de la organización nacional. Urquiza, Alsina, Mitre, 1852–1862*. Buenos Aires: Félix Lajouane editor.
Pendleton Grimes, A. (1983). *American Political Thought*. Lanham, Md.: University Press of America.
Pérez Guilhou, D. (1984). *El pensamiento conservador de Alberdi y la Constitución de 1853*. Buenos Aires: Depalma.

Bibliography

(1989). *Sarmiento y la Constitución*. Mendoza: Fundación Banco de Crédito Argentino.
Pettit, P. (1997). *Republicanism: A Theory of Freedom and Government*. Oxford: Oxford University Press.
Petit Muñoz, E. (1956). *Artigas y su ideario a través de seis series documentales*. Montevideo: Universidad de la República Oriental del Uruguay.
Phillips, A. (1995). *The Politics of Presence*. Oxford: Oxford University Press.
Philp, M. (1996) "Republicanism and Liberalism: On Leadership and Political Order. A Review." *Democratization* 3, no. 4 (Winter): 383–419.
Picón Salas, M. (1953). *Obras selectas*. Caracas.
(1962). *Venezuela independiente, 1810–1960*. Caracas: Fundación E. Mendoza.
Pike, F. (1967). *The Modern History of Peru*. New York: Frederick Praeger.
Pino Iturrieta, E. (1987). *Las ideas de los primeros venezolanos*. Caracas: Fondo Editorial Tropykos.
ed. (1991). *Pensamiento conservador del siglo xix*. Carcas: Monte Ávila editores.
Pivel Devoto, J. (1951). *Las ideas políticas de Bernardo P. Berro*. Montevideo: Cover.
(1955). *Las ideas constitucionales del Dr. José Ellauri*. Montevideo: S.N.
(1956). *Historia de los partidos y de las ideas políticas en el Uruguay*. Vol. 2. Montevideo: Editorial Río de la Plata.
Pivel Devoto, J., and A. Ranieri (1955). *Historia de la República Oriental del Uruguay*. Montevideo: R. Artagaveytia editor.
Planas, P. (1998). *La descentralización en el Perú republicano*. Lima: Municipalidad Metropolitana de Lima.
Pole, J. (1966). *The Gift of Government*. Athens: University of Georgia Press.
Ponce, P. (1987). *Gabriel García Moreno*. Madrid: Historia 16: Quórum: Sociedad Estatal Para la Ejecución Programas del Quinto Centenario.
ed. (1990). *Gabriel García Moreno*. Quito: El Conejo.
Portales, D. (1937). *Epistolario de Don Diego Portales*. Vol. 1. Santiago: Ministerio de Justicia.
Posada-Carbó, E., ed. (1996). *Elections before Democracy: The History of Elections in Europe and Latin America*. London: ILAS, University of London.
Priestley, J. (1791). *Lectures on History and General Policy*. Dublin: L. White and P. Byrne.
Przeworski, A. (1991). *Democracy and the Market*. Cambridge: Cambridge University Press.
Przeworski, A., S. Stokes, and M. Manin, eds., (1999). *Democracy, Accountability and Representation*. Cambridge: Cambridge University Press.
Químper, J. M. (1948). *El principio de la libertad*. Lima: Ediciones Hord del Hombre.
Quintero, I., ed. (1992). *Pensamiento liberal del siglo xix*. Caracas: Monte Ávila editores.
Quiroz Chueca, F. (1988). *La protesta de los artesanos*. Lima: Universidad de San Marcos.
Rabassa, E. (1991). "Historia de las Constituciones mexicanas." In J. L. Soberanes Fernández, ed., *El Derecho en México. Una visión de conjunto*, vol. 1. México: Universidad Nacional Autónoma de México.
Rachal, W., ed. (1975). *The Papers of James Madison*. Chicago: University of Chicago Press.
Rakove, J. (1979). *The Beginnings of National Politics*. New York: Alfred Knopf.

261

Rama, C., ed. (1977). *Utopismo Socialista, 1830–1893*. Caracas: Biblioteca de Ayacucho.
Ramírez, J. A. (1967). *Dos ensayos constitucionales*. Montevideo: Ministerio Instrucción Pública y Previsión Social.
Ravignani, E. (1886). *Asambleas Constituyentes Argentinas*. 6 vols. Buenos Aires: Talleres, S.A., Casa Jacobo Peuser.
Rawls, J. (1971). *A Theory of Justice*. Cambridge, Mass.: Harvard University Press.
(2001). *Justice as Fairness: A Restatement*. Cambridge, Mass.: Harvard University Press.
Rébora, J. (1933). *Ensayo de una doctrina sobre las garantías constitucionales*. La Plata: Anales de la Facultad de Ciencias Jurídicas y sociales.
Recabarren, L. (1972). *Obras selectas*. Santiago de Chile: Ed. Quimantu.
Restrepo Canal, C. (1960). *Nariño periodista*. Bogotá: Academia Nacional de Historia.
Restrepo Piedrahita, C. (1993). *Primeras Constituciones de Colombia y Venezuela, 1811–1830*. Bogotá: Universidad Externado de Colombia.
Reyes, O. E. (1831) *Historia de la República*. Quito: Ecuador.
Reyes Abodie, W., O. Bruschera, and T. Melogno (1968). *El ciclo artiguista*. Montevideo: Universidad de la República.
Reyes Heroles, J. (1957). *El liberalismo mexicano*. México: Universidad Nacional de México.
Rivadeneira Vargas, A. (1978). *Historia Constitucional de Colombia*. Bogotá: Editorial Horizontes.
Rocafuerte, V. (1960). "Ensayos." In *Escritores politicos*. México: editorial Cajica.
Rock, D. (1985). *Argentina 1516–1987*. Madrid: Alianza.
Rodríguez, G. (1970). *Ezequiel Rojas y la república liberal*. Miraflores: Boyaco.
Rodríguez, M. (1978). *The Cádiz Experiment in Central America, 1808 to 1826*. Berkeley: University of California Press.
Rodríguez Albarracín, E., et al., eds. (1988). *La filosofía en Colombia. Historia de las ideas*. Bogotá. Editorial El Búho.
Roig, A. (1984). *El pensamiento social de Montalvo*. Quito: Editorial Tercer Mundo.
Roldán, D. (2002). "La cuestión de la representación en el origen de la política moderna. Una perspectiva comparada." Unpublished manuscript, Univ. Di Tella.
Rollins, R., ed. (1989). *The Autobiography of Noah Webster*. Columbia: University of South Carolina Press.
Romero, J. L. (1969). *Las ideas políticas en la Argentina*. México: Fondo de Cultura Económica.
(1970). *El pensamiento político de la derecha latinoamericana*. Piados, Buenos Aires.
Romero, J. L., and A. Romero, eds. (1977). *Pensamiento político de la emancipación*. Caracas: Biblioteca Ayacucho.
eds. (1978). *Pensamiento Conservador, 1815–1898*. Caracas: Biblioteca de Ayacucho.
Romero, L. A. (1978). *La Sociedad de la Igualdad. Los artesanos de Santiago de Chile y sus primeras experiencias políticas, 1820–1851*. Buenos Aires: Instituto Torcuato Di Tella.
Romero Carranza, A., A. Rodríguez Varela, and F. Ventura Flores (1970). *Historia política de la Argentina*. Buenos Aires: Ediciones Pannedille.
Romero Flores, J. (1959). *Don Melchor de Ocampo. El filósofo de la reforma*. México: Ediciones Botas.

Bibliography

Rosa, J. M. (1955). *Nos los representantes del pueblo*. Buenos Aires: Ed. Theoría.
Rosenn, K. (1990). "The Success of Constitutionalism in the United States and Its Failure in Latin America: An Explanation." *Inter-American Law Review* 22: 1–37.
Ross, J., S. Hoffman, and P. Levack (1979). *Burke's Politics*. New York: Alfred Knopf.
Rossiter, C. (1982). *Conservatism in America*. Cambridge, Mass: Harvard University Press.
Rousseau, J. (1984). *El contrato social*. México: UNAM.
Ruggeri Parra, P. (1949). *Historia política y social de Venezuela*. Caracas: VE Universitaria.
Rutland, R., and W. Rachal, eds. (1975). *The Papers of James Madison*. Chicago: University of Chicago.
Sábato, H. (1999). *Ciudadanía política y formación de las naciones. Perspectivas históricas de América Latina*. México: Fondo de Cultura Económica.
Safford, F. (1984). "The Emergence of Economic Liberalism in Colombia." In J. Love and N. Jacobsen, eds., *Guiding the Invisible Hand: Economic Liberalism and the State in Latin America History*, pp. 35–62, New York: Praeger.
  (1985). "Politics, Ideology and Society in Post-Independence Spanish America." In Leslie Bethell, ed., *The Cambridge History of Latin America*, vol. 3, pp. 347–421. Cambridge: Cambridge University Press.
  (1992). "The Problem of Political Order in Early Republican Spanish America," *Journal of Latin American Studies* 24, quincentenary suppl.: 83–98.
Sala de Touron, N., and J. Rodríguez (1978). *Artigas y su revolución agraria, 1811–1820*. México: Siglo XXI.
Salcedo-Bastardo, J. (1970). *Historia fundamental de Venezuela*. Caracas: Universidad Central de Venezuela.
Saldías, A. (1878). *Ensayo sobre la historia de la Constitución argentina*. Buenos Aires: Imprenta y Libreríode Mayo.
Salvatore, R. (1998). "Consolidación del régimen rosista, 1835–1852." In N. Goldman, ed., *Nueva Historia Argentina*, vol. 3, pp. 320–380. Buenos Aires: Sudamericana.
Sampay, A. (1972). *Las ideas políticas de Juan Manuel de Rosas*. Buenos Aires: Juárez editor.
  (1974). *Las Constituciones de la Argentina (1810–1972)*. Buenos Aires: EUDEBA.
  (1975). *La filosofía jurídica del artículo 19 de la Constitución Nacional*. Buenos Aires: Cooperadora de Derecho y Ciencias Sociales.
Samper, J. M. (1881). *Historia de una alma. Memorias íntimas y de historia contemporánea*. Bogotá: Imprenta de Zalamea hnos.
  (1951). *Derecho Público Interno de Colombia*. 2 vols. Bogotá: Biblioteca Popular de Cultura Colombiana.
Sánchez Viamonte, C. (1948). *Historia institucional de Argentina*. México: Fondo de Cultura Económica.
  (1957). *El pensamiento liberal argentino en el siglo xix*. Buenos Aires: Eds. Gure.
Sandel, M. (1996). *Democracy's Discontent: America in Search of a Public Philosophy*. Cambridge, Mass.: Harvard University Press.
Sarmiento, D. (1972). *A Sarmiento Anthology*. New York: Kennikat Press.
Sayeg Helú, J. (1972). *El constitucionalismo social mexicano*. México: Cultura y Ciencia Política.
  (1978). *Introducción a la historia constitucional de México*. México: Universidad Nacional Autónoma de México.

Bibliography

Scanlon, T. (1975). "The Principles of Justice." In N. Daniels, ed., *Reading Rawls*, pp. 163–189. Oxford: Basil Blackwell.
Schaeffer, J. (1974). "Public Consideration of the 1776 Pennsylvania Constitution." *Pennsylvania Magazine of History and Bibliography* 98, no. 4: 415–437.
Schleifer, J. (1991). "Jefferson and Tocqueville." In K. Misugi, ed., *Interpreting Tocqueville's Democracy in America*, pp. 178–203. New York: Rowman & Littlefield.
Scholes, W. (1967). *Mexican Politics during the Juarez Regime*. Columbia: University of Missouri.
Scully, T. (1992). *Rethinking the Center: Party Politics in 19th and 20th Century Chile*. Stanford, Calif.: Stanford University Press.
Sherman, M. (1991). *A More Perfect Union: Vermont Becomes a State*. Montpelier: Vermont Historical Society.
Shumway, N. (1993). *The Invention of Argentina*. Berkeley: University of California Press.
Sierra, J. (1977). *Evolución política del pueblo mexicano*. Caracas: Biblioteca de Ayacucho.
Sierra Mejía, R. (2002). *Miguel Antonio Caro y la cultura de su época*. Bogotá: Universidad Nacional de Colombia.
Sills, D., ed. (1968). *International Encyclopedia of Social Sciences*. Vols. 1–19. New York: Macmillan and Free Press.
Silva Castro, R. (1969) *Juan Egaña. Antología*. Santiago de Chile: Editora Andrés Bello.
Skidmore, M. (1978). *American Political Thought*. New York: St. Martin's Press.
Snueza, G. (1953). *Santiago Arcos, comunista, millonario y calavera*. Santiago: Ed. Del Pacífico.
Sobrevilla, N. (2001). "The Influence of the European 1848 Revolutions in Peru." In G. Thomson, ed., *The Influence of 1848 Revolutions in Latin America*, pp. 191–216. London: ILAS.
Sowell, D. (1992). *The Early Colombian Labor Movement*. Philadelphia: Temple University Press.
  (1993). "Artisans and Tariff Reform: The Socio-political Consequences of Liberalism in Early Republican Spanish America." In J. Love and N. Jacobsen, eds., *Guiding the Invisible Hand: Economic Liberalism and the State in Latin America History*. New York: Praeger.
Spindler, F. (1987). *Nineteenth Century Ecuador: A Historic Introduction*. Fairfax: George Mason University Press.
Spinrad, William (1970). *Civil Rights*. Chicago: Quadrangle Books.
Starkey, M. (1955). *A Little Rebellion*. New York: Alfred Knopf.
Storing, H. (1981a). *The Complete Anti-Federalist*. 7 vols. Chicago: University of Chicago Press.
  (1981b). *What the Anti-Federalists Were For*. Chicago: University of Chicago Press.
Street, J. (1959). *Artigas and the Emancipation of Uruguay*. Cambridge: Cambridge University Press.
Sunstein, C. (1993). *The Partial Constitution*. Cambridge, Mass.: Harvard University Press.
Svampa, M. (1994). *El dilema argentino: civilización o barbarie*. Buenos Aires: Ediciones El Cielo por Asalto.
Taylor, C. (1989). "Cross-Purposes: The Liberal-Communitarian Debate." In N. Rosenblum, ed., *Liberalism and the Moral Life*, pp. 159–182. Cambridge, Mass.: Harvard University Press.

Bibliography

Taylor, J. (1814). *An Inquiry into the Principles and Policy of the Government of the United States.* Fredericksburg, Va.: Green and Cady.
Taylor, P. (1962). *Government and Politics in Uruguay.* Westport, Conn.: Greenwood Press.
Taylor, R., ed. (1951). *Massachusetts: Colony to Commonwealth.* Chapel Hill: University of North Carolina Press.
Tejeda, J. (1947). *Libertad de la industria.* Lima: Ed. Hora del Hombre.
Terán, O. (2008). *Historia de las ideas en la Argentina.* Buenos Aires: Siglo XXI.
Teresa de Mier, Fray S. (1977). *Idea de la Constitución.* México: Cuadernos de Causa 8.
Ternavasio, M. (1998). "Las reformas rivadavianas en Buenos Aires y el Congreso General Constituyente 1820–1827." In N. Goldman, ed., *Nueva Historia Argentina*, vol. 3, pp. 159–197. Buenos Aires: Sudamericana.
Toro, F. (1954). *Fermín Toro.* Introd. de V. Tosa. Caracas.
Torres Almeida, J. (1984). *Manuel Murillo Toro, caudillo radical y reformador social.* Bogotá: Eds. Del Tiempo.
Tribe, L. (1988). *American Constitutional Law.* New York: Foundation Press.
Trujillo, J. (1993). "El Estado en el pensamiento de Pedro Moncayo." In E. Ayala, ed., *Pensamiento de Pedro Moncayo*, pp. 55–66. Quito: Corporación Editora Nacional.
Tushnet, M. (1999). *Taking the Constitution Away from the Courts.* Princeton: Princeton University Press.
Urbinati, N. (2000). "Representation as Advocacy. A Study of Democratic Deliberation." *Political Theory* 28, no. 6: 758–786.
Uslar Pietri, J. (1962). *Historia de la rebelión popular de 1814.* Caracas: Edine.
Urrutia, M. (1969). *The Development of the Colombian Labor Movement.* New Haven, Conn.: Yale University Press.
Valencia Villa, H. (1987). *Cartas de batalla. Una crítica del constitucionalismo colombiano.* Bogotá: Univ. Nacional de Colombia.
Valenzuela, S. (1996). "Building Aspects of Democracy before Democracy: Electoral Practices in 19th Century Chile." In E. Posada-Carbó, ed., *Elections before Democracy.* London: ILAS, University of London.
Vallenilla Lanz, L. (1919). *Cesarismo democrático. Estudios sobre las bases sociológicas de la Constitución de Venezuela.* Caracas: Empresa EL cojo.
Vanorden Shaw, P. (1930). *The Early Constitutions of Chile, 1810–1833.* New York: Columbia University.
Vanossi, J. (1970). *La influencia de José Benjamín Gorostiaga en la Constitución argentina y en su jurisprudencia.* Buenos Aires: Ed. Pannedille.
Varela, L. (1910). *Historia constitucional de la República Argentina.* La Plata: Taller de Impresiones Oficiales.
Vargas Martínez, G. (1998). *José María Melo. Los artesanos y el socialismo.* Bogotá: Planeta.
Varona, A. (1973). *Francisco Bilbao, revolucionario de América. Vida y pensamiento.* Buenos Aires: Ediciones Excelsior.
Véliz, C. (1984). *La tradición centralista de América Latina.* Barcelona: Ed. Ariel.
Verner, J. (1984). "The Independence of Supreme Courts in Latin America: A Review of Literature." *Journal of Latin American Studies* 16: 463–506.
Vile, M. (1967). *Constitutionalism and the Separation of Powers.* Oxford: Clarendon Press.
    (1991). "The Separation of Powers." In J. Greene and J. Pole, eds., *The Blackwell Encyclopedia of the American Revolution.* Cambridge, Mass.: Basil Blackwell.

Villalva Bustillo, C. (1982). *Los liberales en el poder.* Bogotá: Ediciones Tercer Mundo.
Villamarín, M. (1993). "El liberalismo en la época de la fundación de la república." In E. Ayala, ed., *Pensamiento de Pedro Moncayo*, pp. 43–53. Quito: Corporación Editora Nacional.
Walsh, C. (1969). *The Political Science of John Adams.* New York: Freeport.
Waldron, J. (1993). "A Right-Based Critique of Constitutional Rights." *Oxford Journal of Legal Studies* 13, no. 1: 18–51.
——— (1999). *Law and Disagreement.* Oxford: Oxford University Press.
Walker, F. (1912). *The Making of the Nation.* New York: C. Scribner's Sons.
Walzer, M. (1984). "Liberalism and the Art of Separation." *Political Theory* 12, no. 3: 315–330.
Webster, N. (1788). "Examination of the Constitution of the United States." In P. Ford, ed., *Pamphlets on the Constitution of the United States*, pp. 35–66. New York: Burt Franklin.
Werlich, D. (1978). *Peru: A Short History.* Carbondale: Southern Illinois University Press.
White, M. (1987). *Philosophy, the Federalist, and the Constitution.* Oxford: Oxford University Press.
Wilgus, C., ed. (1937). *South American Dictators.* New York: Russell & Russell.
Williams, M. (1998). *Voice, Trust, and Memory.* Princeton: Princeton University Press.
——— (2000). "The Uneasy Alliance of Group Representation and Deliberative Democracy." In W. Kymlicka and W. Norman, eds., *Citizenship in Diverse Societies*, pp. 124–154. Oxford: Oxford University Press.
Wills, G., ed. (1988). *The Federalist Papers.* New York: Bantam Books.
Wilson, F. (1949). *The American Political Mind.* New York: McGraw-Hill.
Wood, G. (1966). "A Note on Mobs in the American Revolution." *William and Mary Quarterly* 23, no. 4: 635–642.
——— (1969). *The Creation of the American Republic.* New York: W. W. Norton.
——— (1992). *The Radicalism of the American Revolution.* New York: Alfred Knopf.
——— (2002). *The American Revolution: A History.* New York: Modern Library.
Zarco, F. (1957). *Historia del Congreso Constitucional de 1857.* México: Instituto Nacional de Estudios Históricos.
Zarini, H. (1993). *Análisis de la Constitución nacional.* Buenos Aires: Astrea.
Zavala, L. (1966). *Lorenzo de Zavala. Obras.* México: Editorial Porrúa.
——— (1985). *Ensayo histórico de las revoluciones de México.* México: Fondo de Cultura Económica.
Zavaleta Arias, G., ed. (1994). *Partidos políticos y constituciones en Colombia.* Bogotá: Editorial Antillas.
Zea, L. (1970). *The Latin American Mind.* Norman: University of Oklahoma Press.
——— coord. (1993). *América Latina ante la revolución francesa.* México: Universidad Nacional Autónoma de México.
Zevada, R. (1972). *La lucha por la libertad en el congreso constituyente de 1857. El pensamiento de Ponciano Arriaga.* México: Ed. Nuestro Tiempo.
Zevallos Reyre, F. (1947). *Lecciones de derecho constitucional.* Guayaquil.
Zuckerman, M. (1968). "The Social Context of Democracy in Massachusetts." *William and Mary Quarterly* 25, no. 4: 523–544.

Index

Adams, John, 62, 96, 104, 107, 114, 129, 135, 233
agrarian reform, 37, 38, 40, 42, 43, 61, 80, 81, 98, 109, 226
Alamán, Lucas, 5, 11, 30, 81, 98, 100, 113, 115, 122, 123, 136, 137, 142, 143, 152
Alberdi, Juan Bautista, 6, 29, 33, 121, 156, 157, 170, 171, 176, 177, 178, 212, 214
Álvarez, Juan, 42, 74, 184, 218
Ames, Fisher, 12, 27, 62, 77, 104
Amézaga, Mariano, 67
anarchism, 95
anarchy, 4, 30, 75, 84, 85, 93, 95, 99, 108, 109, 113, 121, 122, 124, 130, 132, 134, 153, 154, 155, 162, 222, 223, 232
Antich, Hilarión, 145
Anti-Federalists (U.S.), 10, 15, 24, 25, 27, 32, 34, 48, 59, 63, 77, 78, 88
antifederalism, 74
Arboleda, José Rafael, 102, 139
Arboleda, Julio, 95
Arboleda, Sergio, 94, 95, 102, 109
Arcos, Santiago, 17, 35, 43, 52, 78, 83, 226
Aristocratis, 25
Arriaga, Ponciano, 18, 60, 73, 80, 81, 245
Arrillaga, Basilio, 125, 142
Artigas, José Gervasio, 5, 16, 21, 26, 36, 37, 42, 48, 49, 50, 55, 76, 77, 80, 218, 226
Asamblea del año XIII, 182, 200

Ayutla Revolution, 42, 184.
    See also Revolución de Ayutla
Azuero, Vicente, 168, 190, 191, 204

Balmes, Jaime, 99
Bello, Andrés, 109, 110, 113, 115, 120, 122
Bello, Bernardo, 206
Belzu, Manuel Isidoro, 83, 106, 107, 135
Bentham, Jeremy, 102, 168, 173, 179, 191, 193
Bergasse, Nicolás, 70
bicameralism, 60, 61, 63, 87, 203, 221
Bilbao, Francisco, 5, 17, 21, 26, 35, 36, 43, 51, 52, 55, 56, 67, 77, 83, 239
Bolívar, Simón, 10, 17, 26, 64, 97, 98, 99, 102, 105, 106, 108, 109, 110, 113, 115, 116, 118, 119, 121, 123, 124, 126, 128, 129, 130, 139, 140, 141, 144, 168, 171, 184, 204, 206, 207
Bonaparte, Napoleón, 206
Boves, Juan, 29, 106
Brunhouse, Robert, 47, 192
Burgh, James, 20, 68
Burke, Edmund, 20, 69, 99, 100, 103, 104, 196, 200
Bushnell, David, 174, 175, 193
Bustamente, Anastasio, 106, 122

Cabildo, 21, 192, 193
Calhoun, John, 103, 104
Carbo, Pedro, 187
Caro, José Eusebio, 95, 121

267

Caro, Miguel Antonio, 99, 101, 133, 183
Cartwright, John, 20
Casós, Fernando, 176, 227
Castilla, Ramón, 112, 189
Castillo Velasco, 18, 80, 83, 245
Castro, Manuel Antonio, 200
Catholicism, 7, 91, 101, 102, 123, 131, 132, 133, 134, 135, 141, 151, 160, 183, 186, 187
Catholic religion, 3, 76, 98, 101, 102, 108, 116, 120, 131, 132, 133, 134, 185, 190, 220
caudillo, 28, 29, 36, 42, 75, 87, 98, 113, 122, 123, 134, 135, 153, 154, 170
centralism, 74, 115, 122, 123, 124, 131, 136, 144, 184
checks and balances, 7, 9, 57, 58, 84, 114, 179, 181, 194, 197, 198, 203, 208, 209, 221, 228, 242
Chipman, Nathaniel, 59
church, 3, 22, 35, 51, 65, 66, 67, 77, 78, 91, 92, 95, 98, 99, 101, 102, 123, 132, 133, 136, 138, 143, 146, 150, 151, 152, 155, 157, 159, 160, 161, 162, 169, 171, 173, 174, 176, 182, 183, 184, 185, 186, 187, 189, 190, 194, 219, 221, 222, 245
Cisneros, Benjamín, 188
civic virtue, 33, 39, 48, 114, 125, 132, 137, 138
Comonfort, Ignacio, 184, 185
conservatism, 3, 16, 90, 92, 93, 102, 103, 111, 130, 131, 141, 146, 150, 151, 180, 220, 221, 231
conservative constitutions, 3, 5, 74, 117, 126, 133, 145, 146, 180, 188, 205
Constant, Benjamín, 85, 115, 118, 171, 193
Constitution
of Apatzingán (1814), 5, 26, 35, 48, 50, 58, 64, 66, 75, 116. *See also* Constitution, of México (1814)
of Argentina (1819), 74, 123, 143, 152, 202
of Argentina (1826), 74, 123
of Argentina (1853), 74, 98, 120, 123, 133, 150, 153, 162, 180, 192, 205
of Banda Oriental (1813), 21, 47, 48, 58, 66

of Bolivia (1826), 115, 117, 118, 121
of Bolivia (1831), 121
of Bolivia (1834), 121
of Bolivia (1839), 122
of Bolivia (1843), 121
of Bolivia (1851), 121, 122
of Bolivia (1861), 120
British, 114
Cádiz (1812), 7, 114, 116, 117, 188
of Chile (1818), 126
of Chile (1822), 117, 126, 143
of Chile (1823), 5, 131, 188
of Chile (1828), 74, 113, 116, 122, 180, 188, 208
of Chile (1833), 5, 74, 98, 108, 120, 121, 136, 144, 187, 208, 209
of Colombia (1821), 74. *See also* Constitution, of Cúcuta
of Colombia (1826), 121
of Colombia (1828), 121, 191
of Colombia (1830), 117, 121
of Colombia (1832), 74, 117, 122, 133, 191, 209
of Colombia (1834), 122, 191
of Colombia (1843), 121, 133, 145
of Colombia (1853), 74, 183, 186, 191, 209
of Colombia (1858), 183, 190
of Colombia (1863), 72, 74, 133, 183, 186, 191, 205
of Colombia (1886), 74, 102, 120, 121, 133, 145
of Cúcuta (1821), 117
of Ecuador (1830), 64, 122
of Ecuador (1835), 122
of Ecuador (1843), 127
of Ecuador (1845), 122
of Ecuador (1850), 64
of Ecuador (1851), 122
of Ecuador (1852), 122
of Ecuador (1869), 5, 120, 121, 136, 141, 146
of México (1814), 5, 27, 58. *See also* Constitution, of Apatzingán (1814)
of México (1824), 74, 76, 113, 123, 183, 187, 188
of México (1836), 75, 115, 116
of México (1843), 64, 123
of México (1857), 18, 58, 74, 80, 133, 180, 185
Napoleonic Constitutions, 115, 118

Index

Napoleonic Consular (1799), 114
Napoleonic Consular (1802), 114
of Perú (1823), 63, 65, 116, 168, 205, 209
of Perú (1826), 121
of Perú (1828), 11, 113, 117, 122, 168, 205, 209
of Perú (1834), 122, 168, 205, 209
of Perú (1839), 11, 121, 127, 189
of Venezuela (1811), 10, 16, 25, 50, 64, 74, 116, 118, 124, 182, 209, 218
of Venezuela (1830), 117, 124
of Venezuela (1857), 124
of Venezuela (1858), 74, 124, 190
of Venezuela (1864), 122, 190
of the United States (1776), 9, 13, 61, 69, 199
of the United States (1787), 5, 57, 160, 199, 208
of Uruguay (1830), 117, 206
Córdoba, José María, 204
Correa, Ramón, 186, 205
countermajoritarian institutions, 2, 57, 70, 71, 73, 158, 167, 198, 218, 225, 226, 229, 232, 243
Cruger, Henry, 196

de Alvear, Carlos María, 200
de Bonald, Louis, 99, 100, 101, 117
de Maistre, Joseph, 99, 100, 101
democracy, 15, 17, 23, 28, 29, 36, 41, 43, 46, 47, 55, 62, 64, 69, 80, 87, 88, 90, 94, 103, 107, 108, 115, 125, 126, 129, 148, 165, 166, 168, 170, 171, 172, 198, 210, 214, 217, 224, 225, 227, 236, 239, 241, 243
de Mora, José Joaquín, 116, 188
de Ocampo, Melchor, 18, 23, 67, 73, 184, 185, 218, 245
de Paula Castañeda, Francisco, 96
Dickinson, John, 143
Donoso Cortés, Juan, 99, 101, 125
Dorrego, Manuel, 74, 83, 123, 218
Draconians, 190

Echenique, José, 106
Echeverría, Esteban, 29, 170, 171, 214
education, 22, 35, 77, 96, 102, 128, 131, 132, 133, 138, 139, 140, 160, 170, 183, 187, 190, 238, 239
egalitarianism, 1, 2, 7, 8, 16, 21, 34, 37, 41, 50, 51, 52, 62, 75, 79, 83, 85, 88, 89, 97, 100, 142, 146, 147, 149, 150, 156, 169, 170, 215, 216, 218, 219, 222, 226, 227, 230, 231, 232, 233, 234, 235, 237, 238, 240, 241, 243, 245, 246, 247
Egaña, Juan, 92, 94, 120, 121, 125, 131, 132, 137, 138, 139, 140, 141, 143, 152, 194
Egaña, Mariano, 67, 101, 108, 111, 113, 115, 120, 128, 143
elitism, 62, 93, 124, 142, 214
political, 3, 90, 103, 104, 105, 117, 227
Ellauri, José, 63, 184, 206
Ely, Samuel, 72, 225
equality, 6, 19, 20, 75, 89, 95, 97, 103, 104, 105, 107, 109, 148, 171, 172, 176, 179, 182, 183, 184, 187, 190, 193, 207, 215, 216, 226, 238, 239, 241
political, 19, 105, 226, 227, 228
economic, 38, 39, 226
Errázuriz, Federico, 208
Escudero, Ignacio, 67
Esquiú, Mamerto, 162
European revolution (1848), 17, 189, 237

factions, 28, 39, 108, 165, 166, 195, 205
Falcón, Juan, 79
federal constitution, 9, 10, 14, 25, 46, 49, 57, 59, 60, 63, 85, 87, 192, 198, 199
federal convention, 15, 53, 72, 73, 96, 126, 147, 155, 194, 199, 233
federalism, 48, 49, 52, 72, 73, 74, 75, 79, 83, 109, 110, 113, 122, 123, 124, 125, 133, 169, 175, 178, 180, 188, 209, 218
Federalists (U.S.), 10, 27, 29, 47, 73, 77, 84, 85, 105, 107, 114, 154, 194, 195, 196, 199, 200, 208, 233
Fernández de Lizardi, José Joaquín, 27, 41, 50
Fernando VII, 116
Ferré, Pedro, 134
Flores, Juan, 116, 136, 168, 175, 206, 207
Flores Magón, Ricardo, 53
Franklin, Benjamin, 61
free press, 131, 132, 188

269

Index

freedom of the press, 73, 132, 155, 160, 187, 188
French Revolution, 7, 20, 52, 75, 95, 96, 99, 100, 101
Frías, Félix, 108, 109
fueros, 55, 160, 182, 184
Funes, Gregorio, 200

Gálvez, Pedro, 79, 96, 102, 141, 145, 189
Gamarra, Agustín, 11, 113, 161
Gamboa, José, 60
García de la Sena, Manuel, 21
García del Río, Juan, 109
García Moreno, Gabriel, 93, 102, 121, 132, 136, 141, 207, 221
García, Francisco, 42
Generación del 27, 169, 227
general will, 9, 16, 25, 26, 27, 30, 32, 50, 75, 76, 85, 86, 97
Gerry, Elbridge, 107, 111, 126, 199
Gólgotas, 67, 172, 190, 191
Gómez Farías, Valentín, 171, 183, 184
González, Florentino, 163, 168, 172, 175, 204
González Prada, Manuel, 53, 67
González Vigil, Francisco de Paula, 67, 83, 161, 162, 168, 232, 236
Gorostiaga, José Benjamín, 135, 186
Gorriti, Juan Ignacio,1688a, 175
Goyena, Pedro, 162
Gual, Pedro, 144
Guerrero, Vicente, 30, 74, 75, 106, 122, 218
Guzmán, Antonio Leocadio, 207

Hall, Francisco, 168, 219
Hamilton, Alexander, 27, 71, 96, 104, 105, 110, 114, 118, 125, 126, 128, 129, 130, 147, 166, 167
Hart, Herbert, 31, 94
Haya de la Torre, Víctor Raúl, 53
Henríquez, Camilo, 33
Henry, Patrick, 159
Herrera, Bartolomé, 5, 67, 95, 96, 101, 105, 119, 125, 143, 145, 152, 161, 186
Hidalgo, Miguel, 34, 35, 41, 50, 218
Humble, John, 25

individual autonomy, 8, 89, 97, 224, 229, 230, 231, 232, 235, 237

individualism, 156, 158, 164, 231, 232
inequality, 40, 44, 104, 105, 109, 223, 226, 236
Infante, José, 188

Jarvis, William, 22, 70
Jefferson, Thomas, 15, 20, 22, 23, 24, 31, 32, 38, 39, 40, 41, 54, 58, 59, 70, 80, 87, 105, 148, 157, 159, 213, 215, 216, 225, 233, 238
Jensen, Merrill, 46, 47, 224
Juárez, Benito, 52, 74, 184, 185
judicial power, 115, 117, 202, 203
judicial review, 10, 71, 129, 203, 208, 209, 214, 221, 225, 229, 243
judiciary, 26, 57, 58, 69, 70, 71, 72, 73, 121, 128, 129, 143, 151, 181, 196, 197, 198, 229
Justo, Juan B., 53

King, Rufus, 62, 126
Konvtiz, Morton, 91, 93, 159

Lacordaire, Henri, 35
laissez faire, 43, 44, 51, 172, 174, 175, 176, 235
Lamennais, Robert, 35
Laso, Benito, 27, 145, 168
Lastarria, José Victorino, 35, 162, 169, 181, 208
Lavaysse, Benjamín, 186
Lee, Richard Henry, 25, 34, 88
legislative power, 66, 101, 126, 171
Leiva, Manuel, 134
Lerdo de Tejada, Miguel, 184, 185
Ley Juárez, 184
Ley Lerdo, 184, 185
liberal constitution, 3, 7, 63, 133, 178, 180, 203, 246
liberal-conservative constitutions, 231, 246
liberales puros, 64, 67, 73, 184, 218, 245
liberalism, 4, 6, 109, 153, 155, 156, 160, 161, 164, 167, 168, 171, 172, 175, 179, 180, 191, 194, 203, 204, 208, 209, 210, 219, 220, 221, 222, 227, 231
  economic, 18, 52, 174, 175, 176, 178, 190
  political, 4, 175
Linares, José María, 176

270

Index

Locke, John, 104, 105, 159
López, José Hilario, 18, 43, 175, 221
Lorenzo de Zavala, 30, 42, 49, 74, 218
Luna Pizarro, Francisco, 161, 168, 206

Machado, Prebendo, 144
Madiedo, Manuel María, 37, 44, 83, 245
Madison, James, 6, 14, 15, 28, 34, 39, 46, 58, 59, 71, 125, 126, 127, 129, 147, 148, 153, 155, 158, 159, 195, 199, 200, 203, 204, 227
Maldonado, Francisco Severo, 41, 50
Mariátegui, José Carlos, 53
Marshall, John, 203
Martin, Luther, 107
Mason, George, 25, 38, 78, 107, 125, 126, 127, 158
Matta, Manuel Antonio, 65, 149
Maya, Miguel, 144
Melgarejo, Mariano, 5
Mendoza de Tapia, Lucas, 69
Mercer, John, 25, 144
Michelet, Jules, 51
military forces, 9, 16, 18, 26, 36, 51, 65, 66, 67, 82, 91, 98, 119, 122, 123, 135, 142, 143, 152, 179, 182, 183, 184, 185, 189, 190, 205, 206, 207, 219
Mill, John Stuart, 156, 157, 187
mixed constitution, 82, 114, 225
Monagas, José, 124, 207
Moncayo, Pedro, 149, 155, 161, 168, 187, 207
Montalvo, Juan, 17, 23, 37, 43, 232, 238
Monteagudo, Bernardo, 16, 27, 33, 50
Montesquieu, Charles Louis, 70, 117, 159, 171
Montezuma, 25
Montt, Manuel, 26
Mora, José María, 153, 162, 171, 180, 183, 184, 185, 187, 188, 193, 194, 202, 203
morality, 3, 30, 37, 38, 76, 94, 120, 125, 131, 132, 133, 135, 137, 138, 140, 215, 220, 223, 226
moral neutrality, 3, 157
moral perfectionism, 3, 90, 92, 99, 102, 103, 117, 163, 178
moral populism, 3, 30

Morelos, José María, 34, 35, 37, 41, 50, 76, 88, 218
Moreno, Mariano, 16, 27, 31, 50, 86, 218
Morris, Gouverneur, 126, 144
Mosquera, Tomás, 66, 175, 191, 205
Murillo Toro, Manuel, 18, 22, 23, 43, 79, 155, 175, 219, 237, 238, 239, 245, 246
Myers, Jorge, 98, 220

Nevins, Allan, 14, 15
Nuñez, Rafael, 133, 223

O'Higgins, Bernardo, 126, 136, 143
Olvera, Isidoro, 80, 81
Ospina Rodríguez, Mariano, 95, 97, 101, 102, 106, 107, 115, 121, 133
Otero, Mariano, 73

Páez, José Antonio, 74, 108, 124, 207, 221
Paine, Thomas, 13, 20, 21, 22, 54, 60, 61, 62, 63, 80, 107, 228, 239
Palacios, Alfredo, 53
Palma, Ricardo, 188
Pando, José María, 101, 125
paper money, 9, 10, 14, 29, 61, 106, 126, 172
Paredes y Arrillaga, Mariano, 125, 142
Paso, Juan José, 200
Patronato, 160
Penn, William, 61
Poinsett, Joel, 218
Portales, Diego, 16, 92, 93, 108, 111, 113, 136
powers
 executive, 11, 64, 66, 115, 119, 122, 151, 204, 206, 208, 221
 extraordinary, 117, 120, 128, 130, 137, 151, 205, 206, 208
 separation of, 9, 14, 54, 57
 of veto, 10, 14, 65, 116, 117, 120, 137, 151, 203, 204, 221, 225
presidentialist system, 151
Price, Richard, 19, 68
Priestley, Joseph, 20, 68
Proudhon, Pierre Joseph, 83, 161
Putney debates, 19

Quinet, Edgar, 51
Quíper, José María, 176

271

Index

radicalism, 7, 9, 11, 12, 16, 17, 18, 19, 20, 28, 30, 31, 38, 45, 48, 49, 50, 51, 52, 53, 54, 55, 70, 72, 73, 74, 75, 78, 82, 85, 86, 87, 88, 154, 155, 159, 217, 218, 220, 223, 224, 231, 234, 244
radical constitutions, 3, 10, 20, 21, 49, 50, 57, 80, 199, 218
Ramírez, Ignacio, 18, 23, 60, 64, 81, 245
Randolph, Edmund, 107, 126, 127
Rangel, Francisco José, 29
Rayón, Ignacio, 27, 76, 86
Recabarren, Luis, 53, 73
Reglamento provisorio, 42, 80
religion, 2, 30, 33, 34, 35, 75, 76, 77, 78, 91, 92, 93, 94, 98, 99, 101, 102, 116, 120, 123, 131, 132, 133, 134, 136, 138, 139, 144, 150, 157, 158, 159, 160, 161, 186, 187, 189, 239
representative system, 24, 47, 48, 56, 64, 69, 107, 136, 151, 170, 171, 172, 192, 197, 198, 201, 202, 205, 224, 227
republicanism, 7, 80, 202, 240
Revolución de Ayutla, 18
rights
 bill of, 3, 13, 19, 48, 50, 69, 77, 78, 99, 130, 152, 163, 181, 182, 208, 221
 individual, 3, 4, 9, 28, 30, 31, 49, 75, 77, 78, 88, 119, 123, 131, 132, 133, 152, 181, 188, 189, 190, 210, 221, 229, 235, 239, 241, 246
 political, 11, 45, 54, 78, 79, 82, 119, 121, 123, 141, 143, 144, 145, 190, 191, 192
 property, 10, 81, 86, 106, 142, 169, 193, 224, 241
 social, 245, 246
Rivadavia, Bernardino, 116, 173, 174, 179, 188, 191, 192, 202
Robespierre, Maximilien, 31
Rocafuerte, Vicente, 74, 175, 178, 187, 206
Rodríguez Aldea, José, 126, 143
Rodríguez de Francia, Gaspar, 94, 102, 136
Rodríguez, Martín, 174
Rojas, Ezequiel, 168, 181, 183, 205

Romero, José Luis, 17, 27, 35, 91, 93, 95, 96, 97, 98, 99, 102, 108, 113, 128, 141, 145, 153, 162
Rosas, Juan Manuel, 19, 29, 98, 107, 108, 113, 121, 123, 135, 169, 205, 220, 221
Roscío, Juan Germán, 27
Rousseau, Jean-Jacques, 16, 32, 33, 43, 55, 85, 86, 96
Rush, Benjamin, 33, 62, 87

Safford, Frank, 7, 11, 29, 33, 106, 114, 115, 116, 144
Samper, José María, 164, 165, 168, 175, 202, 205, 212, 227
Samper, Miguel, 43, 44
San Martín, José, 65, 136, 168, 205
Sánchez Carrión, José Faustino, 65, 168
Sandel, Michael, 5, 33, 37, 38, 40, 41, 71, 75, 78, 80, 164, 240
Santa Anna, Antonio, 18, 42, 98, 122, 123, 136, 137, 142, 171, 180, 184, 185
Santa Cruz, Andrés, 116, 206
Santander, Francisco, 102, 133, 174, 175, 179, 183, 193, 204
Sarmiento, Domingo F., 29, 109, 121, 170, 173, 193, 214
Say, John Baptist, 44
Scanlon, Thomas, 103
self-government, 7, 8, 12, 13, 16, 19, 20, 21, 32, 34, 38, 39, 45, 47, 51, 53, 54, 68, 80, 88, 168, 170, 215, 216, 224, 229, 230, 231, 237, 238, 239, 240, 245
Shays, Daniel, 72, 96
Silva Santisteban, José, 176
slavery, 34, 35, 55, 61, 69, 77, 136, 175, 184, 189, 191, 211, 213, 221, 235
social contract, 16, 97, 130, 216
Sociedad de la Igualdad, 17, 18, 26, 35, 43, 51, 52, 65, 79, 219, 239
Soublette, Carlos, 176
sovereignty
 of the people, 16, 36, 55, 56, 97, 167, 170, 227, 239
 popular, 29, 69, 81, 100
 of reason, 29, 167, 170, 227
Spencer, Herbert, 176, 205
state of siege, 17, 26, 117, 120, 151

Index

suffrage, universal, 18, 22, 43, 73, 78, 79, 107, 108, 144, 179, 190, 191, 192, 237
Supreme Court, 47, 71, 72, 73, 123, 143, 185, 196, 202, 207, 214

Taylor, John, 23, 71, 164
Tejada, José Simón, 176, 177
Toro, Fermín, 124, 125
town meetings, 13, 46, 47, 62, 192, 194, 197, 224, 234
tradition, 20, 50, 57, 64, 94, 97, 99, 100, 103, 111, 116, 146, 151, 162, 178, 209, 223, 240
Turner, Charles, 34, 77–78
tyranny, 4, 24, 49, 58, 64, 65, 100, 153, 154, 181, 194, 199, 202, 206, 209, 222, 231

Unger, Roberto, 243
unicameralism, 61, 63, 64
Ureta, Alberto, 188
Urquiza, Justo José, 98, 153

U.S. Declaration of Independence, 9, 10, 15, 20, 31, 194, 216

Valencia Villa, Hernando, 84
Vidaurre, Manuel, 27
Vile, Maurice, 57, 58
Voltaire, 159
von Gentz, Friedrich, 99, 100
von Humbolt, Wilhelm, 99, 100

Waldron, Jeremy, 19, 225, 240, 241, 243
Washington, George, 87
Williams, Roger, 158, 242
Williams, Samuel, 58
Wilson, James, 126
Wood, Gordon, 9, 12, 13, 20, 33, 56, 72, 77, 142, 201, 215, 216

Zamora, Ezequiel, 41, 49
Zarco, Francisco, 60, 80, 185
Zenteno, Pedro, 134

For EU product safety concerns, contact us at Calle de José Abascal, 56–1°, 28003 Madrid, Spain or eugpsr@cambridge.org.

www.ingramcontent.com/pod-product-compliance
Ingram Content Group UK Ltd.
Pitfield, Milton Keynes, MK11 3LW, UK
UKHW020451090825
461507UK00007B/170